Software and System Development using Virtual Platforms

Software and System Development using Virtual Platforms

Full-System Simulation with Wind River® Simics®

Daniel Aarno

Jakob Engblom

AMSTERDAM • BOSTON • HEIDELBERG • LONDON
NEW YORK • OXFORD • PARIS • SAN DIEGO
SAN FRANCISCO • SINGAPORE • SYDNEY • TOKYO

Morgan Kaufmann is an imprint of Elsevier

Acquiring Editor: Todd Green
Editorial Project Manager: Lindsay Lawrence
Project Manager: Priya Kumaraguruparan
Cover Designer: Alan Studholme

Morgan Kaufmann is an imprint of Elsevier
225 Wyman Street, Waltham, MA 02451, USA

Notices

Knowledge and best practice in this field are constantly changing. As new research and experience broaden our understanding, changes in research methods, professional practices, or medical treatment may become necessary.

Practitioners and researchers must always rely on their own experience and knowledge in evaluating and using any information, methods, compounds, or experiments described herein. In using such information or methods they should be mindful of their own safety and the safety of others, including parties for whom they have a professional responsibility.

To the fullest extent of the law, neither the Publisher nor the authors, contributors, or editors, assume any liability for any injury and/or damage to persons or property as a matter of products liability, negligence or otherwise, or from any use or operation of any methods, products, instructions, or ideas contained in the material herein.

ISBN: 978-0-12-800725-9

British Library Cataloguing-in-Publication Data
A catalogue record for this book is available from the British Library

Library of Congress Cataloging-in-Publication Data
Aarno, Daniel.
  Full-system simulation with Simics / Daniel Aarno, Jakob Engblom.
      pages cm
  Includes index.
  1. Virtual computer systems.   2. Simics.   I. Engblom, Jakob.   II. Title.
  QA76.9.V5A76 2014
  005.4′3—dc23

                                                                            2014027622

For information on all Morgan Kaufmann publications
visit our website at http://store.elsevier.com/

This book has been manufactured using Print On Demand technology. Each copy is produced to order and is limited to black ink. The online version of this book will show color figures where appropriate.

www.elsevier.com • www.bookaid.org

Contents

Foreword

In the 19th century a French novelist named Jules Verne imagined and described a lot of surrealistic machines, such as the submarine and the space rocket, that were perceived to be impossible to build; and even if they could be built, why would you even want to go into space or deep water! Years later these places are humankind's backyard. Like science fiction, simulation has set free mankind to solve complex problems by looking at these situations from a different level of abstraction, focusing on what matters for the problem to be solved. Likewise, Wind River Simics has enabled thousands of commercial and academic users to do things that were just not possible to do in simulation—what was not possible in the real world. This book will likely uncover to the reader how powerful simulation tools can be, making the sky the limit for engineers.

Michel Genard
VP and General Manager,
Simulation and Lifecycle Solutions,
Wind River.

Acknowledgments

It is with a smile on our faces that we are putting the final touches on this book—a book that would not have been possible without the support and contributions of a number of people.

We would like to thank Alexey Veselyi and Denis Vladimirov for contributing Chapter 10. Our editor, David Clark, deserves an enormous thank you for providing such excellent proofreading and editing on short notice and in a very short time.

In addition, we would like to thank the entire Simics team for building such a capable product—in particular, Andreas Moestedt and Bengt Werner for providing detailed feedback and suggestions on some of the contents. In addition, we would like to thank the many members of the Wind River Simics sales, support, and engineering teams who read parts of the material and provided encouragement and feedback. It really helped to get early indications that the material was useful!

Finally, we would like to thank Intel and Wind River for supporting this work.

Introduction

1

Fools ignore complexity. Pragmatists suffer it. Some can avoid it.
Geniuses remove it.
—**Alan Perlis, *Epigrams on Programming*, 1982**

In just a few years, electronic systems have become significantly more complex. Now, even comparatively simple designs include multiple processors, a mixture of CPU types, digital signal processing (DSP), application-specific integrated circuits (ASICs), field-programmable gate arrays (FPGAs), and other devices. Complementing the diverse combinations of hardware, today's systems employ a variety of operating systems and application stacks that until recently would not have been combined within a single product or solution.

Unfortunately, however, as these systems have grown in complexity, the development tools and processes that were refined when single processors and basic client–server architectures were the rule have not kept pace. As a result, today's system developers are challenged to find new ways to define system architectures, develop and integrate millions of lines of code, and deploy such complex systems. They must do this in ways that reduce risk and shorten the schedule while simultaneously resulting in a higher-quality product that is easier to support and maintain.

In addition to the growing complexity, the market also expects new systems to be delivered at a much higher pace. The product development lifecycle of most electronic systems has been significantly shortened over the last decade. Thus, today's system developers are faced with two significant challenges: deliver new solutions faster, and develop, debug, and maintain ever more complex systems. Virtual platforms can help in addressing these two challenges.

The goal of this book is to inspire and educate the reader to find new ways to leverage the power of virtual platforms and full system simulation to improve their systems' design and development activities. With this book we seek to share our experience, gathered over more than a decade, from working with our customers to help them realize the advantages of working in a simulation environment. This book is focused on virtual platforms created in Wind River Simics[†], and although Simics offers many unique features, many of the techniques and challenges discussed apply to other virtual platform solutions as well.

At one level the book will address how to use Simics simulations to achieve your development goals as a leader of an organization. At another level, the book will discuss how to use Simics simulations to get actual tasks done. The book offers best practices along with real-life examples to help you understand how to get the most out of your Simics implementation. Design patterns and architectures that have been proven to work when building complex simulation systems involving many separate components are described. While the book is not intended to be a user manual, it is a comprehensive book on simulation using Simics, and we have tried to provide enough details for the book to be useful for someone trying to implement the concepts described.

This chapter introduces the reader to why virtual platforms and full-system simulation like Simics is a critical tool for developing today's complex computer-based systems. The chapter defines the basic terminology and provides a high-level overview of why and where Simics is being applied to solve problems for software and system developers. The chapter concludes with an outline of the remaining chapters of the book.

VIRTUAL PLATFORMS

A *virtual platform* is a model of a hardware system that can run the same software as the hardware it models. The virtual platform is simulated on a *host* computer that may be different from the hardware modeled by the virtual platform. For example, a big-endian Power Architecture system with a controller area network (CAN) bus and other peripherals running VxWorks[†] can be simulated on a typical little-endian Intel[®] Architecture PC running a Linux[†] or Windows[†] operating system. A virtual platform is not limited to modeling a single processor or board, but can represent anything from a basic board with only a processor and memory to a complete system made up of network-connected boards, chassis, racks, and models of physical systems.

The key property of a virtual platform is its ability to run unmodified binaries of the software that will finally run on the real system, and run it fast enough to be useful for software developers. Such software includes low-level firmware and boot loaders, hypervisors, operating systems, drivers, middleware, and applications. Therefore, the virtual platform accurately models the aspects of the real system that are relevant for software, such as CPU instruction sets, device registers, memory maps, interrupts, and the functionality of the different devices. On the other hand, the virtual platform is typically not concerned with modeling the detailed implementation of the hardware, such as internal buses, clocks, pipelines, and caches.

By focusing the model on the hardware—software interface and functionality it is possible to achieve good performance and produce a virtual platform very early in the product lifecycle—two critical features required to address the aforementioned challenges.

TERMINOLOGY

There are many terms in use for the kind of technology that Simics represents. This section defines some of the terminology the reader may come in contact with.

Simulation is a very broad term, used in many different fields. At its core, it means that you use computer software to build a *model* of some phenomenon you want to study and then run this simulator to understand the behavior of the modeled system. A simulation provides more flexibility than the real system, allows parameters to be set freely, provides better insight into the internal workings, and allows for the replay and repetition of scenarios. It also fundamentally avoids the need to build physical prototypes or experiments, which speeds up development. Simulation is used in every field of science and engineering. Simulations are used to predict weather, crash-test cars, design aircraft, understand economic mechanisms, and find new medicines. This book is primarily concerned with the simulation of a digital computer system (the target) using another digital computer system (the host).

Full-system simulation (FSS) is a term commonly used to describe Simics, and it captures the fact that the simulation targets an entire target system. Originally, the point of a full system was that the digital computer hardware model was sufficiently complete to run a real operating system (Magnusson et al., 1998). Over time, it has grown in scope, and today a full system often includes factors external to the digital computer hardware, such as models of the surrounding world and inputs and outputs from the outside. It also includes the use of the simulator to model collections of digital computer systems, such as multiple machines in a network or multiple boards in a rack. A simulation that cannot simulate more than a single system-on-chip (SoC) or board is not really a FSS today.

Virtual platform is the established term in the world of electronic design automation (EDA) for a piece of software that works like a piece of hardware and is capable of running software in lieu of the real hardware. Virtual platforms are used at many levels of abstraction, from cycle-accurate models that correctly emulate all pins and signals on buses and inside devices, to programmer's view (PV) and transaction-level models (TLMs) that essentially work like Simics does. Virtual platforms are considered to be development tools.

Emulation is a term commonly used to indicate a software layer that lets a piece of software run on a platform it was not initially targeted to run on. Well-known examples are the Mac[†] 68k emulator that Apple[†] used in the migration from the 68k-family of processors to the PowerPC[†] family, and the Rosetta emulator that allowed PowerPC binaries to run on Intel® Architecture in Apple's next architectural transition. Simulators for old videogame platforms, such as the Nintendo[†] Entertainment System (NES), are also known as emulators to the public. We thus consider emulation in the software realm to mean something that runs software by translating binaries and operating system calls, where the primary use is to run software, not to develop it.

Virtualization in the IT world means the use of virtual machines to run multiple software loads on a single host. Virtualization as a principle traces its beginnings back to the IBM System/360 line in the 1970s, and today there is a wealth of virtualization solutions available on standard Intel hardware such as KVM, VMware[†], Xen, Hyper-V, Virtualbox, and many others. A virtual machine runs a real operating system, but often employs special drivers and input/output (I/O) mechanisms to optimize performance for disks and networking. The goal is to provide an isolated and manageable container for a particular workload. A key property of virtualization is that it provides virtual clones of the underlying host machine—a virtualization system cannot provide a target system that is fundamentally different from the host.

In EDA some of these terms have specific meanings. An *emulator* is a custom hardware system that runs the register-transfer level (RTL) of a new design without having to actually manufacture a chip. Emulators are optimized for execution speed, even if they also typically support some development. A *simulator* is a software program that simulates the RTL. This is very slow, but it also does not require any special hardware, and it provides very detailed insight into the execution of the system. For understanding and debugging a hardware design, a simulator is the gold standard. A *field-programmable gate array prototype* synthesizes the hardware design to run on an FPGA, rather than for ASIC production. The functionality is the same, but the detailed timing behavior is not. Still, it is much cheaper than using an emulator and runs much faster than a simulator. If seen in software terms, this is the equivalent of using the same source code, but compiling it for a different architecture and operating system.

SIMULATION AND THE SYSTEM DEVELOPMENT LIFECYCLE

Full-system simulation can be applied during the complete system development lifecycle as shown in Figure 1.1. It helps in designing and defining systems by providing an executable model of the hardware interface and hardware setup. FSS supports hardware and software architecture work, and it validates that the hardware can be efficiently used from the software stack. Full-system simulation is

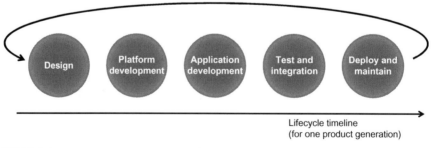

FIGURE 1.1

System development lifecycle.

used to develop low-level firmware, system software, and application-level software. Testing and integration can be performed on the simulator as well as on hardware, providing increased hardware flexibility and developer agility. The software development schedule can be decoupled from the availability of hardware. Using a simulator improves software development productivity by providing a better environment than hardware, especially for reproducing issues, debugging, and automated testing and execution.

The following sections describe various ways in which virtual platforms are being used to make developers more efficient throughout the product lifecycle.

HARDWARE DEVELOPMENT AND DESIGN

A virtual platform is a common tool in the design of new computer systems and new SoC designs. Early hardware design models tend to focus on performance modeling without much care for the actual functionality and what is being computed, which is not really a good match for the Simics-style fast functional simulation. Still, Simics-style virtual platforms are very useful during the hardware design, because Simics provides a means to define and test the functional design of the hardware system. It feeds into pre-silicon software development, as discussed in the next section.

It is also quite common to use fast virtual platforms with a few components swapped out for detailed cycle-accurate and bit-accurate models to perform component-level tests with real workloads and component-level verification and validation work. Chapter 9 discusses how such mixed-level simulations can be built by combining elements from multiple different simulation systems.

PRE-SILICON

When developing a new chip, FSSs like Simics are used to develop software long before the first silicon appears. This allows the entire project to have its schedule "shift left," effectively reducing the time to market and time to revenue for a new product. In the traditional product development flow, hardware development, software development, and integration and testing more or less take place serially. Typically, software developers try to start as early as possible by using different techniques such as cross-compilation to the host machine, working with old revisions of a board, or using previous-generation hardware. These techniques offer significant challenges, especially for low-level code such as firmware and drivers. Using virtual platforms, the software and hardware can be developed more or less in parallel, significantly reducing the time to a releasable product. Additionally, because the schedule pressure is reduced by increased parallelism, there is the option to get more testing done before release, increasing product quality. These benefits from a "shift left" are illustrated in Figure 1.2.

It has been shown many times that by using virtual platforms the time to create a board support package (BSP) for a new design can be pulled in from several

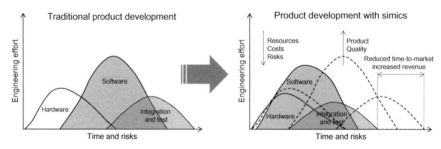

FIGURE 1.2

Product "shift left".

months to only days after the first hardware is available. In the ideal case, the hardware and software teams work closely together, allowing the software team to provide feedback to the hardware designers already before the design is frozen. This can help to avoid costly mistakes in terms of overly complex programming models and performance bottlenecks that appear because of a lack of system optimization.

The software most commonly developed on the pre-silicon virtual platform are boot loaders and basic input/output systems (BIOSs) (Carbonari, 2013), silicon verification and test software (Veseliy and Ayers, 2013), drivers, firmware, and operating system support. Even though the Simics abstraction level hides the detailed timing and implementation of a system, developing software on a functional virtual platform has been proven to work very well. Compared to not using a virtual platform, system developers save weeks and months of time (Koerner et al., 2009).

A variant of pre-silicon development that might not be obvious is the development of software for a new *board*. Even if a new board is based on a familiar SoC and existing network chips, memory, and other functions, a Simics model can still be provided ahead of the arrival of the board and offer the same benefits as for a new silicon chip. Just like a new chip, a new board needs custom boot code and drivers to enable software to use the capabilities of the board.

PLATFORM DEVELOPMENT

Platform development refers to the development of the fundamental software that makes hardware work and that provides a platform for application development. As discussed before, this includes the development of firmware, boot loaders, and BIOS, as well as operating system kernels and BSPs. In addition to such hardware-interface code, it also usually involves integrating various forms of middleware software on top of the operating system. The middleware provides the crucial domain-specific specialization of the generic operating system platform, such as distributed communications systems, fault-tolerance mechanisms, load balancing, databases, and virtual machines for Java, C#, and other languages. The complete software stack can be developed and run on Simics.

Debugging low-level code in Simics is a much nicer experience than using hardware, especially compared to early unstable prototype hardware. As discussed in depth in Chapter 3, Simics enables the debugging of firmware and boot code from the first instruction after power on, and makes it easy to debug device drivers and interrupt handlers. When drivers and the operating system are up, Simics can be used to integrate middleware and services on top of the operating system, taking the setup all the way to a complete running platform, ready for application developers (Tian, 2013).

In larger organizations, there is usually a dedicated platform team who is responsible for developing and delivering ready-to-use integrated platforms for application developers. Virtual platforms can be used to efficiently deliver the platform to application developers, containing both hardware and software, booted, configured, and ready to go. With a virtual platform, a nightly build can become a nightly boot, using checkpoints as discussed in Chapter 3 to deliver a ready-to-use platform to the application development teams.

APPLICATION DEVELOPMENT

Applications provide the software that makes a system useful for its end users. An application can be a single standalone process like a traditional desktop application. More often, an application actually consists of multiple cooperating processes, running on the same machine or spread out across machines to form a distributed application. In the embedded world, there is often an element of hardware involved, interfacing to the world outside of the computer. Fault-tolerant applications containing multiple redundant software and hardware systems are also commonly seen in the embedded world.

Application development with Simics means giving application developers access to virtual hardware, which lets them test their code on the same platform the code will run on in the end. Often, application software development is performed using development boards that only partially match the target system, or by using some form of emulation layer compiled to the host. With Simics, target hardware availability is not an issue, and application developers can work on their standard PCs while still compiling their code for the actual target and running it as part of the real software stack. Simics can simulate networks of machines and the interface between computers and their environment to provide a realistic system for application developers.

As the time available for development gets shorter and continuous integration and continuous deployment are being applied even to traditionally slow-moving embedded systems, the value of working with the actual target hardware increases. The goal is to have every build of the software ready to deploy to customers, and this means that it has to be built with the actual release compilers and get tested on the hardware that is used in the field. This is a very good match for virtual platforms, because they can be built and configured to precisely match the real-world platforms, enabling fast and agile software development while still only using standard laptops, workstations, and servers.

Application development can be supported by various simulation-powered shortcuts to make the work more efficient, such as using back doors to load software and scripts to automate a load-configure-run cycle.

For applications built on top of distributed, parallel, and virtualization-based systems, Simics provides an ideal debug and test platform, because it offers the ability to control and debug the entire system and all parts of the application using a single debugger, regardless of whether the actual system has debug access built into its hardware or software.

DEBUGGING

While not really a part of the product lifecycle, debugging is one of the most time-consuming parts of software development. Even worse, a really bad bug can potentially hold up a release, and cause customer pain, manufacturer embarrassment in case they are discovered post-release, and even force a recall of a product.

Software debugging involves three fundamental activities: provoking the bug, finding and isolating the bug, and fixing the bug. Traditionally, successful debugging requires a high degree of developer skill and experience, often combined with patience and luck. Simics removes luck from the equation by simplifying efforts to repeat and isolate the bug. Several of Wind River's customers previously struggled for months to repeat and isolate bugs on physical hardware only to find them in hours with Simics.

Simics's usage and value as a debugger applies to post-silicon as well as pre-silicon use cases (Tian, 2013). When hardware is available, Simics complements the use of hardware for debugging. Users who test-run their code on Simics can easily debug it using Simics, and Simics can also be used to replicate and debug issues from the field and tricky hard-to-find bugs.

To repeat a bug on physical hardware, developers may have to restart the system or application hundreds or thousands of times, using a new set of input parameters, data streams, or operator actions each time, or hoping for some random fluctuation that will provoke the bug. Simics virtual platforms are different. They operate in a virtual world where the entire system state and all inputs are controllable and recordable. As a result, any simulation can be trivially reproduced. Once a bug is seen inside a Simics simulation, it can be reproduced any number of times at any time or any place in the world. Thus, Simics makes it possible to transport bugs with guaranteed replication.

Once a bug can be reliably repeated, the developer must find the source of the bug. Traditional hardware-centric debug methods require an iterative approach where breakpoints are set, the system is run, registers are reviewed, and the application is restarted or execution is resumed to the next breakpoint. Using this technique, developers can eventually find the precise offending lines of source code. However, attaching a debugger to a hardware system will affect the execution of the system, leading to so-called *Heisenbugs*, whereby the act of debugging changes the observed system and makes the bug disappear. In particular, stopping individual threads or putting in breakpoints will often cause a complex software system to break entirely. In contrast, a simulation-based debugger is nonintrusive, and the system will run exactly the same regardless of whether it is under the inspection of a debugger or not.

With Simics, developers can run the system in reverse, watching the sequence of steps that led up to an issue. Simics will trigger breakpoints in reverse, making it possible to stop at the previous change to a variable or memory location. Such an approach does away with the need to start the debug session over and over again and try to reproduce a bug and plant different sets of breakpoints. Instead, Simics allows debuggers to continue from finding the bug directly to debugging and unearthing the cause of it. Simics can observe all parts of the system state and trace all interactions without disturbing the target execution, which means that it is easy to understand just what the system is doing.

Once a bug has been repeated and isolated, the effort to resolve it may range from trivial to extensive. With Simics, developers may apply standard features such as checkpointing, reverse execution, run-to-run repeatability, and full-system visibility and control while finding the precise bug fix. For complex systems, Simics will make it easier to replicate the particular hardware–software setup involved with a bug report to test fixed code in a relevant environment.

TESTING AND INTEGRATION

Testing and integration are crucial parts of any large-scale software development project. Modules from many sources have to be built, integrated, and tested to make sure they are working together. Hardware has to be integrated with software, and networks and racks configured, brought up, and tested. Using a simulator like Simics for this phase brings great benefits to the development workflow (Magnusson, 2005). As discussed in more detail in Chapter 5, Simics can scale up to truly large systems, making system testing and integration work in simulation a realistic option.

When Simics is used to enable software development before silicon or boards are available, it is natural to also perform *system integration* ahead of hardware. Because Simics models cover the whole system, all the system software and hardware can be integrated in the simulation before the hardware is available. A particularly interesting case is when the new hardware is part of a bigger system containing older hardware, such as rack-based systems where new and old boards coexist. In such cases, Simics makes it possible to virtually integrate the new hardware with the old hardware, allowing system integration and testing to happen before the hardware becomes available.

Creating and managing multiple system and network configurations for testing is often difficult in hardware. The number of hardware lab setups is limited by hardware availability, and reconfiguring a hardware setup with different boards and network connections is time consuming and error-prone. With Simics, it is possible to write scripts and save setups as software, making configuration an

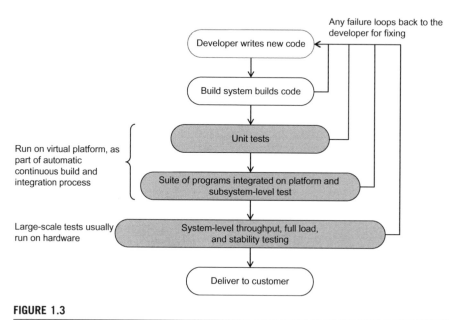

FIGURE 1.3

Continuous integration with Simics.

instant process. Configurations can also be saved in version control systems, allowing hardware and software configurations to be managed together.

Testing can naturally be performed in *parallel*, because virtual platform availability is only limited by the number of servers that can be used to run Simics. This increases the amount of testing that can be performed within a given time, compared to only using hardware setups. Using techniques like *checkpointing*, it is possible to shorten test execution time by starting from booted setups rather than rebooting the test system for each test.

Simics and simulation are enablers for *continuous integration* (Duvall et al., 2007) and automated testing of embedded code. Using hardware is much more difficult than simulators, especially for quick short tests. As illustrated in Figure 1.3, a typical continuous integration workflow starts with a developer submitting new code to the build system. If the build fails, they have to fix it. Once the code actually builds, quick unit tests and other smoke tests are typically run to make sure the code is not totally broken. Such tests should run very fast—no more than a few minutes—to quickly return a reply to the developer.

Once code passes unit testing, it can be subjected to larger-scale tests. First, some form of subsystem test is run where the code is tested in a real context but typically with quite small inputs. The goal is to get the subsystem-level tests done in hours. Code that passes subsystem tests is finally used in system-level tests where it is run along with all other code and functionality of the system, and subjected to long hard tests under high load and lots of traffic.

Simics is a suitable platform for unit tests and subsystem tests, but system-level tests are usually run on hardware. At some point, it is necessary to test what is actually going to be shipped. The maxim is always to "test what you ship and ship what you test." Thus, the physical hardware that will be shipped to the customer must be used for final testing.

Still, using a virtual platform like Simics can drastically reduce the amount of hardware labs needed. If most unit tests and subsystem tests are run on Simics, most developers will be independent of hardware and can run the tests whenever needed, regardless of hardware availability. It is very easy to integrate Simics as an automated testing component in build automation systems like Jenkins. Integration also covers the integration of a computer system with its physical environments. By combining Simics with other simulators, as discussed in Chapter 9, simulation-based testing can cover both a control computer and its environment.

DEPLOYMENT

The pre-silicon use case is easy to appreciate—when there is no hardware available a simulator is a good solution and often the only solution. However, many Simics users find that the benefits of virtual platforms carry on long into the deployment and maintenance phases. For example, some customers embed Simics into their complete virtual environment, allowing them to carry out system-level development and testing in a flexible and powerful environment, at the point in time where systems are actually available in the market and deployed to customers.

In the deployment phase Simics can be used to perform demos for customers. It is easy to bring a fully configurable Simics model to a customer to showcase an application that would otherwise require custom hardware or a large set of hardware to be brought to the customer or maintained in a separate demo lab with obvious resource limitations. A related topic is that of training, which is covered in more detail later in this chapter.

Virtual platforms can also be used to simulate faults that have appeared in deployed systems. For example, if the target system is flying through space somewhere, a virtual platform on Earth can be used to model various faults that have appeared in the physical system during its service life. Software workarounds and patches for hardware issues can then be tested on the ground, in the simulated environment of the virtual platform, before being uploaded to the live system.

MAINTENANCE

Once development is complete and a product version is released, it goes into maintenance. In maintenance the focus is typically on providing incremental improvements and to resolve bugs that were not found during QA testing. The test automation systems discussed previously for testing and integration should still be used to make sure no new errors creep back into the system.

When issues come back from the field, as they invariably will, virtual platforms support the reproduction and analysis of the issues. With a virtual platform, it is possible to reproduce a customer's setup even if the precise hardware needed is not available in physical form. Once a bug has been reproduced on the virtual hardware, it can then be analyzed at leisure.

REAL-WORLD STORY: DEBUGGING A CORRUPTED FILE SYSTEM

One Simics customer had a system that handled large amounts of network data. Every once in a while the system would crash with a corrupted file system. The crash happened in a catastrophic way so the customer was not able to recover any useful information about the crash from the logs on the hard drive. Because this system was deployed in a situation where downtime was very costly, the customer was desperately looking for a solution.

After months of debugging the problem using real hardware, the customer decided to try a different approach. There was already a Simics model available for the system that had been used during development, so the customer cloned the setup of the system in Simics and began trying to reproduce the bug. They realized that the bug was most often triggered when the hard drive was close to full, so they replicated this scenario and started running traffic through the Simics model. By varying timing parameters and traffic data they eventually managed to reproduce the bug in Simics. Because Simics is deterministic they could now reproduce the bug at their leisure.

The next step was to write a script that checked the consistency of the file system automatically. Using this script and checkpoints the customer bisected the workload to pinpoint the time when the file system was corrupted. Attaching the debugger they found that a routine in the operating system was corrupting the stack and overwriting the return address. This was a commercial real-time operating system (RTOS) and the customer did not have access to source code. However, they could go to the OS vendor and pinpoint exactly the routine that was causing the issue. The problem was then identified and fixed by the OS vendor.

Another aspect of maintenance is generational change: once a system is delivered and deployed, it is often the basis for tweaks and upgrades. Components can be upgraded to increase capacity or fix hardware issues, and the virtual platform used to develop the original software can easily be updated to model the updated hardware, enabling another round through the lifecycle.

A virtual platform for a deployed system is often also used as the basis for the development of a next-generation system, especially for SoC, chip designs, and system designs. A next-generation platform can be developed by starting with a model of the current platform and then changing one component at a time from old to new as they become available. The software is then updated to work with the new hardware one component at a time, always maintaining a working hardware—software system that is gradually changing from all-old to all-new. Such a gradual change from one generation to another is very hard to do in hardware, because there is no practical way to build a series of part-way designs (Magnusson et al., 2002).

TRAINING

Virtual platforms can be used for training on the system being simulated. The main benefit of using a virtual platform is that training can be performed without the need to access the real hardware system. Providing large classes with sufficient hardware is often prohibitively expensive. The virtual platform runs the actual software, which means that the behaviors seen are just like the real thing.

For the case of certified software, such as avionics, using exactly the same binary ensures that the training setup can be updated and kept in sync with the real system. In the past, simulators for systems containing avionics systems often relied on porting the software to run on a standard machine, or simply building a behaviorally correct emulation of system components. With increasing system complexity and reliance on software to implement system functionality, these approaches tend to fail. Keeping software ports or behavioral emulators up-to-date with the latest released real-world software is an extra cost and schedule risk, which can be entirely avoided by running the real binary on a virtual platform.

Virtual platforms can also be used in lieu of real systems to simplify training in general concepts. Simics has been used to teach networking, multicore programming, and operating systems at Wind River (Guenzel, 2013). In academia, one particularly interesting area is teaching operating system concepts. With a simulator at the base, it is much easier to debug and understand the behavior of an operating system, enabling much more advanced labs than would be possible on hardware. Once the operating system is up and running on the simulator, it can be moved to real hardware and tested to show the students that what they did actually works in the real world (Blum et al., 2013).

REAL-WORLD STORY:
TEACHING OPERATING SYSTEM WITHOUT SIMICS

In the mid-1990s, before Simics was available, one of the authors of this book was a teaching assistant on a course in operating systems. The course was taught using a set of MIPS R3000-based boards with a small amount of memory and standard serial port for output. Getting an operating system up and running was not entirely easy, and most students ended up pulling a few all-night hack sessions in the computer lab to get their software to work. In the end, most of them did.

However, one very ambitious group of students decided that they would try to make use of the memory management unit (MMU) of the MIPS processor. After all, a real operating system should have memory protection. This turned out to be very hard indeed—setting up the translation look-aside buffer (TLB) entries and moving to a protected memory model is nontrivial. Test run after test run was made, with debug printouts scrolling by on the 24-line terminals in use, each time ending in a complete freeze of the target system. With no hardware debugger available and very limited scroll-back on the terminal, debugging was basically guesswork.

In the end, the students were forced to give up. Had they had Simics around, debugging would probably have been trivial. Check the MMU state, trace the MMU setup operations, and check where the code froze. Still, the students were given passing grades for the course and went on to quite illustrious careers in programming. The lab assistant later worked as an associate professor in the department and introduced Simics as the basis for the operating systems lab. It did make it much easier to debug the students' OS kernels.

LONGEVITY SUPPORT

Full-system simulation has been proven to have tremendous value in the support of *really old hardware*. Indeed, once a system gets old enough, the value of having a simulator for it tends to go up, as the hardware starts getting scarce.

In telecom and other fields, hardware sold a decade ago is often still used in field installations—customers do not upgrade their hardware unless they absolutely have to, and hardware tends to last longer than expected (or planned). Such hardware tends to be built from racks containing lots of boards, and there are usually a large variety of boards with several generations of each board. With a virtual model of the older boards in place, all developers can have their own immediately accessible hardware to work on. In the physical world, these older boards are often in very limited supply, limiting user productivity.

The practice of extending the life of older systems by software upgrades to old hardware is common in the military, aerospace, and transportation fields. The development of a software upgrade requires development hardware, but typically there are very few or no physical units available. Development boards tend to go bad and become unstable or useless over time. Even if a large supply of boards were procured at project start, their half-life tends to be only a few years, and after a decade or two it is rare to have many development boards available at all. Taking electronics units from systems in the field is not a realistic option due to hardware cost, the fact that making systems unavailable is often unacceptable, and that the boards being used in production are not exactly being designed for development tasks.

A virtual platform is thus a very nice solution that provides developers with the rare luxury, in these fields, of ample hardware access. A virtual platform is also stable and available virtually forever, as illustrated in Figure 1.4. The virtual platform will be available as long as Simics continues to be ported to new generations of hosts. And as long as the virtual platform is available, there is the ability to run the decades-old software stack and to test and integrate new software.

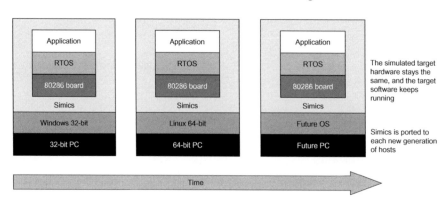

FIGURE 1.4

Virtually infinite platform life.

CERTIFIABLE AND SAFETY-CRITICAL SYSTEMS

Simics is commonly used to help develop certifiable and safety-critical systems. While Simics is not a qualified tool, it can still add tremendous value to the development of such systems, across all the lifecycle phases.

In the aerospace world, Simics is not usually used to actually test software for certification credit directly, but instead it is used to debug and develop the certification tests. By making sure that the certification tests are solid before they are run on hardware, significant effort and schedule time can be saved.

Certified hardware is also usually both expensive and rare, and using Simics to augment hardware availability can remove many hardware-dictated bottlenecks from the development process. For example, with Simics, it is possible to run automated tests in parallel on regular servers, rather than relying on particular hardware. This can enable daily regression testing instead of weekly, reducing the chance of bugs sneaking back into the code base. Certified hardware and software stacks also tend to have poor debug support, because back doors are not a good thing on a critical system. Using a Simics model along with the unintrusive Simics debugger makes debugging much easier.

Safety-critical systems also tend to contain error-handling code. Testing error handlers is about the hardest thing possible, because forcing errors on hardware is very difficult. With a simulator like Simics, fault injection is much simpler, allowing for testing, debugging, and validation of error handlers. In industrial systems, validating fault-handling code is a requirement, and using a simulator like Simics makes it much easier to systematically inject particular states in the system directly into the virtual hardware. The alternative method of using a debugger to control the target system and overwrite values is much more intrusive.

REAL-WORLD STORY: NASA GO-SIM

The NASA IV&V Independent Test Capability (ITC) team joined forces with NASA Goddard Space Flight Center (GSFC) to develop a software-only simulator for the Global Precipitation Measurement (GPM) Operational Simulator (GO-SIM) project. The GPM mission is an international network of satellites providing next-generation global observations of rain and snow. GO-SIM includes the GPM ground system and database, flight software executables, and spacecraft simulators.

GO-SIM was designed as a high-fidelity simulator with no hardware dependencies. Its functions include loading and running unmodified flight software binaries, executing flight scripts, performing single-step debugging, injecting errors via the ground system, stressing the system under testing, and validating findings from other analyses.

Part of GO-SIM is a Simics model of the RAD750[†] processor, which enables the target software to run on the virtual platform the same way it does on physical hardware. Along with Simics' capabilities of scripting, debugging, inspection, and fault injection, it enables users to define, develop, and integrate their systems without the constraints of physical target hardware.

Simics allowed NASA's ITC team to simulate their target hardware, ranging from a single processor to large, complex, and connected electronic systems, and build its GO-SIM product with all the desired features.

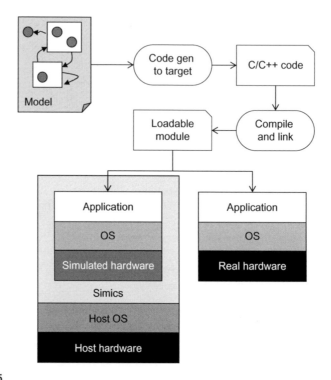

FIGURE 1.5

Simics and autogenerated code.

MODEL-DRIVEN DEVELOPMENT

Model-driven development (MDD) is widely applied in the domain of control systems and is the standard development methodology for automotive, aerospace, avionics, and defense systems. A key part of MDD is to generate code from the model, as illustrated in Figure 1.5, rather than writing it manually. For Simics, whether code is generated or handwritten does not matter—it will run the same on Simics.

PROCESSOR-IN-THE-LOOP TESTING

In a typical model-driven workflow, a model is first tested using model-in-the-loop (MIL) testing within the modeling tool (e.g., Simulink, Labview, MATLAB, or SCADE). In MIL testing, the model of the code to be generated is tested against a model of the world it interacts with. Next, simulation-in-the-loop (SIL) testing is performed, where code is generated to run on the development host, testing the code part against the world model. This makes sure that code generation from the model works. Once this is proven, processor-in-the-loop (PIL) testing is performed where the code is generated to the target system and tested using the actual processor it will run on in the final system. PIL testing makes sure that code generation and compilation for the target system does not introduce any errors, such as those involving word length, endianness, floating-point implementation details, or other target properties. In PIL testing, the model of the world is still used as the counterpart to the code.

PIL testing makes sense to do on Simics, because Simics provides a model of the final target system and thus a model of the final target processor. With Simics used as a PIL target, it is possible to automate the execution of tests from within the model-driven tool (see Chapter 9 for more information on such integration work) and to provide easy and widespread access to target hardware. The alternative to using Simics is to use a development board or even the final hardware, which is always a logistical and practical issue.

HARDWARE-IN-THE-LOOP TESTING

After a control program is proven in PIL testing, it is time to test it for real. This is done by generating code for the real target and running the code on the real target with the actual physical system being controlled instead of the world model used for MIL, SIL, and PIL testing.

Simics can be used for hardware-in-the-loop (HIL) testing in the same way that a physical board can. This requires that the Simics model is connected to the outside world using some form of real-world connection from a connection on the simulated board to a connection on the host machine. As discussed in Chapter 5, Simics provides such connections for a variety of common buses and networks.

INTEGRATION TESTING

The classic MDD flow does not really touch on the issue of system integration. The focus is on generating correct code for the core functionality of the system. That code will need an operating system and a hardware platform to run in the real world, and integration with that platform often happens quite late in the system design cycle. Indeed, even HIL testing is often performed using development hardware rather than the final system.

Simics can be used to move integration earlier and allow earlier testing of the integration. As shown in Figure 1.6, with a Simics model of the target system, the OS port to the target hardware and the integration of the operating system and applications can be tested without hardware.

Something that Simics makes possible is to test that the application works with the actual input and output as provided by the operating system and target hardware platform, while still using a model of the world. Thus, it is possible to create a fully virtual integration environment, where hardware, the operating system, the applications containing control algorithms, and the world can all be run together in simulation.

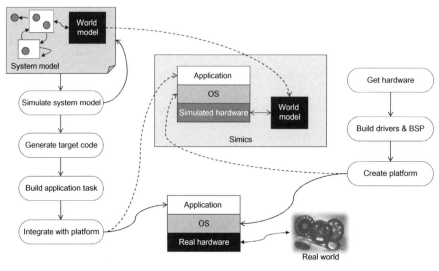

FIGURE 1.6

Model integration testing with Simics.

BOOK OUTLINE

Chapter 2 defines the basic terminology used throughout the book and introduces the reader to the Simics architecture, design, interface, and execution model. It describes how Simics works and why it works the way it does.

The core values of a fast virtual platform—developing, debugging, analyzing, and testing software—are covered in Chapter 3. A virtual platform like Simics lets users run software of all kinds, targeting all kinds of hardware, on a laptop or a development or test server. With the software running on Simics, the benefits of using simulation can be realized: determinism, checkpointing, reverse execution, full control, and insight. Chapter 3 describes how Simics is used to develop and debug software, including the features of the Simics system-level reversible debugger.

Simics structures a virtual platform into a hierarchical structure of reusable components with typed connectors. The components mimic the physical or logical breakdown of a system. The Simics system panel can be used to provide a visualization of a system that makes sense to the end user. Chapter 4 presents the Simics component system, the system panel, and script systems that are used to build systems from individual device and processor models.

Network simulation is an integral part of Simics, and many Simics target systems are networked in one way or another. Simics is used to simulate very large networks of systems, scaling up to several thousand target processors spread across dozens or even hundreds of networked boards. Chapter 5 shows how network simulation is done in Simics and how simulation can be scaled up to very large systems.

Chapter 6 introduces the reader to how to best perform transaction-level modeling of individual devices and how such models are built in Simics. It covers the Device Modeling Language (DML), as well as device modeling in C, C++, Python, and SystemC. Chapter 6 provides detailed step-by-step instructions for how to create a simple device model in Simics.

Following the introduction to modeling, Chapter 7 provides a tutorial-style example on how to develop a model of a direct memory access (DMA) controller, properly connect it to a virtual platform using PCI Express (PCIe), and to enable a device driver to interact with it. The example covers a wide range of important modeling concepts, such as handling, PCIe configuration and inbound/outbound accesses, interrupts, parsing of data structures, and how to model the passing of time.

Simics is designed to be an extensible and programmable system, allowing users to customize the tool to solve their particular problem in the best way possible. Over the years, Simics has been used for things and in situations that were not intended or even imagined by its developers. Chapter 8 discusses how Simics can be extended by its users, including aspects such as cache modeling and fault injection.

Simics users often need to model the physical world or look deep into the implementation of computer components. Rather than using Simics itself to create such models, it sometimes makes more sense to integrate Simics with other simulators, leaving each simulator to do what it does best. Chapter 9 addresses the reasons for, and the main issues involved in, creating such simulator integrations. The chapter provides a discussion on the general issues involved in integrating simulators and proven design patterns for such integrations.

Chapter 10 describes how Intel has used Simics for improving the system development workflow. At Intel, one of the major use cases of Simics is to help software and hardware bring-up, starting from the early pre-silicon stages. With the help of Simics, a functional model of future Intel hardware can be made available to BIOS and driver developers a year or even more ahead of engineering samples. This approach allows development of low-level software, which is very hardware-dependent, in parallel with the development of the hardware. In addition to that, close collaboration with hardware developers allows the team of Simics engineers to perform a certain amount of validation of early hardware specifications, thus speeding up the hardware development process as well. These practices lead to cost savings by reducing product time-to-market—that is, the "shift left."

TRADEMARK INFORMATION

Xeon, Core, Intel and the Intel logo are trademarks of Intel Corporation in the United States and other countries.

[†]Other names and brands may be claimed as the property of others.

Simics fundamentals

> *We may change the name of things; but their nature and their*
> *operation on the understanding never change.*
> **—David Hume**

This chapter defines the basic terminology used throughout the book and introduces the reader to the Simics architecture, design, interface, and execution model. It describes how Simics works, and why it works the way it does.

SIMICS[†] ARCHITECTURE AND TERMINOLOGY

Simics is a modular *full-system simulator* (FSS), which means that it is capable of simulating the user's entire system, while running the real software taken from the real system. The systems simulated with Simics go all the way from individual processor cores, through processors and SoCs, to boards, racks of boards, or even networks of machines, to systems of systems based on arbitrary network topologies. Because of the complexity of the models and the simulation environment it is important to clearly define some concepts and the terminology that is used throughout this book.

Simics itself runs on the simulation *host*, typically a desktop or server in the user's development environment. The host runs a host operating system, such as Microsoft[†] Windows[†] or a Linux distribution.

Inside of the Simics process, we find one or more simulation *targets*. A simulation target corresponds to a specific configuration, including software, of a *virtual platform* (VP) model. The *target hardware* is what Simics simulates, on top of which the *target software* is running. The target software typically includes a target operating system, which may differ from that running on the simulation host, and from other targets within the same simulation.

Simics is modular in the sense that it provides a small simulation core, an API, and the ability to load additional functionality, including models, at runtime. Such additional functionality is loaded from a Simics *module*, which is basically

21

a dynamically linked object file. A module can, for example, contain a single device or processor model, or all the models of an SoC or a set of simulator features relevant for a specific use case. This fine-grained structure makes it possible to supply the exact set of models and features needed for any specific user. An overview of the Simics architecture is shown in Figure 2.1.

Simics modularity enables short rebuild times for large systems, because only the modules that are actually changed have to be recompiled. The rest of the system is unaffected, and each Simics module can be updated and upgraded independently. The modularity also allows for changing the simulation system while it is running, such as adding features and reconfiguring the target hardware.

Simics modules are always distributed in binary form, ensuring that a user does not need to build anything to use Simics. Python modules are distributed as compiled .pyc files, with source code being optional. In practice, a large part of the module set delivered with Simics is also made available in source-code form to help a user customize and extend their Simics environment.

Even central functions of Simics like the Python interpreter and the command-line interface (CLI) are built as modules and loaded dynamically. This means that the actual Simics executable can be kept very small, at just a few hundred kilobytes. As Simics starts and more functions and models are brought into use, they are loaded dynamically as needed.

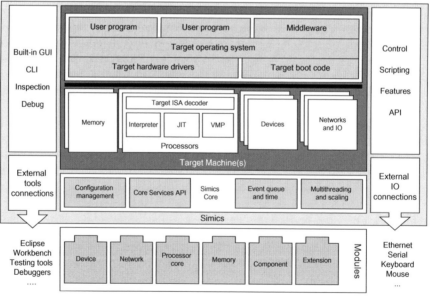

FIGURE 2.1

Overview of the Simics architecture.

RUNNING REAL SOFTWARE STACKS

A key design goal of Simics has always been to run the real software stack, as found on the target system. This includes the boot code or BIOS, operating system, drivers, and the applications and middleware running on top of that. Over the years, Simics has run most types of software, including hypervisors with guest operating systems, small MMU-less embedded operating systems and bare-metal code, as well as Windows, Linux, mainstream RTOSs like VxWorks[†], and major server operating systems.

Running real unmodified software stacks has many benefits. Because Simics is primarily used for software development, running the actual software that is being developed makes eminent sense. The software is compiled using the same tools and compilers that are used with the hardware target, avoiding inconsistencies and deviations introduced by host compilation or other approximations.

Unmodified software also means unmodified build systems, and thus there is no need for users to set up special builds or build targets for creating software to run on Simics. There may also be portions of the system where only machine code is available, such as proprietary libraries, drivers, or operating systems.

Using unmodified software also means that software can be managed and loaded in the same way as on a real system, making Simics useful for testing operations and maintenance of the target system.

To be able to inspect and debug the target software running on Simics, a feature known as *OS awareness* is used. OS awareness is available from the Simics CLI, scripting interface, and debugger. OS awareness looks at the contents of memory and registers in the target hardware and figures out the target software's state, such as the currently running process and thread on a certain processor and all the processes and threads currently active in the target operating system.

Note that there are cases where small modifications to the software stack are appropriate. For example, taking shortcuts early in the development of a target system to get software running without a full boot system in place, or adding drivers to the target software to access simulator features like host file system access. This is discussed in more detail in Chapter 3.

INTERACTING WITH SIMICS

From the very beginning, Simics was designed as an interactive tool that could also be used in automated batch runs. Given the wide range of users and usage scenarios, both CLIs and graphical user interfaces (GUIs) are needed. Today, the primary user interface for new users to Simics is the Eclipse-based GUI, but the CLI is still there for more advanced tasks. Figure 2.2 shows a screenshot of the Simics 4.8 Eclipse GUI, running two simultaneous but separate simulation sessions.

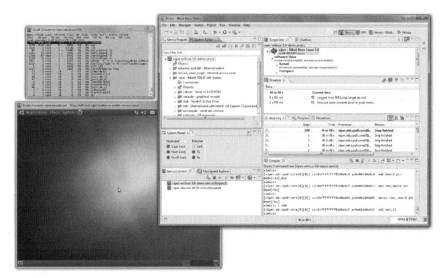

FIGURE 2.2

Simics 4.8 Eclipse GUI, with two Simics simulation sessions running (clockwise from top left: simulated serial text-terminal console, Simics Eclipse GUI, and simulated graphical console).

The currently selected session is running Wind River Linux and uses a serial text-terminal console to interact with the target system (top left). The other session is running Ubuntu Linux on a graphical console (bottom left). In the Eclipse window (right), a number of Simics views that allow inspection and control of the target system can be seen. It is worth noting that the Simics CLI is available and fully integrated into Eclipse, and that actions taken on the CLI are reflected in the state of the GUI and vice versa.

Simics can also be run from a normal command-line shell, on both Linux and Windows hosts. This makes it possible to run Simics without invoking the Eclipse GUI, and this is useful when it comes to automating Simics runs from other tools. Simics behaves just like any other UNIX-style command-line application when needed.

As illustrated in Figure 2.1, the Simics architecture separates the function of the target hardware system from the connections to the outside world. The target consoles shown in Figure 2.2 are not part of the device models of the serial ports and graphics processor unit, but rather they are provided as generic functions by the Simics framework. This means that all consoles behave in the same way, and provide support for command-line scripting, record and replay of inputs, and reverse execution.

In addition to the Simics console windows, a common way to interact with a Simics target machine is via a network connection. In this case, Simics opens up

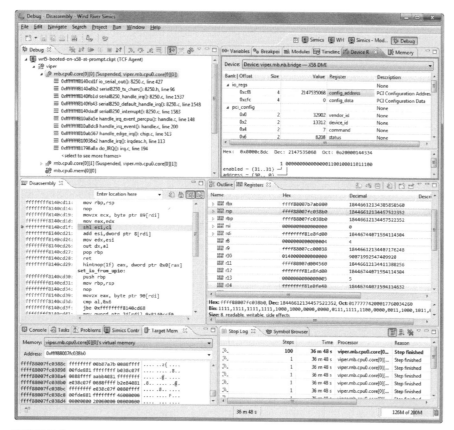

FIGURE 2.3

Simics debugger, looking at various hardware aspects of the target.

a network connection from the virtual network inside of Simics to the host machine or other machines on the network. This feature is known as *real network* in Simics. Users can then connect to Simics with the same tools as they would use to connect to a physical system on their network. Typically, ssh or telnet is used to get to a target command line, and remote debug protocols are used to control a target from an agent on the target machine. This process is described in detail in Chapter 5.

The Simics interface, the simulator scripting commands, and the Simics API provide rich access to the state of the target system and the simulation itself. It is easy to look inside any part of the system and check the state of hardware devices, processors, memory, and interconnects. Figure 2.3 shows an example of how the Simics GUI can be used to inspect various aspects of the state of the target system. The target software is executing inside a serial port driver in the

Linux kernel, as can be seen from the stack trace in the upper left portion of the window. Other views display the device registers, memory contents, processor registers, and disassembly at the point of current execution.

SOFTWARE DEBUGGING

The Simics interface also includes a very powerful debugger, based on the Eclipse CDT and some Wind River extensions. The debugger leverages Simics' OS awareness feature to allow debugging of individual applications and threads, as well as stepping up and down through the software stack layers. Symbolic debug information can be attached to processors for bare-metal debugging and to software stack context, such as a kernel or user application, for debugging at a certain abstraction level.

The debugger functionality is also accessible from the Simics command line, providing the ability to automate debug tasks and control the debugger from the CLI while looking at the state of the system in the GUI.

The Simics debugger can handle debugging both forward and backward in time, as well as user operations that arbitrarily change the target's state and time.

Simics has the ability to trace or put breakpoints on aspects of the target that are inaccessible on the hardware, such as hardware interrupts, processor exceptions, writes to control registers, device accesses, arbitrary memory accesses, software task switches, and log messages from device models. In Simics it is possible to single-step interrupt handling code and to stop an entire system consisting of multiple networked machines synchronously. The advantages of being able to synchronously stop an entire system are discussed in more detail in Chapter 3.

With checkpoints, it is easy to capture a bug in one location and then transfer a perfect reproduction of it to any developer, anywhere in the world, with no need to describe the system setup or bug scenario. Instead, users just provide a recording of the issue and the developer is able to perfectly reproduce it.

SCRIPTING

No matter how Simics is run, the full power of the CLI and its scripting engine is available. Simics scripts work the same way in a Simics simulation started from Eclipse, in an interactive command-line session, and in an automated batch run on a remote compute server. Basic scripts are written in the Simics command-line language, and for more complex tasks there is a full Python environment embedded in Simics. The Python engine has access to all parts of the simulated system and can interact with all Simics API calls. CLI and Python scripts can exchange data and variables with each other, and it is common to find snippets of Python embedded inside of Simics scripts.

An example Simics script is shown in Figure 2.4. It opens a Simics checkpoint and then runs a command on the target. The parameters to the command are sent in as Simics CLI variables to this script, but they are also provided with

```
## Parameters to run:
if not defined opmode        { $opmode = "software_byte" }
if not defined generations   { $generations = 100      }
if not defined packet_length { $packet_length = 1000 }
if not defined packet_count  { $packet_count = 1000 }
if not defined thread_count  { $thread_count = 4       }
if not defined output_level  { $output_level = 0       }

## Ensure stall mode to enable cache analysis
sim->cpu_mode = stall

## Load existing checkpoint
$prev_checkpoint_file  = (lookup-file "%script%") + "/after-ca001-
booted-and-setup.ckpt"

if not (file-exists $prev_checkpoint_file) {
  interrupt-script "Please run ca001 script first to establish the
checkpoint!"
} else {
  read-configuration (lookup-file $prev_checkpoint_file)
}

$system = viper
$con    = $system.console.con

# Script branch that will run the program and wait for it to complete
# by watching the target serial console
$prog_name = "/mnt/rule30_threaded.elf"
$cmd  = ("%s %s %d %d %d %d %d \n" % [$prog_name, $opmode,
$packet_count, $generations, $packet_length,$output_level,
$thread_count])
script-branch {
  local $system = $system
  local $con    = $con
  local $cmd    = $cmd
  local $prompt = "~]#"
  add-session-comment "Starting run"
  $con.input $cmd
  $con.wait-for-string $prompt
  add-session-comment "Run finished"
  stop
}
```

FIGURE 2.4

Example Simics target automation CLI script.

default values in case nothing is provided. The *script branch* at the end is a construct that lets script code run in parallel to the target system and react to events in the simulation. This makes it very easy to automate and script systems containing many different parts where the global order of scripted events is unknown before the simulation starts. Separate scripts can be attached to the different parts.

Scripting in Simics is implemented by an embedded Python interpreter (using Python 2.7 at the time of writing). This Python interpreter has access to the complete Simics API, thanks to an automatic system that generates Python bindings for the Simics API at build time. The Simics CLI is actually implemented using Python, as are large parts of the Simics infrastructure itself, such as the unit test framework.

CONFIGURATIONS AND THE SIMICS OBJECT MODEL

A running simulation in Simics is called a *configuration*. A configuration is a collection of *configuration objects*, each maintaining its own state. Each configuration object is an instance of a *configuration class*. A class represents some "thing" being simulated—typically a model of a processor core, a memory, an I/O device, an interconnect, or a network. A configuration class can register a number of *attributes* and *interfaces*. The attributes can be used to interact with objects and they are available to other objects and to the user, who can directly interact with the objects through the CLI or via scripts. Classes are defined in *modules*, as mentioned before. Simics *checkpoints* save the entire configuration to disk, allowing it to be reconstructed later. Checkpoints are discussed in more detail later in this chapter.

ATTRIBUTES

An *attribute* has a name and a value. The configuration class determines the types and names of its attributes. Attributes allow the user to configure, inspect, and modify the internal state of a configuration object in a controlled way. Rather than directly changing variables in the implementation of a class, attributes provide a level of indirection that allows the *internal implementation* and *external representation* of the state of an object to be separated. It also means that classes can be implemented in any language, and freely mixed in a Simics implementation.

Attributes can have many different types; for example, an attribute may hold a simple integer value representing the state of a register, it may reference another configuration object, or it may contain a complex list of values such as the state of a TLB. Attributes referencing other objects are of particular importance, because that is the way that configuration objects know of each other. If an object *A* needs to call an interface in object *B*, it will have an attribute giving it a reference to *B*. All connections between objects are done in this way, allowing them to be configured, reconfigured, and inspected at any point in the simulation. Object references in attributes are also properly checkpointed and restored—something that would not be the case if a simple memory pointer was maintained in object *A*.

The attributes should capture the entire internal state of the configuration in a way that allows it to be exported and imported on demand. This is important for two key Simics features known as *checkpointing* and *reverse execution*. Checkpointing allows the entire state of the simulation to be stored to disk and then later restored and restarted as if nothing had happened in the target system. Reverse execution allows the simulation to run backwards in time, and this is extremely useful when debugging. Furthermore, attributes are typically not directly used as part of advancing the simulation. For example, objects should avoid querying or modifying attributes of other objects; that is the job of interfaces.

INTERFACES

An *interface* is a set of methods that do specific things, and is the method by which configuration objects communicate with each other. It is analogous to the object-oriented concept of interfaces as used in, for example, Java. A configuration class can implement any number of interfaces, and even implement the same interface multiple times via the concept of named *port interfaces*. When implementing an interface, the class defines the behavior of the interface's methods for all objects of that class. Interfaces are the main mechanism by which objects in the simulation communicate. While technically attributes and interfaces can both be used to query and modify the state of a configuration object, they serve different purposes. Attributes are for the simulation system and the user; interfaces are for other objects and for expressing the target system's behavior.

Interfaces are normally involved in advancing the simulation. Interfaces do not capture any state and are not used by, for instance, the checkpointing mechanism. Interfaces often represent various hardware communications mechanisms, such as simple 1-bit signals for interrupts, Ethernet packet transmission, or more complex interfaces such as NAND flash. One of the most commonly used interfaces is the `io_memory` interface, which is implemented by objects that have a memory-mapped I/O (MMIO) interface. Memory transactions in Simics use the `io_memory` interface.

Unlike languages like SystemC, the Simics interface concept is unidirectional: it describes a set of methods that other objects can call on a particular object. There is no requirement to set up a connection where both objects involved know of each other. This has the nice side effect that it is possible to call many interfaces from the Simics command line, which is useful for interactive testing and performing actions on the target system. In practice, many interfaces are implemented as a pair of interfaces where both sides know about each other. Examples of this are the relationship between a serial device and a serial link, where the link needs to call the device to deliver data in, and the device needs to call the link to send data out.

HAPS

Simics modules can register and fire off global events known as *haps*. Haps can be related to the simulated machine, such as processor exceptions or control register writes, and the simulator itself, such as stopping the simulation. To react to a hap, a module registers a callback function for the hap. This callback function will then be called every time the hap occurs. Any module can react to any hap, and hap names are global within a Simics simulation session. Any module can register haps. The name *hap* was chosen to not overload *event* with yet another meaning, and *happenstance* was deemed too long. It is also easy to associate a hap with any happening that happens to happen in the system.

Haps should not be used to communicate between device models in a simulation. For that purpose, interfaces are the recommended mechanism, because they do not involve a trip through the Simics kernel and have much richer semantics. Another disadvantage of haps for communicating between objects is that they hide the communications channel between the objects. With an interface, the sending object will have an explicit pointer to the receiving object. With haps, this is entirely implicit and impossible to determine from the configuration. Haps are useful to communicate important events to scripts and tooling extensions, because the sending object does not need to know who the recipients are.

PORTS

It would not be sufficient if objects could only implement an interface once. Because interfaces correspond to hardware activities, it is often necessary to implement the same interface multiple times in a single object. For example, a general-purpose I/O (GPIO) controller usually controls multiple I/O pins from the same device. Thus, Simics has the mechanism of named *ports*. A named port is an instance of an interface with a particular name, and to communicate with this interface, you need to reference both the object and the name of the port.

DOCUMENTATION AND METADATA

Every module and class in Simics carries its own documentation and other metadata. This makes it possible for Simics to offer help and descriptive text for literally everything inside a simulation session, including components and objects, all the way down to attributes and individual device registers. This self-description keeps documentation tied to the items it relates to, and keeps most of the documentation inside the source code where it is easy to keep it in sync with the code. A large part of the Simics manuals is actually automatically generated by running Simics and extracting the documentation and metadata from modules and classes. Metadata on modules is used to automatically load modules, as classes in them are required.

CALL CHAIN AND LOCALITY

Simics uses an event-driven simulation model (as discussed in more detail later in the chapter). An important consequence of this is that Simics objects do not run in their own threads, but rather they are only activated by calls from other objects, or the simulation event processor. Each function call into an object over an interface or port is executed immediately and in its entirety before returning to the caller. This provides great locality and the best simulation performance.

CHANGING THE CONFIGURATION

A Simics configuration can be modified at any point during a simulation. New modules can be loaded and new hardware models and Simics extensions can be added. All connections between components and objects can be changed from scripts and the Simics CLI at will. This dynamic nature of a system is necessary to support system-level development work. Reconfiguration can also be used to implement fault injection and test the target software's behavior in the presence of faults in the hardware.

COMPONENTS

To aid configuration and management of a simulation setup, Simics has the concept of *components*. Components describe the aggregations of models that make up the units of a system, such as disks, SoCs, platform controller hubs, memory DIMMs, PCIe cards, Ethernet switches, and similar familiar units. They carry significant metadata and provide a natural map of a system. Figure 2.5 shows an example of a component hierarchy from a simple target called `viper`. The `viper` target has a model of an Intel® Core™ i7 processor and an Intel® X58 chipset.

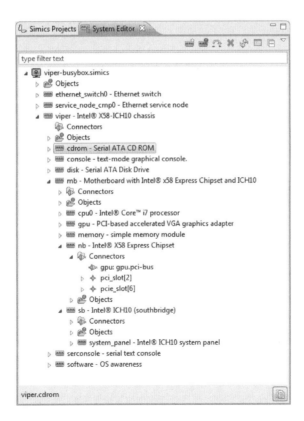

FIGURE 2.5

Example of a component hierarchy from a simple system as shown in the Simics system editor.

Components usually have parameters like the number of processor cores to use in a processor, the size of memories, the clock frequency of a core, or the media access control (MAC) addresses of an Ethernet controller. Components provide the standard way to create Simics simulation setups, and a normal Simics setup script simply creates a number of components and connects them together.

Components encapsulate the details of connections between parts of the system, creating abstractions like DDR memory slots, PCIe slots, and Ethernet ports. Components can be used to change the simulation configuration both during initial setup and at runtime.

Components can contain other components, and normally each board in a simulated system is represented by a single top-level component that in turn creates all the distinct units in the system. This is seen clearly in Figure 2.5, as the `viper` board contains several distinct units that map to the hardware decomposition of the real system. Components are covered in more detail in Chapter 4.

TIME IN SIMICS

The representation and management of time inside the simulation is one of the most fundamental and difficult aspects to consider when creating a simulation environment. This section describes the timing model used by Simics. The first important concept is the difference between *virtual time* and *real time*.

Real time, also referred to as wall-clock time, is the time perceived by humans in the physical world. On the other hand, the virtual time is the time as it is perceived by an observer inside of the simulation. The ratio between the real time and the virtual time, known as the *simulation slowdown*, typically varies during the simulation and can range from zero (simulation is infinitely fast) to infinity (simulation is stopped). A slowdown of one means that the virtual time and the real time progress at the same rate. Simics usually tries to push virtual time forward as quickly as possible to minimize the slowdown.

Simics normally does not attempt to synchronize the virtual time to the real time, because this would destroy determinism and repeatability. Virtual time is part of the state stored in a checkpoint, such that each time the checkpoint is loaded into Simics, the same saved virtual time is used. This makes checkpointing completely invisible to the target software.

Inside of Simics a multiple-clock time model is used. Virtual time is represented locally at one or more *clock objects*. Technically, a clock object is a configuration object that implements the cycle interface, but in most cases it is simply a model of a processor core. Each clock gets to advance time for a certain number of cycles, its time quantum, before the simulation forces a switch to the next clock object. A clock that is advancing time is said to *execute* cycles.

Every processor core in the simulation has its own local representation of time based on the number of cycles it has executed, its frequency, and its offset.

Note that the number of cycles executed may differ from the number of instructions executed, because the execution of an instruction does not need to take exactly one cycle.

Processor models in Simics have a constant rate of instructions per cycle (IPC), with the default value of one IPC. The IPC can be configured by the user and can be changed during runtime to more closely simulate the approximate real-world speed of a processor (Canon et al., 1980). In addition, there are other mechanisms that make a single instruction take more than one cycle. For example, a processor may stall, meaning that it gives up normal execution during some time period. This effectively halts execution of instructions while the cycle queue advances normally with respect to the processor's frequency. Another example is a disabled processor, which works in much the same way. Both stalling and disabled processors will continue to handle events on their cycle queues.

Time is represented in Simics as a 128-bit integer, and the smallest time unit that can be represented in Simics is a picosecond. Using a 128-bit integer places no practical upper bound on the time that can be simulated, which is on the order of a quintillion years. Older versions of Simics used a 64-bit integer, which caused problems for some users, because less than a year in virtual time could be simulated before time maxed out.

ABSTRACTION LEVELS

Simics is mainly used as a fast, functionally accurate simulator for software developers, and it is the authors' opinion that this should be the basic design point for the virtual platform. Where more details are required, individual models or groups of models can be replaced with more detailed variants to study specific behavior. Not only is this efficient in terms of the resources required to create the model, because more detailed models take longer to develop, but it is typically the case that not all parts of the platform need a detailed model. If the foundation for the virtual platform is a more detailed model it is more difficult to abstract "up" and gain simulation performance, because that requires substituting all detailed (slow) models. Figure 2.6 illustrates commonly used abstraction levels and their performance characteristics. The figure also shows the typical users for each abstraction level.

A major division occurs somewhere around the approximately timed (AT) abstraction level. At or below (more detailed) the AT abstraction level models are typically *clocked*. A clocked model drives the simulation by advancing a clock that is propagated out to the different models that are constantly "active" doing work. At or above (less detailed) the AT level it is more common to use *transaction-based modeling*, where the models are driven by higher-level transactions. Such a transaction can correspond to transferring a few bytes of data as a result of a memory load or store, or it can be an even higher level, such as delivery of an Ethernet frame.

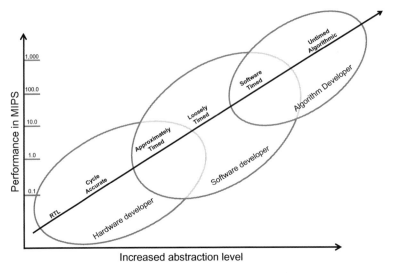

FIGURE 2.6

Virtual platform abstraction levels.

The simulation performance can easily differ by one or two orders of magnitude between two abstraction levels. Similarly, the time required to develop the models is also significantly reduced for the higher abstraction level, although not to such a great extent as the simulation performance is increased.

Simics models are typically developed using the *software timed* (ST) abstraction level to provide maximum performance. The term *software timed* is used to highlight that only enough timing information is added to allow unmodified software to run on the simulated environment. Simics ST is similar to the SystemC[†] TLM 2.0 loosely timed (LT) model (IEEE, 2011) in that a memory access is a blocking call. However, the Simics model is a special case of the LT model with a zero time delay, which sometimes is also known as a programmer's view (PV) model. The most common timing models are illustrated in Figure 2.7. For the rest of the book it should be assumed that models relate to ST models, unless otherwise stated.

The ST abstraction level means that each interaction with a memory-mapped device, such as a processor reading from or writing to the registers of a device, is handled at once: the device is presented with a request, computes the reply, and returns it in a single function call. The device does not add any immediate delay to the operation, and the result is computed before returning to the processor so that the processor can use the result immediately. In the same way, when a device calls an interface method in another device, it can rely on the result being returned immediately, without any time having passed in the simulator.

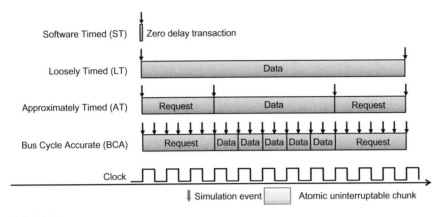

FIGURE 2.7

Different transactions models used to model memory accesses.

EVENT-BASED SIMULATION

The TLM simulation in Simics is *event based*, which means that the simulation is driven by executing a sequence of events. An event is a specific change at a specific point in virtual time. The execution of an event results in the simulation changing from one state to another, and simulation progress is achieved by a sequence of such state transitions. Event-based simulation is typically contrasted with threaded simulation. In an event-based simulation, all actions are taken as a result of events, and once an event is handled, control is returned to the simulation kernel. In a threaded simulation, each model contains (at least) one thread sitting in a main loop, waiting for things to happen. In SystemC, threaded models are coded as SC_THREAD and use wait() to release control to the simulation kernel. In general, event-based simulation has better code locality and higher performance than thread-based simulation.

In Simics, events are scheduled on event queues, which are typically attached to processor models (in the general case, to any clock object). Because each processor has its own representation of local time, it also has its own event queue.

In a single-processor system the event processing is straightforward. The processor maintains two queues: one step queue and one cycle queue. The step queue's main responsibility is to execute instructions and the cycle queue is responsible for executing other events based on the virtual time. Remember that each processor has its own representation of local virtual time based on its cycle count, frequency, and offset. Any object may post an event on the queue of a clock object. When an event is posted on a specific virtual time, the time is first converted to a cycle count on the processor and then posted on the processor's cycle queue.

As mentioned, only clock objects, such as processors, define time inside the simulation.

Device models are passive and only perform actions when activated due to an event on an event queue. The most common case is that a processor executes a load or store instruction. When the load or store terminates in a memory-mapped device, that device is activated and may perform side effects as a result of the memory operation. It is important to note that no virtual time will pass while the device is called. The other way a device is activated is when a timed event that the device posted earlier—for example, as a result of a store to a register—is triggered as part of advancing virtual time. Such events result in a call to a function inside the device model that has been registered with the event. Events are the mechanism by which device models manage tasks that should appear to take virtual time.

Simics device models handle time and delayed actions by posting events on the time queue of a processor to get a callback at a certain point in virtual time. Figure 2.8 shows a simple example of a timer being programmed from a processor. We can see how the timer device model gets activated each time the processor does a memory access to it. While the device model handles the access, the processor is stopped in the middle of the instruction, waiting for the device model to return. At the second memory access, the timer sets up an event callback corresponding to the timer expiry time. This is done by calling the processor model. Some more instructions are executed by the processor, and when the time for the event comes, the processor stops between two instructions and calls the event handler in the timer device. This event handler calls the interrupt controller device model, which calls the processor to trigger an interrupt. The processor notes that the interrupt needs to be handled, and returns. Once the normal processor loop is

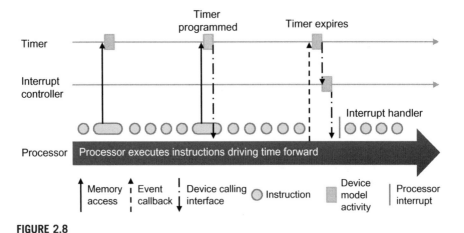

FIGURE 2.8

Device interaction.

back in control, it handles the interrupt by redirecting the instruction flow to the interrupt vector associated with the interrupt triggered by the interrupt controller.

This modeling method is used for anything with a software-noticeable latency. For another example, consider the device driver for an I/O device. The driver expects to be able to run code to prepare for the completion interrupt after writing a register to start an operation in the device. All too often, the driver would crash if the completion interrupt arrived immediately upon starting the operation. The Simics model of such a device would typically compute the device-local effects of the operation immediately upon starting the operation, and then post a timed event at the point in the future when the operation is complete. Only at this time would the processor get the interrupt, and the device driver would see the expected behavior.

MULTIPROCESSOR SCHEDULING

With more than one processor core or clock in the simulation, event scheduling becomes more complicated. To achieve high simulation performance it is important to allow the processors to be *temporally decoupled*. Rather than switching between the units at each step of the simulation, each unit is allowed to run for a certain amount of time, its time quantum, before switching to the next unit. Temporal decoupling has been in use for at least 40 years in computer simulation (Fuchi et al., 1969), and it is a crucial part of all fast virtual platform simulators (Aynsley, 2009; Cornet et al., 2008). Efficient support for temporal decoupling is one of the reasons why Simics processor models have local time instead of a single global time.

The clocks in a configuration take turns to advance time by a small amount. This is done in round-robin order. The amount of time advanced each turn is the *time quantum*, which is sometimes called the CPU *switch time*. For example, assume a system with three clocks and a time quantum Q. Their times would then proceed like the illustration in Figure 2.9.

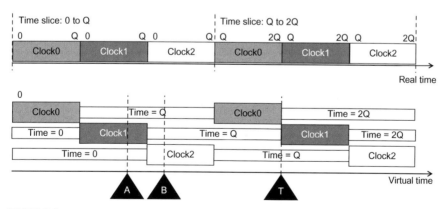

FIGURE 2.9

Round-robin scheduling of temporally decoupled clock objects with time quantum Q.

At the point marked T in Figure 2.9, $Clock_0$ has reached time $2Q$ while both $Clock_1$ and $Clock_2$ are still at time Q. As mentioned before, there is no single global time in the simulation; time always belongs to a clock, and different clocks can have different views of the time.

Because of the time quantum, the clocks are loosely synchronized. For instance, the time of $Clock_1$ at point A is greater than that of $Clock_2$ at point B, although A precedes B in the simulation. This may cause time paradoxes if objects using different clocks interact or share a mutable state. The most common communication channel between clocks is memory shared between processors. If processor $Clock_1$ writes a value to a memory location M and its local time is t, that value might well be read by a later processor $Clock_2$ at a local time that is less than t. This behavior might look odd to an outside observer, but it rarely causes any issues, because the code on $Clock_2$ does not know when the value was written. All it sees is a value in memory. However, there have been cases where code designed to synchronize the clocks of processors have failed due to temporal decoupling, thus requiring special handling.

Another potential issue with temporally decoupling the clocks is that events can be posted in the (local) past if processors post events on each other's queues. Consider the case where $Clock_1$, at some point between local time 0 and time A, posts an event on $Clock_0$'s queue at time A; because $Clock_0$ has already passed time A and is already at time Q, the event will appear to be scheduled in the past.

When clocks have different frequencies, the length of the time quantum in clock cycles will be different between the clocks, while being the same in virtual seconds. The number of cycles in a quantum will sometimes vary between individual activations of a clock to avoid drift in the global time synchronization. The scheduler is perfectly deterministic and will always produce exactly the same schedule for the same set of clocks, as that is necessary for a deterministic simulation.

It is important to note that all events on a time queue are triggered precisely. The Simics semantics allow events to be triggered at any point during a time slice. For example, this means that a timer local to a processor will trigger at the right cycle, regardless of how many processors there are in the simulation. Some other simulation systems use temporal decoupling where events are only allowed to trigger at quantum boundaries. This is not the case in Simics, which makes it possible to model hardware event timing more precisely and allows running with a longer time quantum than is practical in most other simulators.

Managing time and scheduling becomes even more complex when the simulation is running in multithreaded mode. This is covered in more detail when discussing networked simulation in Chapter 5.

CYCLE-ACCURATE SIMULATION

When developing hardware, it is common to use models that are called *cycle accurate* (CA) or *clock-cycle accurate* (CCA). Such models are needed to accurately predict the eventual performance and behavior of the hardware and to validate that the hardware works correctly with respect to bus protocols, cache coherency protocols, and the like.

CCA models are commonly used as a *design tool*, where hardware design teams first build a rough bandwidth and latency model, and then a more detailed model of the internal microarchitecture and pipeline of the hardware. Such models are then used with various forms of input to validate performance goals and find problems in the design. This methodology has been used for processor design since the late 1950s (Brooks, 2010), and it is the dominant paradigm today. From a modeling perspective, such models essentially *prescribe* the timing that the eventual hardware implementation needs to have to satisfy the requirements.

CCA models can also be *generated* from the actual implementation of hardware using tools like the Carbonizer from Carbon Design Systems. Such models essentially serve as a software model of the precise hardware behavior, allowing the simulation of the cycle-by-cycle behavior of hardware as it is actually implemented. This can be very handy for low-level validation of hardware.

Manually programming a CCA model of an existing piece of hardware has been proven impractical. It is very time consuming and almost guaranteed not to match the hardware (Engblom, 2002; Phillips, 2010). Instead, CCA models should focus on the design and validation aspects.

Simics setups can be extended to contain CCA models by building *transactors* that map between Simics ST-level transactions and cycle-level activities. Typically, only a few device models are replaced each time, keeping most of the platform at the native Simics abstraction level. Such hybrid setups are used to support workflows, such as testing detailed models with transaction flows from a full platform, and real software stacks. See Chapter 9 for more details on such hybrid simulations.

MEMORY MAPS

The *memory map* is a fundamental service provided by the Simics framework and is a core component to enabling very fast simulation. Memory maps take care of routing memory accesses from their source to their destination, based on the address of the access. Memory maps replace the explicit modeling of buses in Simics. Memory maps provide the software view of the bus system, but not the hardware view. It is a typical transaction-level abstraction from the hardware behavior. Simics memory maps are dynamic and can be changed during the simulation, both by the user and more commonly from various devices and components that manipulate memory mappings to implement dynamic target behaviors.

Figure 2.10 shows an example of the memory map for a simple system. It is not a complete system, but instead it is just intended to show a few typical cases of memory mappings. The processor has a memory map that shows how RAM and a few devices are mapped, as well as a PCIe memory space in which PCIe devices are mapped.

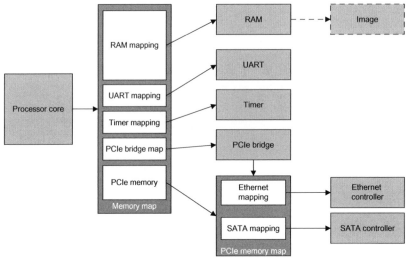

FIGURE 2.10

Memory maps.

HIERARCHICAL MEMORY MAPS

The basic building block for creating memory maps are objects of the memory-space class. When a memory transaction is initiated from an origin, typically a processor model, the address a of the access is passed unmodified to the first memory space. For a processor model, the first memory space typically represents the physical address space of the processor. If nothing is mapped at address a, an access error is signaled to the origin. However, if the access falls within the range of a second memory space that is mapped in the first memory space at offset b, the transaction is passed on to the second memory space with the local address $c = a - b$. Memory spaces are traversed in this fashion until an unmapped address is reached or the transaction terminates in a device model. This process is shown in Figure 2.11.

Figure 2.11 also shows how the final access to a device always ends up using a local offset into the mapped register bank. The device does not need to know where it is mapped in memory to function, and the memory map can be reconfigured without the device being concerned. Figure 2.11 also shows a device being mapped in multiple places. This is trivial to achieve in the Simics memory map system, and the same device can also be mapped multiple times from the same memory space.

RAM, ROM, AND FLASH

When it comes to models of devices like RAM or ROM—that is, memory without side effects—Simics will use efficient caching of the target address to avoid

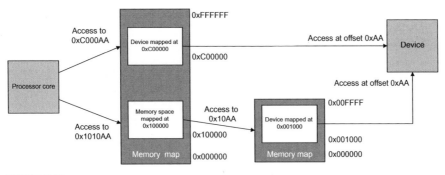

FIGURE 2.11

Hierarchy and multiple mappings.

traversing the memory space hierarchy for every instruction executed, and will instead directly access the underlying memory. Such direct memory access is common in all virtual platforms, and the Simics implementation is based on the information from the memory maps.

In Figure 2.10, we see how the RAM is mapped in the processor's memory map. The RAM object ties the memory map to the image object, which cannot be directly mapped, and implements the support for fast memory access from the processor. The actual data is stored in memory image objects, which are explained in more detail later.

When a Simics model includes a memory controller it is only used to manipulate, initialize, or control the underlying activity of the Simics memory system. The controller is not directly involved in accessing memory.

PCI AND OTHER MEMORY-MAPPED INTERFACES

For the simulation of PCIe and similar interfaces, Simics uses subordinate memory maps cascaded from the primary memory map, configured by the PCIe controller in response to the mappings set up by software following the PCIe probing. The software setup process results in the configuration of a memory map in PCIe space, and devices are mapped into this space. Once configuration is completed, the memory space for PCIe is handled just like any other memory map, with efficient access to resources. The PCIe controller is only used for the configuration.

Figure 2.10 contains a PCIe memory map inside the system's main memory map, containing two devices. Those device mappings are created by the PCIe bridge device when the software probes and configures the PCIe system. The PCIe bridge itself is mapped into the memory map directly accessible to the processor, and it has an arrow down indicating that it configures the PCIe memory map.

Having device models manipulate memory mappings is a very useful implementation trick. For example, it has been used to simulate devices being turned off by replacing the mapping of an actual device with passive RAM. It has been used to implement devices with multiple operation modes, where rather than having each register in the device check the mode on each access, a different register bank is mapped for each mode. When the mode is changed, the device updates the memory map to route transactions to the correct bank.

MULTIPROCESSOR MEMORY MAPS

In a system with multiple processor cores sharing memory, each core typically has its own local memory map. The local memory map provides mappings for core-local devices like interrupt controllers. All accesses that miss the local devices are forwarded on to the shared system-level memory map, as shown in Figure 2.12.

The use of hierarchical memory maps does not affect performance, because the processor models cache accesses to the performance-critical memory where instructions and data are stored. The direct-access mechanisms described earlier function regardless of the depth of nested memory maps.

MEMORY IMAGES

The Simics memory image simulation system provides several features that are unique[1] and enables Simics to tackle simulation of systems far bigger than any

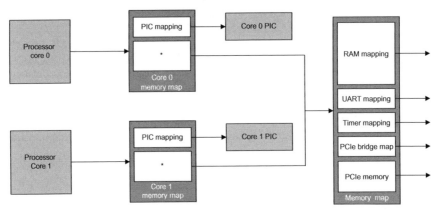

FIGURE 2.12

Memory maps with multiple processors.

---

[1]Unique at the time of writing in mid-2014, to the best knowledge of the authors, compared to other development-oriented virtual platform products and frameworks.

other simulation system. The Simics memory image system is used to simulate all large storage in a system, be it RAM, flash, or disk.

The image system only represents the memory that is actually being used, which means that the host machine only needs to have enough RAM to represent the working set of the target machines. In many cases this is significantly less than the total amount of simulated RAM. Memory images allow Simics to simulate target memory that is larger than the physical memory of the host machine (Alameldeen et al., 2003a; Rechistov, 2013). This is in contrast to a typical virtual machine monitor system or other virtual platforms, where all target memory is explicitly allocated as part of the simulation setup.

REAL-WORLD STORY: VERY BIG MEMORY

Back in the early days of Simics, a customer was building very large 64-bit servers using Simics. Having gone to 64 bits, it was interesting to find out if the operating system actually handled a fully populated 64-bit memory correctly. For example, was there some code that used signed instead of unsigned so that a memory of 2^{64} bytes would be considered -2^{63} instead? Even if there had been a server capable of loading that much RAM, the cost of buying it would have been bigger than the U.S. defense budget at the time. But with Simics, they just set the memory size to the 2^{64}, and off the system went booting. As long as the simulation did not touch too much memory, Simics easily simulated this on a machine with less than a gigabyte of RAM on the host.

Simics can also reduce the RAM needed by representing identical memory pages only once. Unused pages are never explicitly represented, and it is possible to set the default value of unused memory (e.g., for flash, unused memory has the value 0xFF). If two different memory pages have exactly the same content, they can also be merged and represented only once. This is the same idea as the Linux kernel's Kernel SamePage Merging (KSM), or VMware's Transparent Page Sharing (TPS). Such pages are surprisingly common, in particular when simulating many instances of similar boards in networks.

If more RAM is needed to represent the target state than is available, the Simics image system does its own swapping to disk, based on information available to the simulator about what is the best data to swap out. It also means that Simics can simulate system memory larger than the virtual memory of the host. This means that the available disk space is the limit to how large images can be simulated.

Simics images also track the pages that have been changed between operations, such as starting the simulation and taking a checkpoint.

Simics images used to simulate disks are normally read-only; this prevents the simulation from accidentally changing fundamental disk images and makes it safe to share the same disk image between multiple target machines. For example, this means that you can boot several copies of the same Linux system into a simulation without them clobbering each other's state. All changes are considered local to each target machine and will be discarded when the simulation exits. If desired, the changed pages can be saved as "diff" files and later reapplied to achieve the new disk state by combining the original unchanged image file with the diff.

Simics images are not in themselves disks, RAM, or flash—they are used as the storage behind those various types of memory or storage systems. Figure 2.10 shows an example of how an image is used to provide the storage for a RAM object, where the RAM object is mapped into the target memory map and the image is behind it.

CHECKPOINTING

Checkpointing is a very important and useful feature of Simics. Making sure that checkpointing works and works well has been the design goal throughout the history of Simics, and has had a deep influence on a number of design decisions (Magnusson et al., 2002; Engblom et al., 2010a). The Simics object model is crucially designed to allow checkpointing to function. By avoiding threads in models, there is no state hidden on the execution stack. Rather, each time the simulator is stopped, all state is stored inside of the objects of the simulator (and typically accessible via attributes).

It does happen that Simics objects contain state that is not checkpointed; however, such state is defined to be ephemeral and has to be reconstructed each time a checkpoint is opened. Typically, the non-checkpointed state consists of various caches of information from the rest of the simulation, which can be reconstructed from the state of other objects. Such state is cached locally in an object purely as an optimization for performance.

A Simics checkpoint is really a directory in the host file system, which contains several files. An example is shown in Figure 2.13.

- The `config` file describes the current state of all processors, devices, and other checkpointed simulation modules. It is a text file following standard Simics object state syntax.
- The `info` file provides the metadata for the checkpoint, including the versions of Simics used to create the models, and user-provided comments and annotations. This is also a text file following Simics standard object state syntax.
- A set of Simics `craff` (compress random-access file format) files for all memory images in the simulation that have changed because the simulation started or the last checkpoint was saved.

REAL-WORLD STORY: VERY BIG CHECKPOINT

The Simics checkpointing system has proven very robust in the face of demanding users. Sometimes to an extent that even surprised the developers. One example was a customer who built their own custom Simics models and ended up with a very large system model containing a thousand or so instances of a device with a few thousand registers in it. The result was a `config` file that was about 5 gigabytes in size, enough to overload most text editors. But Simics was able to parse and load this checkpoint file without a hitch. It is nice when your product surprises you in this way!

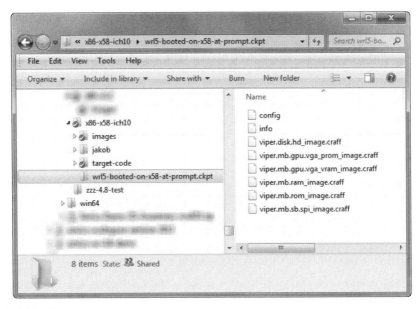

FIGURE 2.13

Example Simics checkpoint.

PORTABILITY AND IMPLEMENTATION INDEPENDENCE

Simics checkpoints are portable across host types and implementations. In practice, this means that a checkpoint of a target system taken on a 32-bit Windows machine using Simics 4.4 can be opened on a 64-bit Linux machine using Simics 4.8 (as long as the same set of simulation models are available). This is enabled by the explicit export and import of state, without assuming any common implementation between the saving of the checkpoint and the later loading of it.

Such portability is not possible with approaches to checkpointing that involve dumping the entire binary state of the target memory to disk and then restoring it into a new process. Such checkpointing only works when the basic simulation code is unchanged and you restore the checkpoint onto the same machine or one with a virtually identical operating system installation. Even the change of a single system library can break such checkpoints if some data structure stored in the checkpoint is affected (Kraemer et al., 2009).

In case the implementation of a model does change enough between model versions to make old checkpoints invalid, Simics allows the model designer to create checkpoint update code that transforms the old checkpoint state of an individual model to a new format that fits the new version of the model.

DIFFERENTIAL CHECKPOINTS

Simics checkpoints make use of the differential memory image system described before to save space and reduce the time needed to save a checkpoint. This means that to open a checkpoint, you need all previous checkpoints that it depends on and any disk or memory images used to set up the initial simulation state.

The advantages of using differential checkpoints are that saving a checkpoint can normally be a very quick process and that checkpoints can remain fairly small. Checkpointing systems that rely on saving the complete target memory state often have to save many gigabytes of memory to disk, even if only a tiny portion of it has changed since the last save. With Simics, only the change is saved, and if nothing has changed, nothing needs to be saved at all. Thus, the size of a checkpoint depends on how much the target system state has changed since the last checkpoint, and not on how large the target system is overall.

SESSION STATE AND SIMULATION STATE

Simics checkpoints are defined to contain the simulation state—that is, the state of the simulated system. By design, they do not save session state such as command-line variables, breakpoints, symbol file associations in the debugger, or running scripts. Excluding the session state is necessary to facilitate sharing checkpoints between users and using checkpoints to archive state for the future.

For example, it would be very confusing to a user who opens a checkpoint and starts an overnight simulation if Simics suddenly stopped on a breakpoint the user had never set and did not know about, just because it was included in the checkpoint by mistake. By cleanly separating the target state (checkpointed) from what the user is doing with the target (not checkpointed), checkpoints remain robust communications tools.

If a user wants to reproduce a particular Simics session setup, it is usually done by running a script after opening the checkpoint to restore the session state. Such a script would start up script branches, add symbol file mappings to the debugger, and set up the values of command-line variables. The Simics Eclipse debugger will save the debugger state in Eclipse, including symbol file associations and breakpoints.

DETERMINISM AND REPEATABILITY

Simics is normally deterministic; this means that from a given starting configuration, the simulation always proceeds in exactly the same way. This is a very useful property, because it allows analysis of the same simulation over and over again, and makes it easier to debug the simulator and its models, as well as the software running on the simulated system. Determinism is also a requirement for reverse simulation.

A simulation is only deterministic if all of its parts are. In particular, all classes that are used in the simulation must be written deterministically. For example, if a module uses random numbers, it must maintain the random number seed as part of its configuration so it can use the same random sequence for each run.

Models that communicate with the outside world require particular care. This includes communication over a real network connection and keyboard or mouse input. In these cases, input has to be recorded using the *recorder module*. This permits subsequent reexecution of the same simulation to be performed with already recorded input instead of reading new data. Simics can save the recorded asynchronous inputs along with a checkpoint so that another user can replay the exact same execution scenario. Input can also be scripted to provide deterministic behavior during testing, for example.

Deterministic does not mean *predetermined*. In a predetermined execution, you would know what is going to happen before it happens, and the exercise would be fairly pointless. Instead, the system's execution on Simics will vary for the same reasons it varies in the real world: the exact code loaded, the timing of asynchronous events, and the accumulation of state over time. Simics executions exhibit the same *variability* as a real system would, with the difference that *repeating* a certain execution is trivial thanks to determinism and recording.

In a variable system, each time an action is performed, the effect might be different. A good example is running a multithreaded program on a multicore computer. Each time it runs, the precise pattern of thread starts, thread switches, locks, thread communications, and other concurrent properties of the program will be different. Sometimes this affects the program results, sometimes not. Such variation will be present on a deterministic virtual platform too, as long as the program starts from a different state each time. For example, running the same program many times in succession within the same simulation will lead to variability because the state of the simulator will be different between runs. Similarly, if nondeterministic user input, such as mouse movements or keyboard input, is provided to the simulator, variability will manifest itself. However, if the simulation is restarted from time zero or from a checkpoint and runs under deterministic script control, each such run will repeat the same execution.

REVERSE EXECUTION

Simics can give the illusion of running the simulation backwards; this is referred to as *reverse execution*. Simics uses an implementation model for reverse that is known as *reconstruction* (Engblom, 2012a). When enabled, the entire simulation state is automatically saved in memory, in what is known as a *micro-checkpoint*, at some interval. The micro-checkpoints permit Simics to restore the configuration to a previously saved state and proceed to any subsequent point.

Figure 2.14 shows the basic technique used to reach a certain previous point in time in Simics. First, the system state is pulled back to a micro-checkpoint, which comes *before* the desired target time. The system then executes forward

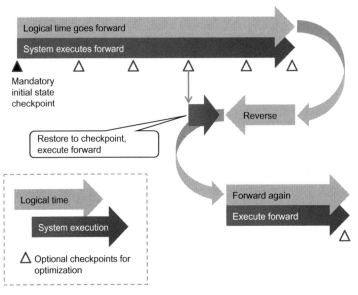

FIGURE 2.14

Reverse execution by reconstruction.

until the desired point in time has been reached. The crucial fact is that the execution of the system model is always in the forward direction, even if the user-perceived time is indeed going backwards.

For reverse execution to work, all models used must be deterministic and checkpoint-safe. This is considered a requirement for normal model development. When using reverse execution for going backward in time, it is not defined how many times interface methods and callbacks are called, or in what sequence. Some special cases, such as console output and breakpoints, are temporally ordered by Simics.

Reverse execution is used to implement reverse debugging, as discussed in Chapter 3.

RECORDERS

As mentioned before, a key part in enabling deterministic behavior, repeatable runs, and reverse execution is the recording of asynchronous inputs to Simics. This is done using the *recorder* class in Simics, a piece of simulation infrastructure provided by the Simics framework. Recorders are used both to replay inputs during a reverse execution run and to provide the ability to save and replay input scenarios associated with checkpoints.

A user module that communicates with the outside world has to make sure to save all inputs using a recorder; see Chapter 9 for more about writing user modules that interact with the world.

SIMICS PERFORMANCE TECHNOLOGY

Simics is designed from the ground up to be a fast simulator. The first use of Simics was to boot a multiprocessor 64-bit Solaris OS on a simulated Sun Workstation (Magnusson, 2013; Magnusson et al., 1998), which required pretty good performance. Since then, many different performance technologies have been added to Simics. Some of them are described in detail in later chapters, when they are applied.

- Transaction-level modeling (TLM) improves simulation performance by reducing the amount of detail in the model.
- The Simics memory map abstraction speeds access to devices and target memory.
- *Just-in-time (JIT) compilation* where the Instruction Set Simulator (ISS) translates target instructions to host instructions for faster execution. The JIT can run in a thread parallel to the main simulator thread, reducing the impact of the JIT compilation phase on the overall simulation.
- For Intel® Architecture targets on Intel® Architecture hosts, *Simics VMP* uses Intel® Virtualization Technology (Intel® VT) for IA-32, Intel® 64, and Intel® Architecture (Intel® VT-x) virtualization instructions to directly execute target code on the host processor. This makes it possible to get close to native speed.
- *Direct memory access* and instruction and data TLB caching enables the ISS to directly access the host memory used to simulate target memory, without checking the target MMU mappings and simulator location of target memory pages for each access.
- *Temporal decoupling* improves simulation locality.
- *Multithreaded simulation* lets Simics use multiple host processors to simulate multiple target machines and multiple target processors.
- *Hypersimulation*, also known as idle optimization, allows the simulator to skip ahead in virtual time when a processor is idle. Idleness is either executing an architecturally defined idle instruction such as HALT, MWAIT, or WFE; executing a branch to self (common idiom); or spinning in a loop that will not terminate until something happens in the target machine. Such loops are automatically detected by analysis of the executing target code or manually defined for cases where Simics cannot automatically detect them.
- The Simics image system reduces host memory pressure, allowing larger systems to be efficiently simulated.
- Distributed simulation extends the multithreaded simulation paradigm across multiple host machines to simulate really large target systems.

SIMULATION SPEED MEASURES

When discussing simulation speed, it is important to understand that there are several ways to measure simulation performance. The two main ways to measure the target system's progress are simulation *time* and simulated *instructions*.

For a software-oriented, fast, transaction-based simulator like Simics, Qemu, ARM Fastsim, SystemC TLM, or IBM CECSim, the preferred measure is the number of target instructions executed per host second. This is the simulated instructions-per-second (IPS) number. Hopefully, a prefix such as *mega* or *giga* can be applied to the IPS, giving up to MIPS or even GIPS to work with.

For hardware-oriented simulators, such as RTL simulators, SystemC used for cycle-accurate simulation, or hardware emulators, *time* is the better measure. Time is measured in target cycles per host second, which is usually expressed as hertz, or Hz (1 Hz equals one target cycle per host second).

IPS and Hz are not directly comparable, because it typically requires several cycles to process one instruction. The activities in a fast transactional simulator do not translate directly to the activities of a cycle-level simulator. Still, at a rough level it usually works to compare IPS and Hz to get an idea for how quickly software can progress on the simulator.

Another popular measurement is *slowdown*—compared to a physical machine running the same workload, how much slower (or faster) is the simulator? This is a very practical measurement because it relates performance to the work a user wants to get done, but it is also very hard to define in a precise way in the simulator without a clear external reference. Simics provides slowdown measurements by looking at the clock frequencies set for its target processors and comparing this to the progress of time in Simics. This means that the same simulation speed can correspond to widely different slowdowns, if the processor clock frequency is different. As a measure of the inherent speed of a particular simulator, a slowdown number is meaningless. IPS and Hz do indicate the speed of a simulator in a way that can be compared between simulators, as they are based in absolute numbers. The inverse of slowdown is sometimes also used and is referred to as the *real-time factor* (RTF).

Domain-specific measurements can also be used when simulating particular workloads to indicate the simulation progress in terms interesting to the user. For example, network application users might be interested in network *packets processed per second* or *network data volume transmitted per second*. Multimedia applications can be measured by their *frame rates*. Such measurements require some custom tool that is able to observe the simulation output and interpret it in domain-specific terms. While similar to slowdown, they allow the comparison of different ways of doing things regardless of any particular speed reference.

MULTIPROCESSOR SIMULATION SPEED MEASUREMENT

When simulating multiple processors, simulated *time* per host second (RTF) works just fine. Target time will progress at some speed, and simulating a larger system typically just makes this move slower. However, simulated *instructions* per host second (IPS) becomes a bit trickier because it can be considered both for each processor individually or for the simulation as a whole.

Starting with an ISS that progresses at N IPS for a single target processor and running P such processors in the same simulation using round-robin scheduling means each ISS will run for $1/P$ of each real-world second. Thus, the progress of each individual ISS will be N/P IPS. However, the progress of the simulation as a whole will be $P \cdot (N/P)$, which is N. Thus, it is fair to call this an N IPS simulator regardless of the number of processors simulated. For clarity, the overall IPS might be called *aggregate IPS*, indicating the sum of progress on all processors in one host second.

A domain-specific measurement like frames per second or packets per second might or might not reflect the effect of the round-robin simulation; it depends on the behavior and load balance of the software being run on the simulator. Slowdown tends to go up as more processors are simulated using a single host processor.

When using multiple host cores to simulate multiple target processors or processor cores, there are essentially multiple ISSs running in parallel. Thus, if there are H host cores being used to run N IPS ISSs, the aggregate IPS is going to be $H \cdot N$. To measure the fundamental technology, the N IPS of the basic ISS still seems the most appropriate. Note that the $N \cdot H$ number assumes linear scaling as the number of host cores increases, which is only reasonable if the target software parallelizes perfectly and there is insignificant communication needed between the simulated cores.

SPEED VARIABILITY

Given the complexity of a full-system simulator and the many different performance techniques used, it should not come as a surprise that simulation speed tends to vary greatly during a run and between different runs. The actual performance of a simulator like Simics depends on the nature of the code being executed, the type of the processor being simulated, target code and simulator code locality, achievable parallelism in the simulation, and many other factors. This often changes during a simulation run, as the target code goes through different phases. To give an idea for the variability, Figure 2.15 shows a performance profile of Simics running a boot of a dual-core embedded target system running a real-time operating system. The horizontal axis shows the *virtual* time, and the vertical axis shows the measured MIPS as well as the slowdown. Note that the vertical scale is logarithmic to capture the very large magnitude changes over the run.

It can be seen in Figure 2.15 that early in the boot, the slowdown is close to 10. This is due to the software performing many device accesses, which is an expensive operation in any Simics-style simulator. After about one second, the boot speeds up for a short while when the target waits for some tasks to complete. Then there is another bout of intense processing, and finally at around three virtual seconds, the target is booted to prompt and starts idling at many billion instructions per host seconds (the top number was around 50 GIPS), executing

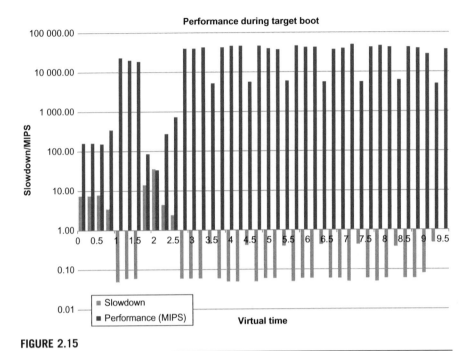

FIGURE 2.15

Relationship between virtual and real time.

with a slowdown below one, which indicates that it executes faster than a real machine would. It can also be seen that once every virtual second, the target executes a bit slower for one measurement interval. This is caused by periodic operating system processing making the target less idle, reducing the effect of hypersimulation.

TEMPORAL DECOUPLING

As mentioned before, the length of the time quantum used in temporal decoupling has a huge effect on the performance of the simulation. A time quantum of a few cycles will slow the simulation down, even if everything is operating as a transaction-level model with no timing details added, because it reduces the locality of the code and invokes the overhead of switching between processors more often. Having a too short time quantum also disables performance techniques such as JIT compilation or direct host execution (VMP).

Typically, Simics systems ship with a temporal decoupling time quantum of 10,000 to 100,000 clock cycles. Experience has shown that this range offers the best balance between reasonable software behavior in a multicore system and simulation performance. See below for more on this subject.

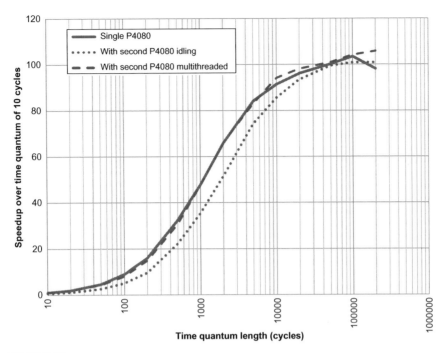

FIGURE 2.16

Performance scaling with different time quanta.

Figure 2.16 shows how the performance improves as the time quantum is changed from 10 to 500,000 cycles on an eight-core Power Architecture target. The target system processors are simulated on the Simics JIT-compiled ISS and run a computationally intense benchmark on all eight cores. Performance improves radically before peaking at around 100,000 cycles.

We also see the effect of Simics hypersimulation; when adding a second identical machine to the setup, performance does not suffer very much as long as the machine is idling. When using multithreading to simulate the second machine, there is no impact on the performance on the first machine.

Figure 2.17 shows the runtime of a checksum computation running on an Intel® Architecture target system, as the time quantum (called CPU switch time in Simics) changes from 100 to 100 million cycles. The Intel Architecture system is different from the Power Architecture system because it uses the Simics VMP technology to directly execute code on the host. This makes the simulator more sensitive to being interrupted in the middle of executing instructions, and thus it makes sense to use a longer time quantum. Peak simulation performance is thus reached at a longer time quantum than for a JIT-based simulator, at around 1 million cycles.

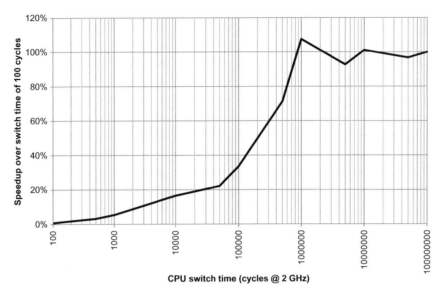

FIGURE 2.17

Temporal decoupling and performance with VMP.

The target system used in the example shown in Figure 2.17 is an Intel® X58 chipset with a quad-core CPU implementing the Intel® microarchitecture code name Nehalem, with two threads per core. The data is generated by running four instances of the md5sum program to calculate the checksum of data received from a pipe, thus no disk I/O is involved in the process. The checksum computation is a compute-bound process.

In addition to affecting Simics performance, the time quantum length used in a run might have an effect on how the software executes. For a target processor operating in the GHz range, the Simics default time quantum is on the order of microseconds, which is usually short enough not to be noticeable by the target operating system and software load.

However, temporal decoupling can affect the order in which events happen, and this might have software-visible effects. For example, consider the scenario in Figure 2.9. With the given time quantum Q, A will be simulated before B, even though the virtual time stamp of the event B is lower than that of A. However, if the time quantum is reduced to half of Q, B would happen before A, as illustrated in Figure 2.18. If A and B involved side effects such as sending data to an output device, those side effects would occur in a different order in the two simulation runs.

Another example is if the computation performed at A and B involves some shared state that is read and modified. In such a case, the value computed in the two runs will most likely be different, because A and B happen in different orders. It is very similar to the nondeterministic effects seen in parallel software, except

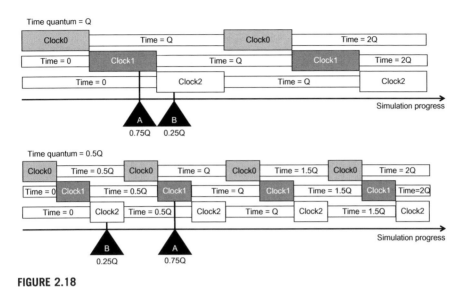

FIGURE 2.18

Event order and temporal decoupling.

that in Simics it is repeatable—as long as the time quantum is kept the same, it will behave the same way. It is also important to note that when this code is running on physical hardware, typically both event orders are possible, due to weak memory models, thread scheduling decisions by an operating system, and other system noise. The Simics simulation corresponds to one possible real-world scenario. Varying the time quantum length in Simics has proven to be a fairly effective way to cause varying event orders, and thus finding and repeating timing-dependent bugs that can be very hard to find on physical hardware. Chapter 3 describes one such case.

There have been examples of multicore software loads that require a fairly short time quantum to work properly. Such software loads tend to be concerned about time and will check the current time across processor cores using some high-precision local timer. A time quantum of 100,000 or even 10,000 cycles might be enough to be noticeable for such software, and the solution is simply to lower the time quantum length to a point where the software functions correctly.

Exceedingly long time quanta can also have effects on a system. When time quanta reach into virtual seconds, even standard non-real-time operating systems will notice and will generate errors indicating that the operating system believes that processor cores are stuck or crashed.

When multiple cores are competing for shared resources, longer time quanta can have the effect that one core gets an unfair share of time. Assume that a program running on a core locks a resource, operates on it for some time, and then releases it. If the program is such that the resource is mostly locked, the core that first gets the lock will most likely lock out the other cores. Figure 2.19 illustrates

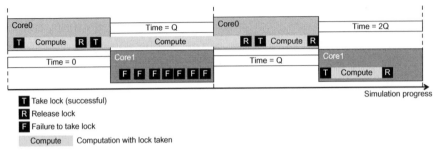

FIGURE 2.19

Temporal decoupling and locking.

this issue. Within its time quantum, *Core0* takes the lock, computes, releases it, and immediately takes it again. Because *Core1* does not run between the release and the take, it will not have a chance to take the lock. On physical hardware, it is quite possible for *Core1* to grab the lock from *Core0* at this point, but with temporal decoupling that will not happen. In the second time quantum, *Core0* releases the lock just before its quantum is up, and then *Core1* is able to come in and take it. But if the compute had taken just a little more time, the scenario from the first time quantum would have been repeated.

The issue illustrated in Figure 2.19 is real, but it is usually not noticeable in real systems. There is a lot of noise in a modern multithreaded, multitasking, multicore system, and it is highly unlikely that software will be "hogging" a lock in the manner presented here—that is bad for performance on a real system too and would have other undesirable effects.

One case where the locking time for shared resources does matter is the simulation of multiprocessor cache systems and shared buses, as well as when studying multicore synchronization at the level of individual instructions. For such work, it is necessary to use a very short time quantum to get reasonable results. Chapter 9 has some more discussions on this issue. Still, the experience from many decades of multiprocessor simulation is that using a time quantum between 1,000 and 100,000 cycles works well for most software stacks.

PERFORMANCE EFFECTS OF CHANGING TARGET TIMING

In general, Simics tries to push the simulation forward as quickly as possible. This means that the amount of real time spent executing a workload is useless as an indicator of the target speed. Even if the target processor clock speed is changed, Simics should complete the same workload in approximately the same amount of real time, even if the virtual time spent is radically different. The only exception is if Simics is running with real-time mode enabled, as discussed in Chapter 9.

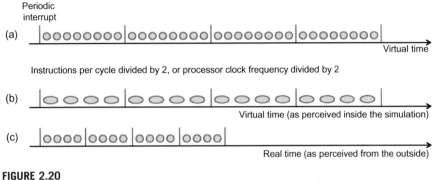

FIGURE 2.20

Performance effects of changing IPC or processor frequency.

Still, changing parameters such as instructions per cycle or the clock frequency of a simulated processor can have relevant effects on the perceived performance of a target system. Normally, Simics runs software as quickly as it can, and the instructions per second executed should not change as the operating frequency or IPC of a simulated processor changes. All that changes is how virtual time relates to the instructions executed. This does have an observable effect in most cases, because OS work and thus overhead is typically scheduled based on intervals of virtual time, such as periodic timers triggering 1,000 times per (virtual) second.

Consider the case shown in Figure 2.20. Figure 2.20(a) shows the normal execution of the system, where an interrupt hits every eight units of work. If we change the IPC to be ½, or change the virtual operating frequency to be half of its original setting, the net result will be that each instruction takes twice as much *virtual* time to execute, and thus that each unit of work takes longer to complete.

Figure 2.20(b) shows the effect in virtual time. The periodic interrupts hit at the same point in virtual time, but instead of eight there are only four units of work executed in each period. If each interrupt invoked the operating system for some periodic work, this increases the proportion of work spent in the operating system. Less virtual time will be left for user code to get work done, essentially slowing down user code processing. However, Figure 2.20(c) shows the effect from an observer looking at the system from the *outside*. Because each unit of work still takes the same amount of *real* time to execute, the periodic interrupts will hit more often in real time, and virtual time will appear to run faster in relationship to real time.

As long as the target system is mostly idle, this can be a very useful effect to exploit to improve the performance apparent to a user. For example, in case a system is spinning waiting for a timer to expire, setting the cycles per instruction to a value like 10 or even 30 will make the simulation get to the end of the loop much faster (assuming the loop cannot be hypersimulated due to some

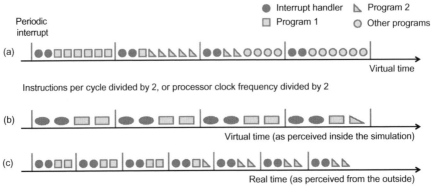

FIGURE 2.21

Performance effects under heavy load.

complexity). It has also been used to make GUIs more responsive, because they typically pick up mouse movements using a periodic interrupt.

However, if a system is heavily loaded, the net effect will be to slow down user processing due to increased OS overhead, as shown in Figure 2.21. Figure 2.21(a) shows the original scenario, with two programs (program 1 and program 2) running, along with an operating system. Each time a periodic interrupt happens, the operating system does some processing. The OS processing overhead is greatly exaggerated for clarity, at about 25% of total CPU time. We then lower the operating frequency by a factor of two. As illustrated in Figure 2.21(b), this means that the OS consumes 50% of the CPU time, and the programs require more virtual time to complete. Program 1 finishes after four periodic interrupts instead of after two. Figure 2.21(c) shows the effect apparent in real time. The behavior in real time is not as bad, but the end of both program 1 and program 2 are clearly delayed compared to the original execution. Thus, changing the IPC or operating frequency was a bad idea in this scenario.

MODELS AND EXTENSIONS

Simics users have the ability to create arbitrary extensions to the simulator, in addition to hardware models. Hardware models are supposed to use a small defined set of APIs to make it easy to maintain determinism, reversibility, checkpointing, and high simulation performance. Extensions have access to the full Simics API and can do anything inside of Simics. Simics itself comes with a large set of extensions, implementing its user interfaces, debug connections, and most of the features of the simulator. In theory, any Simics user could reimplement any part of this, but in practice, user extensions tend to focus on building application-specific inspection and connection functionality. Typical examples include customized instruction and data trace modules, race condition detectors, and connections between the Simics-simulated computer system and external simulators for the physical world.

Often, extensions begin their life as Python scripts. Python scripting is used to prototype the functionality, but as the desired functionality is clarified and the complexity of the task increases, it typically makes sense to move things into a Simics extension module.

Extensions are described further in Chapter 8, and modeling is described in Chapters 4, 6, and 7.

Develop and debug software on Simics

3

DEVELOPMENT MEANS TESTING

When people talk about software development, they often focus on the constructive activities of design, architecture, and coding. However, a fundamental part of development is testing what you have built. A piece of software that does not run is a pretty pointless piece of software, and the truth of a program is not seen until you have seen it running. As noted in the quote at the head of this chapter, we have always had to try our software live to see what it really does. Developing software means running software, and running software is testing it, even if it is not part of a formal test process or done by specialist test engineers. Thus, test runs are integral to the software development process.

Simics offers a very powerful way to run software—be it for a machine very similar to the PC you are running it on, or a machine very much unlike it. A fundamental benefit of a virtual platform like Simics is that you can run software of all kinds, targeting all kinds of hardware, on your local desktop or favorite development server.

Still, at its core, a virtual platform simulator like Simics is a computer executing the binary code. What it sees is a sequence of processor instructions being executed by a processor, and memory accesses and device accesses from this code. At this level, debugging means planting breakpoints on memory locations and watching memory accesses. There is no notion of what software is running or the abstractions of the operating system. To make sense of the software, Simics has been extended with a wide variety of debugger tools, including standard features like symbolic debugging and OS awareness, as well as more exotic features like reverse debugging.

With the software running on Simics, the benefits of using simulation can be realized: determinism, checkpointing, reverse execution, full control, and insight. This chapter describes how Simics is used to develop and debug software.

A HISTORICAL PERSPECTIVE ON SOFTWARE DEVELOPMENT ON VIRTUAL PLATFORMS

The idea of using a virtual platform or simulation to run, test, and debug software is an old one; actually, almost as old as programmable computers themselves. The quote at the beginning of this chapter is from a paper presented in 1951, describing the late 1940's experience from the University of Cambridge. They had built a machine called the EDSAC, which was a pretty sophisticated machine for its time. More interestingly, a key focus for the research team in Cambridge was software and software development.

What they discovered was that software had a life of its own once it was put into a machine, and that you had to look at it in action to understand what it did and why it did not do what the programmer intended it to do. The EDSAC did not have any hardware support for debugging, and the Cambridge researchers ended up coding the world's first single-stepping debugger using a simulation of the EDSAC running on the EDSAC. Before this, they had already discovered basic stop-on-error, postmortem memory dump, and printf debugging. The simulation system was the solution to capturing each step of a program as it executed (Gill, 1951).

Another important paper is from 1969, where a group at the Japanese Government Electrotechnical Laboratory describes a full-system simulator capable of running a real interactive multiuser multiprocessor operating system on top of a simulated HITAC-8400 data center computer. The paper describes most of the performance techniques and abstractions in use today, including temporal decoupling, transaction-level modeling of input and output devices, hypersimulation, and recorded input to drive deterministic replay. With this simulator, they debugged an operating system kernel, in particular chasing race conditions (Fuchi et al., 1969; Engblom, 2008).

A decade later, the engineers at Data General who were developing the Eclipse MV/8000 superminicomputer made very good use of a cycle-accurate simulator that they developed as part of the hardware project. The architecture was microcoded, which meant that a significant chunk of firmware had to be developed in parallel with the finalization of the hardware design. The team had access to two wire-wrapped prototype machines, which turned into a serious bottleneck for testing the microcode. Despite believing that it would not be ready in time, a simulator was developed, and once it was in place it basically saved the project. With the simulator, they got access to many more hardware systems. It also supported a record–replay debugger, allowing programmers to step through a failed test case at leisure, and without impacting the testing activities of others by tying up crucial prototype hardware. This case is also noteworthy in that it is a cross-simulator: the new machine was simulated using a computer with a different architecture (Kidder, 1981; Engblom, 2012b).

All of those examples show how simulation has been used many times in the past, but usually as internal tools for internal projects, or as research prototypes. In all cases, it has proven incredibly useful. It is really only in the past decade that commercial computer simulation tools have become available that make such technology available to anyone, not just engineers capable of building the tools for themselves.

AGENT-BASED DEBUGGER

When debugging software on a piece of hardware, the most common method is to use a debugging agent that runs as part of the target system software stack. Sometimes, it is an OS component, sometimes it is a user-level application with some help from the operating system, and sometimes it is part of a hypervisor or similar partitioned system. A debugging agent can make use of the target's OS API to inspect and control the target, making it fairly easy to access software abstractions like processes, threads, and file systems. Debugging agents can usually download new software to a target system, start programs, and attach the debugger. Debugging using an on-target agent is common with Simics, even if it does give up some of the benefits of using a simulator.

When running the software stack on a simulator, using a debugging agent is just like running on a real system. As illustrated in Figure 3.1, the agent is part of the target's software stack, and it uses the networking, or serial ports, of the target system to connect to the debugger. To the debugger, the Simics target looks just like a regular target with an IP address and a port to connect to. To Simics, the debugging agent looks like any other network-connected program running on the target system; it has no idea that this happens to be part of a debug chain. This makes it very easy to integrate Simics with existing tools, fitting into existing development and debugging flows.

When using an agent-based debugger, Simics has to keep running all the time to keep the debugger happy. If Simics stops, the debugger's connection to the debugging agent will eventually time out and drop the connection. The agent-based debugger is also completely unaware of Simics' capabilities like reverse execution and breakpoints on hardware accesses. If such features were used, the result would be a confused debugger and a disconnected debug session.

An agent-based debugger is *intrusive*, in that it changes the state of the target system. Attaching a debugger to a Simics system that contains a target agent will

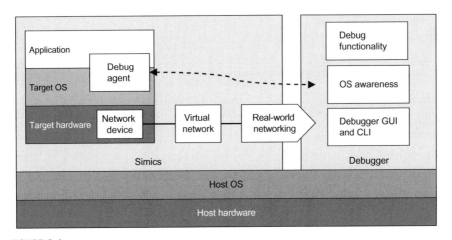

FIGURE 3.1

Agent-based debugger.

change how the target behaves compared to a run when the debugger is not attached, thus giving rise to classic problems like *Heisenbugs* that disappear as soon as a debugger or log printouts are added to a system to try to find them.

Agent-based debuggers can be used alongside Simics features like checkpointing. Just make sure to disconnect the debugger before taking a checkpoint and reconnect it after the checkpoint has been opened. It makes perfect sense to boot a machine and save a checkpoint, and then open that checkpoint and attach the agent-based debugger.

DEBUGGING USING SIMICS

The Simics debugger allows Simics to rise above the level of assembly-language debugging. The debugger is designed to support *nonintrusive* debugging, and to enable all Simics features while debugging. *The debugger is implemented as a Simics module*, and the software stack does not have to contain a debugging agent. As shown in Figure 3.2, the Eclipse-based Simics debugger talks to Simics directly, using the Target Connection Framework (TCF) protocol, and does not connect to the target itself system in any way.

The Simics debugger works both when the target is stopped and when it is running. It allows for all Simics breakpoints to be used, and supports reverse execution and reverse debugging. No matter how the simulation is stopped, the Simics debugger is able to display the state of the system. The debugger is completely asynchronous and does not assume that it has exclusive control over the target system, unlike most other debuggers. It is even possible to attach multiple debuggers to the same target system.

As shown in Figure 3.2, TCF (Eclipse, 2013) is used to connect the debug module inside of Simics and the Eclipse-based debugger. TCF is used both for

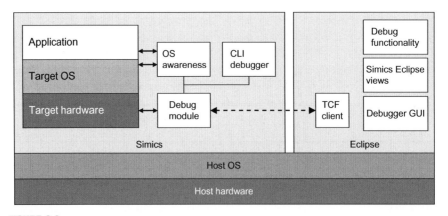

FIGURE 3.2

Simics debugger architecture.

the debugger and to drive all other Simics views in Eclipse, in particular the Simics CLI console.

The Simics debugger is similar in principle to a traditional hardware-based Joint Test Action Group (JTAG) debugger like the Wind River on-chip debugging (OCD). When using hardware debuggers, the software stack is unmodified and debugging happens without the software being aware of it. The JTAG debugger is similar to Simics in that you need OS awareness to make sense of the software stack. OS awareness provides the ability to determine which processes, tasks, and threads are running on which processors. OS awareness can capture system calls and investigate the state of an operating system and its processes. OS awareness provides insight into the software of a target system, not just the hardware.

Because the debugger is nonintrusive, it does not itself load software onto the target system. How to load software onto the target system is described later in this chapter.

SYSTEM-LEVEL DEBUGGER

A key difference between Simics and other debugging systems is that Simics has realized a *system-level debugger*. With Simics, there is a single debug session for each Simics simulation process, and the attached debugger has access to the *entire target system* over a single connection. This includes multiple processor cores, multiple boards connected in a network, and all the operating systems running on all the processors in the system. Even if the system contains many different types of processor cores and many different operating systems, the Simics debugger still controls and debugs the entire system as a unit.

Because the Simics debugger is nonintrusive, the debugger will see exactly the same execution that would happen when the debugger was not attached. Investigating a part of the system does not disturb the execution of any part of the system, allowing system-wide events such as interprocessor interrupts (IPIs) to be observed, and its effects on all parts of the system investigated. In most real systems, stopping a part of the system in a debugger quickly leads to system failure as other parts of the system notice that it has stopped and have to abort their processing.

Simics lets a developer cut through all the layers of the target system: it allows the simultaneous debugging of hypervisors, OS kernels, middleware, and user-level code. With OS awareness, it is possible to restrict debugging to a single process, but it is just as possible to step from a process through a system call into the OS kernel.

OS AWARENESS

Simics OS awareness is a Simics module that understands the data structures and abstractions of the operating system running on the Simics target system. With OS awareness, Simics and the Simics debugger know about kernel space, user space, processes, threads, and tasks.

Fundamentally, OS awareness performs two tasks: *live tracking* of events as they happen, and investigating the *instantaneous state* of the operating system. The live tracking of events means that OS awareness detects when the operating system performs a task switch, when software does a system call, or when interrupts happen. Indeed, the most common way to detect such events is to wait for interrupts in the target system—as long as no interrupts happen, the same user-level software is running. When an interrupt happens, the operating system takes over and the running process is considered to have been switched out. When the operating system returns back to user space, some process is considered to have been switched in.

Live tracking determines *when* something happens, but determining *what* happened requires investigating the *instantaneous state* of the operating system. For example, when an interrupt triggers, what are the active threads on the processor that received the interrupt? To determine that, OS awareness needs to know the structure of the OS queues of running and waiting processes, the contents of the task structs or process control blocks, and other data structures. Provided that this has been configured correctly, OS awareness can then traverse the lists in target memory and determine the name of the currently active process on a particular processor, all existing processes, dynamically loaded software modules and their relocation addresses, and anything else of interest.

Because the precise contents of task structs and the offsets of particular fields can vary between operating system builds and versions, OS awareness has to be configured before it can be used. Most often, it is possible to determine the parameters for OS awareness by looking at a symbol table or kernel file with debug information from the OS build. However, there are operating systems where the precise parameters cannot be determined until runtime, and in such cases the configuration will have to wait until the target system has booted. In any case, once determined, the set of parameters can be saved and used the next time the same target setup is run.

The use of parameter files makes it possible to have OS awareness configurations be distributed along with the OS images that they refer to. This means that a platform team can build an OS image, configure OS awareness for it, save the parameters, and supply its users with the OS and its OS awareness parameters without having to provide symbol files or debug information. The OS awareness parameters file is simply part of the software stack provided, and it is activated in the startup scripts used to start Simics. The users of the system do not need to know how to configure OS awareness—they just get it working as soon as they start the provided target system setups. OS awareness parameters are also saved inside of Simics checkpoint files, so that OS awareness keeps working across checkpoint save and restore operations.

OS awareness makes it possible to have Simics features work on only a particular subset of the software stack, such as having breakpoints set only inside a certain process, or tracing only memory accesses performed by the kernel and not by user-level tasks. A user-written Simics extension or script can listen to the events from OS awareness and take actions based on which software is currently running in the target system. It is possible to ask the OS awareness system for notifications only for a certain process, or to see all actions for all processes.

FIGURE 3.3

OS awareness tree.

The OS awareness system in Simics operates with the concept of a *node tree*. Each node in the tree represents an abstraction level in the OS process model. Typically, the top node is the operating system itself, which is then split into kernel and user-level tasks. In an operating system like Linux, each user-level task contains one or more threads. In the kernel, OS awareness normally distinguishes kernel threads from the idle task, because that helps account for target execution time. Figure 3.3 shows an example of a node tree from a barebones Linux system.

In the Simics CLI and debugger GUI, *process queries* are used to find processes of interest. These queries can match process names, process ID numbers, or other properties made available by OS awareness. In most cases, the name of a process is sufficient to identify it, but in complex systems more complex matches are needed such as "the process named foo on the board named bar." In a long-running system where a certain program is run many times, the process ID can be used to identify a particular start of a process.

Simics OS awareness supports nested operating systems to handle OS awareness for hypervisor-based systems. In a system with a hypervisor, it is necessary to track the scheduling of guest operating systems on the target processor cores. Once the active operating system on a core has been determined it is possible to then apply OS awareness for that operating system to determine the active process or thread. A single tree is thus used for the entire system, rooted at the hypervisor.

The details of what OS awareness can track and discover about the target software stack varies depending on the guest operating system and how much work has been spent building OS awareness for it.

Compared to the OS awareness systems used with hardware-based (JTAG) debuggers, a simulator's ability to precisely track task switches is unique. Such features have proven impractical to implement in hardware-based debuggers, because they would incur a significant overhead and overwhelm the availability of hardware breakpoints. The inspection of the instantaneous state is essentially the same as a hardware debugger's inspection of system state after halting the system, and indeed the same code as used for hardware debuggers has been used with Simics to determine facts like relocation addresses for dynamically loaded modules.

An agent-based debugger does not need OS awareness, because it is running inside the target system and can use OS APIs to ask the target OS about running tasks, loaded modules, and other information.

SIMICS BREAKPOINTS

A simulator like Simics makes it possible to break on most events in the target system, including those that are inaccessible even to JTAG debuggers. The Simics breakpoint system supports breakpoints on a wide variety of events in the target system software, target system hardware, and simulator itself.

Execution breakpoints can be set on single instructions, as well as arbitrary ranges of addresses. There is no limit to the number of breakpoints, nor on how much memory they cover. Breakpoints can be set on instructions matching particular encodings, allowing a user to catch all jumps or all arithmetic instructions of a particular type, for example. Breakpoints are available for both physical and virtual addresses.

Data memory access breakpoints can be set on reads, writes, or both; on any address; on any access size; and on physical or virtual addresses; and they can cover arbitrary ranges of memory.

Magic instructions are special instructions that are NOPs on real hardware, but that Simics intercepts. Simics' magic instructions can be used to break the execution when target software reaches a particular point by setting a *magic breakpoint*. To use magic instructions as markers, they have to be compiled into the target software. The advantage of magic instructions is that they are automatically moved around as code is changed and recompiled, with no need to map a location in a program to memory addresses using debug information. They can be used without needing debug information for the software.

Accesses to memory-mapped devices are intercepted at the device itself. The Simics `break-io` and `trace-io` commands take a device name as their argument and make Simics stop on each access to the device or trace all accesses to the device. In this way, it is not necessary to know where in memory a device is mapped. A device that is mapped in multiple memory locations or in multiple memory spaces stops on all accesses to it (such multiple mappings are commonly found for multiprocessor interrupt controllers and other system control hardware). Figuring out where a device is mapped can be fairly complicated in modern architectures where PCI configuration and flexible chip selects make the memory mapping for a system something the software sets up at runtime rather than a fixed property of the hardware.

Simics processor core models also provide a set of breakpoints on process actions. In particular, Simics can break on any interrupt or exception that is triggered in a processor core and on changes to processor control registers. Exception breakpoints make it much easier to debug low-level code such as drivers, exception handlers, and page fault code.

When OS awareness is available for the target software stack, Simics can also break on OS-level events—in particular, on processes and threads being created, destroyed, and switched in and out by the OS scheduler. Putting breakpoints on processes and threads being switched in or out is not really feasible on hardware, because the overhead of such checking is simply too big. It allows Simics to do things like reverse until the point where process X crashed and died—which is expressed as reverse until the point where process X was last switched out from a processor.

As discussed later, Simics device models and extensions can emit log messages during a simulation run. Simics is able to break when a log message is printed, which makes it very easy to pinpoint the code that puts bad data into a configuration register or causes some other log to be printed.

Simics haps can also be used for breakpoints. Some Simics devices and other modules register haps to offer a hook for scripts and breakpoints. Chapter 2 provides more information on haps.

Some Simics features offer their own breakpoint commands. In particular, the Simics serial console is able to break on strings being printed to the console. This is used both to stop when particular messages are printed and to automate interaction with a target system.

Most breakpoints can also be used as waiting points in script branches. This makes it possible to write simple scripts that set breakpoints and then wait for them to trigger before taking some other scripted action. This is a powerful method for building automatic solutions that interact with and observe the simulated system.

REVERSE DEBUGGING

Simics supports jumping to a particular point in time, single-stepping backwards, and reversing until a breakpoint hits. Reverse debugging is supported by the

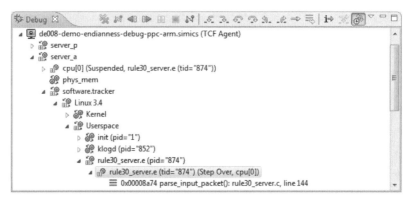

FIGURE 3.4

Reverse debugger toolbar.

Eclipse GUI, as shown in Figure 3.4. Reverse execution works for all Simics breakpoints, which means that it is possible to do things like reversing until the last time a certain I/O device was accessed or a log message complaining about a specification violation was printed by a device.

Reverse debugging in Simics applies at the system level, just like all Simics features. This makes it different from the reverse debuggers that only apply to user-level code, such as GDB, UndoDB (UndoDB, 2013), and Totalview (Gottbrath, 2009). There is no other system-level reverse debugger available at the time of writing, even though there have been several research prototypes produced over the years (Engblom, 2012).

Reverse execution in Simics uses in-memory checkpoints to enable fast restore during reverse-execution operations. These checkpoints are known as *micro-checkpoints*, because they are smaller than the regular checkpoints saved to disk. To a user, the micro-checkpoints are largely invisible, because they are managed by the reverse-execution machinery in Simics.

The backwards breakpoint is implemented as shown in Figure 3.5. The state is rewound to a micro-checkpoint and then the system is executed forward once with breakpoints set. When a breakpoint is hit during this first rerun, the time of the breakpoint is noted, and execution is resumed without notifying the user. Once Simics reaches the current point in time, execution stops. Simics then uses the reverse-execution machinery to reverse time back to the point of the last breakpoint seen. This process is repeated for each successive checkpoint stored, starting with the most recent and going backwards in time. The assumption is that most of the time the breakpoint will hit close to the current time, so the most recent time should be evaluated first.

NAVIGATING IN TIME

Reverse debugging adds time as an important parameter to the debugger interface, compared to a classic debugger. When moving backwards and forwards through

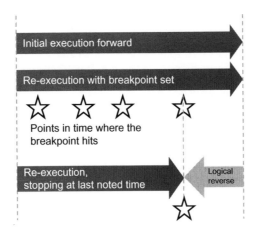

FIGURE 3.5

Reverse breakpoint.

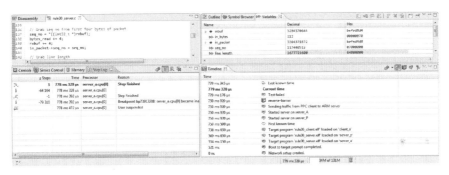

FIGURE 3.6

Navigating in time.

the execution history, it has proven to be very helpful to have an idea for how much target time has passed since the last stop. Because virtual time often develops at a very different rate compared to real time (as discussed in Chapter 2), users cannot use intuition to tell if a run takes a long time or a short time.

To resolve these issues, there are two novel views in the Simics debugger. The Stop Log view and the Timeline view, both shown in Figure 3.6. The Stop Log view shows the target time change of the debugger operations performed, making it easy to tell if a breakpoint was hit after a cycle or after a minute. It also shows if the simulation is moving backwards or forwards in time.

The Timeline view shows the current time, along with the earliest and latest known times in the simulation. When reversing, the current time will be less than the latest known time. The Timeline view also offers the user the ability to set *bookmarks* to mark interesting points in the execution. Later, a user can simply select a bookmark to jump to that point in the execution. In addition, as shown in Figure 3.6, the Timeline view allows a user and scripts to add *comments* to the execution. Such comments annotate the execution and help a programmer understand where the current time is in the history of the system. Bookmarks and comments can also be used from the Simics CLI as well as from scripts and extensions.

DEBUGGING HARD-TO-TALK-TO TARGETS

The Simics debugger works even when the target system does not have any kind of external connections at all. It is not uncommon to find deeply embedded systems where the computer component has no Ethernet, USB, or serial connections to the outside, and no accessible debugging ports. Other targets might have connections, but they are all used for live data and cannot be allocated for debugging. Yet another class of targets is forbidden from having any kind of debugging agent in place, because that would complicate the certification of the software stack or be a potential security vulnerability.

In such cases, having a Simics model is really the only reasonable way to do software debugging. Simics provides the target software with the encapsulated environment it expects, and the debugger comes in from the side completely without affecting the target system.

MULTICORE DEBUGGING

Debugging systems containing multiple processor cores was one of the original use cases for Simics, and it has only become more relevant as multicore architectures have become pervasive. A simulator has huge advantages when debugging parallel software compared to running the same software on a hardware platform.

The key problem with debugging a parallel system is its inherently chaotic behavior. The slightest change in timing can cause very large divergence in how a parallel program executes. Races between unsynchronized threads sometimes—but not always—affect the execution. Rerunning the same program is almost guaranteed *not* to repeat the same execution (Alameldeen and Wood, 2003b). In debug practice, this often manifests itself in the form of Heisenbugs.

The Simics ability to trivially reproduce any execution of a system, any number of times, makes the chaotic behavior reproducible. The precise execution that happens is still impossible to predict ahead of time, but once a run is complete, it can be reproduced with ease. Simics' nonintrusive debug, trace, and other inspection facilities avoid Heisenbugs. System-level stop means that it is possible to look at a simultaneous cross-section of the state on all cores in the system, something that is not possible on hardware. Simics breakpoints apply across all cores in a system, and they will catch accesses to shared data from anywhere in the system.

Figure 3.7 shows an example debugging session targeting a parallel program with multiple threads. The program is stopped in a function updating a shared variable, and all the threads in the program are in this function or in code called from it. The Stop Log view shows that the program has stopped each time a new core started running the function.

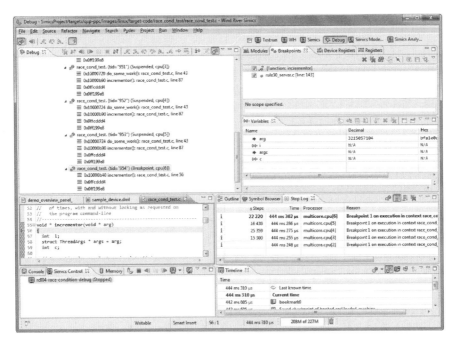

FIGURE 3.7

Multicore debug.

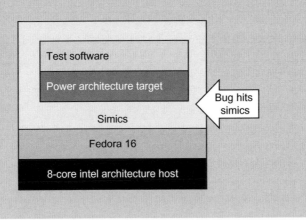

REAL-WORLD STORY: DEBUGGING SIMICS ON SIMICS

Simics is a really good tool for debugging parallel software. Simics itself is a parallel program, and we have used Simics to debug tricky bugs in Simics. This requires running Simics on Simics, which is achieved by simply installing a Linux matching the host Linux on an Intel® Architecture target machine.

In one particular case, the Simics target was a Power Architecture machine. This Power Architecture machine was running some bare-metal test code testing the processor simulation. Occasionally, this setup would crash Simics, due to some bug in Simics or the models. It was a difficult bug to track down, as it only happened in 1 run out of 50 or so. When attaching a debugger to try to diagnose it, it invariably did not happen (a classic Heisenbug). The initial situation looked like the illustration shown below.

To debug this using Simics, the development code tree from the host was packaged up as a tar file and put on a DVD image file. Simics was started from a checkpoint of a booted Linux system, the DVD image was inserted into the virtual DVD drive, and the image was mounted by the Fedora Linux running on Simics. The tar file was copied to the file system on the target and unpacked. A new checkpoint was taken after the Simics installation was completed and Simics could run on Simics. The result at this point was a completely self-contained, controllable, and repeatable environment.

The next step was to replicate the bug inside of Simics. To this end, a shell command was used that repeatedly ran the inner Simics until the bug hit. This session was started from the checkpoint after the Simics installation. The outer Simics was also running a Simics script setup that searched for the problem and set things up to easily replicate the issue if it was found. The complete setup looked like the illustration shown below.

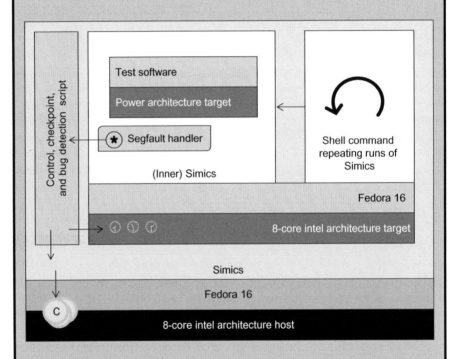

The outer Simics script varied the time quanta given to the processors in the Intel Architecture target system. This caused greater variation in scheduling of concurrent processes and threads in the Simics-simulated Fedora 16 operating system, which in turn helped provoke the bug so that it appeared faster (after fewer runs of the inner Simics).

A checkpoint was taken each time that the inner Simics had been started and the timing variation applied to the Intel Architecture processors—but before it had started executing the test case. This meant that a checkpoint would be available that led straight to the bug, with no need to do any warm-up of the target or particular configuration of Simics. The checkpoint would in effect be a self-contained bug report for the issue.

A magic instruction (shows as a star in the illustration) was planted in the segfault handler of the inner Simics, making it very simple to catch the crash of the inner Simics. Often, using a magic instruction like this is simpler than trying to capture the right page fault or putting a breakpoint at the right place.

Eventually, after some 20 runs of the inner Simics, the bug was triggered. Thanks to the checkpoint and Simics repeatability, reproducing the bug was trivial. The Simics crash could now be reproduced any number of times, and it was time to go debug and figure out why Simics crashed. An occasional Heisenbug had been converted into a 100% reproducible Bohrbug.

The next step of debugging was to open the checkpoint again, configure symbol information for the inner Simics to enable source-code debugging, and turn on reverse execution. Once everything was set up, the outer Simics was run forward until the magic instruction hit. Then, OS awareness was used to back up until the last time that the inner Simics was running prior to hitting the segfault handler. This placed the execution of the outer Simics at the precise instruction where the inner Simics crashed.

It turned out that Simics was trying to execute code in a location (let's call it BCDE) where no code was to be found. Stepping back one instruction led to a JMP instruction to the location BCDE. So where did this JMP BCDE come from? It was clearly not part of the static code of Simics, but something that was generated at runtime by the Simics JIT compiler.

To find out how the bad JMP was created, a memory write breakpoint was put on the instruction (JMP BCDE) and the execution reversed. Simics stopped at the point where the JMP part of the instruction was written to memory. Doing a stack backtrace at this point showed the code that was trying to write a 5-byte JMP XYZQ instruction into the JIT-generated code stream. Because the breakpoint had hit on the write of the byte containing the JMP instruction code, this meant that the other 4 bytes (containing the actual JMP target location of XYZQ) were yet to be written when the instruction got executed and Simics crashed, as shown in the illustration below.

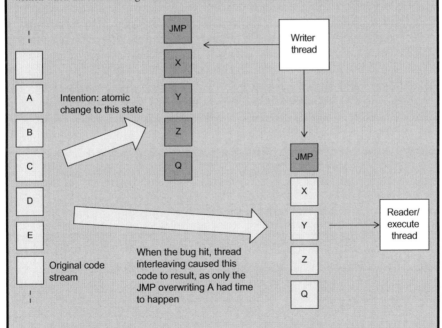

Stepping forward (on the processor) revealed that a thread switch happened in the inner Simics, and that the incoming thread immediately executed the 5-byte JMP instruction, such as it was. As shown in in the picture above, because only the JMP byte had been written, this was a jump to location BCDE, rather than the intended XYZQ (it would also have been okay to execute the original ABDCE code). Thus, the issue was diagnosed to be a read—write race condition, with

> the twist that the read was an execution of the memory as code and the write a regular data write. As soon as the problem was identified it was easy to fix.
>
> With the same setup, several other race conditions in Simics have been found and fixed, many of them involving the more common case of multiple concurrent threads updating and reading a shared data structure without sufficient synchronization. The mechanism of varying the length of time quanta for the processors has proven surprisingly effective to trigger parallel bugs.

LOW-LEVEL DEBUG

Simics makes it possible to debug low-level code, such as boot loaders and BIOS, firmware, drivers, and OS kernels, in a way that cannot be done using any other debug solution. In Simics, it is possible to debug a system from cycle zero, single-stepping even the first few instructions after reset. The nonintrusive nature of the debugger is incredibly important when debugging code that depends on interrupts, timing, and coordination across cores. Thanks to the global stop property of the simulator, interrupt-handling code can be single-stepped without affecting the system behavior.

Hardware state inspection, as discussed in detail later in the chapter, along with breakpoints on device accesses and exceptions, are incredibly useful to debug software interacting with hardware. Being able to precisely trace all accesses to a hardware device makes it much easier to investigate driver issues. A particularly interesting application of tracing is to determine whether the hardware or software is to blame for a driver issue for hardware in development. Given a trace of all software writes to the hardware, and comparing it to the specification of the hardware, it is easy to see if the software design or the hardware design is to blame. This can save many roundtrips compared to working only on prototype hardware; when the hardware is unstable, telling software and hardware issues apart is usually incredibly challenging (Condon et al., 1980).

Simics lets programmers look at the state of a processor in great details. User-level registers, supervisor-level registers, model-specific registers, and the MMU are all available for inspection without altering their state. They can also be inspected irrespective of the current operation mode of the processor.

REAL-WORLD BUG: U-BOOT COMMAND LOSS

Simics was being used to develop a model of a new Power Architecture–based system. The U-Boot boot loader was being used, as is common for Power Architecture targets. When U-Boot boots up, it normally presents the user with a CLI, where a sequence of commands are given to tell it where in memory the operating system to boot is located, how to configure the target network, and similar information. Finally, the boot command is given to boot the target.

However, the Simics developers on the project noticed that U-Boot occasionally would not accept the boot command, instead indicating that boot was an unknown command. Obviously, something had broken. Firing up the Simics debugger and working through the issue revealed that a string compare between the command input from the U-Boot command line and the command names stored in the U-Boot data area failed—basically, the string boot appeared to have disappeared from the list of commands. Looking closer at the memory contents, it was clear that the area where U-Boot stored the names of its commands was overwritten with garbage, at some point between the time the power was (virtually) turned on and when we needed to type the command.

But why, and how, and who? To debug this, it was critical to be able to repeat the bug. In this case, one of the Simics scripts that had been created to automatically boot the target system (by typing a sequence of commands at the U-Boot prompt) triggered the bug. Thanks to the repeatability and determinism of Simics, the bug could thus be reproduced any number of times and on demand.

Putting a data breakpoint (watch point) on the strings area, it was found that the cause was an interrupt service routine (ISR). The ISR pushed some data onto the stack to be able to restore the machine state after it had finished, and the stack pointer would then wander into the strings area. However, this would only happen if the stack pointer was close to the string area when the ISR was called. That means the interrupt triggering the ISR had to happen when the call stack was unusually deep. Most of the time, the stack pointer was far enough away that running the ISR was harmless.

Backing up toward power-on, it was found that the stack pointer was so close to the data not by design, but by a mistake in the early `boot` code. Just after the initial power-on, some assembly-language code used the `r1` register (which holds the stack pointer on Power Architecture) as a scratch register, without correctly saving its prior value. Thus, the stack pointer became corrupted. By pure luck the system kept working in most circumstances.

Essentially, the code created a broken system, but the issue only manifested itself as a real error when the circumstances were right.

The creators of the software acknowledged the error and were quite astonished as to how it could have been found and diagnosed. It would not have been possible except by using a deterministic and repeatable system like Simics.

As discussed in more depth in Chapter 6, Simics contains a powerful and flexible logging system where devices can emit diagnostic messages at several levels. For debugging software, log messages can provide invaluable insight into the interplay between hardware devices and software drivers.

Simics devices emit warnings and errors when software performs operations that are not legal according to the hardware specification. Typical examples are writing to offsets in device register banks where there are no registers, changing the value of bits that are marked as "reserved," or writing illegal values to configuration registers. These warnings are very useful to software developers, because they expose incorrect hardware use that cannot be seen or debugged on hardware.

In an ideal world, software should run on Simics without triggering any warning messages. However, very often the code works just fine on the physical hardware even with the issues that Simics spot. Hardware can be a lot more forgiving than most people realize. Writes to reserved bits and accesses to nonexistent register offsets are usually ignored in a hardware system, but they might become active in future systems. One classic example of this was the change from 24-bit to 32-bit physical addresses that happened on Macintosh systems in the 1980s—plenty of software had used 32-bit words to hold a 24-bit address along with an 8-bit tag of some kind. This failed badly when the 68020 processor started interpreting all the address bits. The universal lesson is that it is a very good idea to respect the hardware specification, even if the actions seem harmless for the moment.

Bad configuration values are truncated, misinterpreted, or fall back on some default behavior. What happens depends on accidental properties of the implementation, and it might not be immediately fatal. For a hardware designer, adding logic to detect bad accesses is a waste of silicon, and what could the hardware do about the error anyway? Warnings make a lot more sense within the user interface of a virtual platform. Being helpful for a software developer is not necessarily the same as being correct in the view of a hardware designer.

Even if software works on the physical hardware available right now, it is worth fixing bad behavior. Simics implements the documented and specified interface of hardware, and that is the interface guaranteed by the hardware designer. We have seen many cases where a new implementation of a particular hardware device or a new generation of a family of devices reacts very differently to accesses where there previously was nothing mapped at all. More than once, such accesses have proven fatal as code was ported from old devices to new devices. Simics model warnings have flushed out pretty serious bugs in drivers over the years, such as driver code completely miscalculating register offsets or an OS setup actually mistakenly containing a driver for a different set of hardware than intended. Particularly insidious are bugs that do not cause any issues on hardware until software actually starts using a particular function of a hardware device, such as configuration code for a network interface that writes to completely wrong locations, but as long as no attempt is made to actually communicate using the interface, no error will be seen on the hardware. On Simics, such accesses will be spotted very early.

REAL-WORLD STORY: FORCE-ALIGNED MMU WARNING

When running an operating system on a Simics model, Simics emitted a warning message that a 64 MB page was being force-aligned to the next lower 64 MB boundary. In effect, an MMU mapping that tried to put a 64 MB page at 0xefe0_0000 was in practice putting it at 0xec00_0000. The specification for the architecture makes it clear that if an MMU page is not aligned on its own size, the mapping will be implicitly force-aligned, and the processor will keep executing. Simics was doing the same thing as the real processor, and the code kept running, but in addition Simics also emitted the warning (because this is likely an error).

Indeed it was an error on the part of the programmers. The intention had been to map just 1 MB at 0xefe0_0000 (which is perfectly okay), but the effect was to also map 62 MB below the address, reserving it for the operating system. This bug had been latent for a few years, until a user finally managed to create some tasks that made the operating system attempt to use the erroneously mapped area for user data. The access failed, resulting in a crashed task and a bug report to the OS vendor. This shows the value of looking at the warnings being produced by Simics—even if the code appears to work on hardware, it can have latent issues that Simics spots even if the hardware does not complain.

Warnings can also be added to devices for the explicit purpose of helping software developers. When developing new silicon that is being constantly revised, extra checks are often added to models to pinpoint places where software has missed to do required workarounds. Such checks can later be removed when the hardware stabilizes and the model is updated to reflect the revised silicon. Particular types of code can also benefit from extra warnings being permanently added to a model. Intel Architecture BIOS bringup is such an example, where the source address decoder (SAD) registers need to be set up correctly very early, but where any errors do not manifest themselves until much later in the boot. Intel added special checks to the SAD addresses, helping BIOS developers get the code right much more efficiently than if they had been working on hardware (Carbonari, 2013).

Simics device models should also implement informational log messages that can be turned on to help a user understand how a device works and what the software is programming it to do. Such informational log messages are often invaluable when debugging code, because they reveal the precise sequence of hardware events and actions that result from software actions. To track down which code causes logs to be emitted, Simics provides the ability to break when a log message is emitted. This will stop the execution right at the instruction or cycle when a log is emitted, making it very easy to find the code that performs the access that triggered the log message.

Chapter 6 contains an in-depth discussion on how to model accesses to reserved registers, missing registers, and other operations. The modeling strategy used depends on both the hardware specification and the prevalent software interpretation of it.

UEFI BIOS DEBUGGING

Debugging a Unified Extensible Firmware Interface (UEFI) BIOS on an Intel Architecture platform is a special case of low-level debugging. Most boot loaders are fairly simple systems that can be treated as a single program running on bare metal and debugged without any software-specific support from the debugger. UEFI, on the other hand, is a much more sophisticated setup with a defined architecture, modularity, runtime loading, multiple execution phases, and several special data structures (Doran et al., 2011). A UEFI BIOS also contains system error-handling code that can be invoked by system management interrupts, which means that the BIOS is resident as part of the software stack for the entire runtime of the system.

Debugging UEFI BIOS in Simics thus requires some special support, and Simics uses a simple OS awareness system to identify the current UEFI execution phase as well as to enumerate loaded modules. UEFI OS awareness makes it possible to set breakpoints in modules before the module gets loaded, and it automatically determines the relocation address of a module once it is loaded.

USER-LEVEL DEBUGGING

To debug user-level code, Simics needs to have OS awareness in place for the operating system being used. With OS awareness, the debugger can restrict its actions to within a user-level process.

Breakpoints set within a process will only hit when the process is active. Without OS awareness, breakpoints would be set on a logical address, and hit

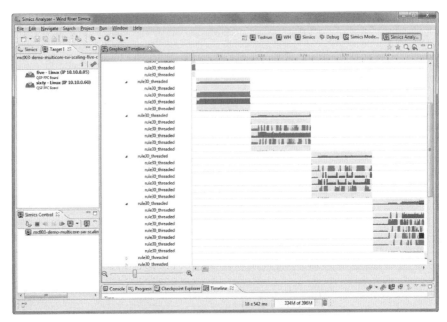

FIGURE 3.8

Thread scheduling visualized.

regardless of the active process because the machine does not know about the program abstraction implemented by the operating system. In the same way, single-stepping will step to the next step inside the process, not on the machine. If the process switches out while stepping, the step will not complete until the process switches back in again. In this way, a user can work on a process in the same way as when using the typical host-based or agent-based debugger.

OS awareness also provides the ability to observe and break when a process is switched in or switched out by the operating system, something that is not feasible when using a hardware debugger or an agent debugger. This helps when debugging issues involving several threads or processes, because it makes it possible to observe the precise activation patterns of software. Figure 3.8 shows an example of looking at the scheduling pattern of the threads in a multithreaded program, where it can be seen that scheduling becomes quite inefficient as the number of threads move from four to five, six, and seven. The top left run using four threads has two threads keeping two processor cores busy, but the later runs do not scale nicely, instead having the threads bounce around between different processor cores and spending most of their lifetime waiting to be scheduled.

Because the Simics debugger is a system-level debugger, it can debug multiple user-level programs at once. This makes it possible to debug distributed and parallel systems, where multiple user-level processes interact to realize the system's functionality.

PERFORMANCE ANALYSIS

Analyzing running software on a simulator like Simics can provide quite a bit of insight into the performance of the code. Even if the timing model used by Simics does not lend itself to the analysis of the *absolute* performance of a system, it can still be used to find bottlenecks in the code and understand the *relative* performance of software and system variants. In practice, the number of instructions executed by code plus the time spent waiting for hardware devices to complete their operation is usually sufficient to get a good understanding for how the system performance can be improved.

PROFILING INSTRUCTION COUNTS

Simics can count the number of instructions executed in any piece of code in the system. In most cases, this provides a useful approximation for software performance and allows work on analyzing and optimizing the code. Algorithm complexity as well as wasted work will manifest itself as the execution of more instructions, and optimizations usually correspond to reductions in the number of executed instructions.

In most of the current 32-bit and 64-bit processors modeled by Simics, the details of instruction cycle counts disappear in the noise of pipelines, speculative execution, branch prediction, and caches. Changes in instruction counts are also likely to be significant for code that is ported between different machines, while precise cycle counts are often peculiar to the particular machine used. Still, assigning an average execution speed to the processor through the means of the CPI setting (Chapter 2) can produce a useful number when combined with interrupt latencies and models of hardware delays. In particular for large workloads, the effect of the microarchitecture can be approximated with an average throughput number (Canon et al., 1980).

There are cases where the number of cycles that a particular instruction takes to execute does matter, in particular for low-end microcontrollers where an instruction like divide can take an order of magnitude more time than a simple add. There are also cases where single instructions in the hardware can cause very expensive operations, such as a trap instruction changing from the user level to the OS kernel. If such operations dominate a workload, the instruction count might be misleading (Kågström et al., 2006).

CACHE AND MEMORY

Cache hierarchy models can be optionally added to a Simics system, and the system configured to send data accesses and instruction fetches to the model of the cache system. Based on the cache simulation, it is possible to determine the hit and miss rate of caches at different levels of the cache hierarchy. The cache operations can be tied to locations in the code to find hot spots. Different data structures and loop structures can also be compared to determine how well they use the caches.

Because Simics runs the complete software stack, cache studies performed using Simics will reflect the operating system and the effect of the OS scheduling processes and threads on different processors in a multicore system. Studies done using only user-level code typically fail to see the OS effect. Another nice advantage of Simics is that the cache analysis can be kept unintrusive, because no code needs to be added to the target system to collect statistics (Kågström, 2008).

Cache simulation can also be used to provide timing penalties to code that misses the cache, which can be used to get a measure of how code performance improves as its cache behavior improves. The effect of NUMA memory setups can also be simulated (Guenzel, 2013). It should be noted that when timing penalties are applied, the functional behavior of the target software will most likely change, because changes in timing affects communications between cores and how the scheduling of the operating system interacts with the user-level software (Alameldeen and Wood, 2003b).

The `gcache` module provided with Simics provides a configurable generic cache model that has been successfully used to model a wide variety of real machines. In reality, the precise details of the cache of any modern system are kept closely guarded, but by configuring the `gcache` to match the size, line lengths, and associativity of a real cache, it is possible to get close enough to get very useful results. Cache models can be added to just a few processors in a system to study the behavior of one particular subsystem or board in a bigger system in detail while keeping the rest of the system fast. Chapter 8 contains more details on memory system modeling with Simics.

IMPACT OF HARDWARE ACCELERATORS

Full-system simulation provides the ability to profile and analyze the interaction among devices, device drivers, the operating system, and user-level code. When using hardware to accelerate software tasks, for example, it is necessary to also take the device driver layer into account. A bad device driver can completely negate any benefit from hardware offload.

In Simics, the performance of the hardware is typically modeled by the time it takes from the submission of a job to the hardware to the time the processor sees the results. The availability of a result is typically reported by an interrupt or by setting a flag in a register. A device driver would react to the interrupt or poll flag registers for completion (for short-duration waits). This models the latency of the operation as seen from the software.

When exploring the architecture and requirements on a hardware accelerator, varying the completion time of an operation makes it possible to explore the actual performance effects of hardware speed when taking the entire software stack into account. When the hardware accelerator is known, the analysis tends to focus on how best to drive it, trying different variants of drivers within the complete system context.

INSPECTING THE HARDWARE STATE

Being able to inspect the current state of the target hardware is a great benefit of virtual platforms. In a virtual platform, what is opaque (a black box) in hardware becomes crystal clear (a white box).

COUNTING HARDWARE EVENTS

A virtual platform makes it possible to count and profile events that are impossible to get access to on physical hardware, or in the case where hardware only provides a very approximate view of the situation via performance counters. In a virtual platform, events like TLB misses and interrupts can be intercepted, counted, and possibly analyzed with respect to the code running at the time of the event. Hardware device accesses can be counted. For particular events inside of devices, it is possible to extend the devices with hooks that allow custom modules or scripts to count and react to the events.

DEVICE REGISTERS

The most obvious part of hardware inspection is the inspection of the values of device registers. In a simulator like Simics, all devices and registers are available for inspection, regardless of whether they are currently mapped into memory or not.

On hardware, the best you can do is try to read memory-mapped registers, which often has side effects such as clearing interrupt states. In a virtual platform, on the other hand, it is possible to see the current state of registers without altering them and without causing the side effects associated with reads or writes to a register. The simulator offers a fundamentally different way to inspect the state, where the values of registers are brought out through a back door and presented to the user.

As shown in Figure 3.9, Simics also adds metadata about the register to increase the inspection power, including annotations on register fields. The metadata about a device is part of the device model, and the GUI is driven by the Simics simulator itself. Thus, there is no need for the Simics GUI to have a separate memory map and device description file for a target—the model itself is sufficient, while hardware-based debuggers always need a separate description file that has to match the target.

Such register views are also available in most JTAG/hardware-based debuggers, but then they are implemented by reading and writing memory, and thus subject to changing the state of the system unless care is taken to avoid registers with side effects. Hardware-based debuggers also have to rely on description files to document the register layout, bit fields, and add other metadata, because hardware is not self-describing in the same way as a Simics virtual platform model.

Simics can present the user with the memory mappings of a particular device register from the CLI as well, because all the same information is available in the GUI and CLI. As noted in Chapter 2, Simics features are typically made

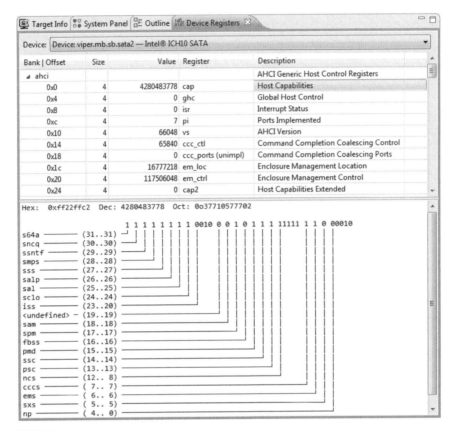

FIGURE 3.9

Register inspection.

available both as a GUI and CLI feature. Figure 3.10 shows an example of register inspection from the CLI.

MEMORY MAPPINGS

The virtual platform makes it quite easy to understand and inspect the memory map of a target system. When working on hardware, memory maps are typically determined by reading documentation and possibly inspecting configuration registers and PCI mappings from target software. On a virtual platform, the memory maps are part of the state explicitly represented in the simulator and thus easy to inspect and change. In Simics, memory maps are handled by a special memory_ space class, which offers inspection via the CLI and GUI views.

Figure 3.11 shows an example system setup and its many memory spaces. As discussed in Chapter 2, Simics uses memory spaces to implement PCIe dynamic

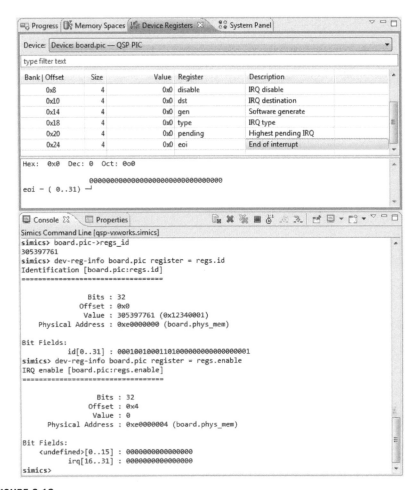

FIGURE 3.10

CLI device register inspection.

configuration, and that is clearly visible here. It is also worth noting that there are several top-level memory maps. The physical memory map of the processor is separate from the PCI configuration space (managed by the PCIe bus controller), port memory, and the Industry Standard Architecture (ISA) memory.

SYSTEM PANEL

The Simics system panel (described in more detail in Chapter 4) models the front panel of a real system and offers a quick way to inspect the state of a system, just like on a real board. In a model of a typical real-world system, the state of LEDs

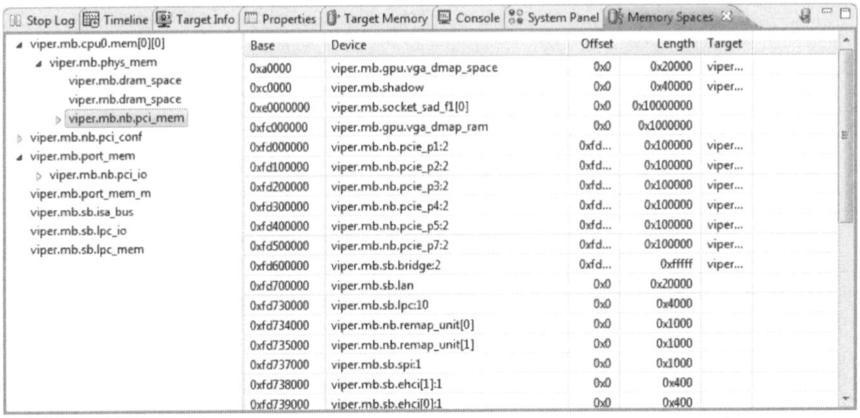

Stop Log
Timeline
Target Info
Properties
Target Memory
Console
System Panel
Memory Spaces
viper.mb.cpu0.mem[0][0]
viper.mb.phys_mem
viper.mb.dram_space
viper.mb.dram_space
viper.mb.nb.pci_mem
viper.mb.nb.pci_conf
viper.mb.port_mem
viper.mb.nb.pci_io
viper.mb.port_mem_m
viper.mb.sb.isa_bus
viper.mb.sb.lpc_io
viper.mb.sb.lpc_mem
Base
Device
Offset
Length
Target
0xa0000 viper.mb.gpu.vga_dmap_space 0x0 0x20000 viper...
0xc0000 viper.mb.shadow 0x0 0x40000 viper...
0xe0000000 viper.mb.socket_sad_f1[0] 0x0 0x10000000
0xfc000000 viper.mb.gpu.vga_dmap_ram 0x0 0x1000000
0xfd000000 viper.mb.nb.pcie_p1:2 0xfd... 0x100000 viper...
0xfd100000 viper.mb.nb.pcie_p2:2 0xfd... 0x100000 viper...
0xfd200000 viper.mb.nb.pcie_p3:2 0xfd... 0x100000 viper...
0xfd300000 viper.mb.nb.pcie_p4:2 0xfd... 0x100000 viper...
0xfd400000 viper.mb.nb.pcie_p5:2 0xfd... 0x100000 viper...
0xfd500000 viper.mb.nb.pcie_p7:2 0xfd... 0x100000 viper...
0xfd600000 viper.mb.sb.bridge:2 0xfd... 0xfffff viper...
0xfd700000 viper.mb.sb.lan 0x0 0x20000
0xfd730000 viper.mb.sb.lpc:10 0x0 0x4000
0xfd734000 viper.mb.nb.remap_unit[0] 0x0 0x1000
0xfd735000 viper.mb.nb.remap_unit[1] 0x0 0x1000
0xfd737000 viper.mb.sb.spi:1 0x0 0x1000
0xfd738000 viper.mb.sb.ehci[1]:1 0x0 0x400
0xfd739000 viper.mb.sb.ehci[0]:1 0x0 0x400

FIGURE 3.11

Memory Spaces view in Eclipse.

and values on numerical displays can tell an experienced user quite a bit about the system health. This lets users translate their real-world understanding of a system into the virtual world.

FAULT-INJECTION AND BOUNDARY CONDITIONS

One advantage of simulation over the real thing is that the simulation can be controlled to explore scenarios that are very unlikely or hard to achieve in the real world. When simulating computer systems, this manifests itself as the ability to provoke software errors by changing the state of the simulated system, a process commonly known as *fault injection*. The purpose of fault injection is to test system behavior in the presence of faults, and in particular to exercise system error-detection and -recovery mechanisms. Testing the code that is supposed to handle rare and erroneous situations is usually very hard to do in hardware, with the result that the error-handling code is often the least tested code in the system. In simulation, activating error-handling code and testing its correctness is quite simple. A related concept is the testing of extreme cases in terms of the system configuration or load, also known as *boundary condition* testing.

CONFIGURATION CHANGES

Most Simics targets make it easy to change basic system parameters like the number of processors, the speed of the processor, and the size of memory and disks. Such changes can have quite profound effects on the software and can expose bugs when unforeseen configurations are used. On physical hardware, the range of possible configurations is much smaller, because chips are only sold in certain configurations, memory slots are limited in number, and particular boards might only support a few clock configurations.

For a configuration change to matter to the software, the software must be able to detect the change and change its behavior accordingly. Adding processors is pretty pointless if the operating system does not notice them and does not make use of them. On Intel Architecture hardware, most interesting parameters tend to be detected by the BIOS at boot, making it very easy to vary hardware setups. On Power Architecture designs in particular, Linux uses device trees to describe the hardware. Thus, after changing the virtual platform configuration, it is also necessary to update the device trees used by the operating system. It can also happen that the OS kernel must be reconfigured and recompiled to adjust to hardware changes.

There are a few systems where the architecture and design is such that the simulator cannot do much in terms of configuration change. For example, if there is no register to enable more processors, or no way to route IPIs for more processors than are present in the actual hardware design, there is little Simics can do. Typically, such limits come in the form of control registers with a certain number of bits allocated for control functions, or dual-core designs where the assumption is that there is the current processor and the other processor.

Varying the processing speed of a processor can often be effective even if the software is not quite aware of what is going on. The effect of executing fewer or more instructions between each periodic timer interrupt or task switch will affect the software, even if it does not know what the current speed is. In cases where the clock frequency is hard to change, varying the number of instructions executed per clock can create a virtually very fast or very slow system in terms of instruction throughput per unit of virtual time, but without breaking the OS assumptions on various clock frequencies.

Memory size variation can be very useful, in particular to see how a system deals with running out of memory or when memory is extremely large. We told a real-world story about this in Chapter 2.

For networked systems, it has proven useful to vary the number of nodes in networks. In particular, for systems that use various forms of self-organization like leadership election or automatic route optimization, being able to try out particular topologies or extremely large numbers of nodes is very important. More often than not, hardware board access limits the scale on which tests can be run. With Simics, it is just a matter of trading execution speed for system scale, as discussed in Chapter 5.

As discussed in the real-world story about debugging Simics on Simics earlier in this chapter, changing the length of the time quantum given to the processors in Simics can be an effective tool to reveal parallel bugs. The reason this works is that it makes OS task switches as well as the Simics time quantum switches move to different locations in the code, increasing the chance that a switch happens between a read and a write in a badly synchronized program.

CHANGING THE SOFTWARE STATE

Given knowledge about the software stack and how it stores its state, the simulator can be used to directly change the software state. This has been exploited to examine software behavior under boundary conditions and to explore many different execution scenarios to systematically search for errors. In particular, the testing of parallel and distributed software has attracted interest, because controlling and debugging such software on hardware is very difficult.

Test systems need to know about how the target system works. Randomly perturbing the system is not likely to produce interesting results, while software-aware control has been shown to be quite effective at exposing problems in the software (Albertsson, 2006; Blum et al., 2013; Yu et al., 2013). Such control methods rely on information like debug information (Albertsson, 2006; Yu et al., 2013), instrumentation points built into the software (Blum et al., 2013), and programmer guesses of what could be sensitive areas of code (Yu et al., 2013) to know where and when to act to trigger software bugs. The goal is to bring latent issues out into the open and expose them as bugs that can be detected, diagnosed, and corrected.

The most common target is to force the operating system to change the scheduling order of threads. To achieve this, it is possible to change the values in OS data structures, trigger timer interrupts at precise times to cause task switches, and disable individual processor cores to make them freeze in time while the rest of the system executes. The methods chosen will depend on the operating system being investigated. When testing device drivers, changing the timing of various interrupts is a good way to test robustness, including triggering interrupts when already inside an interrupt handler, or triggering interrupts just after accesses to shared data.

HARDWARE FAULT INJECTION

Injecting various faulty behaviors into the hardware of a system is something uniquely suitable for simulation. In the physical world, injecting faults is hard work that requires special hardware support and sometimes the actual destruction of the unit under test. Faults can be injected by pulling boards out of racks, putting chips inside radiation chambers, or taking an axe to a running system and breaking cables to test the ability to withstand sudden shocks. Computer hardware might be designed to facilitate the injection of faults, such as having special backdoor registers to allow software to set up bad values and error conditions that other parts of the software and hardware can then detect (Chessin, 2010). There are also hardware units designed to attach to various types of networks and buses, and inject erroneous traffic.

> It is worth noting what an expert in the field had to say on fault injection on hardware:
>
> *"Handling errors is just attention to detail. Injecting errors is rocket science."*
> —**Steve Chessin (2010)**

On a simulator like Simics, on the other hand, injecting errors is as simple as writing some code that affects the state of the target platform. Exactly how the injection of a fault is done depends on the nature of the fault and the implementation of the simulation for the affected piece of hardware.

In the simplest case, transient faults can be injected by changing the values of processor registers, device registers, and memory from a Simics script or even from the debugger or CLI. When the value is next used, hopefully something will go wrong. It is also easy to trigger an interrupt; just call the appropriate interface or port on the system interrupt controller.

Simulating permanent errors in read—write memory requires the fault injector to intercept writes to memory and patching up memory values after the write. To do this, a Simics extension needs to be used that is hooked into the memory transactions. Given such a module, all kinds of errors can be simulated, including particular bits stuck at 0 or 1, or entire words with a fixed value.

Device models can be extended to support fault injection. If faults can be simulated by setting values in error-reporting registers, device models need to include such registers, and possibly also some efficient ways to create valid fault configurations. While Simics device model registers can always be set using attribute accesses, generating valid sets of values for an error-reporting device might take some work. Device models can also add specific fault-injection features, such as a sensor that can be set to an explicit faulty mode where readings are randomly perturbed.

In many cases, faults in hardware are best simulated by using the hardware's built-in error-reporting mechanisms. Most robust computer systems contain such error-detection and -reporting hardware, and fault injection is performed by simulating the error reporting that results from a certain hardware fault. Trying to simulate the actual fault and the actual detection mechanism is likely to be much more complex and also risks having to include a large number of low-level implementation details. For example, an error-correcting code (ECC) memory error is really not an issue of reading bad values from memory, but rather of the memory controller detecting that some piece of memory has gone bad by comparing its values with the invisible ECC data stored alongside it. The result of such a detection is to raise an error exception with the responsible processor core, and setting error-reporting registers to values describing the nature of the error and where it occurred. The exception causes a jump to the OS error handler or the BIOS system management interrupt (SMI) handler, which will then proceed to diagnose and report the error. The interesting behavior is to see what the error handler does when the error is detected, not to actually represent the faulty value in memory and simulate the memory ECC mechanism and extra bits.

Communications buses and networks might need to be extended to include error states, so that endpoint devices can indeed detect that data has been corrupted in transmission. For example, Ethernet network simulations offer the ability to inspect and optionally drop and modify packets in flight, as discussed in Chapter 5. To make use of such mechanisms, it is usually necessary to write a custom Simics fault-injection module, as discussed in Chapters 5 and 8.

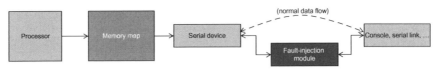

FIGURE 3.12

Serial intercept.

When data is flowing across Simics interfaces like serial, I^{2}C, SPI, MDIO, and custom interfaces between closely coupled hardware units, a simple implementation is to put a fault-injection module into the data flow. As shown in Figure 3.12, this module replaces the direct connection between two devices, forwarding data and corrupting it when appropriate. No change is needed to the connected devices, except updating the system configuration so that both of them point to the fault-injection module rather than directly to each other.

At the system level, faults can be injected by stopping processors and disconnecting networks to make entire subsystems, boards, or machines become unresponsive. Testing system recovery mechanisms and high-level fault-detection mechanisms is actually a fairly common use for Simics.

Injecting errors into a virtual platform does not have to be rocket science, but it certainly does require some attention to detail to make sure relevant error states are modeled in a way that makes them amenable to fault injection. For reliable systems, testing error handling is necessary, and a virtual platform is a great tool for doing it in a cheap and nondestructive way.

See Chapter 8 for more on how fault injection can be implemented using Simics extensions.

REAL-WORLD STORY: QUICK CARD CHANGE

At one point in the history of Simics, we built a model of a custom system where a user could take interface cards out and swap in new ones in a few card slots. The interface cards were hot-pluggable, and when a swap happened, some software actions were taken to reconfigure the system. These software actions were the responsibility of a certain task running in the system.

In Simics, when we stopped the simulation, virtually pulled out a card, and then immediately inserted a new card, this software task would reliably crash. Each time we did the change, the task crashed. On real hardware, we did not see this behavior when swapping cards. The immediate conclusion was that there was something wrong with the model. However, some more investigation revealed that if we stopped the simulation, virtually pulled a card, resumed the simulation again and let it run for a short while, and then inserted the new card, things worked just fine.

The problem was that the swap happened too quickly, in zero time. This was not sufficient for the configuration management task to react to the pull before the insertion happened, and so it crashed. The problem was actually reproduced on the hardware by quickly just shaking a card so it briefly lost contact with the system and then came back online. This caused the crash to happen on the hardware too.

In summary, we had accidentally provoked a real problem on the simulator, one that could conceivably happen in the real world too if someone were to swap cards really fast. This demonstrates how a simulator can test boundary conditions and extreme timing in a way that just cannot be done using real hardware, and do so repeatedly and reliably. Each time this scenario

> was played out on Simics, the same thing happened. It would also have been quite easy to vary the waiting time between the operations to find the longest time that would crash the configuration management process.

TEST RESULT CHECK

Simics checkpoints are handy to determine whether an injected fault has any effect on the final state of the system. By starting from a checkpoint of known state and then performing two runs, one with a change and one without change, the effect of the change can be ascertained. It should be noted that the check for changes needs to be targeted at particular software variables or system output values—there are quite likely to be many other changes in the system from most forms of intervention, changes that are basically the result of the fault injection itself. For example, if a network packet is dropped, the OS network stack state will be different in terms of allocated buffers, network packet numbers, and the like.

USING CHECKPOINTS

The Simics checkpoint feature is simple in concept, but very powerful in practice. Using checkpoints, the state of the target system becomes a document that a user can save, open, comment on, and pass to other users. Thus, it provides a mechanism for communication and collaboration, in addition to making individual users more efficient in their work. Checkpoints can have long lives and can be passed between users of a model. Thus, as discussed in Chapter 2, Simics checkpoints are designed to be independent of the host machine, Simics version, and model version.

SAVE THE BOOT TIME

The first use for checkpointing that most people encounter is to save the state of a target system after it has been booted and set up, so that the boot process and setup process need not be repeated over and over again. Instead, the user can simply pick up a ready-to-use booted system from the checkpoint and get to work immediately. Depending on the time to boot, the time savings from this basic use can be significant. Note that the person reusing the booted system might be a different user from the one doing the boot in the first place—with Simics, it is possible to share the booted system state between users of the same system.

SAVE WORK AND CONTINUE LATER

When closing down after a workday, users can use a checkpoint to save the current state of the target system they are working with. This ensures that they can pick up and continue the next day, exactly where they were. Using physical hardware, this is often an iffy proposition, because leaving a system running over-night is likely to make something happen or its state change in unknown ways. With Simics, users can reliably save their work and later pick up where they were, with no change to the target's state.

POSITIONING FOR ANALYSIS

Checkpoints can be used to save a particular run at a point where it gets interesting and needs to be analyzed, such as at the lead-up to a particular issue with the target system. Normally, the run up to the interesting point will be done without attaching a debugger, activating OS awareness, or using any other tools that could slow down Simics.

Once the checkpoint of the right position is established, more costly tools can be used because the work will be interactive and it is more important to gain a deep understanding of the system behavior. Tracing all instructions executed or all memory accesses to a device are typical examples of tools that slow down Simics and benefit from a positioning approach. The same checkpoint is normally opened many times, with different tools and scripts applied to the target system. Because Simics is repeatable and its tools are nonintrusive, the same problem can be examined from many different angles.

SHARE SETUPS

Simics checkpoints can be used to share a combined hardware and software setup between different users and teams. This means that a user can set up an arbitrarily complex setup of software and hardware and do a number of operations on it to configure the system, start programs, connect networks, and anything else they need to do. Once the setup is complete, a checkpoint is saved and given to other users who instantly have the same setup. See later under "Bug Transportation" for the particular case of sharing setups containing bugs.

Using checkpoints is different from sharing Simics target setup scripts (see Chapter 4 for more on Simics setups) in that a Simics script starts Simics from scratch and then automates a series of operations on the target to reach a certain state. Usually, such setup scripts assume that some part of the setup can change, like changing the OS kernel or the compiled programs loaded on the target. Thus, to rep-licate an exactly identical state, you need to ensure that the other user has exactly the same binaries and images. With a checkpoint, you know exactly what they get.

NIGHTLY BOOT

Making setup sharing and saving the boot part of the defined workflow and pro-cess in a company provides what we call the "nightly boot." Just like a nightly build centralizes the build of all software, a nightly boot centralizes and auto-mates the setup and boot of the system.

Typically, there is a platform team responsible for the hardware, operating system, and middleware platform used for a certain product or project. This team configures the simulated hardware and loads the newly built target software, boots it, performs any setup actions needed, and takes a checkpoint. This checkpoint is then provided to application software developers, instead of having them configure and set up hardware and software themselves.

Using Simics and checkpoints for this process results in a number of benefits:

- *Time savings*—no user needs to set up and boot up a system before going to work on the application software.
- *Consistency of setup*—all users get exactly the same known-good setup, and there is no risk that some boards or systems are still running an older version of the platform software.
- *Lower support costs*—the platform team does not have to handle support for cases where users fail to properly set up their hardware and software.

ADDING ACTIONS

A checkpoint fundamentally represents the state of the system at a certain point in time. In addition to the state, it is often desirable to capture and communicate a set of actions to be taken from the point of the checkpoint to demonstrate a bug or other interesting behavior of the system. Such action sequences can be added to checkpoints in a number of ways.

The simplest way to add actions to a checkpoint is to use Simics' *session checkpoints*. Such checkpoints include the starting state of the target system, as well as all asynchronous inputs recorded during the simulation run. Session checkpoints are explicitly started by the user at the first point in time that is to be recorded. Simics saves the current state at that point in time as a standard checkpoint and also starts recording all asynchronous actions. When the Simics session is closed or the recording is explicitly stopped by the user, all the recorded actions are saved with the checkpoint of the initial state. When a session checkpoint is opened and the simulation started, Simics automatically starts to replay the recorded actions. The starting state of the new Simics session is the initial state where the recording was started.

Another common way to add actions to a checkpoint is to use a script. Before the advent of session checkpoints, this was the most common way to add actions to a checkpoint. Typically, a script is created that first opens a checkpoint and then uses script branches or plain CLI scripting to perform actions on the system. Listing 3.1 shows a simple example of such a script, which first opens a checkpoint file and then starts a program called `temp_display` on the target system by typing in its serial console.

Using scripts like this is appropriate if the actions to be performed are scripted anyway as part of automated testing or automated setups. Scripts are also often built as part of the work of nailing down a particular bug: if a long sequence of

```
1    read-configuration "%script%/water-heater-after-001.ckpt"
2    $system = controller
3
4    script-branch {
5      local $con = $system.console.con
6      local $cpu = $system.cpu[0]
7      add-session-comment "Started session from checkpoint"
8      $con.input "temp_display\n"
9      $con.wait-for-string "->"
10     $cpu.wait-for-time 0.1 -relative
11     add-session-comment "Started temperature display task"
12     stop
13   }
```

LISTING 3.1

Script Adding Actions to a Checkpoint.

target commands is needed to cause a particular event to happen it makes sense to capture those commands in a script.

Another advantage of scripts is that they are not tied to the checkpoint directly and can thus be used even if the checkpoint changes. For example, if a script is used to drive a test case for software, it can be used even if the software is recompiled with a bug fix and reloaded onto the target system. You could not use a session checkpoint for this, because the recording loses its validity unless you start from the checkpointed initial state.

ANNOTATIONS

In all cases where checkpoints are shared between users or just saved for a long time, it becomes necessary to annotate the checkpoints to explain what they contain. Fundamentally, opening a Simics checkpoint gives you the system state, but a system state alone is not necessarily very informative. A user needs to know why the state is interesting, how the setup was created, and the reason for looking at it. A "why" is needed in addition to the obvious "what" of the checkpoint's contents.

To allow users to provide the why, Simics provides the ability to add a free-text informational comment to a checkpoint, as shown in Figure 3.13. The informational text is saved within the checkpoint and can thus not be accidentally lost. It is longer and stickier than just giving the checkpoint a good name. A user can edit the text later to add more observations and clarifications.

Furthermore, as shown earlier in Figure 3.6, Simics allows users to add time-stamped comments to the execution of a system. Each comment is stamped with the time it happened, and is displayed in a time-ordered list in the Simics GUI or from the Simics CLI. This makes it possible to add comments as a system is executing, describing how it arrived at its current state.

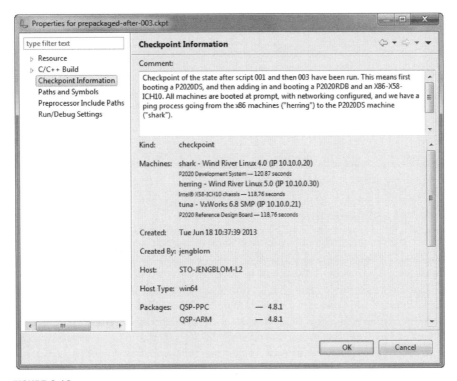

FIGURE 3.13

Checkpoint metadata in Simics Eclipse.

It is important to note that both session comments and checkpoint information can be added from the CLI and from scripts. This means that a script that does a sequence of nontrivial actions on a target can document its progress in comments, so that all later users of the checkpoint can understand how the automated scripts drove the system to its current state. Figure 3.6 shows some examples of such automatic comments, where a script is noting how it is loading software and starting processes on the target.

> **MOTIVATIONAL STORY:** TEST.CKPT, **TWO MONTHS LATER**
>
> The personal view of one of the authors, Jakob Engblom:
>
> *As a big Simics user myself, I have found that being able to add annotations to checkpoints is a huge help. Before we had this ability, I would find my Simics projects full of checkpoints with names like* bug2.ckpt *and* test.ckpt *where I found some bug (which) or testing something (what). I would often find these checkpoints a few months later and wonder if it was safe to delete them.*
>
> *It is really hard to know from just the file name whether the checkpoint is necessary to save (because I sent in a bug report to engineering based on* bug2.ckpt *and they will*

> *come back and ask me about it later), or whether it was just something I saved and then never did anything more about.*
>
> *With checkpoint comments, I now discipline myself to make sure that I always enter at least some kind of comment to describe the nature of the checkpoint. Now, when I find a forgotten checkpoint somewhere, I have a fighting chance to evaluate whether it is important to save or should be thrown away. Because it is possible to come back and add to and change the checkpoint comment later, I can also note in a checkpoint that it is related to some bug report after I have saved the checkpoint and reported the bug related to it. I would not know the bug number before saving the checkpoint, because I would file the checkpoint after I made sure to save the state related to the bug.*

BUG TRANSPORTATION

One of the hardest problems in debugging is to correctly and reliably reproduce a bug found by someone else. Typically, test departments and other users of software create long and brittle instructions to reproduce errors in bug-tracking systems. Accompanying each bug report is a list of relevant facts such as the version of the software, the OS version on the machine, the nature of the hardware, any attached external hardware, and anything else deemed relevant. With Simics checkpoints, all of this can be captured in a checkpoint and sent on from the bug reporter to the developer responsible. Using checkpoints in this way is called *bug transportation* (Engblom, 2010).

Thanks to the portability of Simics checkpoints and the determinism of the simulator, a checkpoint saved in one office by one user can be opened in any other office by any other user, and he or she will see exactly the same system setup and exactly the same system behavior when executing from the checkpoint. To ensure that the behavior seen repeats itself, it might be necessary to accompany the checkpoint with a series of actions taken on the target system.

Sometimes, no action is needed to reproduce a bug starting from a checkpoint. A typical example is a bug in an OS boot that has no external interaction, or inside of compute-bound software that does not receive inputs during the run. Common problems characterized by this are hardware—software interaction issues and threaded software where something goes wrong under particular system setups or initial states.

However, often inputs are needed to drive the system from the checkpointed state to the failing state. In some cases, the best solution is to use a Simics script that automates target inputs. A typical example would be a failure in a test case automated using Simics scripts. In such a case, using the same scripts for the bug report makes perfect sense.

When bugs are caused by asynchronous external inputs such as network traffic from the real world or a user typing commands on a serial console, the Simics recording feature and session checkpoints should be used to save all the input traffic for deterministic replay. To help the recipient make sense of the checkpoint and its inputs, it is a good idea to use the Simics checkpoint information and session comments to explain to the recipient just what is being communicated.

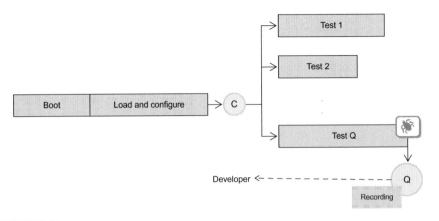

FIGURE 3.14

Cloning and parallelizing testing.

CLONING SETUPS

Checkpoints can be used to *clone* a particular setup to use for multiple runs. A developer or test engineer configures the system hardware and software to a point of interest, such as a particular set of programs being loaded on a booted target system. A checkpoint is then taken, and this checkpoint is used as the starting point for multiple test runs with different parameters.

Figure 3.14 shows an outline of this process. The target system is booted, and then software is loaded onto the system and configured. Once a useful configuration has been reached, the checkpoint named C is taken. This checkpoint is then used as the starting point of a number of test runs, where each test adds some variable input to the software on the target system. In this way, there is no need to repeat the expensive boot and load and configuration before each test run and on each test machine. It is also very useful to know that all tests start from the same clean machine configuration.

If a bug hits in a test run, Simics session checkpoints (as discussed before) can be used to report the bug back to engineering. It is a simple matter of recording the simulation session and then passing it back to the developer as a checkpoint. The developer can then easily reproduce the issue and address the bug.

RECORD–REPLAY DEBUGGING

Record–replay debugging is the use of Simics session checkpoints to record a target execution in one Simics session and then replay it into a second Simics session. Record–replay is an effective technique to use when live debugging does not work. For example, if a simulated system needs to interact with the outside world, it is often impossible to stop the simulated system during the run. However, if the entire run is recorded while it is live, it can then be replayed into a new Simics session where the debugger can be used at ease. Another example is running Simics in batch mode in a test system, recording every test run and then bringing failures back to engineering for replay and debugging.

Record–replay debugging is particularly powerful with a simulator like Simics, where the whole system state is available for inspection. There is no need to determine at recording time what will be investigated—the entire system is available during replay. Breakpoints can be used freely, and reverse execution can be applied to the replay session. Indeed, the best way to transport a reverse debugging session between users is to use a recording (typically in a session checkpoint). From the perspective of the debugger, there is no difference between a replayed session and a live session.

In a replay session, the debugger essentially operates over a finite and predetermined slice of time. Continuing the execution beyond the end of the recording is usually pointless, because no input is available to drive the system forward. Fault injection and changes to the target system state are not compatible with record–replay debugging, because the goal is to reproduce one particular run and investigate it without disturbing the system. Changing the system state will lead to a divergence between the recorded and the replayed session, and the recorded input might become incompatible with the system state.

Record–replay is a way to perform bug transportation, but it is also a useful technique for an individual developer working with a system where live debugging is impractical. It has been used with virtual platforms at least as far back as 1979 (Kidder, 1981).

DIFFERENTIAL CHECKPOINT SAVING

Simics checkpoints are normally chained to previous checkpoints, saving only the difference from the last time a checkpoint was taken or the simulation was started. This has great performance benefits, but it does mean that some care needs to be taken when dealing with checkpoints. If a checkpoint that a later checkpoint depends on is deleted, that later checkpoint becomes useless. Thus, checkpoints should be deleted in reverse chronological order. Because several checkpoints can be based off of the same checkpoint (forming a tree of dependencies as shown in Figure 3.15), you need to make sure that *all* dependent checkpoints are deleted before deleting the base checkpoint. The Simics Eclipse Checkpoint Explorer shown in Figure 3.15 helps you manage your checkpoints and avoid the accidental deletion of checkpoints that are needed to support other checkpoints.

Sometimes, having a very long chain of dependent checkpoints becomes impractical. For this case, Simics provides the ability to merge several dependent checkpoints and the disk images they are based on into a single checkpoint. For disk images, it is possible to either merge a chain of diffs into a single large diff, or to merge all diffs with the basic disk image. It depends on whether the recipient of the merged checkpoint has access to the basic disk image. In case they do, it makes sense to exclude it to reduce the size of the checkpoint. Merging checkpoints is recommended before sending a checkpoint to a recipient, because it can

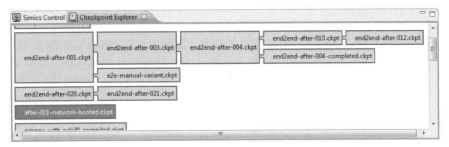

FIGURE 3.15

Simics Checkpoint Explorer showing checkpoint chains.

easily make the checkpoint self-contained or at least depend on only a few external files. Another reason to merge checkpoints is to reduce the number of files that Simics needs to keep open during a run.

REAL-WORLD STORY: TOO MANY OPEN FILES

For security reasons, Unix-style operating systems typically limit the number of files that each user can have open simultaneously. This is intended to prevent denial-of-service attacks against other users on the same machine by limiting how much of the system resources each user can occupy. Unfortunately, sometimes this causes problems for users.

With Simics, we have hit this a few times when users have been aggressively using checkpoints during a long simulation run. In a large simulation encompassing many boards and processors, you can get upwards of 100 memory images, and if you have many simulation sessions running on a shared server, each using a long chain of dependent checkpoints, you can actually run out of open file handles.

Among the first such cases we encountered was a really interesting one. An academic researcher using Simics ended up with tens of thousands of checkpoints for each target system. The reason was that he wanted to use the checkpoints to switch from fast functional simulation to detailed computer-architecture simulation, and to be able to do this at almost arbitrary points in a workload. This would be used to support sampled simulation (Hardavellas et al., 2004). The ideal setup was thus to run Simics forward and save a checkpoint every 10 million target instructions (for runs encompassing many billion target instructions). However, this long sequence of dependent checkpoints quickly overwhelmed the number of files that could be kept open on Solaris.

His final solution was to use a hierarchical checkpointing scheme, where major checkpoints were established every 100 million instructions, from which a sequence of minor checkpoints were derived each 10 million instructions. This got around the open file count issue and did not unduly impact the use of the checkpoints. The checkpoints could be opened just as normal, while the code to establish them was a bit more complicated.

GEAR SHIFT

In fact, the original use for checkpointing in full-system simulation was not to save time for software developers. Rather, the goal was to provide a way to let a user boot and set up a system using a fast simulator and then switch to a detailed system model for architectural studies (Rosenblum and Varadarajan, 1994; Magnusson et al., 2002).

An important property of designing checkpointing for this use case is that the data in the checkpoint describes the architectural state of the target system, rather than the internal state of the simulation itself, as discussed previously in Chapter 2.

This use case is supported by Simics checkpoints, and Simics state has been imported into a variety of detailed simulators from various companies (Magnusson, 2002; Liong, 2008; Engblom, 2010b). Usually this is done as part of customer-internal projects targeting internal simulators. Such customers use Simics simulation runs to establish a system state save a checkpoint, and then import the state into their own models for more detailed simulations. There used to be a framework for building cycle-accurate simulators with Simics, but this turned out to be commercially unviable and was dropped after Simics 3.0. A few other simulators apart from Simics support this use case, which requires collaboration between the developers of the fast functional simulator and the detailed simulator (Peterson et al., 2006; Neifert and Kaye, 2012).

The gear change is conceptually similar to the positioning use of Simics, but in gear change you change the implementation of the target system rather than the tools applied to the target system.

LOADING SOFTWARE

Before tests can be run on a Simics target system, it is necessary to get software on to the target system. Because the Simics debugger in itself does not have an agent on the target, it does not have the ability to load and run software on the target that an agent-based debugger has. Instead, loading and starting software has to be achieved using other mechanisms. Some mechanisms are peculiar to the simulator, while others simply use real-world mechanisms with the virtual target.

The simplest way to change the software on the target system is to boot from a *different binary image*. When the software stack being tested is a boot loader, BIOS, OS kernel, monolithic OS image, or a complete file system image, putting software on the target is simply a matter of changing the image used when setting up the target system. It is fairly common that real-world software builds end up rebuilding the entire system image or boot file system image, and thus loading the result of a new build into Simics requires rebooting the Simics target system with the new image or images.

When using a Linux host, it is possible to *loopback-mount the disk image* of the target's file system. This offers a fast way to move large numbers of files and folders into the target file system at the cost of having to convert the disk image into a raw file instead of the compact Simics craff format. Loopback-mounted disk images can also be used to create new Linux root file systems from scratch. Most embedded Linux build environments take care of this without manual intervention.

New software can be added to a system by using *removable drives*. Models of Intel's systems often feature CD-ROM/DVD readers or even floppy disks, where disk images can be virtually inserted. Virtual USB disks can be connected to most target systems that feature USB ports. Once a removable disk is mounted in the target system, its contents can be used directly or copied into the target's main file system. Using a virtual disk based on a disk image file does not affect Simics repeatability as long as the file is not changed. It is also possible to directly connect a host drive to the simulation so that Simics can directly use physical disks or CD-ROMs/DVDs present in the host machine. However, working directly with the host's physical disks can lead to some problems. For example, checkpoints cannot easily be moved to another host, because they will depend on having the same disks attached to the host. Similarly, if the content of the mounted physical disk is changed, Simics determinism may be compromised. It is therefore often best to copy any required files from the physical disk and unmount and eject the removable disk from the target before taking a checkpoint.

The *SimicsFS file system* is available for Linux target systems. SimicsFS provides the target with access to the host file system via a special device added to the Simics target hardware setup, and a special device driver in the target operating system. The result is that a Linux system can mount some part of the host file system and copy files in and out. Typically, SimicsFS is used to copy files into the system and then unmounted before starting test runs, because it potentially interferes with repeatability. If the host file system contents change, it could change the timing of operations on a mounted SimicsFS file system. SimicsFS facilitates adding files to an existing running system and does not require rebooting the target system. To repeat actions using SimicsFS, it is necessary to write a script that goes through the copy actions, such as that shown in Listing 3.2.

```
 1 ## Load program $filename from location $host_path on the host
 2 ## into $destdir on the target. $system is the name of the target
 3 ## in Simics.  SimicsFS assumed to be mounted to /host.
 4 $system.hfs.root $host_path
 5 script-branch {
 6   local $con = $system.console.con
 7   local $prompt = "~#"
 8   $con.input "\n"
 9   $con.wait-then-write $prompt
       ("mount -t simicsfs none /host \n")
10   $con.wait-then-write $prompt
       ("cp /host/%s %s\n" % [$filename, $destdir])
11   $con.wait-then-write $prompt
       ("umount /host \n" )
12   $con.wait-then-write $prompt
       ("chmod a+x /host/%s\n" % [$filename])
13   $con.wait-for-string $prompt
       add-session-comment ("Target program '%s' loaded into '%s'" %
       [$filename,$system])
   }
```

LISTING 3.2

Script Loading Software via SimicsFS.

The *Simics agent* system puts a user-level agent into the target system. This agent communicates with Simics using magic instructions and does not require a device to be present in the target system hardware setup, nor any device driver in the target's software stack. It runs as a user-level program, making it quite easy

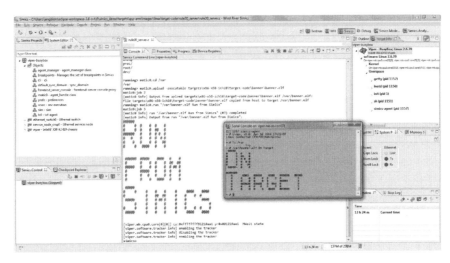

FIGURE 3.16

Simics agent in action.

to provide precompiled target agents that work for a large variety of target systems, such as any Windows version since XP and any Linux version. The Simics agent on the target periodically checks if there is anything for it to do, with a back-off algorithm to avoid taking up target system cycles in case the agent is not being actively used. The Simics agent is able to copy executables and other files onto the target, copy files from the target, and perform actions such as starting programs. Figure 3.16 shows an example session involving the Simics agent. When the agent runs the target program, the output is reported back to Simics and is displayed on the Simics command line, instead of appearing on the target console. In the Target Info view, the `simics-agent` process is visible, and in the System Editor view, the `agent-manager` and connection handle (`matic0`) are shown.

The *target agent* used by an agent-based debugger typically provides the ability to copy files and load and link software onto a target system. The agent can be connected to load software into the target system and then disconnected. Determinism is ensured as long as the debugger is disconnected before starting to run tests. Taking a checkpoint after software has been loaded is always a good idea. A debugger target agent is similar to the Simics agent in that it runs on the target system, but it connects to the outside world using a network rather than magic instructions. A debugger agent is also used to drive a debugger, while the Simics agent is strictly for file transfers and target system control.

It is also quite common that loading is *handled by the target software*. Most real-world systems have some defined way to get new software onto the target when in deployment, and when Simics models such a system, the same mechanism can be used. The mechanisms vary widely and usually cover both loading and starting software. For example, the system modeled in Simics has an operations and management (OM) system running as part of the target software stack. The OM system on the target connects to an external OM client over a real network. Operators or automation using the OM client can push new applications and new versions of applications to the target, and it will restart software systems as necessary to activate the new applications' code. As far as the OM system is concerned, Simics is just a real machine. Another example is the use of on-target shell scripts that connect to an FTP server and pull in new software, or using packaging tools on Linux to pull in new software from a repository.

For targets running Linux, it is quite common to mount the root file system over a *network file system* (NFS). Changes to the mounted file system reflect immediately into the target system. NFS is connected using a real network to a server in the physical world, or by using an NFS server provided by the Simics service node (see Chapter 5).

In general, any real-world file copying or file-access mechanism built on networks can be used with Simics. It is strongly recommended to explicitly copy everything into a Simics disk or other storage before running software, because that ensures repeatability and checkpointability.

If users install the same operating system over and over again on the same Simics model, it is possible to automate the process of selecting installation options, clicking OK in the right dialog boxes, and generally driving the installation process forward. For Simics academic users, scripts like this have been used to simplify the installation of operating systems that would run on Simics but that could not be packaged with the product itself due to licensing restrictions.

CONTINUOUS INTEGRATION

Having a simulator available enables continuous integration (Duvall et al., 2007) for any system that can be simulated. A key part of continuous integration workflows is to automatically test new code as it is built. Usually, automatic testing and continuous integration have problems with code that requires anything except a standard server or laptop to run, but with a simulator like Simics it can be applied to specialized, next-generation, or complicated hardware. Simics provides access to any number of instances of the special hardware, using a standard server.

In a typical continuous integration workflow, the code is tested in several steps. There are small tests that are run often, intermediate tests that are run slightly less often, and the final long complete system tests. Simics is most commonly used for small and intermediate tests, because the complete system tests need to run on the real hardware to assess actual performance and ensure that the software works on the physical system just as well as it does on the virtual system. Still, being able to run more small and intermediate tests without having to procure more hardware is a great benefit from using virtual platforms.

The simulator makes it possible to run tests on a *variety of hardware configurations* as part of the automated build and test cycle. At the end of the build cycle, multiple Simics configurations can be booted and checkpoints taken. For parts of a system that do not change, checkpoints can be stored between builds. Once the build has completed, a server farm can be used to distribute tests that run on the various configurations available in the checkpoints. As long as the setup of the target systems and their boot-up is automated, this can be done as part of the automatic build cycle and without manual intervention.

Running the tests on a simulator has a number of benefits, such as the ability to test many different network configurations, or to include fault injections as part of the automated build/test cycle. In addition, the deterministic nature of Simics enables test failures to be easily reproduced and resolved.

**REAL WORLD STORY: CONTINUOUS INTEGRATION
FOR BIOS DEVELOPERS**

Intel's BIOS developers rely on Simics for pre-silicon BIOS development (Carbonari, 2013). They use a server farm for automated building and testing of new BIOS code that integrates a source code control system, a build infrastructure, a test framework, and a simulator server farm. The workflow of the BIOS teams is as follows (Carbonari, 2013):

1. A BIOS code developer checks in code into the source control system.
2. The build system is triggered by the check-in. The BIOS binary for a variety of targets is built and the binaries are placed on a file server with the status of the build recorded in a database. Each code change can affect multiple BIOS targets because much of the code is shared.
3. The test launch service finds that a job is available in the database and initiates a request to the test server to run a simulator test on a specific VM. A monitoring agent is activated to manage the request.
4. The test server receives the request and queues the job for the specified VM. When the VM becomes available, the test server pushes the job to the simulator and updates the database with the status of the job and VM.
5. The test monitor on the specific VM receives the test request and kicks off a simulator automated test.
6. The simulator performs all the tasks of the specified job request initiated from the test server.
7. After the job is complete, the simulator pushes the logs to the file server for examination by the test server.

A key goal of this is to test the BIOS code on a variety of particular Intel Architecture platforms. If Simics was not used, there would need to be a very large lab with many different customer reference boards and internal prototype boards. Managing automatic tests on such real boards is not easy, and the supply of each platform and board variant is severely restricted. Simics also provides the ability to integrate pre-silicon future platforms into the automatic testing—something that simply would not be possible with hardware.

SOFTWARE TEST AUTOMATION ON SIMICS

The typical way to automate test runs on Simics is to load a checkpoint from the point where the target software has been loaded and then run either a single or a

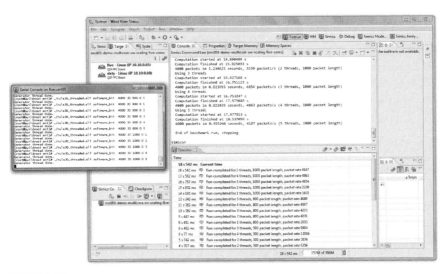

FIGURE 3.17

Example of an automated test run.

series of tests. This is illustrated in Figure 3.14. A single test is run when it is important that all tests are run from the same initial state. When running on hardware, getting to a consistent starting point for all tests often involves resetting and rebooting the target system, as well as cleaning out any files that might have been created by the program under testing. In Simics, opening the checkpoint instantly achieves a complete cleanup of the state, with no reboot or other actions needed. Running multiple tests in sequence is useful when the goal is to indeed run the program under testing from various initial conditions.

Figure 3.17 shows a screenshot of a demonstration setup where a script runs the same program with a large number of different inputs. The script also measures the time for each run, computing the execution time and throughput numbers echoed in the Simics CLI console and the Timeline view (as automatically generated annotations).

No matter which test strategy is used, Simics checkpointing and repeatability means that any issues found can easily be passed back to engineering from the test system. Once an issue has been fixed, repeating the same tests with the new software is done by going back to the load phase, loading the new software, and then rerunning the automated tests.

SHORTCUTS IN THE SOFTWARE STACK

Simulators like Simics can be used to take *shortcuts* in the development and testing of software and systems. One of the key benefits of a simulator is that what used to be hard hardware is now soft software, and it would be foolish not to take advantage of this to simplify workflows and speed things up. Sometimes this involves modifying the target software stack, or making it detect that it is running on Simics. Even if the end goal is a software stack that will run the same on the real hardware, there are cases when a software development team can take advantage of the presence of a simulator during the development of the software.

INCOMPLETE SOFTWARE

Because the simulator can be configured from scripts and software loaded into memory directly with no need for a traditional boot loader, it is quite possible to run incomplete software stacks on top of Simics. The goal is to quickly get to some interesting point, which usually involves at least running an OS kernel on Simics. For example, both RTOS and Linux operating systems have booted on Simics without a boot loader, by loading the kernel straight into memory, pointing the PC at the start of the kernel, and starting the simulation.

Another way that software can be incomplete is in having a very small set of hardware drivers. A normal operating system needs quite a few drivers to function, including timers, serial ports, PCIe controllers, memory management, and other infrastructure. However, on Simics, it often possible to run a kernel without most of these drivers in place, and indeed without having the corresponding devices in the hardware setup either. Dynamic hardware detection can be replaced with hard-coded values, and drivers entirely stubbed out. Such incomplete software is often used early in the development of a new platform and its model, where both design and device models might be missing from significant parts of the system.

SIMULATOR-AWARE SOFTWARE

Simulator-aware software is software that intentionally behaves differently when running on Simics compared to running on physical hardware.

Any software application can be modified to include Simics magic instructions. Given a magic instruction, Simics can stop the simulation (magic breakpoints) or activate script code. A particular common case of using magic instructions is to delineate interesting points in the code base so that simulator scripts can take action when the points are reached. Typical examples include enabling instrumentation only for a certain part of a software stack, or counting the number of times some certain operation is done in the software. Compared to detecting a point in the code using debug information and code breakpoints, magic instructions work regardless of the availability of OS awareness, debug information, and a configured debugger, and are insensitive to compiler optimizations.

Magic instructions can also be used actively to communicate between software and Simics. For example, values can be put into processor registers by the target code, and then using a magic instruction to "call Simics." Simics scripts or modules can then put values into processor registers to return values to the target code. In this way, it is possible to write code that interacts with the simulator directly, with no device drivers needed.

If the target software can detect the simulation environment, it can skip steps that would be needed on real hardware but where the simulator can run without as much initialization or setup. For example, Intel's BIOS developers check for the presence of a simulator to allow an incomplete BIOS to run (Carbonari, 2013). An incomplete BIOS would normally fail to run due to insufficient hardware initialization, but on the simulator it can still run. The simulator relaxes the hard rules of the hardware, because the simulator usually provides a functioning system without the detailed initialization needed to configure real hardware. This lets software development proceed for the large proportion of the software that is not directly involved in hardware setup.

The software stack running on Simics can also be altered to replace hardware drivers for a real piece of hardware with a purely virtual hardware unit. This can be used to replace some difficult-to-model hardware functionality with a simplified Simics-only model. For example, a real-world Ethernet switch chip is a very complicated piece of machinery, but it can often be replaced with a configuration of a Simics-generic Ethernet Virtual Local Area Network (VLAN) switch. However, the VLAN configuration done by the software has to be communicated to Simics, and one way to achieve this is to replace the driver for the actual Ethernet switch with a simple driver for a simple Simics device. This driver replacement relies on having some API in the target system, behind which more than one type of switch can be placed.

The SimicsFS file system discussed previously is another example of modifying the software stack to simplify workflows, as is the Simics Agent.

REAL-WORLD STORY: SLOW, SLOW FLASH

A customer reported that writing to the flash memory of a simulated target was taking a very long time. It took minutes to upload even rather small files, which was not quite expected because the Simics flash memory simulation itself is supposed to be very fast. It took minutes on the hardware too, but the expectation was that Simics would be faster. The story unfolded into an excellent example of how you sometimes need to tweak the target software a bit to take full advantage of the simulator.

The flash driver being used had a very raw interface to the flash memory. Each word written was followed by a delay in order not to violate the write access times of the flash. That busy-wait loop consumed almost all the simulation time, and the speed of the flash memory model itself was irrelevant to the system performance. The delay needed was on the order of 10 microseconds, which is the kind of timeframe where a busy-wait loop is the only reasonable implementation. You cannot set a timer to 100 kHz and fill the flash using an interrupt driver.

On physical hardware, the delay is absolutely necessary for correct operation. On a Simics virtual platform, it is not, because the flash model in a functional simulator does not require wait time for a write to go through. We can just write each word immediately following the end of the previous word, which would save some 90—99% of the execution time of the flash write operation.

There were several ways to remove the wait loop, and we are not sure which one the customer ended up using in the end. One solution is to replace the call to the delay function with a NOP after the code has been loaded on the virtual platform. This would rely on having reasonably precise symbolic debug information. Patching the delay function so that it starts with a return instruction is another open, which needs less support from the debug information (all you need is the list of starting addresses of the functions in the program). Finally, the programming software itself could be modified to detect that it is running on Simics, and then make a very quick programming loop.

This example shows how modifying the software can enable more efficient simulation and save developer time.

BACKDOOR OUTPUTS

Simulator backdoors can be used to communicate with the outside world using methods that just would not work on the real hardware. Magic instructions and memory-mapped special devices enable communication that would not be possible to do in real hardware. The simulator can also peek at what the software is doing and output information that is hard to get at on the real hardware.

It is quite common for integrated and deployed systems to lack communication channels usable for testing and development. All I/O on such systems is often dedicated to system functionality, not to helping developers. With Simics, the real board (in simulation) can be used, along with the complete real software stack, and usually a model of the surrounding physical reality. Inside this setting, test drivers can be added to communicate to the outside using Simics backdoors. This compares to physical hardware in quite an interesting way—in hardware, you would either not be able to do interactive work with the real system, or you would use a development system quite different from the real thing. With Simics, you get something that is the real system, with added interactivity. It is not quite the real thing, but much closer than any other alternative, and for software testing in particular, it has the operating system, drivers, and I/O of the real system in place. Backdoor devices range from the fairly complex SimicsFS device that allows a target Linux to map the host file system as a file system on the target, to simple single-byte outputs.

REAL BACKDOOR: DEEPLY EMBEDDED CODE COVERAGE OUTPUT

In 2012, we worked together with a Wind River partner called LDRA, a company building tools for safety-critical and certified systems, to create a Simics solution to an intriguing problem. The problem was that when doing code coverage on deeply embedded targets, it was really difficult to get the results out. The code coverage tools would take a target program, add instrumentation to it to collect coverage, and then run it on the target. Typically, the test cases and the target program would be combined into a single binary that could run without any external control or input needed.

As the target program was running, the instrumentation would collect information. To be useful, this information needed to get back to the analysis tools. In practice, this part has turned out to be one of the hardest practical problems to solve. It requires the target system to have a working hardware debugger connection, serial cable, USB connection, or Ethernet network connection to the host. On hardware intended for deployment, such connections are hard to come by. Even when they do exist, it means that the test software needs to be integrated with some form of driver or communications stack to get the data out.

In Simics, we instead came up with a solution where a very simple trace device was created and mapped into target system memory, as shown in the illustration below.

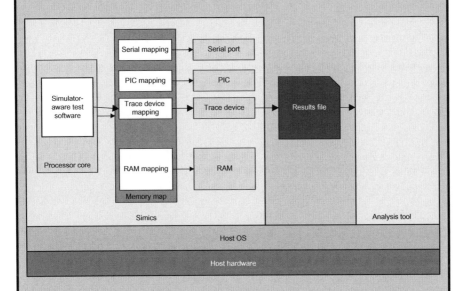

The trace device would take any character written to its single-byte memory map and write it to a file on the host machine. It allowed the test software running on the target system to dump information straight to the host with no need to do anything more complex than writing a stream of bytes to a particular memory location. The benefit is that as long as you are testing on Simics, there is no need to integrate the test code with drivers. Just add the trace device to any Simics platform, tell the software where it is located, and you can start testing and collecting code coverage.

This is a good example of how simulator-aware software can make use of backdoors to achieve efficient workflows that are not possible in the real world. See Thomas and Engblom (2012) for an interview with the people involved in this project.

The simulator can also peek at what is going on inside the target system using breakpoints on writes or certain function calls. This makes it possible to capture output that is happening inside the target system, but that isn't visible or accessible. The most common example of this is using scripts to capture kernel debugging printouts as they happen—usually such printouts will not be seen until serial ports have been initialized or a user logged in. With Simics, Linux `printk()` and similar calls can be watched as they happen. If the OS kernel crashes, the Simics trace of printouts will still be available to allow for diagnosis.

System configuration
in Simics

4

*I must create a system or be enslaved by another mans; I will
not reason and compare: my business is to create.*
—William Blake

As outlined in Chapter 2, a Simics configuration can consist of an arbitrary number of virtual platforms, and it is made up of a set of configuration objects that are configured through their attributes. The configuration objects communicate with each other and the simulation infrastructure using a set of interfaces.

In theory, a Simics virtual platform can be built from a collection of individual configuration objects, such as devices, processors, memories, interconnects, and memory maps, using the Simics CLI or scripts to instantiate and connect individual objects and assign the appropriate attributes. However, users require something that is easier to work with, and modelers need structures that support encapsulation of logically isolated components and the reuse of models.

The model structure needs to reflect the structure of the physical hardware to facilitate maintenance and user recognition. Subsystems should be easy to instantiate in any number of copies without worrying about name clashes or connections accidentally connecting unrelated objects. The proper way to assemble the virtual platform in Simics is by using *components*. Components provide a standardized way to connect configuration objects and allow organization of the objects into a hierarchy.

There are actually three levels of programming in a Simics setup. At the basic level there are the device models (see Chapter 6), which implement the functionality of the simulation. These are grouped into Simics components. The components provide the second level of configuration. While it is possible to construct a system by creating components manually on the Simics command line, this is both tiresome and a bad way to create flexible and reusable setups. For this reason, Simics sessions are, in practice, started from a Simics *script* that contains Simics commands that instantiate components and connects them to each other. The scripts also provide automation, such as loading of software and typing commands into the boot-prompt. This process is illustrated in Figure 4.1. Scripts can call other scripts to create a system, and components in turn can create subcomponents.

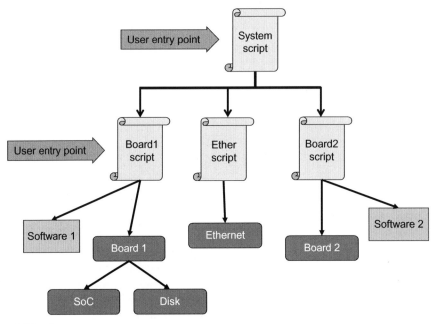

FIGURE 4.1

Overview of a Simics setup system.

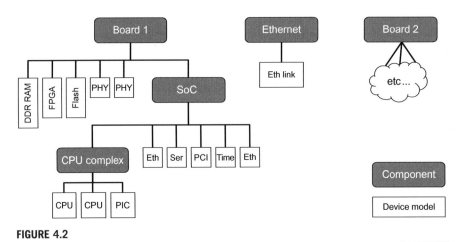

FIGURE 4.2

Simics virtual platform structure.

Figure 4.2 shows that a Simics configuration normally contains several separate component trees, each of which is the root of its own hierarchy. It is certainly possible to merge all of these under a single top component, but, in practice, using a set of components without a single component tying them together provides more flexibility.

SIMICS COMPONENT SYSTEM

A component typically corresponds to a physical unit like a board, processor, SoC, memory module, hard disk, PCIe card, or other unit that is typically found on a system block diagram. Components can also correspond to useful logical groupings of devices that recur in multiple systems.

The components are implemented as Python classes that create their contents using arbitrary control flow, which means that it is very easy to build components that can vary their exact configuration based on parameters supplied when they are created. For example, some systems can be configured with 1–128 cores using exactly the same component. The user only has to provide a different value for the parameter for the number of cores, and the component code creates the cores and wires them up to the interrupt controller and memory using a simple loop. If a component had a static configuration, this would be hard to do. Most components have a set of parameters to allow users to easily change aspects like memory sizes, operating frequencies, and names of firmware files.

Components also usually create subordinate components. In the example shown in Figure 4.2, creating the Board1 component would instantiate all its subordinate components. The component system also provides the basis for Simics's hierarchical namespaces. For example, the PCI device in Figure 4.2 would be referred to as Board1.SoC.PCI. Components in the global namespace are normally *top-level* components, the main responsibility of which is to provide informational metadata in some standardized attributes, which are mainly used by Simicss' graphical tools. Top-level components are shown in the list of systems in the Target Info view. Figure 4.3 shows a screenshot of a simple setup in the GUI, where only the viper component is seen in the Target Info view (top right), despite being accompanied by two more components at the global level in the System Editor view (top left). This is because the ethernet_switch0 and service_node_cmp0 components are not coded to present themselves as top-level components. Note the value of the Top Level property in the Properties view for the viper component. By default, each top-level component is associated with its own *cell*. Each cell can execute in parallel, providing improved simulation performance for multi-machine systems. Cells are covered in more detail when discussing networking in Chapter 5.

Whether a particular component is a top-level component or not is context dependent and is determined when the system is assembled. For example, a compact PCI single-board computer can either be the top-level component in a standalone system or part of a chassis-based system, where the chassis would be the top-level component.

PRECONFIGURATION OBJECTS

When creating a configuration in Simics it is not uncommon to have cyclic dependencies between objects—for example, when there are two objects that

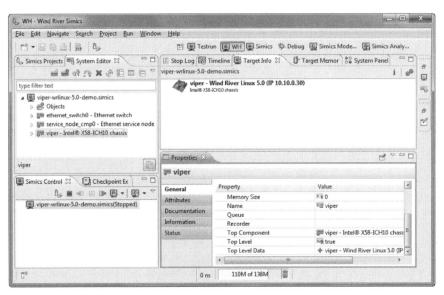

FIGURE 4.3

A top-level component in the Simics GUI.

both need to hold a reference to each other. To overcome this problem, the assembly and instantiation of the configuration is done in two steps: first a *pre-configuration* object is created, and then all preconfiguration objects are turned into configuration objects. The preconfiguration objects do not need to have their required attributes set until they are turned into configuration objects (instantiated). With this scheme the virtual platform is assembled using preconfiguration objects, and then all these objects are instantiated at once. Contrary to many other virtual platform solutions, Simics allows new objects (models) to be instantiated and added to the simulation at any time. The ability to modify the target system while it is running is often very useful when working interactively with the system. For example, it is possible to add a new machine to the simulation and connect it to the rest of the simulated network using a newly instantiated Ethernet cable.

Listing 4.1 shows an example of a basic component. The component first creates a clock and two memory spaces, and then proceeds to map one memory space into the other. As is common in Simics, the code is self-documenting and the documentation automatically shows up in the built-in help and in reference documentation.

As mentioned in Chapter 2, any object in Simics that handles time must be associated with a clock so that it may post events to the clock's queue. The component system automatically sets the queue attribute for all objects at instantiation time, based on the component hierarchy.

```
1    from comp import *
2
3    class c4_basic_comp(StandardComponent):
4        """Component documentation goes here."""
5        _class_desc = 'Short description goes here'
6
7        def setup(self):
8            StandardComponent.setup(self)
9            if not self.instantiated.val:
10               self.add_objects()
11
12       def add_objects(self):
13           p = self.add_pre_obj('p_mem', 'memory-space')
14           v = self.add_pre_obj('v_mem', 'memory-space')
15           c = self.add_pre_obj('clock', 'clock',freq_mhz = 10)
16           p.map = [[0x100, v, 0, 0, 0x10]]
```

LISTING 4.1

Basic component.

COMPONENT CONNECTORS

Components are connected using typed and directional *connectors* that make sure that only components that can usefully talk to each other can be connected. Constraint-checking is part of the connection process to ensure that connections make sense. Some common connector types provided by Simics are agp-bus, compact-pci-bus, ethernet-link, graphics-console, i2c-link, ide-slot, isa-bus, mem-bus, mmc, ms_1553_link, pci-bus, phy, sata-slot, scsi-bus, serial, and usb-port. In addition, a number of target- and architecture-specific connectors exist.

To make the concept of connectors more concrete, consider the example of connecting a USB device to a USB controller. The component that contains the object for the USB controller would add a connector object with type usb-port and the direction down. The component encapsulating the USB device, on the other hand, would add a connector object of the same type (usb-port) but with the direction up. The code for the USB connectors is provided in Listing 4.2.

The semantics for the USB connector is that the model of the USB device should have an attribute named usb_host that should refer to an object implementing the usb interface. By the definition of the usb interface, a device connects to the host by calling the connect_device method of the usb interface in the model of the USB controller. The USB controller model then stores a reference to all attached devices in an attribute containing a list of objects (called usb_devices in this example). This is illustrated in Figure 4.4; refer to the *Simics Model Builder User's Guide* for more details (Wind River, 2014b).

SYSTEM METADATA

An important role of components is to help a user understand the structure of a system and work on the level of user-relevant components. For this purpose, they carry metadata describing themselves, just like all Simics objects do. All components and

```
1     # USB port
2     class UsbPortDownConnector(StandardConnector):
3         '''The UsbPortDownConnector class handles usb-port down connections.
4     The first argument to the init method is the name of the USB device.'''
5
6         type = 'usb-port'
7         direction = simics.Sim_Connector_Direction_Down
8         required = False
9         hotpluggable = True
10        multi = False
11
12        def __init__(self, usb):
13            self.usb = usb
14
15        def get_connect_data(self, cmp, cnt):
16            return [cmp.get_slot(self.usb)]
17
18        def connect(self, cmp, cnt, attr):
19            pass
20
21        def disconnect(self, cmp, cnt):
22            pass
23
24    class UsbPortUpConnector(StandardConnector):
25        '''The UsbPortUpConnector class handles usb-port up connections.
26    The first argument to the init method is the name of the USB device.'''
27
28        type = 'usb-port'
29        direction = simics.Sim_Connector_Direction_Up
30        required = False
31        hotpluggable = True
32        multi = False
33
34        def __init__(self, usb):
35            self.usb = usb
36
37        def get_connect_data(self, cmp, cnt):
38            return [cmp.get_slot(self.usb)]
39
40        def connect(self, cmp, cnt, attr):
41            (usb_host,) = attr
42            cmp.get_slot(self.usb).usb_host = usb_host
43
44        def disconnect(self, cmp, cnt):
45            cmp.get_slot(self.usb).usb_host = None
```

LISTING 4.2

USB connector code.

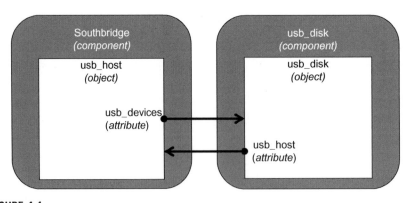

FIGURE 4.4

Component connectors.

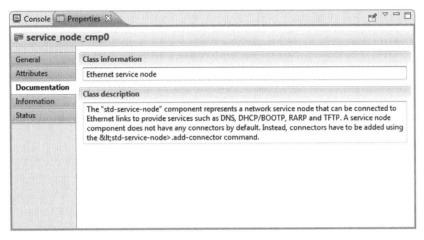

FIGURE 4.5

Documentation for a component.

Simics objects have a name, short description string, and long description string. These are accessed using the Simics `help` command, or in the Properties view in Eclipse when the object is selected in the System Editor, as shown in Figure 4.5.

When creating a new component class, it is important to give the component and its connectors good names that are easy to understand and map to the target system setup. If other components contain the same kind of connector, it is usually a good idea to use the same name, because that makes it much easier for users to employ different types of systems. When creating components from scripts, the names assigned to the components should also make sense and make the system easy to navigate. Often, a number is used at the end of the name to distinguish multiple different objects of the same type at the same level of the hierarchy. If you look at the System Editor view in Figure 4.3, `ethernet_switch_0`, `service_node_cmp0`, and `viper` are the names of the components. `Intel X58-ICH10 Chassis`, `Ethernet switch`, and `Ethernet service node` are the description strings for the component classes.

Top-level components also have a picture of the system they represent for use in the Target Info view, which helps make a system a bit more concrete to a user (along with the use of the System Panel feature, discussed later).

As shown in Figure 4.6, top-level components can also be queried for certain common information: the number and type of processors, total memory, total disk storage, and the total number of Ethernet connections in the simulated system.

SETUP SCRIPTS

Simics scripts are text files containing Simics commands that are used to set up a configuration or run specific command sequences. Simics script files have the

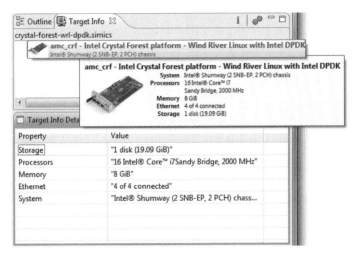

FIGURE 4.6

Top-level component presentation in target Info view.

extension .simics for scripts that are intended to be run directly, or .include for files that are intended to be included into other Simics scripts but not run directly by a user. The Simics GUI only shows .simics files when a user is starting a session.

A simulation session is typically started from a *target script* that will load and configure one or more target machines. Simics scripts are based on the Simics command-line language, and any command that can be executed on the CLI can be put into a script for automation. Simics scripts can be combined with Python scripts or inline Python code to create advanced configurations and test environments.

Most advanced scripting and automation in Simics is done using Python scripts. However, there are a number of situations where it may make sense to use the scripting support in the CLI due to its advantages over Python. For example, Simics scripts provide the same environment as the CLI. The CLI is suitable for interactive use with its simple syntax and features, such as context-sensitive tab completion. Being able to script using the same set of commands simplifies writing scripts. Another benefit is that the CLI hides some Simics API restrictions. The Simics API has restrictions on when certain API functions may be called. For example, some functions cannot be used while an instruction is executing. The CLI scripting environment will only run commands in a context where the full API is available, greatly simplifying scripting. Using CLI scripting, it is also much easier to write sequential code that waits for events to occur by using a mechanism called a *script branch*. By using script branches it is easy to write sequential code that can wait for various events in the system, postponing the rest of the script until these events occur.

HARDWARE SETUP SCRIPTS

Simics target scripts are often divided into two categories: a hardware setup script and a software setup script. The hardware setup script is typically a `.include` file and configures the hardware of the target system based on user-supplied parameters. For example, the `viper` target in Simics is constructed from the `x86-x58-ich10-system.include` script. This script is responsible for assembling a target system based on an Intel® X58 Express Chipset. The script does this by instantiating a chassis (the system enclosure), motherboard, processor, memory, disk, dynamic random-access memory (DRAM), and so forth. The script is parameterized so that the script calling the hardware setup script can configure the hardware. For example, it is possible to configure the amount of memory, the processor speed, the MAC address of the built-in local area network (LAN) adapter, whether a traditional IDE or SATA drive should be used, and whether a tablet or mouse should be connected.

The parameters to Simics hardware scripts will depend on the nature of the target system. Where possible, the same parameters are used for analogous configurations, such as the amount of RAM or clock frequency of a processor. In many cases, however, parameters are unique to a single target or group of targets, such as parameters to control the frequency of an on-board clock or determine the absence or presence of a cryptographic accelerator unit. Most targets do not have a visible on-board clock, and the cryptographic acceleration setup is specific to a particular target system or SoC.

As shown in Figure 4.1, the main activity of a hardware setup script is to create Simics components and connect them to each other. A hardware setup script is what actually builds a complete target *system* from the pieces provided as components.

SOFTWARE SETUP SCRIPTS

The software setup scripts are responsible for loading software onto the targets, configuring debugging contexts, and performing any scripted sequences required during boot. There are usually multiple software setups for each hardware platform, and thus multiple software scripts will be used along with a single hardware setup script.

Listing 4.3 shows the setup script for the `viper` target with the lightweight Linux variant Busybox. As can be seen, the script calls the `x86-x58-ich10-system.include` script to instantiate the hardware, as well as some additional scripts to configure the GRand Unified Bootloader (GRUB) boot loader and the network topology.

The script shown in Listing 4.3 is the one that a user would tell Simics to run to start a simulation. Some of the parameters that can be supplied to the target script are the Linux kernel image to use, whether the script should automatically press Enter in the boot menu, and whether the machine should be connected to the simulated network. Such parameters make it easy to make small changes to

```
1    if not defined vmlinux_image       {
2        $vmlinux_image = "viper-vmlinuz-2.6.39-x86_64" }
3    if not defined tracker_params      {
4        $tracker_params = "%script%/viper-busybox-2.6.39.params" }
5    if not defined initrd_image        {
6        $initrd_image = "viper-busybox-1.cpio" }
7    if not defined enter_in_boot_menu { $enter_in_boot_menu = TRUE }
8    if not defined text_console        { $text_console = TRUE }
9    if not defined uart0_text_console { $uart0_text_console = TRUE }
10   if not defined create_network {$create_network = TRUE}
11   if not defined connect_real_network {$connect_real_network = TRUE}
12   if not defined network_connection {$network_connection = "napt"}
13
14   run-command-file "%script%/x86-x58-ich10-system.include"
15
16   instantiate-components
17
18   # set a time quantum that provides a reasonable boot time
19   $system.cell->time_quantum = 0.0001
20
21   run-command-file "%simics%/targets/common/grub-setup.include"
22
23   $system->system_info = "Viper - BusyBox; Linux 2.6.39"
24
25   # Automatically select linux in the grub menu
26   if $enter_in_boot_menu {
27       script-branch {
28           local $con = ($system.serconsole.con)
29           $con.wait-for-string "Press any key"
30           $con.input "\n\n"
31       }
32   }
33
34   if $tracker_params != "" {
35       $system.software.load-parameters $tracker_params
36   }
37
38   $eth_comp = $system.mb.sb
39   $eth_cnt = eth_slot
40   run-command-file "%simics%/targets/common/add-eth-link.include"
41
42   if defined service_node {
43       local $sn = ($service_node.sn)
44
45       if $connect_real_network {
46           if $network_connection == "napt" {
47               $eth_link.connect-real-network-napt
48               $sn.enable-real-dns
49           }
50       }
51   }
```

LISTING 4.3

Viper busybox script

the configuration using a script that calls the software setup script. If, for example, users would like to use their own Busybox image, they could build a two-line script such as that shown in Listing 4.4.

Another example of such hierarchical scripting is shown in Listing 4.5. In the example, the script from Listing 4.3 is called repeatedly to create multiple machines in the same simulation session and connect them via the simulated

```
1    $initrd_image = "viper-busybox-my-build.cpio"
2    run-command-file "%script%/viper-busybox.simics"
```

LISTING 4.4

Small variation to a target.

```
1    if not defined machine_count {$machine_count = 2}
2    if not defined id          {$id = 0}
3    if not defined mac_address  {$mac_address = "00:19:A0:E1:1C:10"}
4
5    @def next_mac(mac):
6        return mac[0:15] + hex(int(mac[15:17], 16) + 1)[2:]
7
8    foreach $count in (range $machine_count) {
9        $host_name = "viper" + $id
10       run-command-file -local "%script%/viper-busybox.simics"
11       $id += 1
12       $mac_address = `next_mac(simenv.mac_address)`
13   }
```

LISTING 4.5

Multi-machine script.

Line 5: Inline Python function to compute the next MAC address.

Line 12: Assignment to a CLI variable based on the result of a Python function.

network. The example in Listing 4.5 also shows how Python can be inlined into the script to perform an arbitrary computation; in this case to compute a unique MAC address for each system.

SCRIPT PARAMETERS

As is evident from the examples shown, Simics script parameters are expressed using normal Simics CLI variables. Typically, a parameter has a default value provided by the script, with the option to have it overridden by a calling script. Lines 1-3 of Listing 4.3 shows the idiom used to implement parameter overrides: the use of the defined command in Simics CLI to determine whether a variable has been defined (given a value). If it is defined, it is not changed. If it is not defined, the variable is created and given a default value. This is similar to how a C header includes work. Well-behaved scripts should also error-check variable values and try to report readable errors when a value given is invalid. In such cases, scripts should provide helpful output and abort cleanly using the interrupt-script command.

SCRIPT BRANCHES

Script branches allow the user to write sequences of CLI commands that are postponed waiting for things to happen in the simulator, without breaking the sequential flow of commands. An example of a simple script branch is shown in Listing 4.6. In the example, a configuration is loaded using `run-command-file` and some informative text is displayed using the `echo` command. The text shown is: "`Loaded configuration`", followed by "`Start of script branch, let's sleep`", and finally "`Script completed, start the simulation!`". Because the simulation is not running, the script branch will be "stuck" at the `wait-for-time` command until the user starts the simulation. Once the simulation is started and the target has progressed one second of virtual time, the `echo` command will display the text "`Processor registers after 1.0 seconds`", followed by the registers of the processor (`pregs`).

A big difference between script branches and the main script is that the main script, also called the main branch, may be interrupted by the user pressing the Stop button or typing Ctrl-C. The script branches are unaffected by such actions and can exist in the background, coexisting with any interactive command line use.

When a script branch is started, using `script-branch`, it begins executing immediately, and runs until a `wait-for-` command is issued. Execution is then resumed in the main script and there is never any concurrent activity. When some activity occurs that a script branch is waiting for, the branch continues executing

■ Simics script

```
1   run-command-file "%simics%/targets/x86-x58-ich10/viper-busybox.simics"
2   echo "Loaded configuration"
3   script-branch {
4       echo "Start of script branch, let's sleep"
5       $system.mb.cpu0.core[0][0].wait-for-time 1.0
6       echo "Processor registers after 1.0 seconds"
7       $system.mb.cpu0.core[0][0].pregs
8   }
9   echo "Script completed, start the simulation!"
```

■ Simics output

```
1   Loaded configuration
2   Start of script branch, let's sleep
3   Script completed, start the simulation!
4   simics> c
5   Processor registers after 1.0 seconds
6   16-bit legacy real mode
7   rax = 0x00000000c39f0017          r8  = 0x0000000000000000
8   rcx = 0x00000000ded10000          r9  = 0x0000000000000000
9   rdx = 0x0000000069da000f          r10 = 0x0000000000000000
10  rbx = 0x0000000027ad0000          r11 = 0x0000000000000000
11  rsp = 0x0000000000006960          r12 = 0x0000000000000000
12  rbp = 0x00000000c38c0000          r13 = 0x0000000000000000
13  rsi = 0x0000000069da0000          r14 = 0x0000000000000000
14  rdi = 0x0000000069da0242          r15 = 0x0000000000000000
15
16  rip = 0x00000000000054e5, linear = 0x00000000000f54e5
17
18  eflags = 0 0 0 0 0 0 0 0 0 0 0 1 0 0 0 0 0 0 1 0 = 0x00000202
19           I V V A V R - N I I O D I T S Z - A - P - C
20           D I I C M F   T O O F F F F F F   F   F   F
21             P F                 P P
22                               L L
```

LISTING 4.6

Script branch.

```
1    $con = $system.console.con
2
3    ##-----------------------------------------------------------
4    ## Boiler v1
5    ##-----------------------------------------------------------
6    ## $con.wait-for-string is a simple way to detect that target software
7    ## has started using the program output.
8
9    script-branch {
10     local $con = $con
11     while TRUE {
12       # Infinite loop
13       $con.wait-for-string "Boiler version 1"
14       add-session-comment "boil_v1 started"
15     }
16   }
```

LISTING 4.7

Script branch annotating a target.

once the currently simulated instruction is ready. The *Hindsight User's Guide* contains the complete list of commands available in a script branch (Wind River, 2014a).

Multiple script branches can be running at once, operating on the same target machine or different target machines. This means that it is simple to control parallel target systems in parallel. When setting up or booting multiple targets in a single Simics simulation, they can all be controlled at once using their own local script branches.

Script branches can also be used to provide feedback to a user about what is happening in a simulation, and annotate the Timeline view as discussed in Chapter 3. Listing 4.7 shows one such example, where the script branch waits for output on the target system serial console and then adds a comment to the Timeline view.

SYSTEM PANEL

The Simics System Panel feature enables users to create a virtual representation of their physical hardware's user interface and connect it to the Simics virtual platform. This ability allows familiar user interaction with the virtual platform, and it also lets a Simics system designer create a custom UI for quick inspection of, and interaction with, simulator extensions.

Figure 4.7 shows a typical example where the System Panel shows the status lights of a standard PC. This is a very minimal example, but still useful because it communicates information that is not part of what is seen on the target consoles, nor in any other part of the Simics UI. For rack-based systems, the System Panel contains a picture or diagram of the front panel of each board, decorated with live LEDs and sometimes simple numerical outputs. The Quick Start Platform (QSP) panel shown in Figure 4.8 is a simple example of such a panel.

The System Panel can also be used to visualize and control simulator extensions, such as physics models and fault-injection systems. This is not really

FIGURE 4.7

System panel for a standard PC.

visualizing the front panel of a target system, because it corresponds to something that has no direct physical counterpart. However, it makes it much easier to understand the state of the system and to control the target simulation, for example, by turning faults on and off interactively. Figure 4.8 shows an example of a System Panel for such a system. The electric kettle is controlled by the control computer, and there is the option to inject faults into the running simulation using the buttons in the fault-injection System Panel.

It is also worth noting that the physics system has its own top-level component, as can be seen in the Target Info view in Figure 4.8 (where it is called a

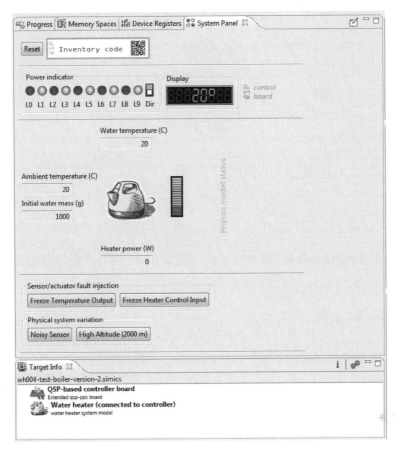

FIGURE 4.8

System panel for a physics simulator and control computer.

water heater and not an electric kettle). The System Panels for all components in a simulation are put into the same view so that the panel will show all machines in a network or all boards in a rack.

A System Panel is implemented by a Simics component, usually as a subcomponent of the target system that the System Panel is supposed to visualize. Figure 4.9 shows the component hierarchy of the setup shown in Figure 4.8, with the System Panel editor active so that the name of each component is shown.

AUTOMATING TARGET CONFIGURATION AND BOOT

With Simics, it is easy to automate target configuration tasks that are time consuming and require extensive manual intervention in the physical world. Both

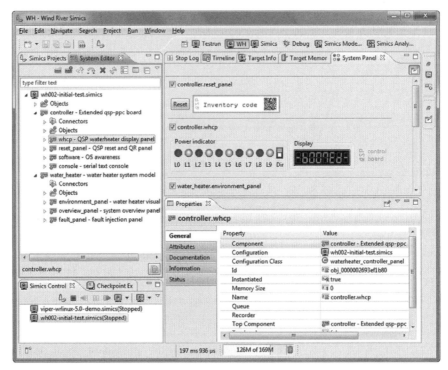

FIGURE 4.9

System panels as hierarchical components.

inputs to the target software and actions on the target hardware can be turned into Simics scripts and repeated any number of times, and they can be parameterized as well. Using a full script language makes it possible to create very flexible and smart configuration systems.

Automated target configuration in Simics covers both the hardware and software components of the target system, using settings for configuration variables and custom actions. Each time the script is run, the same target system setup is created, which makes it easy to recreate a particular setup over and over again in virtually no time at all.

Booting a system to a useful prompt often involves setting various parameters on the boot prompt, as well as logging in with a username and password. With Simics, such tasks are automated using scripts that wait for prompts to appear and then supply the requisite responses. The scripts are typically parameterized to allow other scripts and the user to control aspects of the system boot, such as changing the disk images, login names, and password used.

Target boot-up scripts are also used to vary the configuration of a target system automatically. For example, a script that boots up VxWorks on Simics can intercept the VxWorks boot ROM prompt and use its configuration commands to set the network addresses of the target system. In this way, a single boot ROM and OS image can be used, with its networking parameters set when the target system is booted.

REAL-WORLD STORY: ONE OS IMAGE PER MAC

Sometimes, software is not very cooperative in the quest for flexible configuration. Software built to run on real systems does not necessarily include easy ways to change things like network addresses or hardware MACs—after all, that is a very dangerous operation in a real system. In many cases, this can be fixed with post-boot scripts doing `ifconfig` on a system. However, if there is no simple way to fix it, the only solution is to use brute force. One example of this was an early RTOS configuration for a model of the PPC440-based Ebony development board. The Ebony BSP was really just an example intended to get a customer going, and it made some simplifying assumptions, including using a MAC address hard-coded in the compiled code. Because we needed to run more than one Ebony instance at a time, there was only one solution: compile a set of OS images, each with a different hard-coded MAC and IP address.

The startup scripts would track how many Ebony instances had been created and use a new OS image for each successive start until we ran out of images. We ended up using five different images, which was sufficient to prove what we wanted to prove—namely, that we could run interestingly large networks in Simics using the PPC440 and the RTOS of interest.

Simics scripts can also automate the creation of networks of machines, including mixed networks and racks. In some cases, a script will list the precise set of machines to be created, while in other cases variables guide the number of machines to create. Most Simics target systems come with a "multi" script that creates several identical machines, except that each machine has its own Ethernet MAC address and IP address generated. The code in the script simply generates a new address for each successive machine, usually just by adding 1 to the address of the previous machine. More complex cases can involve automatically building setups containing multiple networks and multiple types of machines to fit certain test scenarios.

REAL-WORLD STORY: NETWORK EDUCATION USING SIMICS

Wind River Education Services provides user training for a variety of topics, including Wind River operating systems and tools, as well as more general topics like networking. Training always includes hands-on labs, which can complicate logistics for training sessions. Shipping boards and configuring networks is time consuming and error-prone. It is also not feasible to build network lab setups for every student, because even a small network involves five or more pieces of hardware plus cables to connect them (Guenzel, 2013). One such setup per class might be possible, but it would be hard to maintain its reliability as it was moved around. Simics offers a very nice alternative, and Wind River Education Services uses some generator scripts that take parameters for the type of network to build, and then generates a setup with multiple networks and machines of different types.

One example, shown in the illustration , has four router machines all running VxWorks, alongside four "node" machines that communicate via the routers. The node machines use both Wind River Linux and VxWorks as their operating systems.

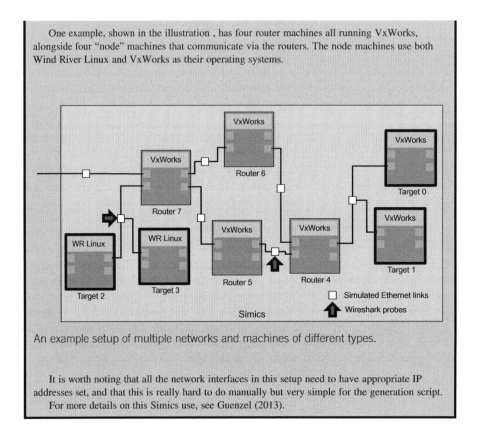

An example setup of multiple networks and machines of different types.

It is worth noting that all the network interfaces in this setup need to have appropriate IP addresses set, and that this is really hard to do manually but very simple for the generation script. For more details on this Simics use, see Guenzel (2013).

Networking

5

The network is the computer.
—**John Gage, Sun Microsystems, 1984**

Network simulation is an integral part of Simics, and many Simics target systems are networked in one way or another. Simics is used in the real world to simulate very large networks of systems, scaling up to several thousand target processors spread across dozens or even hundreds of networked boards.

Networks are used in Simics target systems in many different ways. The simplest case is a single computer board that is connected to the outside world via an Ethernet link. There are target systems that just combine a few separate computers over Ethernet to model a small office network. Scaling up, target systems can be racks where a sophisticated backplane containing tens of separate network links connect ten or more boards into a single system. Networks are often built into hierarchies where systems with internal networks (e.g., a rack) are connected to other systems over long-distance links. Simics models and simulates even these systems. Simics has been used to model a range of different networks, including Ethernet, serial, I^2C, MIL-STD-1553, ARINC 429, Packet-over-Sonet (POS), Asynchronous Transfer Mode (ATM), and Controller Area Network (CAN).

NETWORK SIMULATION IN SIMICS

The standard network simulation method in Simics is to put *all* the target machines in a network inside the same Simics simulation process. The virtual networks can be self-contained or connected to the outside world, depending on the use case for a setup. This section explains how network simulation is performed in Simics.

NETWORK INTERFACES

As shown in Figure 5.1, networks are normally simulated by modeling concrete network interface devices and running the same drivers as the the real hardware would use. The simulated system uses the same path—from software through the

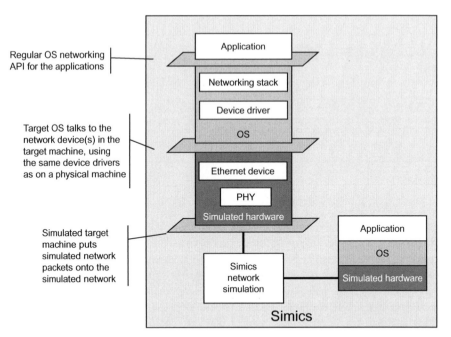

FIGURE 5.1

Real software and simulated networks.

network stacks to network device drivers to the network—as on the real system. There is no special simulation connection for the software on a target system to the network, and Simics simulates networks at the hardware packet level, not the protocol level.

This way of network simulation provides enormous value to users of Simics, because it means that Simics can be used to test the actual integration of operating systems, drivers, middleware, and applications just as they would on a real system. By modeling real network interfaces, Simics is able to run real unmodified network drivers and complete software stacks. Thus, it is a crucial part of delivering the promise of working like the real hardware as far as the software is concerned.

As part of modeling a network, the physical interface (PHY) devices connecting the network interface devices to the network cabling are normally modeled explicitly as their own separate device models. This has been proven to be the simplest way to model real-world network interfaces and make the software and system happy. Most systems have more than one network connection. Even a low-end networking SoC will have three or four Ethernet ports, and high-end systems often feature ten or more gigabit and 40-gigabit ports.

Real-time control systems based on AFDX, CAN, MIL-STD-1553, and ARINC 429 commonly have multiple redundant buses, which means that each network node will have multiple interfaces. The typical way to model a real-time redundant bus network is described later in this chapter. Because an interface is really just a normal Simics device, modeling this is a simple matter of instantiating more copies of the network interface model and connecting them to more copies of the network link.

PACKET-BASED PHYSICAL-LEVEL TRANSPORT

Network simulation in a transaction-oriented framework like Simics is naturally done by considering *each network packet or network message to be a transaction*. The transfer of a packet is handled as a unit, and there is no model of the physical transfer of the packet just like there is no model of the detailed clocking and protocol of a memory bus for memory transactions.

What constitutes a packet depends on the nature of the network; in some cases packet structure has to be imposed on a continuous-stream network, and in some cases performance requires using larger packets than the physical standard (e.g., ATM simulation in Simics moves multiple ATM cells in a single simulation transaction to reduce the simulation overhead per cell).

The virtual network transports the bytes in a simulated packet from the sender to its recipients. Simics only cares about the physical-level transmission and addressing of network packets, which means that it is possible to run arbitrary protocols on top of Simics networks. Simics does not make use of the host machine to bridge traffic between different target machines. (This is unlike typical IT-oriented virtual machines like VMware or other simulators like Qemu that rely on the host to move traffic between different target machines.)

ETHERNET MODELING

For Ethernet, each transaction is a complete Ethernet packet, including its MAC address and checksum—basically, the same set of bits that is put on the wire, but normally excluding the preamble. There is no attempt to model the collision sense and backoff, because that would require too tight a synchronization between network nodes to be practical (see later).

Packets are sent to recipients based on their hardware MAC addresses, and Simics can faithfully model the effects of duplicate MAC addresses in a network. It is up to the models of the Ethernet controllers in the target systems to handle MAC addressing, normally by discarding packets with MAC addresses that they do not own (just like in hardware). Some controllers can have multiple MAC addresses registered, and they will thus accept packets to all these MAC addresses. Interfaces can be set to promiscuous mode, and they will then accept all packets, just like in a real network.

Figure 5.1 shows how the target machines' software (and sometimes hardware devices) put protocols on top of the Ethernet hardware, just like on a real machine. IP addressing is handled by the network stacks on the targets, and then

User Datagram Protocol (UDP) and Transmission Control Protocol (TCP) are built on top of that. More unusual protocols such as Stream Control Transmission Protocol (SCTP) work without any modifications to Simics, because they are just higher-level abstractions that use Ethernet. Protocols that use Ethernet MAC addressing for the physical transport but without using IP on top also work in Simics.

As shown in Figure 5.2, Simics network simulation follows the architectural pattern of isolating the network devices from the real world via a simulated network link. Making the virtual network explicit greatly simplifies modeling, because all a device model for a network device needs to concern itself with is how to put packets on the network and how to receive packets from the network. There is no need to build traffic inspection or real-world connection features into the network device models themselves; all of that is handled in the network simulation module for the particular network in question. The architecture shown in Figure 5.2 is used for all network simulation in Simics. The service node, traffic generators, and inspection are covered in more detail later in this chapter.

Network packet transmission is a unidirectional operation where the network nodes send a packet to the network simulation, returning control immediately to the device model. There is no knowledge of whether the packet was correctly delivered to the destination(s), and thus no need to wait for a reply from anything except the network simulation. This closely correlates to how the physical world works where network packet senders usually do not receive a confirmation that the packet has indeed reached the destination.

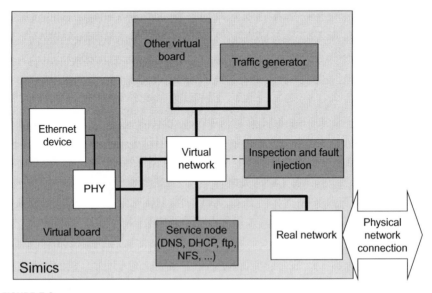

FIGURE 5.2

Ethernet network simulation in Simics.

Simics offers several different types of Ethernet links (the "virtual network" in Figure 5.2). The *cable* goes between two machines and forwards all packets; it is often used as the basis for modeling complex real-world topologies inside individual boards or in rack backplanes. The cable is appropriate when the machines being connected are working as switches—the target machine could have dozens of PHY devices, all connected to cables, modeling a real-world setup. The *hub* connects any number of machines and forwards all packets. The *switch* connects any number of machines and learns the MAC addresses associated with different network ports, just like a real switch. A switch is the default for basic networking, because it reduces the number of packets each target machine sees, improving simulation performance some.

It is important to note that the inspection and modification module shown in Figure 5.2 is *invisible* to the target network and does not have addresses on the network. This is indicated by the dashed line.

WAR STORY: ETHERNET PREAMBLE

The Simics modeling of the Ethernet preamble offers a lesson in real-world transaction-level modeling, and how you have to balance efficiency, complexity, and completeness.

By default, Simics does not model the preamble, because it is really a hardware mechanism that is used to synchronize the receiver clock. On a standard PC or server, there is normally no way to get at the preamble, because the hardware strips it out and the operating system offers no way to access the data. Thus, for Ethernet modeling, adding an 8-byte constant set of bytes to the front of every packet would be wasteful. It would also complicate the interaction with tools like Wireshark that do not expect the preamble to be part of packet dumps.

However, there are Simics users who build systems that dig deeply into the network data. It turns out that many Simics target machines actually have Ethernet controllers that allow software to see and set the preamble for packets. These features are not enabled by default, but they are available in case the device drivers request them. Because nobody was using those features, they were initially modeled as unimplemented. However, as tends to happen, one day a customer use case turned up that relied on being able to see the Ethernet preamble from software.

Because the preamble was now software-visible, we had to extend the network interface models to support reporting the preamble to the software. To get the preamble into the device, a special interface was created, which a local device or a script can use to insert the values for the preamble and read the preamble of an outgoing packet. Changing the semantics of the general Ethernet interface to always transport a preamble as part of all packages was not really an option, because it would affect every Ethernet device in the Simics library for very limited gain. Thus, a solution local to the affected device and network node was used, which was sufficient to make the software happy but did not affect other devices and network infrastructure. In general terms, the common case is still fast and simple, and the unusual case has to deal with a small bit of complexity.

OTHER NETWORKS

While Ethernet is the most common network and the one with the most complex behavior and features in Simics today, many other network types have been modeled in Simics. This section presents some of these network types and the abstraction level chosen for each.

For *serial lines*, each transaction is a single character, transmitted as an 8-bit byte in the simulator (but with high bits masked to 0 in case the originating device is set to transmit less than 8 bits). There is no model of the conversion into a serialized stream of bits, the transmission rate, start/stop bits, or parity. Only the transfer of the payload of interest to software is modeled, the characters (or bytes) themselves. This model excludes the ability to model transmission rate mismatches over a serial line, but such errors are not considered common enough to burden the basic model with. Each serial connection is point-to-point, with exactly one sender and one receiver.

For *CAN*, each packet in the simulation is a complete packet including the priority field and the trailing status bits. The status bits are updated locally in each receiving device to avoid the need for expensive global communication between the network nodes. The priority-based network access protocol is not modeled; rather it is assumed that all messages can be successfully put on the network and reach their destination. It is essentially a broadcast network where each packet sent reaches all recipients, which then filter reception in the same way as on a physical network; the network device knows the message IDs that it is waiting to receive and ignores all others.

MIL-STD-1553 is modeled with a link that connects one master to all the slaves and optional bus monitors. The transactions contain the protocol data, but do not include parity information and synchronization of the physical bus. Simics offers users the ability to model errors in the Manchester encoding and parity by injecting errors explicitly. The 1553 link in Simics keeps track of the protocol state and warns when any device breaks the specification, which is helpful both to debug software on the master and any badly modeled remote terminals. The link supports inspection of the data sent on it to help users debug 1553 setups. It is common to see redundant setups in 1553, as discussed later.

NETWORK TIMING AND CONFIGURATION CELLS

To improve the performance of simulations containing several target systems, Simics provides the capability to simulate loosely coupled systems in parallel. Configuration cells are the concept used to manage parallel simulation in Simics. Each cell contains a set of objects that can be run in parallel to objects in other cells, but that cannot run in parallel to objects in the same cell. Typically, each cell contains a single target machine, with all its components and devices. In most cases the cell partitioning is done automatically by Simics by creating a cell for each top-level component. For some advanced use cases it can be necessary to manually configure the cell partitioning in the simulation. This is covered in detail in Wind River (2014d).

Multithreaded Simics is still deterministic, repeatable, reversible, and checkpointable. The behavior is identical to a single-threaded simulation of the same system. To maintain these properties, objects in different cells may only communicate with each other using *links*. A link transmits messages between objects with a latency measured in simulated time—for example, an Ethernet cable. This section provides some details on how multithreading in Simics affects timing and system configuration and will be the foundation for understanding network timing.

To allow multithreaded simulation to perform well, Simics lets each thread run for a certain amount of virtual time on its own before it needs to resynchronize with the other threads. This timespan is the *synchronization latency*. Because of the synchronization latency, Simics does not allow direct communication between objects of different cells. Even if all accesses were properly locked and performed in a thread-safe way, the objects would have no way to control at what time their access would be done in the other cell, so the simulation would stop being deterministic. This is why all communication between cells should happen over links. A model very similar to this has been applied to SystemC simulations (Weinstock et al., 2014), and it has proven to work well in practice for more than a decade with Simics (Magnusson et al., 2002).

To achieve repeatable and deterministic timing between different runs and different hosts, each link is assigned a user-defined *minimum latency*. Figure 5.3 illustrates this concept using a network link as an example. There are two nodes, A and B, connected over a network with an assigned latency of l, which is greater or equal to the minimum latency. A and B are typically simulated in parallel, using one host thread to run each target. A network packet sent from node A at its local time t will be delivered in node B at its local time $t + l$, even if the packet in practice reaches B much sooner than that. The Simics synchronization mechanism guarantees that A and B will not be separated by more simulated time than the minimum latency and thus will ensure synchronization in less virtual time than l. This fact ensures that the packet will always be available for B to deliver

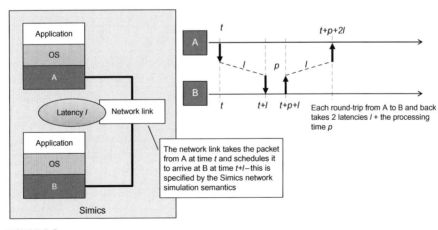

FIGURE 5.3

Network timing in Simics.

at the right time no matter how the actual execution of *A* and *B* evolves on a particular host during a particular run.

Once the packet has reached *B*, it might compute a reply back to *A*. The time to compute a reply is shown as *p* in the diagram in Figure 5.3. At time $t + l + p$, *B* sends the reply toward *A*. Thus, the network latency is applied to all communications over the link and is visible to user software. Figure 5.4 illustrates this: the network latency is set to 1 second, and the ping time reported from one target machine to another is about 2,000 milliseconds (in the serial console titled `Serial Console on client_a.uart[0]`). If you look closely, you can see that the time reported is 10−20 microseconds more than 2,000 milliseconds, which is the overhead of processing packets in the network stacks on both sides of the connection.

Tweaking the network latency is a common performance optimization for networked simulations. In general, the simulation will run faster with a higher latency, because the amount of synchronization in the simulation is reduced. This will result in the highest aggregate instruction throughput (simulated target instructions per host second) across the network nodes. However, in the case that the target software has a pinglike behavior, sending data to another node and waiting for a reply before continuing, it is often better to lower the latency. With a lower latency, we get more synchronization in Simics itself and lower aggregate instruction throughput (simulated target instructions per host second). However,

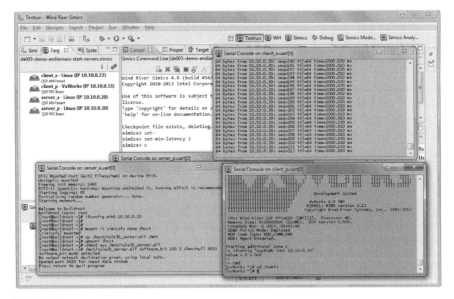

FIGURE 5.4

Ping roundtrip times with a network latency of 1,000 milliseconds.

more of those instructions will be spent doing useful work, and thus the overall progress of the target software will be faster (in terms of user-perceived relevant work per host second).

Latency is also relevant for network throughput for protocols like TCP/IP, where only a certain number of packets are allowed to be in flight at any point in time. A high latency requires a long TCP window to provide the best throughput, and if the latency is too high it might force waits onto TCP. However, Simics latencies are rarely on the order of magnitude needed to truly starve TCP.

The most appropriate network latency will depend on the application, but in practice we have found that latencies of a few milliseconds offer a good compromise for most workloads under most circumstances. It is long enough to allow useful parallel execution, while being short enough that most applications will work well.

LATENCY MANAGEMENT

The example in Figure 5.3 shows the simplest, and most common, case of multi-threaded simulation where there is only a single synchronization latency in the entire system. Synchronization latencies can be controlled in a much finer way. Synchronization domains can be organized in a hierarchy that allows different cells to be synchronized with different latencies. This is illustrated in Figure 5.5 where cell 0 is tightly coupled with cell 1, and cell 2 is tightly coupled with cell 3. These two groups of cells are then more loosely coupled over the long-latency I2C bus, and can diverge further in terms of virtual time before requiring synchronization.

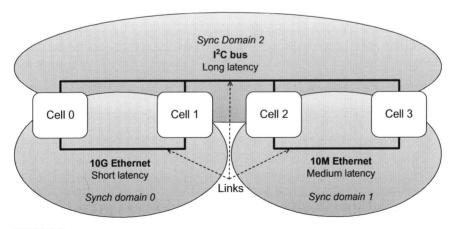

FIGURE 5.5

Synchronization domains.

For the synchronization domains to work properly, links must obey certain rules:

- The time quantum of a multiprocessor cell must be less than half the latency of the domain that contains the cell. The reason for this restriction is that the synchronization system considers a cell as a single unit and does not cope with the fact that the processors inside the cell are scheduled in a round-robin fashion. Simics checks this requirement and prints an error message if a domain's latency is incompatible with a cell's time quantum.
- The latency of a child domain must be less than half the latency of its parent domain. This restriction is once again related to how synchronization events are scheduled. Simics checks for this requirement and adjusts the latency of the child domain automatically while printing a warning. In the example in Figure 5.5, sync domain 2 is the parent for sync domains 0 and 1, and it makes sense because the latencies required by sync domains 0 and 1 are much lower than that required by sync domain 2.
- The latency of a domain must be greater than the length of two cycles of the slowest processor it contains. Simics uses cycles as the lowest time unit for posting events, so synchronization cannot be ensured if the latency resolution is too small. Simics checks this requirement and prints an error message if a domain's latency is incompatible with one of the processors.
- A link may not have a latency smaller than the one of the lowest domain in the hierarchy that contains the cells the link is connected in. In other words, the link must obey the highest latency between the systems it is connected to. Simics checks this requirement and adjust the link latency automatically upward if necessary while printing a warning.
- Once set, latencies may not be changed. This is a limitation in Simics that may be removed in future versions.

In addition to multithreading, Simics also provides the ability to perform distributed simulations where multiple hosts are running separate instances of Simics. With today's multicore host systems this feature is not often used, but it is required for very large-scale simulations. Distributed simulation is discussed later in this chapter when discussing how to scale up the network size.

SCHEDULING AND MULTITHREADING

A multithreaded, parallel Simics simulation is split into a number of cells for simultaneous execution on multiple processor cores in the host system. Figure 5.6 shows how the cells are managed—they are not directly mapped to host cores, but rather executed using a number of worker threads. The Simics scheduler takes care of balancing the load from the cells onto the worker threads and maintaining the virtual time latencies discussed before. Each cell can provide quite a different level of load—a busy multicore compute node will require much more host time to simulate than an idling single-core service processor or a sensor node.

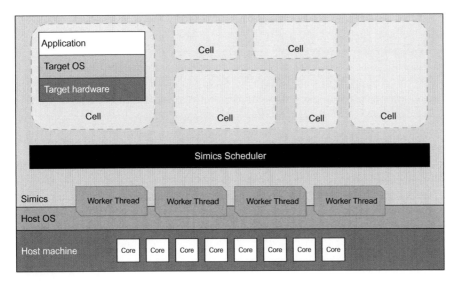

FIGURE 5.6

Cells, worker threads, and cores.

The number of worker threads employed by Simics can change over time and vary between runs of the same system. There is no point to having more threads than cells, and thus the number of cells puts an upper limit on the number of threads used. There is also no point to using more threads than host cores available. However, it also quite common to limit the number of threads further to, for example, use a single massive multicore server to run multiple Simics simulations at the same time. In such a scenario, each Simics process can be limited to only use a certain fraction of the available cores, rather than having them fight over resources. When a cell contains multiple processors, they are executed in the normal Simics temporally decoupled manner. It is possible to set the time quantum individually for each cell to tune execution behavior to optimize performance.

NETWORK TIMING AND BANDWIDTH SIMULATION

Simics does not try to faithfully reproduce the timing of network traffic in the real world. This is a natural consequence of the Simics modeling philosophy of modeling the "what" and not the "how" of hardware. The basic model assumes perfect transmissions and infinite bandwidth. Quite often, this is sufficient to successfully develop and test software that uses networking to communicate between different network nodes. On top of this basic model, contention and constraints can be added as needed to implement use cases and create a network simulation that is realistic enough for the software and system under testing to function correctly.

To faithfully simulate the timing of network traffic (e.g., latencies, transmission times, contention, and other factors), it is necessary to model the shared medium with a very fine-grained notion of time. Even ignoring analog effects, at the very least each defined cycle of the shared medium would need to be made explicit and effects calculated cycle by cycle. This is equivalent to simulating a computer memory system or shared bus in a cycle-accurate manner. The need to simulate the medium with short time intervals propagates to the connected network nodes, which need to interact with the network simulation on each network cycle. For example, a CAN bus simulation would need to get the output of all attached controllers on each bus cycle, do a logical AND between them, and then return the result to all nodes. For example, assuming a 2 GHz processor clock, a 1 MHz CAN bus would result in a time quantum of at most 2,000 instructions, and that is an extremely good case due to the combination of a slow bus with a fast processor. If we use a faster bus with shorter cycles, it very quickly gets down to 100 or less processor cycles, slowing down the simulation by a factor of 10 or more, as discussed in Chapter 2.

For a network such as switched Ethernet, contention becomes an issue at the points where multiple packet flows cross. In this case, the switch or router model needs to see all simultaneous packets coming in from the connected nodes, meaning that we need a synchronization interval close to the length of the shortest packet that can be sent. For example, the maximum packet rate for 1 Gb Ethernet is approximately 1.5 million packets per second, or 600 nanoseconds per packet. For the average 2 GHz processor, this means around 1,500 target system cycles before we have to synchronize with the network, again severely hampering performance. Instead, Simics tends to operate with a network latency (and thus synchronization interval) of at least a few milliseconds, covering the time to transmit several thousand minimum-size maximum-rate packets before synchronizing.

Thus, precise modeling of network contention is fundamentally at odds with fast simulation of the networks. Instead, what is done is to implement simple measures that can be decided locally and that provide a sufficient throttle on traffic to leave reasonably realistic traffic patterns. The simplest solution is to have the network device implement a certain maximum outbound packet rate or bandwidth using a local counter, which still provides backpressure to software that tries to push too much traffic. A local limit like this has to be configurable using a Simics attribute in the network device model so that it can be tuned for each use case. It should not be a hard-coded constant.

SIMULATED NETWORK NODES

A simulated network in Simics can contain nodes other than full machines with a full software stack of the type shown in Figure 5.1. It is fairly common to see simpler simulations being used for some network nodes to drive data to the fully simulated nodes.

SERVICE NODE

Modern computer systems often rely on network support to function at all. It is common for machines to obtain IP addresses from Dynamic Host Configuration Protocol (DHCP) servers, to pick their root file systems from NFS, or to load kernels over FTP or TFTP. To simplify the simulation of such systems, Simics provides a s*ervice node* for Ethernet and TCP/IP. As shown in Figure 5.2, the service node is a member of the simulated network with its own Ethernet MAC and IP address. It provides the most common TCP/IP network services, including DHCP, DNS, PING, RARP, FTP, TFTP, and NFS.

With the service node, it is easy to create a self-contained Simics setup that lets a target machine boot from the network or load user files over FTP without having to connect the simulated network to the real world and set up a server on the simulation host. This means that the execution is deterministic, checkpointable, and repeatable, and that setups can be trivially provided from one user to another without needing anything except Simics.

A CAUTIONARY TALE: WRECKING THE HOST NETWORK

It has happened more than once that Simics users have left a service node active in their virtual network as they connected it to the physical office network. If you use a sufficiently low-level connection mechanism like raw sockets or low-level bridging, this implies that the Simics service node finds itself on the office network. This means that it will see and reply to DHCP requests from real machines. For some reason it has proven to be very fast at replying and will often win over the real DHCP servers. Thus, when other machines on the office network do DHCP requests, the Simics service node would reply, giving them addresses that are quite bogus from the perspective of the real world, neatly shutting down network communications and generally causing mayhem.

The lesson is that there is a reason that raw sockets are restricted on all modern operating systems (it is far too easy to accidentally do bad things with them, not to mention what can be done intentionally). It is also important to know what you are doing when starting to connect different networks—if you bridge a virtual network to the real network, you essentially become an IT administrator for the entire office network. As discussed later, the NAT-based real-network connection does not have this problem and is sufficient for many use cases.

SENSORS AND ACTUATORS

In networks like MIL-STD-1553 and ARINC 429, most network nodes are not actually compute nodes but just fairly dumb sensors and actuators. While their physical implementation might contain a microcontroller (and even this is not always the case), in simulation they are best simulated as fixed-function devices attached to the network. Figure 5.7 shows an example of such a network, with a single master computer controlling a single sensor and a single actuator node (also using a redundant network). Note that the remote nodes do not have any software running on them in Simics; all their functionality is implemented as part of the hardware model.

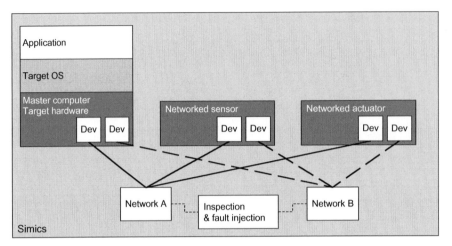

FIGURE 5.7

Redundant real-time bus network.

Depending on the complexity of the devices, the network nodes are either just run using the clock of some processor in the system or have their own internal clock and are thus capable of running in their own simulation thread. In practice, because real-time buses often have hard limits on the time that it takes for a message to propagate from the master to a remote node and then back with a reply, it is simplest to model the remote nodes in the same time domain as the master. The simulation work involved in simulating a remote node is usually very small.

TRAFFIC GENERATORS

A *traffic generator* is used to put traffic onto a network for other machines to consume. Logically, a traffic generator has a physical layer address (and usually higher-level address), because it is supposed to look like a machine on the network to the target machines receiving the traffic. In terms of implementation, they are attached to the network using the same interfaces as other machines, because they are creating new packets that would not otherwise exist. Sometimes, a generator needs to be able to respond to traffic from other machines—for example, to implement Address Resolution Protocol (ARP) in IP networks, or TCP connections.

Packet generators can be based on recordings of traffic from the real world, manually crafted streams of packets, or random data built using an algorithm in the generator. Generators are often existing software adapted to feed a traffic stream into Simics or ported to run inside a Simics module as part of the Simics simulation. Simics has a standard `eth-injector` class that supports injecting `pcap`-format traffic recordings into a Simics network.

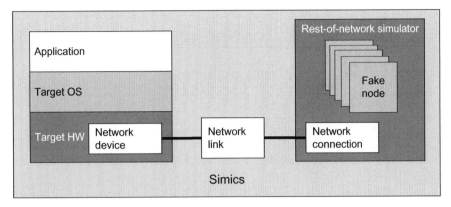

FIGURE 5.8

Rest-of-network simulation.

NETWORK TESTERS

A *network tester* is a network node akin to a traffic generator, except that it also checks the replies from the target machine being tested. Typically, a network tester is attached with one or more simulated Ethernet cables to one or more network ports on the target machine. It sends one specific packet at a time to the target system and checks that the packet or packets generated in response are as expected. For example, a network tester could attach to all ports of a simulated router and check that traffic sent into the router with a certain destination comes out on the correct port. Very powerful and precise tests can be carried out inside a simulation, because we have control over time and perfect access to all network traffic.

Attaching a real-world network test device is discussed in the section "Connecting the Real World."

REST-OF-NETWORK SIMULATION

A *rest-of-network simulator* is a node in the simulated network that pretends to be multiple network nodes, creating the illusion of a large number of active machines in the network. Figure 5.8 illustrates the principle: the rest-of-network simulator has a single network connection to the simulated network, but internally it maintains a state corresponding to many fake network nodes.

The purpose of a rest-of-network simulator is to provide a large environment to a target machine (or sometimes a small group of target machines) without the overhead of fully simulating all the other nodes. This provides flexibility to the simulator user and reduces the amount of work needed to accomplish a certain simulation goal.

For example, this methodology is commonly used in automotive CAN network testing where a node is given a simulated environment corresponding to an

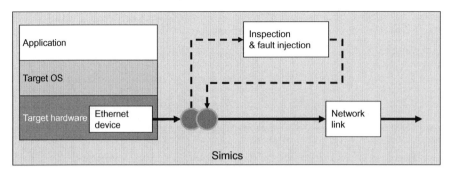

FIGURE 5.9

Network inspection.

entire network. In telecommunications, a single network simulator can provide the illusion of hundreds or thousands of mobile phones generating data traffic and calls. In server computing, the simulation of many clients to a server for load testing or robustness testing is an example of rest-of-network simulation.

TRAFFIC INSPECTION AND MODIFICATION

Being able to inspect and modify network traffic is a huge benefit of simulation over using a physical network. In Simics, each type of network simulation provides its own set of interfaces to allow the modification of network packets, because the nature of operations can be quite different depending on the network type.

TRAFFIC MODIFICATION

The canonical design for traffic interception in Simics is the Ethernet design, which is illustrated in Figure 5.9. The instrumentation is attached to some endpoint of the Ethernet network (in this case, to the device side of the connection to the network link) and receives callbacks when a packet arrives at that point. In the callback function, the instrumentation module has a choice of three actions: it can forward the packet as it is, meaning that it gets transmitted as normal; it can ignore forwarding the packet, in which case it is lost to the network and will not reach any recipient; or it can modify the packet and forward the modified packet to simulate some kind of network disturbance that causes packets to forward with broken contents.

By attaching instrumentation to the endpoints in the network, it is possible to use instrumentation even with distributed setups. The instrumentation module works purely locally and can run in parallel to other threads of the simulation. If we tried

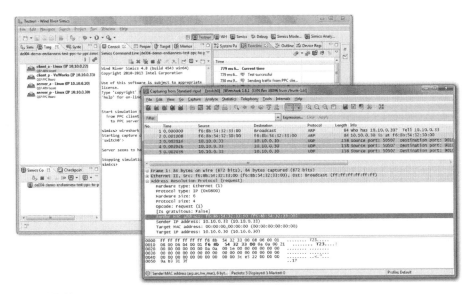

FIGURE 5.10

Wireshark tracing a Simics session.

to provide access from the network link itself, it would greatly complicate the implementation in the case of a multithreaded and distributed simulation (where the link object is actually present in multiple copies, one inside each simulation cell).

ETHERNET INSPECTION WITH WIRESHARK

Simics provides built-in support for capturing Ethernet packets as packet capture (pcap) files as used by the common open-source Wireshark packet analysis tool. It also provides the ability to stream traffic directly to a Wireshark program running concurrently with Simics, providing a live view of the traffic. From the perspective of Wireshark, Simics is a just a network capturing device, and because Simics simulates networks at the level of individual physical-layer packets, it has the same data to work with as it would have with a real physical packet capture tool. Figure 5.10 shows an example session where traffic is sent from one simulated machine to another, and the network traffic is fed live to Wireshark running in parallel to Simics.

SCALING UP THE NETWORK SIZE

The network size needed to do something that is useful and interesting varies greatly between applications. Sometimes a single machine is sufficient, but often several machines are needed to produce interesting results. There is a range of technologies used in Simics to help simulate large networks efficiently, reaching up to hundreds of network nodes and thousands of target processors.

INFINITE INVENTORY

A simulation like Simics has a fundamental advantage over physical network labs in that there is an infinite supply of cards, boards, machines, or whatever you call your network nodes. In most labs, there is a limit to how many nodes of a certain type are available in physical form, and this limits the size and variants of networks that can be set up. In contrast, in Simics each type of node can be instantiated any number of times with no supply limit.

This makes it possible to do much richer testing of a system as variants are limited only by the imagination of the tester and the constraints of the system design. It also means that there is no need to wait for lab hardware to become available to run a particular test setup, greatly improving the efficiency of lab work. As mentioned in Chapter 3, the setup can be automated, and completed setups can be saved as checkpoints, making the configuration work much quicker than with physical hardware. The size of the system to be run is really only limited by the performance of the simulator, and this also means that the system's size is a soft limit, not a hard limit. Given a particular setup, it is always possible to add one more node to it, at the cost of making the simulation run a little bit slower. As discussed in the following sections, Simics has implemented a wide range of technologies to enable this scaling up to go as far as possible.

HYPERSIMULATION

Simics hypersimulation (as described in Chapter 2) is often very useful to speed up the execution of a networked target system. It is rare to have a system where all target machines are busy all the time. Usually, some parts of the system are idle or lightly loaded, and hypersimulation effectively removes these from the work the simulator needs to do. Thus, hypersimulation makes it possible to simulate larger (and sometimes much larger) systems using the same host hardware. It automatically exploits the behavior of the target system to increase the simulation scalability.

REAL-WORLD STORY: A THOUSAND SLEEPING NODES

We once developed a model of a low-power sensor node and its processor for the "RUNES" EU project (Engblom et al., 2005). The sensor nodes ran software that was idle a very large proportion of the time, waking up occasionally to blink the LED on the devices. With this software running on the simulated nodes, 1,000 nodes were simulated in a single Simics process, using a single host processor, at a speed of 12,000 MIPS. Given that the native speed of each node was on order of a few MIPS, this simulated the system at a speed faster than real time! If we had only simulated a single node, it would have run thousands of times faster than real time. Hypersimulation really works.

MULTITHREADING SIMICS

As described earlier in this chapter, Simics can use multiple host threads to simulate multiple target machines. This provides a very easy and simple way to scale up Simics to simulate networks of 10 or 20 machines at a speed comparable to simulating a single machine on a single host core. Multithreading puts more processor power into the simulation of a large target system and works well when the simulation is limited by CPU power. If the simulation is limited by memory usage, a host machine with more RAM tends to be a better option than one with more cores.

For efficient simulation, the network latency set between machines needs to be high enough to allow parallel execution. If the latency is too low, Simics will spend more time synchronizing than doing useful work. Network latencies can be set to different values for different networks in a system, reflecting the particular latency requirements and performance implications of each network link.

CRAZY SIMICS SCALING: 1792 TARGET PROCESSORS

In an article published in 2013, Grigory Rechistov at Intel® describes the largest Simics target system that has been described publicly to date. He used multiple Simics instances running on a cluster of 16 multicore servers with Intel® Xeon® processors to simulate a target system consisting of 112 multicore servers with Intel® Xeon® processors. Taking advantage of both multithreading and distribution, the target system finally contained 1792 target processor cores, running a distributed OpenMP-based application (Rechistov, 2013).

DISTRIBUTION

Simics can connect multiple Simics processes (Simics instances) running on multiple different machines into a single coordinated and coherent simulation system. Such *distributed* simulation is used when multithreading cannot provide sufficient performance for really large target systems. It used to be that distribution was the only way to parallelize Simics, but after Simics 4.0 introduced multithreading within a single Simics instance, multithreaded Simics has replaced almost all uses of distributed simulation.

Using distributed simulation is less convenient, requires more work in the simulation setup, and requires statical division of the target machines between hosts. Thus, using distribution is a second step in scaling up, which should only be done once the option to use a more powerful host has been exhausted. Distributed simulation has the advantage of adding both host processor cores and host memory, and it might be a necessary solution for scaling up in cases where Simics is limited by host RAM size rather than by processor cycles. It is being used, but it is being used in cases where the target setup is truly enormous and a single 24-core server cannot handle the load.

IMPRESSIVE DEMO: ESC 2004 KILO-MACHINE SETUP

Back in 2004, Simics was being developed by the startup company Virtutech, and the Embedded Systems Conference was the place to be to show off your tools for embedded developers. We wanted to make a splash, and thus we cooked up an insane demo containing 1,002 target machines. The target system consisted of 1,000 automated Internet relay chat (IRC) clients connected to an IRC server, along with one interactive client displaying the chat traffic. The automated IRC clients were run on Linux on PowerPC 440GP–based target machines, the server was a PowerPC 750–based target machine, and the interactive client was a SunFire 3500 UltraSPARC running Solaris 9 and a graphical desktop showing the Mozilla IRC client.

To run this, we brought a rack of Linux servers onto the show floor, running a total of 13 Simics instances all networked together in a single virtual network. There were 10 Simics instances running 100 automated clients each, along with 1 instance running the server and another containing the interactive client. Finally, a thirteenth instance ran the coordinated network simulation. The automated clients were run on 5 dual-core Linux hosts (back then, Simics was not multithreaded and multicore processors were still exotic beasts only found in servers). We used Simics checkpoints sharing basic state to achieve the same effect as memory page sharing in Simics today.

Given the state of Simics and hardware in 2014, we could likely pull this off on a single powerful server today, using a single Simics process to contain the entire target system. Still, back in 2004, we were mighty proud of our achievement, and it did duly impress the people on the show floor who actually managed to understand what was going on.

Booth setup.

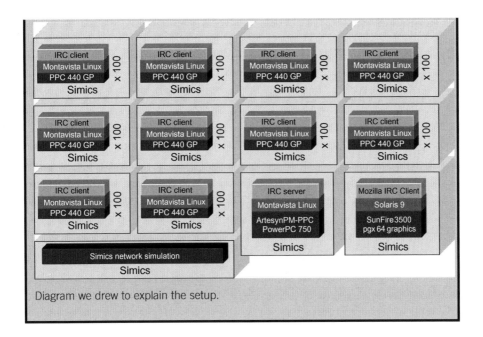

Diagram we drew to explain the setup.

MEMORY PAGE SHARING

Memory page sharing was described in Chapter 2. It can be a very effective tool to reduce the amount of host RAM needed to simulate a large number of target machines as long as the machines run similar software stacks. In practice, this is often the case, because multiple nodes in a network or multiple boards in a rack are based on the same software stack or at least the same basic OS setup. If nothing else, many large setups use some measure of redundancy for fault tolerance and resiliency, leading to software and data being the same across multiple nodes.

STUBBING NETWORK NODES

Some nodes in a network might not need to be fully simulated to make the system work or be useful for a particular simulation use case. If this is the case, an entire network node can be replaced with a simpler simulation, similar in principle to the Simics service node described earlier (but customized for the particular application). Such simplified nodes are called *stubs*, as they have the same purpose as stubs in software—to provide the impression that a part of the system exists when it is not actually fully implemented. A stubbed node typically does not contain any instruction-set simulation (ISS) and does not run software. Stubbing nodes in this way reduces the cost to run a simulation in terms of processor cycles and host RAM, and usually saves development time compared to a full model of a node.

For example, rack-based systems used in telecommunications and data networking tend to contain boards that do not need to be fully simulated. A board that implements the Ethernet switch for an Ethernet backplane can be replaced with a Simics standard Ethernet link. Boards that provide precise clocking to the other boards can often be ignored entirely or simulated as a very simple stub. If a use case does not involve actually processing line data, line cards and DSP boards can be stubbed without implementing their full data-transforming functions.

The most important aspect of stubbed boards and network nodes is that the stub has to convince the rest of the system that the missing piece is still there. Typically, this is done by sending out heartbeat messages or replying to status requests from control boards. As long as the right information is seen by the checking software, the system will keep working.

The key to stubbing is to define and understand the use cases for the simulation setup being built. Stubbing can only be defined from the perspective of what needs to be achieved with the simulator—if the full functionality of a node is needed to complete some use case, or the use case is to develop and test software for that node, it is typically not a good idea to stub the node.

CONNECTING THE REAL WORLD

Connecting the virtual network inside a Simics simulation to the outside world is common. The reasons for connecting the virtual and real networks vary widely and depend on what Simics is being used for. A real network can give a machine access to the Internet for web browsing and updating its software. It can be used to connect an on-target debugging agent (see Chapter 3) to an external tool and to make a Simics target system look like a physical development board on a lab network. Some target systems, in particular those running Linux, like to boot from an NFS mount or a specific FTP server on the external network.

A real network has also been used to connect Simics-simulated control systems to real-world physical hardware. Such an application is shown in Figure 5.11. The idea is to validate the control application by testing it with a real system, but without having to use a real control computer. Quite often the controlled hardware (or a mechanical simulator of the real mechanics) might exist even when the controlling computer hardware is not yet ready or available in very small volumes. In such cases, using Simics as a virtual computer together with real hardware makes perfect sense.

The Simics-simulated system might connect to external machinery for hardware-in-the-loop simulation. External operations and management tools can connect to the Simics-simulated target to update or load new software on the target, and the

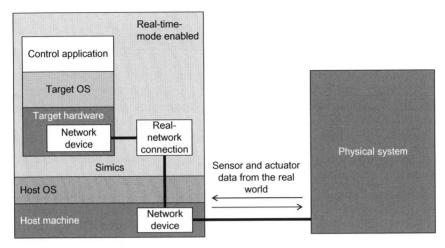

FIGURE 5.11

Real hardware in the loop.

interface between the target software and such tools might be part of what is being tested. Network testing equipment used with physical machines might be used with simulated machines, reusing existing tests and tools with Simics.

There are some cases where the use of an external resource can be replaced with a special simulation node in Simics (as discussed before), but real networking is in general something that is expected in most real applications of Simics.

DEDICATED REAL-NETWORK MODULES

Real-network connections in Simics are handled by dedicated real-network modules, as shown in Figure 5.2. A naïve implementation of a real-network connection builds the connection directly into the simulated network device, but this is not a good idea. It means that each time a new device is implemented, it needs to reimplement the same functionality, and it also complicates the use case of an entirely virtual network. In IT virtual machine applications, it makes sense to use pass-through devices such as `virtio` to improve network performance, but for Simics, this destroys much of the value of the simulator.

The dedicated real-network module can also perform tasks like replaying the interaction with the real world for reverse execution and maintaining settings for how to connect to the real world. Indeed, a properly designed real-network module should offer record and replay facilities that enable saving checkpoints including real-network traffic and the reproduction of a simulation run involving the real world any number of times. The real world is unpredictable, especially in timing, but by recording all inputs, any particular scenario can be made repeatable.

AVAILABILITY OF HARDWARE PORTS

A key requirement for the implementation of a real-network solution in Simics is that there is a way to connect the network of interest to the host PC. This is usually the biggest problem for widespread use of real networking for non-PC-standard networks. Today, Ethernet in wired or wireless form is found on all hosts, but classic serial ports are getting rare. For industrial and embedded buses such as ARINC 429, MIL-STD-1553, and CAN, real-network solutions require that some PCIe card or USB adapter is available.

There also needs to be an API or driver that provides access to the network. For Ethernet, this is part of the host operating system and it is available in standard form on all host machines. It is sometimes necessary to install a TAP device or a TAP driver to enable real networking, but this is also standardized and works with all Ethernet network cards. Thus, Ethernet real networking is available on any Simics host.

For other buses, there is typically no common API available, and real-network solutions are tied to a particular type of interface card or USB adapter. A different host interface card for the same bus most likely would require a new real-network module.

By nature, real-network connections involve putting real-network packets into a real network connected to the host machine, affecting other computers apart from the Simics host. Thus, it is a potentially dangerous operation, and it is normally restricted in contemporary operating systems. Once upon a time, Microsoft Windows XP featured raw sockets as a standard feature, but this was withdrawn because it became a great tool for malware, saboteurs, and Internet miscreants (Menzies, 2002). Today, such functions require the installation of special drivers on Windows, and administrative privileges on both Linux and Windows. In some IT environments, this is not permitted for regular users, and therefore the only way to do real-network connections is to use TCP/IP and a network address translation (NAT) solution.

TIMING ISSUES

The real world runs in real-world time, while the machines inside of a Simics simulation run in virtual time. This can lead to issues when external systems expect the Simics-simulated systems to have the same time and the same speed of execution as the real world. Instead, as discussed in Chapter 2, Simics simulations can run much faster or much slower than the real world, and the speed relative to the real world will change over time.

The most common time-related problem that occurs is that real-world test systems trigger timeouts when communicating with Simics-simulated systems that run slower than the real-world machines they are modeling. The simplest solution is just to extend the timeouts in the test system with some constant factor to allow the Simics-simulated targets enough real-world time to complete their work before the timeouts trigger. Note that if Simics is much faster than the real world (thanks to hypersimulation or the real targets being very slow), timeouts will instead wait for far too long to trigger as seen from the target systems' local virtual time. Such a case is rarely harmful, however, because all that will happen is that a failed system will run in its failed state for a while longer.

To make it possible for external tools to work with Simics time, Simics provides the Simics *Time Server* and *Time Client* libraries. To use these features, external programs need to include the Simics Time Client library and change the time-handling code to get their time from this library instead of from the host system clock. Time handling has to be virtualized to work with a virtual system. By handling time in this way, timeouts in test systems can be kept at the same values as used with real hardware and still work correctly with virtual hardware. It is the best solution in terms of keeping tests consistent between real hardware and virtual hardware, because the tests do not need to be changed, only the way that time is handled in the test system used.

When the real-world counterpart that Simics is communicating with is another simulator, there is the option to use the Simics *Time Synchronization* library. This library allows virtual time to be synchronized between Simics and another program, in a bidirectional peer-to-peer fashion. The Time Server library only exports the Simics time to another program, while the Time Synchronization library allows the other program to affect the time in Simics.

Another potential problem is when the Simics target and the real-world exchange information are based on date and time. The date and time of the Simics system can be set arbitrarily and will increase at a pace that is not necessarily consistent with the real world. To solve this, the date and time in the Simics target needs to be updated regularly to match the real world. This makes the simulation nondeterministic and nonrepeatable unless all time corrections are recorded for later replay.

REAL-TIME MODE

If Simics is consistently faster than the real-world system, Simics *real-time mode* can be used to keep Simics and the real world in sync. Real-time mode can be configured to throttle Simics at any given rate, including much slower than real time. If desired, the simulator can be slowed down to a fraction of real-time speed, allowing fast processes to be observed in slow motion.

For single-processor embedded control systems, such as those employed in current aircraft or spacecraft, Simics running on a modern PC is often fast enough to keep up with the real world. Simics VMP also means that Intel® Architecture targets can often run faster than real time if the host is a little faster than the target. If Simics executes code slower than the real world, it might still keep up with the real world on average thanks to hypersimulation of idle periods. This is sufficient for many cases, but often fails for real-time hardware-in-the-loop control algorithms that require a soft or hard real-time guarantee on the response.

When Simics is used to control real-world equipment in real time, the throttling of Simics has to be done with great care. Simics does not simply run fast and then stop dead for a noticeable amount of time, but it keeps the delays evenly spread out over real time. Such smooth timing has proven crucial when driving real-world mechanical and electrical systems from control algorithms running on Simics.

Real-time mode has also been used to slow down hypersimulating targets to allow user names and passwords to be entered. In particular, for Intel® Architecture models running Linux, the timeout for entering the user's password during login would trigger too quickly to allow a password to be entered manually. To get around this issue, real-time mode is often used during login.

ETHERNET REAL-NETWORK VARIANTS

Ethernet is the most frequently used and most complex Simics real-network variant. There are several different ways available to connect the target systems inside of Simics to the outside world, each with their own benefits and issues. This discussion also provides an idea for how real networking can be implemented for other types of networks and buses.

NETWORK ADDRESS TRANSLATION AND PORT FORWARDING

NAT hides the internal network from the external world by rewriting the return address of outgoing packets to the NAT router and rerouting incoming packets to the correct device on the internal network. In a NAT real-network solution, the Simics machines sit behind a virtual NAT router, just like a home or office network usually sits behind a NAT router when connected to the Internet. The virtual NAT router in Simics allows port forwarding so that the external world can initiate connections to simulated machines.

As shown in Figure 5.12, the IP address of the Simics target machine is hidden from the external world. The NAT bridge rewrites the source of outbound packets to match the host address. For inbound port-forwarding, the NAT bridge is configured to map particular host-side ports to particular IP addresses and ports inside of the virtual network. For example, to contact a web server at 10.10.0.20:80, the external computer would contact 192.168.1.10:4080 (or any other chosen port on the host). The NAT bridge would then rewrite the incoming traffic to go to port 80 on the Simics target.

Because NAT needs to rewrite packets, it only works for UDP and TCP. Some protocols such as FTP require some extra awareness in the NAT to work— for example, including IP addresses in the payloads. For such cases, the NAT code needs to rewrite packets based on application knowledge. This is common to all NAT solutions and not specific to Simics.

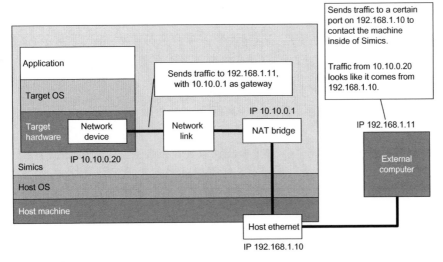

Sends traffic to a certain
port on 192.168.1.10 to
contact the machine
inside of Simics.

Traffic from 10.10.0.20
looks like it comes from
192.168.1.10.

Sends traffic to 192.168.1.11,
with 10.10.0.1 as gateway

IP 10.10.0.1

IP 192.168.1.11

Application

Target OS

Target
hardware

Network
device

Network
link

NAT bridge

External
computer

IP 10.10.0.20

Simics

Host OS

Host machine

Host ethernet

IP 192.168.1.10

FIGURE 5.12

Real-network NAT.

NAT offers a simple way to connect out from Simics targets to the outside
world, requiring no administrative privileges. The Simics process on the host simply opens up TCP/IP ports, and the external world does not need to know that
they correspond to ports on simulated computers.

ETHERNET BRIDGING

An Ethernet bridge connector puts the simulated target systems on the host network. Ethernet packets are picked up from the real network and passed unmodified into the simulation, and Ethernet packets generated inside of Simics are sent
to the external network unmodified.

As illustrated in Figure 5.13, Simics essentially takes over an Ethernet port
from the host, using it to communicate with the outside world. The implementation uses a TAP interface in the host operating system bridged to the host
Ethernet interface using host OS facilities. The host itself is not on the network
that the Simics target machines are on, and it cannot communicate with them. It
is recommended that the host Ethernet interface used by Simics is a secondary
interface connected to a lab network, so that the host does not lose its connection
with the regular office network.

The Simics target machines are on the same IP range as the external computers, and no special routes are needed to direct traffic to them. They reply to ARP
traffic and obtain addresses from DHCP servers just like any real machine would.

Setting up a bridged connection requires administrative privileges, but once
it has been configured, using the connection can be done with regular user

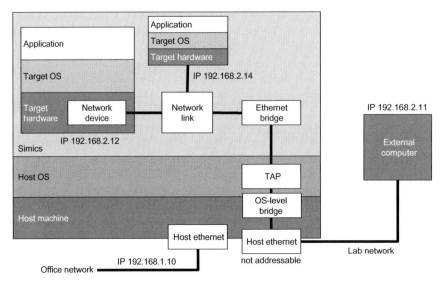

FIGURE 5.13

Real-network bridge.

privileges. This means that Simics runs as a regular user, not as a privileged user, which is both more practical and more security-aware.

HOST ACCESS

Host networking connects the Simics target machines to the host machine, using a virtual network interface on the host (a TAP interface). The TAP interface on the host becomes part of the virtual network, and Simics target machines reach the host at an IP that is local to the virtual network. On the host, Simics targets appear on a separate network accessed via a separate Ethernet device (the TAP device).

Host networking is illustrated in Figure 5.14. Simics contains a virtual network with its own range of IP addresses, and the host is added as a machine to this network. Because the Simics network and the external real-world network appear as two different Ethernet interfaces to the host operating system, it can be configured to do IP forwarding, routing traffic between the external real-world network and the virtual network.

The primary use case of host networking is to provide other programs on the host with network connections to the Simics target machines. Host networking is commonly used to communicate between Simics and debugging agents in the target software stack (see Chapter 3 for more on agent-based debugging with Simics), and to provide Simics targets with access to servers running on the host, such as NFS for target OS root file systems. It also makes servers running on Simics targets easily accessible from the host.

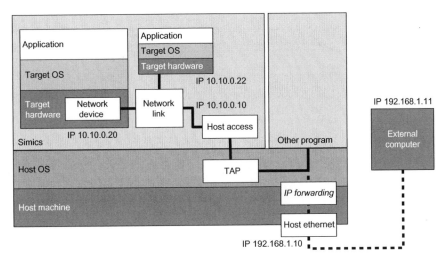

FIGURE 5.14

Host networking.

Just like with Ethernet bridging, configuring the TAP device requires administrator privileges. Once it is set up, Simics can run with user privileges. Host networking is often called *TAP networking* in Simics, which is a bit of a misnomer because TAP devices are also used to implement Ethernet bridging.

REAL-WORLD STORY: WINDOWS FILE SHARING TO POWER ARCHITECTURE VXWORKS 6.9 USING SIMICS

CIFS (also known as SMB or SMB2 depending on the version) is the Microsoft file-sharing protocol that is used for Windows file sharing. This protocol is used in many more places than one might expect, and in one publicly documented case we have had it running on Simics simulating a big-endian Power Architecture machine. The key to the puzzle was the Visuality NQ Server from Visuality Systems, which runs on embedded systems including non-Intel® targets and non-Windows operating systems. We ran the Visuality server on a Simics QSP-PPC target, on top of VxWorks, and successfully shared files from multiple servers to multiple clients on the host Windows machines, using a real-network connection via a TAP interface on the host. The setup looked like this:

The setup let us drag and drop files from the host into the flash disk images on the target. Each target flash disk was started using a single common initial disk image, and then as they diverged, only the difference was saved using the differential image system that was discussed in Chapter 2.

During the setup process, we also hit an interesting issue. Once the two targets were booted, we tried starting the Visuality NQ servers, but we just could not get both running. If the servers were started simultaneously on both machines (using scripting it is trivial to type the same command at the same exact time on both targets), they both immediately shut down. If we started first one and then a second server, the first one kept running but the second shut down. The reason turned out to be that all CIFS nodes need to have a unique name (actually the guilty protocols are NetBIOS and DNS but let's call this CIFS for the sake of simplicity), and the VxWorks instances we had configured did not have any names set at all. Thus, a name collision ensued. The solution was simple enough: provide each target with a unique name from the scripted command-line setup.

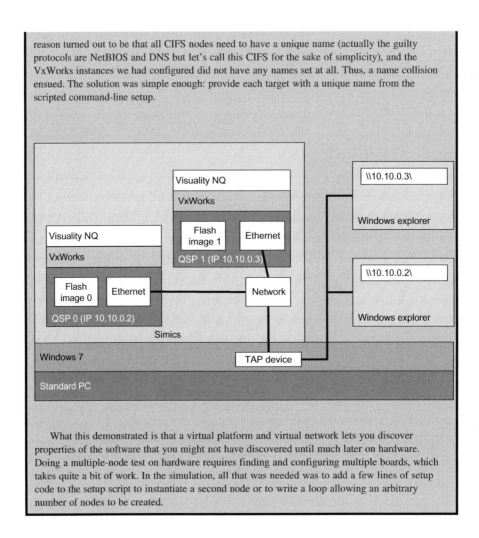

What this demonstrated is that a virtual platform and virtual network lets you discover properties of the software that you might not have discovered until much later on hardware. Doing a multiple-node test on hardware requires finding and configuring multiple boards, which takes quite a bit of work. In the simulation, all that was needed was to add a few lines of setup code to the setup script to instantiate a second node or to write a loop allowing an arbitrary number of nodes to be created.

PROGRAMMING NEW NETWORKS

Any Simics user can add new network links to Simics. It is part of the general extensibility of Simics. In its simplest form, a network link is just another Simics object implemented by some Simics class. Along with the network link object, there needs to be a Simics interface (or several) defined for the network. The interface presents the function calls that network interface devices and the network link use to exchange messages.

As shown in Figure 5.15, a network interface is commonly asymmetric with a different interface used in the device direction and link direction. For example,

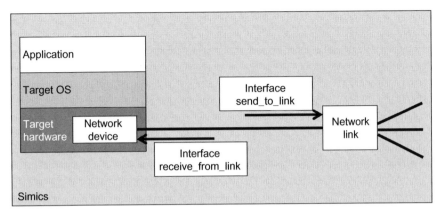

FIGURE 5.15

Implementing a new network.

the link might need to inform the device about link up/down, which is not needed from the device to the link, or the device might need to register its address with the link before it can send traffic.

The network link needs to implement the hardware-level addressing used by the network being modeled and deliver the incoming packets to the correct recipient or recipients. It might also implement functionality to allow users to inspect the packets being sent or trace traffic to external files.

For a local network link that connects devices inside a single machine and simulation cell, immediate delivery of messages is probably the simplest function to implement. This can be done with very little code. Typically, such a "network" would really just be an on-chip or single-board bus, like local I^2C.

A network that connects machines in different cells needs to implement additional logic to support sending messages between cells. It also needs to have network latencies implemented to provide repeatable semantics. To simplify the creation of new links that implement latencies and support crossing cell boundaries, Simics provides the Link library. The Link library provides the basic primitives needed to correctly implement a thread-safe and parallelizable link.

In simple cases, the Simics `datagram_link` example code can be used to simulate a new network. The `datagram_link` provides a simple broadcast bus, where a device can send a string of bytes to all other devices connected to the same link. The `datagram_link` provides no addressing, so all messages reach all other connected devices. If anything more complex is needed, it is better to create a new link implementation based on the Link library. Implementing a protocol on top of the byte stream of the `datagram_link` has proven much more complex and time consuming than just implementing a new link type with proper addressing and traffic-routing logic.

Building virtual platforms

Essentially, all models are wrong, but some are useful.
—**George Edward Pelham Box (1987)**

A virtual platform is a software model of an existing or future hardware system. The model has the ability to run the same software, including operating systems and drivers, as the actual hardware. This chapter introduces the reader to how the parts that make up a virtual platform are developed and how to assemble those parts into a virtual platform and even into a system of many connected virtual platforms.

THE PURPOSE OF THE MODEL

When creating a model it is important to consider the purpose of that model. What is the problem it is going to solve? To what use cases will it be applied? When it comes to virtual platforms, the problems addressed typically fall into one of four main classes based on the point in time (pre- or post-silicon) the virtual platform is used and if it is targeting hardware or software development use cases. The four main classes, labeled A−D, are illustrated in Figure 6.1. Depending on the class of problems addressed, different tradeoffs need to be considered.

As the virtual platform evolves along the time axis, from pre- to post-silicon, the fidelity and completeness of the platform must increase. In pre-silicon use cases it is typically enough to model only a piece of the final system—up to the board level, for example. In post-silicon use cases it is often necessary to view the virtual platform as only a part of a larger system of virtual platforms that are required to support full-system simulation. Thus in the early stages of hardware development, fast development and modifications of the virtual platform are key factors to be able to follow the evolution of the hardware design. However, later on stability, fidelity, flexibility, and the availability of good tools become key factors for the success of the virtual platform. The broader user base later in the development process tends to view the virtual platform as a means to achieve their own goals, such as software development or OS porting, and not as a particularly interesting object in its own right.

When considering tradeoffs along the hardware−software axis the key distinguishing factors are performance versus accuracy. When addressing hardware-related use cases the internal implementation details of a particular part become

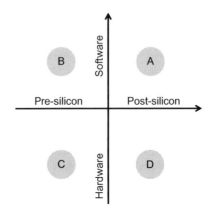

FIGURE 6.1

Four main classes of problems addressed by virtual platforms.

important. Modeling those details comes at a cost of simulation performance, and performance is the number-one concern for software-related use cases. Software developers often do not concern themselves with the internal implementation details of a particular hardware device. It is enough that the hardware−software interface is modeled accurately.

Simics virtual platforms are used extensively both in pre- and post-silicon use cases but have a significantly higher number of software-related use cases than hardware-related use cases. The focus of this chapter is therefore on creating models for class A and class B types of problems.

WHAT TO MODEL

As discussed in the introduction to this chapter, it is important to consider the goal, use cases, and purpose of the virtual platform before starting the development. Understanding the use cases for the model is paramount for an efficient development of the virtual platform. It is easy to fall into the trap of thinking that the virtual platform must be a complete and accurate model of the actual hardware platform. This is sometimes the case, but more often than not it is not the most effective way.

For example, it may be necessary to transfer data into the model, but the problem the model is meant to solve has nothing to do with the specific SATA controller. In this case it may not be necessary to model the specific SATA controller, but rather a generic one can be used and simply added as a PCI card in an available PCI slot. Alternatively, it may be acceptable to use a USB mass-storage device to transfer the files into the virtual platform.

Another common example is device initialization from an erasable programmable read-only memory (EPROM). In the real hardware this often takes place by the device reading a program or configuration data from an EPROM via a SPI or I^2C interface. Often the details of the communication interface between the device and the EPROM is of no concern and the device can be allowed direct access to the internal memory of the EPROM model. This simplifies implementation and enhances performance. Often the EPROM model can be omitted altogether and the corresponding configuration can be done by the configuration layer in the simulator; in Simics that is the *component system*.

In models of systems containing multiple boards, it is commonly the case that only some boards need to be modeled and run software. The other boards just need to be there as stubs, giving the software of interest the impression that the system is complete.

The lesson to take away is to *avoid modeling anything that is not necessary to support the use cases for the model*. In addition to saving time by not modeling things that are not required, anything that is not modeled will be infinitely fast and have no bugs.

Another important aspect is to consider the difference between the *architectural specification* and the *actual implementation*. For each system or component to be modeled there is an architecture specification, typically described in a programmer's reference manual, and one or more implementations. The architecture is the contract between the hardware, or model, and the software. Any software that is written according to the specification should run on any implementation. However, software that intentionally or accidentally depends on the details of a specific implementation is likely to end up being run on a different implementation of the same architecture. Therefore, it is important to focus on modeling the architecture and not a particular implementation of the hardware.

The model can also be seen as a specific implementation of the architecture that is different from the actual hardware finally produced, just as a second revision of the hardware may differ in some aspects, such as timing. The architecture often has very limited requirements on timing, and this is one of the reasons functional models of the architecture can be simplified to a great extent compared to modeling the actual implementation, something that is typically required for detailed performance models.

To understand the difference between the architecture and the implementation, consider the following architectural description: "Writing a 1 to the E bit will start the DMA transfer." The corresponding implementation may implement this so that when the E bit is written the internal state will be updated and a DMA transfer will start after 100 cycles. Any software that relies on the 100-cycles delay is likely to fail when run on a different implementation, such as model or a second generation of the hardware where the delay is perhaps only 50 cycles. Some, but not most, software will make this type of assumption. Sometimes this is by design—for example, to optimize performance—but often it is simply the fact that software has been developed and tested on a single implementation, and when it happens to work it is assumed to be correct, even though it may not be architecturally correct.

Because the architecture is what is modeled and some software makes assumptions about the implementation, there will be cases where software will run on hardware but not on the model. This does not mean the model is "wrong"; it is simply another implementation of the specific architecture, and the software is not written according to the architectural specification.

Two options exist to resolve this conundrum: change the software or change the model. The preferred solution is typically to change the software, because the software is fundamentally flawed in that it may not run on the next revision of the hardware. Our experience shows that it might be difficult to convince software developers that the software is incorrect. They often take the position that if it works on hardware it must be the fault of the model. Hardware designers, on the other hand, tend to immediately recognize the risk in having software depend on features that are not specified in the architecture. The model should only be changed if it is not possible to change software. For example, to run legacy systems where there may be software that is not controllable. Such changes should be made in a way that clearly documents what was done and why.

REAL-WORLD STORY: FAILING CHECKSUM

When booting a customer's software stack on Simics it failed with a checksum error when validating the boot image. The customer complained loudly that this was a bug in the model, because the software had been tested on the real hardware without problems.

After some debugging it was found that in Simics an interrupt happened in the middle of the checksum routine and the interrupt handler did not properly restore the carry bit, causing the following computation to fail. By slightly changing the timing parameters of the Simics models the checksum error went away. To us this was an obvious latent bug in the software, as any minor change could easily make this manifest on the real hardware, or perhaps it already was, but only rarely. However, it took several weeks to convince the customer to update the interrupt handler to correctly restore the state for the checksum computation to finish correctly in the event of an interrupt.

HOW TO MODEL

Once it is decided *what* should be modeled it is time to think about *how* it should be modeled. One of the most important decisions facing the developer of a device model for a virtual platform is the abstraction level to use.

To better understand the importance of choosing the right abstraction level, consider the analogy with physics. In modern physics there are four major abstraction levels, or models, used: classical (Newtonian) mechanics, relativistic mechanics, quantum mechanics, and quantum field theory.

Classical mechanics is very good at dealing with everyday conditions—that is, objects typically found on Earth moving at speeds far below the speed of light. However, once an object starts to move at speeds close to the speed of light or they start to approach the size of atoms, other models are needed. Trying to calculate the motion of planets using quantum field theory becomes intractable, because the chosen model is too detailed for the purpose. Similarly, trying to calculate the motion of subatomic particles using relativistic or even classical mechanics is not possible because the model is too abstract.

The analogy carries over to virtual platform models. If the abstraction level is too low there is a risk that the model will become a performance bottleneck and bring the entire simulation down to an unacceptable speed, not to mention the increased time it takes to create the model. On the other hand, if the abstraction level is too high it may not be possible to perform all tasks required. The various abstraction levels commonly used are described in Chapter 2.

THE MODELER

Building fast and efficient transaction-level models of hardware is a special skill. It requires understanding what the software needs to function correctly, and how to implement that with maximum efficiency while still staying sufficiently true to the behavior of the hardware. In our experience, most hardware designers that try to build TLM models tend to end up with models that contain too many details and with insufficiently abstract timing. Developers familiar with device driver development and OS kernels are typically the best candidates for device modeling, because they have seen the functional, software-facing side of the hardware.

It is crucial that new modelers get proper training in tools and methods. The best way to learn to become a good modeler is to have an experienced modeler available as a mentor for the first few modeling projects, and have the mentor review the design and implementation of a few models. Organizationally, as with any programming job, it is recommended that modelers work on modeling continuously so that skills stay fresh and improve. Using a language or framework that provides the right abstraction level can significantly simplify the task for new modelers. This is why Simics provides its own domain-specific language, which is covered later in this chapter.

VIRTUAL PLATFORMS IN SIMICS

A virtual platform in Simics typically consists of three main parts: an *instruction set simulator* (ISS), a number of *device models*, and a number of *components*. In addition, there is typically a *target script* that is used to instantiate the system that is to be simulated.

The ISS should be highly optimized to achieve good simulation performance. Fortunately, a limited amount of processor types are available on the market and Simics already provides an ISS for many of them. Although it is possible to create a new ISS for Simics, this is rarely done outside of the Simics core team, because it requires a lot of work and special skills to develop these models.

The components are a passive part of the virtual platform and are only used during configuration. They provide a hierarchical structure for the model that mirrors the organization of the real system. Typical components correspond to chips, PCIe plug-in cards, boards, and networks. However, note that configuration can take place both before the virtual platform is started and during runtime. Components are described in Chapter 4 and an example of how to implement a component is provided in Chapter 7.

Device models make up the bulk of the virtual platform and they come in all sorts of flavors, such as interrupt controllers, memory controllers, network adapters, timers, analog–digital converters, cryptographic offload engines, and any other function implemented in the hardware. How to create device models is covered in the next section. A device model essentially has four interfaces:

- *Software visible register map.* The memory-mapped register map is where the device driver software writes and reads registers in the device to control the behavior of the device. This is often known as the *frontend* of a device model. It can be as simple as a few bytes or contain many thousands of registers with varying size.
- *Communication networks and links.* Communication buses and networks are where the device model communicates with the external world (i.e., external to the chip it is contained in). Typical examples are I^2C, serial lines, and Ethernet networks. In Simics, most such interfaces are implemented with an explicit network or communications link. This makes it easier to support multithreaded simulation and also ensures that all input and output to a device model can be recorded and replayed. This is covered in more detail in Chapter 5.
- *Tightly coupled devices.* Devices can also be tightly coupled to each other. Typically, devices within the same chip need to access specific functions of other devices that are not really suitable to model as explicit communications networks. For example, a multiprocessor system controller will need to route interrupts from devices to processors and pass interrupts between processors in the system. Network processing accelerators could have direct data connections to the network interfaces of an SoC where network frames go directly without touching system memory. Devices also often access target memory to do DMA operations and grab descriptor tables for operations.
- *Simulator core.* The interface to the simulator core is used to drive time forward and to perform housekeeping and infrastructure tasks. In Simics, this includes checkpointing, support for attributes, reverse execution, logging, and posting and reacting to events. The part of the model that interacts with the simulator core is also the part that ties the activity on the other interfaces together. A large portion of the kernel interface code is automatically generated for models developed in Simics's native Device Modeling Language (DML), covered in the next section.

When a new virtual platform is being created in Simics, the process roughly follows the following outline:

1. Map the system by collecting and reading design specifications, programmers' reference manuals, and other relevant documents. This creates a list of devices and processors that make up the system and how they are connected.
2. Based on an analysis of the foreseen system usage, make a preliminary decision on the necessary level of modeling of each device. Can it be ignored, stubbed out, or does it need to be fully implemented? If the software load already exists, analyze it to see what it actually uses. If the software is yet to arrive, the system deployment planning or marketing plan for a new SoC can be very helpful to determine initial priorities.
3. Reuse existing device models and processor models from the Simics library. The library makes it faster to produce an initial model, because models for many common standard parts already exist. Reuse often means adapting an existing model of a similar device, which is much faster than writing a new model from scratch. Simics also provides frameworks for writing models for devices attached to common system interconnects like PCI, PCI Express†, RapidIO†, Ethernet, I^2C, and others.
4. Create the initial model; ignore and simplify as much functionality as possible initially to quickly get to a basic model. Add functional device tests as features are added to the model. The features to add are guided by the usage analysis from step 2.
5. If there is already software available, test the virtual platform using that software and add any missing functionality or devices required by the software.
6. Refine the model until it runs the available software or passes all defined test cases as determined in step 2.
7. Evolve the virtual platform as the physical hardware design stabilizes and is updated during a design project or system lifecycle.

This is a classic iterative software development methodology, where the software being developed—the hardware model—is tested early and often to explore the precise requirements. It goes by many names, from spiral model to agile methods to test-driven development. The iterative approach can be applied to help develop and debug the hardware design, considering the hardware model as a software object that can be updated to reflect a new and better understanding of the target domain and software interface requirements.

Virtual platform design can be, and is often, started before the final hardware specification is finalized. This is not a problem, as the virtual platform can be updated as the hardware specification changes or is completed.

As illustrated in Figure 6.2, as the physical hardware design becomes more definite (going from a vague idea to a concrete board), the virtual platform adapts and expands. Over time, the virtual platform adds more and more functions and device models, as well as changing the setup to mirror the design. Thus, the

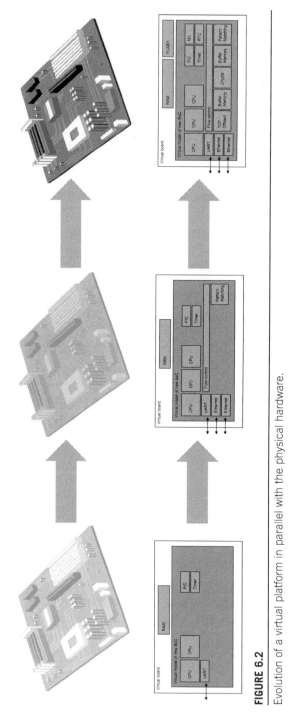

FIGURE 6.2

Evolution of a virtual platform in parallel with the physical hardware.

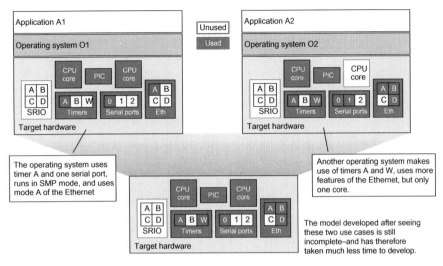

FIGURE 6.3

Use cases drive model depth and breadth.

virtual platform can be used as an executable specification of the hardware, a specification that can run software and be used to validate and evaluate the design (Carbonari, 2013).

During the hardware development process, the virtual platform is used to start software development early and also to get feedback from the software team to the hardware developers. This is an important added value from building a virtual platform for a new piece of hardware that should not be overlooked.

Often, it is possible to start using a virtual system almost immediately after starting to develop the model. Even a basic system that does not yet contain all components can be used to get development started. For example, a boot loader typically requires less virtual hardware to be in place than a full OS port. Such a limited system can be used both as an early start for a design that is finalized or as the early approximation for a system design that is not yet final. Because a virtual platform is designed and extended for particular use cases, it will typically deepen and broaden its coverage of the target system over time. As shown in Figure 6.3, each use case will require a certain set of devices and functions in the devices to be modeled. The final model is a union of all that was found to be needed.

In general, each individual device model can start out quite simple, implementing only the basic operation mode(s) and later have more complex, optimized operating modes added. Over time, more devices and more details for each model will be added to the virtual system, evolving toward the final model. This happens both from changes to the design in the pre-silicon and early design stages, as well as from covering more and different use cases over time.

FOLLOWING THE HARDWARE STRUCTURE

In general, Simics virtual platforms follow the overall structure and architecture of the hardware. This usually makes things easier in the long run, even if it might seem to require extra coding initially. However, it is also necessary to stick to the Simics level of abstraction. Typically, this means looking at the target system's memory map and the most prominent real-world interfaces. There is also an element of smart reuse of existing Simics models and functions to reduce the amount of coding needed.

Figure 6.4 shows a number of examples of how common hardware functions are modeled in Simics, from the perspective of the processor. At the top is a regular RAM. This is modeled using a memory-mapped RAM model, which uses a Simics image object for its storage. At runtime, there is no model of individual dual in-line memory modules (DIMMs) or memory banks, just a single functional RAM. This corresponds well to the software's understanding of RAM.

Next is a NOR flash memory. Flash is more complicated than RAM, because writes have to be interpreted as commands. This interpretation is performed by the flash model. However, reads can often be handled just like RAM reads. For this reason, a RAM model is put behind the flash model, and some accesses are redirected to it from the flash model. In this way, the memory access system for RAM is simply reused, simplifying the flash memory model. Once again, the software perception is modeled correctly.

In the lowest part of Figure 6.4 are two devices attached using PCIe. The PCIe bridge sets up memory mappings for the Ethernet controller and the SATA controller in a separate PCIe memory map. Using a separate memory map simplifies the implementation and follows the logical structure of the real system. Inside the PCIe memory map, each device maps its set of memory-mapped registers.

Simics Ethernet network models tend to split the Ethernet controller from the PHYs. This split makes it easier to model the software view of the networking devices, as it is possible to identify and control individual PHYs from software via the Ethernet controller. Chapter 5 has a deeper discussion on how to model networks and network devices in Simics.

The model of a SATA disk system splits the disk from the SATA controller. This follows the split in the physical hardware, and allows Simics to provide a set of generic device models for SATA disks, CD-Roms/DVDs, etc., which can be attached to any model of a SATA controller. A SATA controller model only has to model the particulars of the controller itself, and does not need to concern itself with the modeling of a disk. The disk model, in turn, relies on the Simics image system to manage storage and allow the modeling of arbitrarily large disks.

Beginning modelers often try to merge all these aspects into a single model, because it seems easier to write a single model rather than a whole chain of models. However, this monolithic model breaks down as soon as a second variant is needed, quickly leading to copied and inconsistent code. Separating the model into several modules with well-defined interfaces following the hardware structure increases reuse and allows faster evolution of the device models and the system setup.

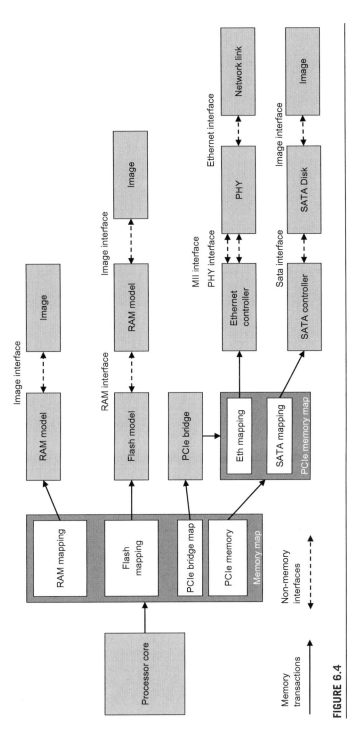

FIGURE 6.4

Following the hardware structure.

DEVICE MODELING LANGUAGE

Simics provides a C API and ABI, meaning that models written in almost any language can be integrated into a Simics virtual platform. When Simics was initially created, device models were written in C directly calling into the Simics API, but over time this was found to be very inefficient. To improve modeling efficiency, a domain-specific language, DML, was created. DML is specifically designed to allow rapid development of robust ST-level models for Simics. Besides DML, the most common languages used for creating device models are C, C++ (including SystemC), and Python. For the purpose of this book DML is considered the language of choice for creating device models.

OVERVIEW OF DML

DML is a textual language that provides a way to write transaction-level device models with less code and fewer mistakes than plain C/C++ with calls to the simulator API. DML models are much more concise, and much easier to write, read, understand, and maintain.

DML explicitly supports an iterative development style for device models by providing default implementations for many device aspects and strong support for marking unimplemented aspects in a way that makes them easy to find during test runs. DML supports and encourages inline documentation in a model, and documentation is extracted and used to help Simics provide a better end-user interface for a model.

DML COMPILATION PROCESS

DML does not compile directly to binary models; rather, DML is compiled to C code that is then compiled by the native C compiler. The DML compiler also generates the plumbing code needed to connect a particular model to Simics, reducing the Simics API knowledge needed to create models and keeping the code relatively free from explicit Simics API calls. This includes automatic support for checkpointing, attributes, reverse execution, logging, and other Simics features. Figure 6.5 illustrates the steps of the DML compilation process. Note that the entire process is transparent to DML users, who just need to invoke the Simics module Makefile that is automatically generated by Simics to compile a DML module. The C code is compiled like a Simics module written in C, using the same Simics API header files as all other Simics modules.

The common denominator for all Simics modules is the C-level Simics API. By generating C code with Simics API calls, DML code integrates naturally with any other Simics module. It also makes it possible to combine C and DML source

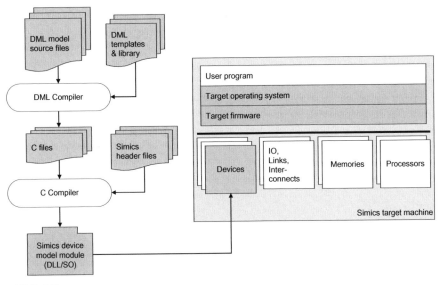

FIGURE 6.5

DML compilation process.

code into a single module, which can be used to wrap existing C-language simulations behind a DML frontend, or make use of particular C-language libraries to implement module functionality.

REACTIVE MODELING STYLE

DML is designed to code models in a reactive style. DML describes models as a set of methods (functions) that are called from the simulation kernel and across the device interfaces whenever something occurs that the model has to respond to. There is no main loop in a DML model; the simulation kernel and DML compiler takes care of sequencing and activation of the different pieces of sequential code in a model.

This is the industry-standard way to write high-performance transaction-level models. In SystemC terms, it is equivalent to using SC_METHOD and explicit events rather than SC_THREAD and wait statements. In C, it means creating a model to be driven by function calls from other parts of the simulation rather than running multiple threads and using interthread communication and coordination.

The benefit of a reactive model is, first of all, higher performance, because no thread-level context-switching cost is incurred when activating models. Creating a reactive model also makes it easier to stop the simulation at any time and to investigate and checkpoint its state, because no state is hidden on the call stack.

MODEL PERFORMANCE

Not all models are equal, and the final performance of the simulation is directly affected by how models are designed and written. Modelers need to think carefully about the design of a model to make it fast and make sure that no implementation details accidentally spoil performance.

With DML, it is harder to make performance mistakes. The DML itself encourages a reactive TLM style of coding that does not rely on periodic updates to implement functionality. The DML compiler generates the integration code to the simulation platform, which removes the risk of misusing the platform API in a performance-degrading way. DML itself does not introduce any overhead compared to native C coding of a model.

REUSING EXISTING INFORMATION

When creating device models, it is beneficial to reduce the amount of manual work and new work needed to create Simics models. One important way to do this is to reuse existing information when creating Simics models. The reuse of entire models is discussed in Chapter 9.

REGISTER MAPS

It is very common to find some form of machine-readable documentation or list of device programming register maps. Such descriptions can be converted into Simics DML source code to automatically provide register map layouts, without any need to manually transcribe documentation into source code. Over the years, register layouts have been created from a wide variety of formats. Plaintext files, Excel sheets, custom XML document formats, IP-XACT specifications, SystemRDL programs, and even reference manuals in PDF have been used as a source for register lists.

Depending on the source format, sometimes all that are generated are offsets to registers, while other source formats contain enough information to add initial values, reset values, and bit fields to the registers. In some cases, it is possible to assign basic behavior to the registers as well, using DML templates expressing behaviors like *read only, clear on write,* or *reserved for future use.*

DML allows the modeler to split the declaration of register offsets and sizes from the definition of their behavior, and this is often exploited when generating DML from register lists. One bank declaration is used to hold all the register offsets and other generated information, and another one is used to add behavior to the registers that need to have their behavior modeled. In practice, it is often not necessary to deeply model the behavior of all registers, at least not initially.

DEVICE FUNCTIONALITY

DML code can call into existing C code. This is useful to take advantage of existing libraries for complicated computations, such as compression, crypto, and media-coding libraries. Using existing libraries saves development time and often leads to faster execution as well.

The ability to call from DML into C can also be used to wrap models of the functionality of a device into a Simics device that can be integrated into a full system and driven by software, such as, for example, to put a register map onto a basic algorithm model for a hardware accelerator or signal-processing block. This is often used to import device functionality kernels written in C and C++ for the benefit of algorithm and hardware design flows into Simics models.

There is actually no need for the existing code to be available in source form, as long as there is a header file and a linkable library file available. For example, DML can be used to create a memory-map frontend interface for a function call–driven model of a piece of hardware that is provided as a dynamically linked library or a linker archive. It also makes it possible to reuse pieces of functionality from existing TLM models written without framework support or for different simulation APIs.

DML FEATURES

This is not a textbook on DML or even a comprehensive guide on how to write device models for Simics. Therefore, it only covers enough of DML to explain the broader concepts and to give the reader a good foundation for further exploring device modeling with DML. Chapter 7 is a case study that builds a complete DMA controller model, which is complex enough to show how to use the most of the important aspects of DML. The following section describes some of the fundamental features of DML.

In the section "Creating Device Models" a simple but complete device model is developed to illustrate how a device model is typically built using Simics and DML. The device being modeled is not a real device; it is a very simple example that contains just enough complexity to show the fundamentals of the modeling process and of DML. A more in-depth example is shown in Chapter 7.

The device being modeled has one register data that can be written to and that can have its value read back. In addition, there are two registers that count the number of reads and writes to the register data. The final two registers of the device are the interrupt control register, which allows enabling and disabling and masking of interrupts and the interrupt status register that holds the interrupt status. A specification for the registers as it could appear in a programmer's reference manual is shown in Figure 6.6.

The DML terminology can sometimes be a bit confusing. DML has its own object model, which is completely separate from the Simics object model with

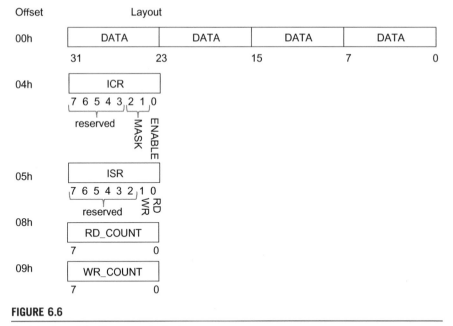

FIGURE 6.6

Register layout for the example device.

configuration classes. The DML objects are only relevant when working on the DML code and have no real significance during simulation time. Examples of DML objects are device, register, connect, and attribute. These are all covered in the following subsections. As can be expected there are also statements and expressions, such as try, log, foreach, new, and cast.

INLINE DOCUMENTATION

In DML many objects can be documented in the code. This encourages the developer to add relevant information and makes the code more readable. The same information could, of course, be added as comments instead, but the documentation contained in a DML file is exposed to the user (as opposed to the model developer) in several ways. The documentation is used in the GUI in the device register viewer, as shown in Figure 6.7, and it is also accessible from the Simics help system from the command line, as shown in Figure 6.8. The register layout and bit fields are automatically generated from the device structure described in the DML source code.

Listing 6.1 shows a minimal device model in DML. The device does not declare any interfaces, so although it can be instantiated inside Simics, it cannot be connected to the virtual platform.

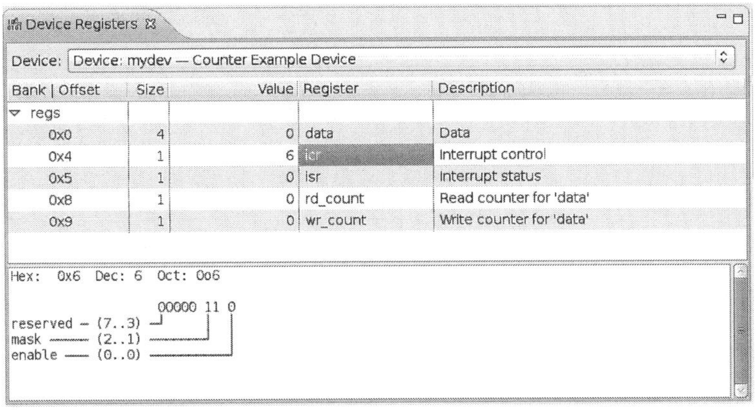

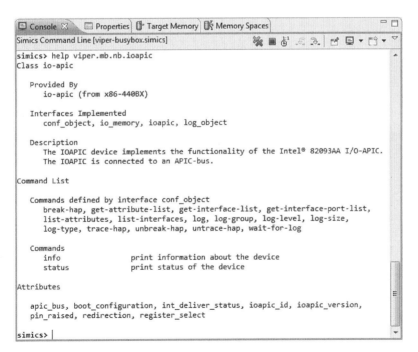

FIGURE 6.7

Simics device register viewer.

FIGURE 6.8

Simics help on a device in the CLI.

```
1    dml 1.2;
2    device c6_counter;
3
4    parameter desc = "Counter Example Device";
5
6    parameter documentation =
7        "This device implements a register that can be read and
     written and two counters that keep track of the number of times
     the device is read and written. When one of the counters overflow
     the device can optionally raise an interrupt.";
```

LISTING 6.1

Minimal device definition.

Line 1: Mandatory DML declaration to indicate it is a DML file.

Line 2: The device object means that this file will define a new Simics class with the corresponding name. Objects of this class can then be instantiated inside Simics.

Line 4: The desc parameter is an optional, but highly recommended, short description that shows up in the help, device register viewer, and other places.

Lines 6–7: The documentation parameter is optional and holds the documentation for the device that shows up in the help. If undefined, the desc parameter is used instead.

To make the device model useful it must be able to interact with the rest of the simulation. This is done through various interfaces, and the most fundamental one is the I/O-memory interface used for memory-mapped I/O. The next step is to define the register layout of the device as per the specification in Figure 6.6.

REGISTER MAPS

The most obvious contribution of DML is in simplifying the specification and implementation of a device's memory-mapped registers. This was the main problem that DML was designed to solve. The typical way a device's register map decoder is written in a C-style language is a "big switch" as illustrated in Listing 6.2.

The code needs to work out if a memory access is a read or write, and then look at the address and take the appropriate action. The result is normally two large switch statements, one for the read case and one for the write case. The drawbacks of this coding style are that it mixes the definition of the register map with the implementation of the behavior for each register, and that read and write behaviors tend to end up in two separate locations.

Note that doing the outer switch on the address accessed, and then for each case determining whether the operation is a read or write, ends up being just as hard to read. The core problem here is that doing this type of dispatch is not part of the C-style languages, and you end up coding a particular implementation of the decoder rather than simply declaring it. The situation can be somewhat alleviated by carefully structuring the code or using a library such as Synopsys' SystemC Modeling Library (SCML) to formalize the register dispatching to some extent.

```
1    switch (n) {
2        case 0x10:
3            if (do_log)
4                SIM_LOG_INFO(DBG_1, vga_ptr->obj, 0,
5                            "write to Attrib: Mode Control");
6            vga_ptr->attrib.palette_size = (value & 0x80) >> 7;
7            vga_ptr->attrib.pixel_clock = (value & 0x40) >> 6;
8            vga_ptr->attrib.pixel_panning = (value & 0x20) >> 5;
9            vga_ptr->attrib.enable_blink = (value & 0x08) >> 3;
10           vga_ptr->attrib.enable_line_gfx = (value & 0x04) >> 2;
11           vga_ptr->attrib.display_type = (value & 0x02) >> 1;
12           vga_ptr->attrib.graphics_mode = value & 0x01;
13           if (vga_ptr->tty_con
14               && vga_ptr->etty_int.graphics_mode)
15               vga_ptr->etty_int.graphics_mode(gm));
16           vga_ptr->update_cache(vga_ptr->obj);
17           break;
18       case 0x11:
19           if (do_log)
20               SIM_LOG_INFO(DBG_1, vga_ptr->obj, 0,
21                           "write to Attrib: overscan-color");
22           vga_ptr->attrib.overscan_color = value;
23           break;
24       case 0x12:
25           if (do_log)
26               SIM_LOG_INFO(DBG_1, vga_ptr->obj, 0,
27                           "write to Attrib: color"
28                           " plane enable");
29           vga_ptr->attrib.color_plane_en = value;
30           vga_ptr->need_update = 1;
31           break;
32       case 0x13:
33           if (do_log)
34               SIM_LOG_INFO(DBG_1, vga_ptr->obj, 0,
35                           "write to Attrib: Horizontal"
36                           " Panning");
37           vga_ptOr->attrib.horiz_pan = value;
38           break;
39       }
```

LISTING 6.2

VGA register decoder in C, "Big Switch".

In DML, the definition of the register map is much more declarative in style. As shown in Listing 6.3, the model source code can describe the register layout (which registers have which addresses) separately from the implementation, making it much easier to read.

```
 1    bank regs {
 2        parameter register_size = 1;
 3        parameter byte_order = "big-endian";
 4
 5        register data size 4 @ 0x00 "Data";
 6        register icr @ 0x4 "Interrupt control";
 7        register isr @ 0x5 "Interrupt status";
 8        register rd_count @ 0x08 "Read counter for 'data'";
 9        register wr_count @ 0x09 "Write counter for 'data'";
10    }
```

LISTING 6.3

DML register layout.

The actions to be taken on memory accesses are described in separate read and write methods for each register, and these are usually defined in a block of code separate from the main register map definition. You are allowed to put both the declaration of the register sizes and offsets and the definition of the actual functionality into the same block of code, but it is strongly recommended that you separate them to make the source code easier to read. Note that there is no need to repeat the size or offset of a register when declaring the functionality; the DML compiler takes care of combining all information specified for a register.

Note the use of parameters in Listing 6.3 to specify the endianness and default register size for the register bank called regs. Such parameters are common throughout DML, providing values for defaults or specifying the particular behavior of a particular object. Later, Listing 6.5 also shows some parameters giving the reset values of a register, which is another way in which DML makes device coding easier.

Combining the code from Listings 6.1 and 6.3 produces a minimal device that can be added into a Simics virtual platform and accessed through MMIO. The device has a single bank object named regs. A device can have many banks and each bank can be mapped into any number of locations in a *memory space* to allow software to access it using load and store instructions. This is explained in detail in the section "Creating Device Models."

The device model only provides the default read—write semantics for the registers. This is not good, because the model is not actually performing according to the specification. If an access is terminated in one of the registers, it would be good if the model could warn that unimplemented functionality is being triggered. This can help greatly during the early phase of the virtual platform development when there are many functions missing from the virtual platform. To provide this behavior the *unimplemented template* can be applied to the registers.

TEMPLATES

To reduce code duplication, DML uses templates to describe recurring functionality—for example, *always zero* or *clear on read*. Users can define their

Table 6.1 Example of Standard Templates in DML

Template	Behavior
clear_on_read	When read, return the current value and set the value to 0.
ignore	Writes have no effect, reads always return 0.
read_constant	All reads return the value set in the model source code; writes have no effect.
reserved	Log accesses as reading or writing reserved bits, remember written values, and read last value written.
read_only	Writes are ignored and logged.
unimplemented	Log accesses as accessing unimplemented feature to Simics console, remember written values, and read last value written.
write_1_clears	Writes clear the bits marked by ones in the written value.

own templates. Groups and arrays are provided in DML to describe repeating patterns and register structures. Using DML mechanisms, even very large and complex register banks can be described succinctly. There are many examples of devices with several thousand registers modeled in DML. Note that templates in DML are completely different from templates in C++.

The DML standard library comes with a set of predefined templates for common register types. A single register or field can combine several templates, as long as the templates do not affect the same aspect of the register's behavior. Table 6.1 gives some examples of DML templates available in DML 1.2.

Templates usually carry parameters that specify aspects of their behavior, making them quite general in applicability. For example, the read_constant template carries a value parameter providing the value to which it is fixed.

Applying the unimplemented template to relevant registers gives the starting point for the development of the example model. The code is shown in its entirety in Listing 6.4.

The code shown in Listing 6.4 is a complete device model that can be used as a part of a Simics virtual platform. It already provides a lot of functionality. Every register can be read and written by software and the user alike. When software is accessing an unimplemented register, a warning is displayed to the user in the Simics console. Documentation is provided in the help system, and the model can be configured to display log messages on each read or write to any register.

BIT FIELD DECODING

As shown in Figure 6.6, some registers, such as ISR and ICR, are divided into fields. Device registers tend to be divided up into fields consisting of a few

```
1    dml 1.2;
2
3    device c6_counter;
4
5    parameter desc = "Counter Example Device";
6
7    parameter documentation =
8        "This device implements a register that can be read and
     written and two counters that keep track of the number of times
     the device is read and written. When one of the counters overflow
     the device can optionally raise an interrupt.";
9
10   import "utility.dml";
11
12   bank regs {
13       parameter register_size = 1;
14       parameter byte_order = "big-endian";
15
16       register data size 4 @ 0x00 "Data";
17       register icr @ 0x4 is (unimplemented)
18           "Interrupt control";
19       register isr @ 0x5 is (unimplemented)
20           "Interrupt status";
21       register rd_count @ 0x08 is (unimplemented)
22           "Read counter for 'data'";
23       register wr_count @ 0x09 is (unimplemented)
24           "Write counter for 'data'";
25   }
```

LISTING 6.4

Initial device model.

> **Line 10:** Import common utilities, including many standard templates, such as
> unimplemented. The registers annotated with is (unimplemented) will
> automatically log an unimplemented message—for example, [mydevice unimpl]
> Read from unimplemented register regs.icr (0x4) (contents = 0).

bits each, and decoding the contents of such fields ends up as a series of very error-prone bit masking and shifting operations in most C code. DML allows the user to declare the bits inside each register that make up each field as illustrated in Listing 6.5. It is possible to use both little-endian and big-endian bit field numbering to align with how the device manuals describe the bit fields.

In addition to specifying named fields in a register, bit-slicing operations are available for integer types, including registers and fields. To access bit 1 of the MASK field in the ICR register it is possible to write $mask[1]. Note that it would be possible to separate the 2-bit MASK field into two 1-bit fields—for example, mask_wr and mask_rd—but to be consistent with the specification from Figure 6.6, the same partitioning of fields is kept.

```
 1    register icr {
 2        parameter hard_reset_value = 0x06;
 3        parameter soft_reset_value = $hard_reset_value;
 4
 5        field reserved[7:3] is (reserved);
 6        field mask[2:1];
 7        field enable[0];
 8    }
 9
10    register isr {
11        field reserved[7:2] is (reserved);
12        field wr[1];
13        field rd[0];
14    }
```

LISTING 6.5

Register definition and bit fields in DML.

> **Lines 5, 11:** Another standard template called `reserved` is being applied, this time to a field. The reserved template will issue a spec-violation warning if software tries to change the value of the field: `[mydevice spec-viol] Write to reserved field regs.icr.reserved (value written = 0x15, contents = 0), will not warn again`. Note that the reserved field may be read or written by software as long as the content is not changed. This is because, to update other fields in the register, software will read the register, modify the relevant bits, and write back the entire register. On the other hand, an entire register that is marked as reserved will produce a warning on any read or write.

ENDIANNESS AND PARTIAL ACCESSES

An advantage of using a declarative style for register maps is that the DML compiler knows the register layout explicitly. This enables the DML compiler to automatically generate code supporting tricky cases like accesses that hit only part of a register (e.g., a single byte in a 16-bit register) and accesses that cover several registers in a single memory operation. Depending on the specification of the target device, such accesses are either flagged as software errors or handled by routing accesses to the correct parts of a device. This is set by a simple parameter in the source code for a bank.

Endianness is also explicitly declared for a register bank, and endianness is handled correctly regardless of the endianness of the target. Note that there is both byte-endianness, which determines how data arriving in a memory transaction is interpreted, and bit-endianness, which deals with how bits are numbered inside a register. These two are independent.

DML makes handling cases like a 2-byte access in the middle of an 8-byte big-endian register on a little-endian host trivial. Coding such an access in C is fraught with problems and risks for error. It also reduces the mental strain on the programmer who has to deal with mixed endianness in a target system.

C-LIKE CORE LANGUAGE

The code that actually performs the work in DML is an extended subset of C. The code can access DML objects using a $ prefix to names, and define and call methods. The DML compiler ties the local definitions of behavior together into a coherent device model; the programmer need not care about the sequencing.

Compared to normal C, some additional features are available in DML. In particular, C++-style new and delete are used to manage dynamic memory, and there is support for simple try-catch exception handling. Other extensions help express common simulation functions like logging information, error reporting, and asserts concisely.

MEMORY LAYOUTS

Hardware devices quite often operate on data structures in main memory without involvement of the main processor in a system. Typical cases are descriptors, structures describing a set of work for a device to do, and data network packets that are processed (or deposited in memory) by devices. To support the modeling of such devices, DML has a memory layout data type. Memory layouts look similar to structure types in C, and are used as types for variables. Unlike C structs, DML layouts explicitly map directly to the data layout in memory, while in C, the compiler may insert padding between fields to ensure proper alignment of the data.

Listing 6.6 shows a snippet of DML code involving a layout. Note that the layout has an explicit endianness and includes single bits in bit fields as

```
1    typedef layout "big-endian" {
2        uint32 addr;
3        uint16 len;
4        uint8 offset;
5        bitfields 8 {
6            uint1 ext @ [0:0];
7        } flags;
8    } sg_list_block_row_t;
9
10   ...
11   {
12       // local variable of layout type
13       local sg_list_block_row_t row;
14       memcpy(&row, ptr, sizeof(row));
15       ptr += sizeof(row);
16       if (row.flags.ext) {
17           ...
18       }
19   }
```

LISTING 6.6

Memory layout in DML.

addressable units. It is used as the data type for a local variable into which the bytes from a block of memory are copied. The manipulation of a layout is local to the code of the device, which avoids repeated calls to the simulated memory system to collect the data, enhancing locality and speed in the simulator. Dealing with layouts is covered in more detail in Chapter 7.

INTERFACES TO OTHER MODELS

As discussed before, models also need to interface to other models within the same tightly coupled system component and to various interconnect links outside. In Simics, all such interfaces are expressed as sets of function calls called interfaces, which a model implements to let other models call it over that interface. It is essentially the same as an interface in Java or a pure abstract public base class in C++. The interfaces are unidirectional, providing a way for one device to call into another device. In DML, this is provided by the `connect` and `implement` objects. This is illustrated in Listing 6.7. Note that the `connect` and `implement` objects appear in different devices.

Incoming connections are defined in an `implement` object, and define the behavior for each function call in the implemented interface. Outgoing connections in `connect` objects provide the model with a configuration attribute that can be used to tell it which device to connect to. The connection is then done by the system configuration that assigns an object reference to the `connect` attribute. It is important to store the reference to the connected object in an attribute so that it can be checkpointed and configured at runtime.

Simics provides common header files and base implementations for interfaces like PCI, RapidIO, Serial, I^2C, and Ethernet to ensure model interoperability and design reuse.

SIMICS ATTRIBUTES

A key feature of the Simics simulation infrastructure is the use of *attributes* to make the state of the simulation explicit. The relevant state in a Simics model is stored in attributes, and by reading all attributes from a simulation object, you get a complete representation of its state that you can later restore. In a Simics model written in C or C++, attributes have to be manually registered with the simulation infrastructure. DML makes this process much simpler by automatically generating attribute creation and support code for all registers and connects in a model.

Sometimes it is necessary to define new model attributes explicitly in DML. This is used to do things that do not really fit into the categories of "registers" or "connects." For example, to support device configuration that results from the platform setup rather than from software, such as configuring the interrupt latency of a device; or to maintain other relevant state in the device, such as keeping track of if an interrupt signal is high or low. Other examples include attributes used to disable and enable fault injection in a model or maintaining various activity counters.

Listing 6.8 shows how an explicit attribute is defined in DML. The default behavior is to store a single value, but users can also override the attribute's `get` and `set` methods to have attributes do anything when accessed.

```
1    connect irq {        // Connect in device A
2        parameter documentation =
3            "Connection to an interrupt controller that"
4            + " implements level triggered interrupts"
5            + " through the signal interface.";
6        parameter required = true;
7        interface signal;
8    }

    . . .

9    implement signal {       // Implement in device B
10       method signal_raise() { /* TODO */ }
11       method signal_lower() { /* TODO */ }
12   }
```

LISTING 6.7

Using connect and implement.

Line 1: Connect object in device A, which can call the methods in the signal interface of the connected device B via, for example, `$irq.signal.signal_raise();`.

Line 3: This `connect` object is marked as required, meaning that a `configuration` object needs to be assigned to the corresponding attribute before the device can be instantiated. If a `connect` object is declared optional, the device must ensure that an object is actually assigned to the attribute before attempting to call an interface.

Line 7: The interface object defines the interfaces an object B must implement to be allowed to be assigned to the `irq` attribute. If an object is connected that does not implement all the specified interfaces, an error will be generated.

Line 9: Device B defines an `implement` object for the signal interface. This allows the device to be connected to the `irq` attribute in device A. If a device needs to implement the same interface more than once, the `interface` object can be placed inside a named `port` object.

Lines 10–11: Implementation of the methods defined by the signal interface.

```
1    attribute is_interrupt_raised {
2        parameter documentation =
3            "Keeps track of the interrupt signal's state.";
4        parameter allocate_type = "bool";
5    }
```

LISTING 6.8

Explicit attribute definition.

For comparison, Listing 6.9 shows the code needed to register an attribute in plain C using the Simics API. It is very repetitive and quite voluminous. Similar things would have to be done in any simulation infrastructure supporting the same features as Simics does, even if the exact way of expressing it might differ. Using explicit API calls to implement functionality is always more expansive in terms of code lines than using implicit generation of the API calls from a higher-level language like DML.

```
1    // Storage for the value attribute contents have to be
2    // put in the device model internal data
3    // representation structure
4    typedef struct sample_device {
5        log_object_t log;
6        int value;
7    } sample_device_t;
8
...
9
10   // get and set functions to convert attribute value to
11   // and from interoperability format and checkpoints
12   static set_error_t
13   set_value_attribute(void *arg, conf_object_t *obj,
14                       attr_value_t *val, attr_value_t *idx)
15   {
16       sample_device_t *sample = (sample_device_t *)obj;
17       sample->value = val->u.integer;
18       return Sim_Set_Ok;
19   }
20
21   static attr_value_t
22   get_value_attribute(void *arg, conf_object_t *obj,
23                       attr_value_t *idx)
24   {
25       sample_device_t *sample = (sample_device_t *)obj;
26       return SIM_make_attr_integer(sample->value);
27   }
28
...
29
30   // API call actually creating the attribute
31   SIM_register_typed_attribute(
32       sample_class, "value",
33       get_value_attribute, NULL,
34       set_value_attribute, NULL,
35       Sim_Attr_Optional, "i", NULL,
36       "The <i>value</i> field.");
```

LISTING 6.9

Defining a Simics attribute in C.

FUNCTIONALITY TEMPLATES

Simics also provides ready-made packages of templates and related code to provide a quick start in modeling devices with particular interfaces. DML has been designed to facilitate the provision of such reusable code in a way that makes it easy to extend in arbitrary ways. This makes creating even fairly complex device models much easier and reduces the code size, because repetitive code is hidden inside the standard template files included with Simics.

Listing 6.10 shows a minimal PCI device implemented in DML for Simics. The crucial part is the directive `import "pci/common.dml"`, which imports the basic PCI skeleton from Simics into the device. The `pci_config` bank is then filled in with some required parameters and register definitions. In Chapter 7, a PCI device is created and connected to the PCI bus of a target system.

CREATING DEVICE MODELS

Armed with the knowledge from the previous sections it is time to look at the process of developing the complete model for the device described in Figure 6.6. The starting point is the code shown in Listing 6.4, which implements a minimal but useful device model. All registers are there, and if software tries to access functionality that is not yet implemented, a log message will be displayed.

SETTING UP THE ENVIRONMENT

To be able to test the examples provided in this section you need to set up a working model-building environment. This requires installing and configuring the Wind River Simics Hindsight and the Wind River Simics Model Builder products. The process to install and configure the relevant products is described in the *Wind River Simics Installation Guide* (Wind River, 2014c) and *Wind River Simics Model Builder User's Guide* (Wind River, 2014b), respectively. You do not need to install any additional products or model libraries, but you may want to install the Eclipse package for Simics.

TEST METHODOLOGY

As in any nontrivial software project it is paramount to the quality and productivity to create automated tests for the model being developed. Depending on the situation, different strategies can be employed to set up the functional and system tests for a model.

If software already exists and the model is developed only to enable that software stack, it may be enough to use the software stack as a test. This modeling strategy is sometimes referred to as "follow the software"; and the purpose is to spend as little time as possible to get a model that enables the workload. It is

```dml
1    dml 1.2;
2
3    device sample_pci_device;
4    parameter desc = "sample PCI device";
5    parameter documentation =
6        "This is a very simple PCI device.";
7
8    import "pci/common.dml";
9    is pci_device;
10
11   parameter pci_hotplug = true;
12
13   bank pci_config {
14       /* This attribute should contain a list of all BAR
15          registers */
16       parameter base_address_registers =
17           ["base_address_0"];
18
19       register vendor_id { // Texas Instruments
20           parameter hard_reset_value = 0x104C;
21       }
22       register device_id { // PC Card Controller
23           parameter hard_reset_value = 0xAC10;
24       }
25
26       register base_address_0 @ 0x10 {
27           is memory_base_address_32;
28           parameter size_bits = 8;
29           parameter map_func = 1;
30       }
31       register base_address_1 @ 0x14
32           is (no_base_address_32);
33       register base_address_2 @ 0x18
34           is (no_base_address_32);
35       register base_address_3 @ 0x1C
36           is (no_base_address_32);
37       register base_address_4 @ 0x20
38           is (no_base_address_32);
39       register base_address_5 @ 0x24
40           is (no_base_address_32);
41   }
42
43   bank reg {
44       parameter function = 1;
45       // TODO: add registers here
46   }
```

LISTING 6.10

Sample PCI device in DML.

basically using a system-level test to test a particular device, and it will most likely mean that the device is incomplete when reused for a different software stack. On the other hand, it also ensures that the device works in the context where it needs to work at the moment. Often, functional tests for the device are also built over time to simplify testing and formally encode knowledge gained about the device-driving behavior of the software stack.

Another approach is to "follow the hardware"; that basically means creating a complete model (or one with known limitations) from the device specification, and creating functional tests for each part based on the specification. Ideally, a test-driven development approach is used where tests are created from the specification, and the device model is then developed to satisfy the tests. Over time, software drivers will become available for the model, and those software stacks will also be included in the testing.

Because no software exists for the example model, this example utilizes the "follow the hardware" approach.

ADDING A MODEL TO THE SIMULATION

As mentioned before, the model from Listing 6.4 is already useful and can be added into a simulation. As an example, start the "vacuum" target, which is a minimal configuration that only contains a clock and a memory space with some RAM. At the Simics command prompt an instance of the sample device can be created by calling the Simics API function SIM_create_object. The device can then be mapped into the memory space and the registers read and written from the CLI or from software. This is shown in Listing 6.11. It is also possible to inspect the registers of the device model in the Device Register view in Eclipse, as shown in Figure 6.7.

```
1    simics> @SIM_create_object('c6_counter', 'mydevice', [])
2    <the c6_counter 'mydevice'>
3
4    simics> phys_mem.add-map mydevice:regs 0x1000 0x10
5    Mapped 'mydevice:regs' in 'phys_mem' at address 0x1000.
6
7    simics> phys_mem.read 0x1004 1
8    [mydevice unimpl] Read from unimplemented register regs.icr (0x4)
     (contents = 0).
9    0 (LE)
```

LISTING 6.11

Adding a model to the simulation.

Line 1: Instantiation of an object mydevice of type c6_counter using the Simics API.
Line 4: The mydevice object is mapped into the phys_mem memory space at offset 0x1000 and with a size of 0x10. This allows memory transactions that hit phys_mem in the range 00x1000-0x1010 to be terminated in the model.
Lines 7-8: Issue a 1-byte memory load from address 0x1004 in phys_mem.
The transaction will terminate in mydevice. Because the register is marked as unimplemented, a log message is displayed.
Line 9: The result from the load operation on line 7 is shown. The register has the default reset value of 0.

This type of simple testing can be very useful for early experimentation when developing the model, but it is no replacement for proper tests. In the next section the device model is completed, including relevant test cases.

COMPLETING THE DEVICE MODEL

To complete the model according to the specification, more functionality must be added and tested. Because in this case we have decided to start with writing functional tests from the hardware specification, a good place to start is to add a simple test that verifies that the model can be instantiated and that the reset values for all registers are correct.

Functional tests are typically written in Python and are placed in a test directory in the module being tested. Instantiating the device is a common task for all tests, so it makes sense to put it in a separate file. Other useful things to place in the common file are the definition for the register layout and import statements for common testing utilities. The code required for the basic reset test is shown in Listing 6.12. Note that this test will fail because most registers have not yet been implemented. The tests can be run by simply running `make test` in the project directory or by using the Test Runner in Eclipse.

It is easy to make the test pass; simply define the proper reset values for the `ICR` register as shown in Listing 6.5.

The next step is to add some interesting functionality. The basic functionality for the device model is that reads and writes to the data register should increase the `rd_count` and `wr_count` registers. Listing 6.13 shows an updated model with the basic functionality in place and it should be easy to understand based on the examples from the previous sections. Interrupts are not yet supported.

The code for the updated model is shown in its entirety and provides the basic functionality for the device. In addition to implementing reset values and read—write counters, all the field definitions have been added.

Because new functionality has been added there should also be tests. The previous tests should of course still work, but it is necessary to add a test for the read and write counters. Such a test is also shown in Listing 6.13.

To complete the device model one more piece is required. The device should send an interrupt to the interrupt controller when the read or write counters overflow. In Simics, interrupts are typically modeled using the simple signal interface. Thus, to add support for interrupts the device should provide a connect object where an interrupt controller implementing the signal interface can be connected. In addition, an attribute will be added to keep track of the state of the interrupt signal. The code required for this is shown in Listing 6.14.

Listing 6.14 also adds a method `update_interrupt` that updates the interrupt status based on the `ISR` and `ICR` registers. This method should be called whenever something that may change the interrupt status takes place in the device. In this

■ File c6_counter_common.py

```
1    import simics
2    import conf
3    import dev_util as du
4    import pyobj
5    from stest import expect_equal
6
7    class Registers:
8        def __init__(self, dut):
9            Reg = du.Register_BE
10           Field = du.Bitfield_LE
11           self.data = Reg((dut, 'regs', 0), 4)
12           self.icr = Reg((dut, 'regs', 4), 1,
13                          Field(('mask': (2,1),
14                                 'enable': 0)))
15           self.isr = Reg((dut, 'regs', 5), 1,
16                          Field(('wr': 1, 'rd': 0)))
17           self.rd_count = Reg((dut, 'regs', 8), 1)
18           self.wr_count = Reg((dut, 'regs', 9), 1)
19
20   def create_c6_counter(name = None):
21       '''Create a new c6_counter object'''
22       obj = simics.pre_conf_object(name, 'c6_counter')
23       simics.SIM_add_configuration([obj], None)
24   return simics.SIM_get_object(obj.name)
```

■ File s-reset.py

```
25   # Test that registers have correct reset values.
26
27   from c6_counter_common import *
28   regs = Registers(create_c6_counter())
29
30   # Check reset values, data last to avoid affecting
31   # rd_count
32   expect_equal(regs.icr.read(), 0x6)
33   expect_equal(regs.isr.read(), 0)
34   expect_equal(regs.rd_count.read(), 0)
35   expect_equal(regs.wr_count.read(), 0)
36   expect_equal(regs.data.read(), 0)
```

LISTING 6.12

A first test—reset values.

Line 7: The dev_util module provides some useful tools for writing functional device tests, such as easily specifying register layouts. Here a helper class Registers is defined that contains the necessary information to easily access registers in the device under test.

Line 20: Definition of a function that creates an instance of the class that is going to be tested. The object can be given a name but it is typically not required for testing purposes.

Line 27: Instantiation of a device to tests and a Registers object to help with registers accesses.

Lines 32—36: This is the actual test part where the reset values of the various registers are compared with those from the specification. Line 35 will fail because all reset values are 0 by default.

- File c6-counter.dml

```
1    dml 1.2;
2
3    device c6_counter;
4
5    parameter desc = "Counter Example Device";
6
7    parameter documentation =
8        "This device implements a register that can be read and
     written and two counters that keep track of the number of times
     the device is read and written. When one of the counters
     overflows the device can optionally raise an interrupt.";
9
10   import "utility.dml";
11
12   bank regs {
13       parameter register_size = 1;
14       parameter byte_order = "big-endian";
15
16       register data size 4 @ 0x00 "Data";
17       register icr @ 0x4 is (unimplemented)
18           "Interrupt control";
19       register isr @ 0x5 is (unimplemented)
20           "Interrupt status";
21       register rd_count @ 0x08
22           "Read counter for 'data'";
23       register wr_count @ 0x09
24           "Write counter for 'data'";
25   }
26
27   bank regs {
28       register data {
29           method after_write(mop) {
30               call $wr_count.inc();
31           }
32           method after_read(mop) {
33               call $rd_count.inc();
34           }
35       }
36
37       register icr {
38           parameter hard_reset_value = 0x06;
39           parameter soft_reset_value = $hard_reset_value;
40
41           field reserved[7:3] is (reserved);
42           field mask[2:1];
43           field enable[0];
44       }
45
46       register isr {
```

LISTING 6.13

Basic functionality of the model.

```
47              field reserved[7:2] is (reserved);
48              field wr[1];
49              field rd[0];
50          }
51
52      register rd_count {
53          method inc() {
54              ++$this;
55          }
56      }
57
58      register wr_count {
59          method inc() {
60              ++$this;
61          }
62      }
63  }
```

■   File s-counter.py

```
1   # Test that the counter registers increment when the
2   # data register is read/written.
3
4   from c6_counter_common import *
5   dut = create_c6_counter()
6   regs = Registers(dut)
7
8   # Reading data should increase rd_count...
9   for n in xrange(10):
10      expect_equal(regs.rd_count.read(), n)
11      expect_equal(regs.data.read(), 0)
12      # ... but not wr_count
13      expect_equal(regs.wr_count.read(), 0)
14
15  # Writing data should increase wr_count...
16  for n in xrange(10):
17      expect_equal(regs.wr_count.read(), n)
18      regs.data.write(n)
19      expect_equal(dut.regs_data, n)
20      # ... but not rd_count
21      expect_equal(regs.rd_count.read(), 10)
```

LISTING 6.13

(Continued)

case writes to ISR or ICR and overflow of the read or write counter will potentially change the interrupt status. To facilitate reuse, two templates can be defined and applied to the relevant registers, as shown in Listing 6.15.

What is left is to provide a test for the interrupt functionality. In addition to checking the values of the ISR registers under various conditions, it is also necessary to make sure that the interrupt signal is raised and lowered appropriately.

```
1     import "simics/devs/signal.dml";
2
3     connect irq {
4         parameter documentation =
5             "Connection to an interrupt controller that"
6             + " implements level triggered interrupts"
7             + " through the signal interface.";
8         parameter required = true;
9         interface signal;
10    }
11
12    attribute is_interrupt_raised {
13        parameter documentation =
14            "Keeps track of the interrupt signal's state.";
15        parameter allocate_type = "bool";
16    }


      ...


17    bank regs {
18        method update_interrupt() {
19            if (($isr.wr || $isr.rd) && $icr.enable) {
20                if (!$is_interrupt_raised) {
21                    $is_interrupt_raised = true;
22                    $irq.signal.signal_raise();
23                }
24            } else {
25                if ($is_interrupt_raised) {
26                    $is_interrupt_raised = false;
27                    $irq.signal.signal_lower();
28                }
29            }
```

LISTING 6.14

Adding interrupt support.

To test the interrupt signal it is necessary to hook up some object to the `irq` attribute of the device. Of course, it is possible to test the device using a real interrupt controller model or by adding it into a full system. However, the recommended approach is to try to test the device in as much isolation as possible. This minimizes the coupling between device models and reduces the risk that, for example, bugs in the interrupt controller manifest themselves as failed tests for the device that is actually being tested. Using more focused testing typically leads to faster running tests, which in turn means they can be run more frequently—preferably as part of the compilation step. This methodology is in line with sound software testing strategies. Testing a device in isolation also simplifies reuse of the model in another system where a particular interrupt controller might not be appropriate or available.

Simics provides a simple facility to create such Simics configuration objects for use in tests. As mentioned previously, it is possible to develop models for Simics in many languages, and one of them is Python. It is simple to implement a

```
1     template irq_updater {
2         method after_write(mop) {
3             call $update_interrupt();
4         }
5     }
6
7     template overflow_ctr {
8         parameter interrupt_status default undefined;
9         parameter mask_bit default undefined;
10
11        method inc() {
12            if (++$this == 0)
13                call $overflow();
14        }
15
16        method overflow() {
17            if (!$icr.mask[$mask_bit])
18                $interrupt_status = 1;
19
20            call $update_interrupt();
21        }
22    }


             ...


23        register icr is (irq_updater) {
24            parameter hard_reset_value = 0x06;
25            parameter soft_reset_value = $hard_reset_value;
26
27            field reserved[7:3] is (reserved);
28            field mask[2:1];
29            field enable[0];
30        }
31
32        register isr is (irq_updater) {
33            field reserved[7:2] is (reserved);
34            field wr[1];
35            field rd[0];
36        }
37
38        register rd_count is (overflow_ctr) {
39            parameter interrupt_status = $isr.rd;
40            parameter mask_bit = 0;
41        }
42
43        register wr_count is (overflow_ctr) {
44            parameter interrupt_status = $isr.wr;
45            parameter mask_bit = 1;
46        }
```

LISTING 6.15

Using templates to update interrupt status.

```
1    import pyobj
2
3    class InterruptController(pyobj.ConfObject):
4        class count(pyobj.SimpleAttribute(0, 'i')): pass
5        class signal(pyobj.Interface):
6            def signal_raise(self):
7                self._up.count.val += 1
8            def signal_lower(self):
9                self._up.count.val -= 1
```

LISTING 6.16

Use python mock objects for testing.

Line 3: Define a new configuration class named InterruptController. Inheriting from pyobj.ConfObject turns this Python class into a Simics class.

Line 4: Define an integer attribute to hold the count for the number of times the interrupt has been raised and lowered.

Lines 5–9: Define the implementation of the signal interface and increment or decrement the counter depending on whether the interrupt is raised or lowered.

configuration object in Python that can be used for testing the interrupt functionality of the device under test. A simple example that counts the number of times an interrupt has been raised or lowered is illustrated in Listing 6.16, and can be added to the file of common test functions for the device.

With the knowledge of how to create mock objects for testing, the basics for device modeling has been covered. The source code for the finished device model and all tests are available in Appendix A.

In Chapter 7, a more realistic model of a DMA device will be created and it will be shown how the model can be connected to a complete virtual platform in various ways.

RESERVED REGISTERS AND MISSED ACCESSES

A memory transaction that is not terminated in a device's register bank, RAM, or similar is called a *miss-access*. As discussed in Chapter 3, when software runs on real hardware miss-accesses can often go undetected for a long time because they may not cause immediate problems or program termination. If correctly designed, virtual platforms can improve developer productivity by early detection of such potential problems. This section discusses how to deal with miss-accesses and reserved registers from a modeling perspective.

Miss-accesses typically come in two categories. Either the miss-access does not terminate in a device or RAM at all, or it occurs *inside* a device's register bank, but at an offset where there is no register mapped. The first category of miss-accesses usually corresponds to a misunderstanding or misconfiguration of the target's memory map, the software, or the virtual platform model. The second category, missing registers inside a bank, is more complicated and also relates to how the model handles reserved registers. Reserved registers are often not modeled as parts of the register set in a Simics model, and thus turn into miss-accesses.

It is not always obvious what the best approach is to modeling reserved registers or miss-accesses. This section tries to outline some of the different methods that can be used. To understand what can be done, it is necessary to understand how a miss-access is handled in Simics. When a miss-access occurs, a `Core_Address_Not_Mapped` hap is generated (see Chapter 2). The default handler for this hap stops the simulation and generates a log message:

```
[ebony.soc.plb error] Access at 0×148300605 where nothing is mapped.
[ebony.soc.plb] Address not mapped
[ebony.soc.cpu] v:0×00101b70 p:0×000101b70 blr
```

Often such errors are bugs in the target software, or sometimes in the model, that should ideally be corrected. However, sometimes this is not possible—for example, if the software is a proprietary operating system as in the preceding example where QNX[†] is booted on a PowerPC[†] system. It can also be time consuming to fix all of the software issues, which often are relatively harmless, as discussed in Chapter 3.

One solution that often works well is to simply map some memory where the miss-access occurs. It is surprising how often drivers make spurious accesses that really have no impact on the simulation, as long as they hit something. Simics provides the `set-memory` class for this purpose. The `set-memory` class implements a device used to represent memory that is all set to a specific value. This class can also be used to model generic unmapped memory ranges that should return a default value on read—for example, the unmapped BIOS area in a PC that should return `0xff` for every byte. Using `set-memory` also has the advantage that the model does not have to be modified, so it does not require source access to the model. The `set-memory` object can be added in the target script for a particular OS setup, so that the miss-access can be suppressed on a single hardware—software combination. A drawback is that if the device is dynamically mapped by the operating system, it can be difficult to maintain a consistent memory map.

Another method to prevent the default handler for the `Core_Address_Not_Mapped` hap from stopping the simulation is to use the `outside_memory_whitelist` attribute that every processor in Simics has. The attribute contains a set of physical address ranges where the hap handler should not stop the simulation. This is very useful when quickly trying to bring up a new software stack on the target, as many missed accesses can simply be ignored. Using the `outside_memory_whitelist` also has the advantage of being applied at runtime, requiring no access to the model's source code and being applicable on a per-software basis. However, the whitelist can be hard to maintain if the number of accesses grows or when the software is dynamically remapping memory.

The Simics memory spaces also provide a mechanism for handling unmapped read accesses by returning a default value and to ignore unmapped write accesses. This can be controlled via the `ignore_unmapped_writes` and `unmapped_read_value` attributes. The byte pattern defined in the `unmapped_read_value` attribute will be replicated across the memory space to represent the value read from unmapped addresses.

RESERVED REGISTERS

It is not uncommon for hardware to have reserved registers that the software is not supposed to read or write. For example, different variants of the same hardware may present slightly different programming interfaces, or some registers may be reserved for planned future expansion or for hardware debugging purposes. Although software should not read or write such registers, it often does. For example, it is common that a single driver source is used for many different variants of the same piece of hardware and it is difficult to ensure that what is a valid register in one variant is reserved in another. One of the reasons for this is that it is often possible to read or write reserved registers without causing the system to fail, thus it is very difficult to find these spurious accesses when working on real hardware.

However, once in a while a new piece of hardware will show up where it is not safe to access a previously reserved register. This can cause bugs that are very hard to find.

Reserved registers should typically not be explicitly modeled in Simics. Experience has shown that it is better to leave reserved registers unimplemented and thus trigger the miss-access handler if software tries to access them. This makes it clear that the software is doing something it should not do or that the modeler has misunderstood the device's specification. Silently suppressing such activity will just hide the issue, leading to bigger problems later.

The default behavior of DML models is to generate a spec-violation log message and a `Sim_PE_IO_Not_Taken` exception, resulting in a `Core_Address_Not_Mapped` hap:

```
[device spec-viol] 1 byte read access at offset 0 in reg (addr
0×148300605) outside registers or misaligned access
```

As discussed in Chapter 3, the simulator is more helpful when it flags potential software bugs by being more restrictive than actual hardware. However, for some reserved registers that are commonly accessed by software it may make sense to model them explicitly. For example, using DML a reserved register can be added like this, possibly with an additional log message on access:

```
register reserved @ 0xadd9 (read_zero, ignore_write) "Reserved" {
  parameter configuration = "none";

}
```

Another common hardware design makes it explicit that all accesses to missing offsets should have a particular behavior, such as ignoring writes and reading zero. As new generations of devices are created, the reserved offsets are taken into use to implement new functionality. This is used to allow device drivers to simply target the newest generations of devices, but be used on all devices, old and new. This means that an old device will see many accesses to reserved locations, but that this is well-defined behavior. If the number of registers involved is fairly small, the best solution is often to add the "new" registers as reserved registers to the older devices.

For some types of devices this behavior is not desirable. For example, the configuration space in a PCIe device is defined so that the software is allowed to probe any byte. This is part of the device's specification, and thus has to be implemented. To catch accesses that fall between explicitly modeled registers in a bank, the `miss_pattern` parameter of the bank can be defined to return a default value, for example:

```
bank regs {
    parameter miss_pattern = 0xff;
    parameter overlapping = true;

    ...
```

If there is a large number of locations that need to be handled, the DML bank methods `miss_access`, `miss_read_access`, and `miss_write_access` can be used. These methods are called when no matching register is found, and can be used to implement logging, simulation stop, or other complex functionality.

Handling reserved registers and miss-access in the best way is not trivial and the best solution depends on the use case. Our experience shows that it is typically best to start out by being as restrictive as possible, thus causing miss-accesses to stop the simulation. The urge to add registers and miss-access handlers to a model to make software work because "it works on real hardware" should be resisted; it is simply too easy to hide errors in this way. The goal is always to help programmers write better code, not just to get the code that exists to run.

CREATING MODELS IN OTHER LANGUAGES

While it is recommended to write device models in DML because it allows the programmer to focus on the functionality of the device without having to worry about the mechanics of interacting with Simics, it sometimes makes sense to use another language. For example, a model may already exist that is written for another simulator, or a model must be able to run in several simulators; in which case it makes sense to use C or C++ for maximum interoperability. Additionally, Simics devices are sometimes created only to act as part of a test suite, in which case it can make sense to use Python due to its more dynamic nature and the possibility to easily integrate with the module test system. No matter what the reason is, it should be recognized that some special care needs to be taken to preserve core Simics features, such as checkpointing and reverse execution.

As mentioned earlier in this chapter, Simics provides a C API and ABI for maximum flexibility and interoperability. Simics also provides a C++ API on top of the C API. The C++ API is not a replacement for the C API, but rather an addition on top of it to simplify some common tasks. The C API must still be used for some tasks when writing models in C++. Most of the C API is also exported to Python, allowing Python code to be used for device models.

MODULE SCANNING

Classes registered in a module should be listed in the `MODULE_CLASSES` variable in the module's Makefile. The declaration puts metadata into the module file that is read by Simics during module scanning, so that Simics knows which classes are declared by a module. Later, when a class is needed, the most recent module containing it will be loaded. This mechanism allows Simics to automatically load the required modules when reading a configuration file or checkpoint.

MODULE LOADING

Most modules need to do some work when initially loaded into Simics. Typically this work includes registering the classes implemented by the module, their attributes, interfaces, and ports. It can also include loading libraries and registering new event types and custom haps. A module written in C/C++ must implement the function `void init_local(void)`. It must exist, even if it is empty. The function will be run by Simics when the module is loaded, and it is responsible for registering the class or classes in the module with Simics. If the module is written in C++, this function must be declared `extern "C"` for C linkage.

A module written in Python must have a structured comment before the first statement:

```
# MODULE: module-name
# CLASS: class-name
```

These comments indicate to Simics that this Python file is a Simics module and that it should be run during an initial scan of available modules. As the Python file is executed as a program at load time, all Python statements in global scope will be executed. Normally some of these statements will register classes and attributes with Simics performing the same function as the body of an `init_local` function in C.

CLASS REGISTRATION

For Simics to use a class to create configuration objects, the details of the class have to be registered with Simics. This is performed in the init_local function when the module is loaded. In detail, registering a class is done by creating and filling a class_data_t structure, and then calling the function SIM_register_ class with the new class name and the class_data_t structure that describes it. The important members in the class_data_t structure are:

- init_object—a function called when creating an instance of the class.
- finalize_instance—this function is called once init_object has returned, and all attributes in a configuration have been set.
- description—a string that should contain a description of the class.
- kind—this class tells Simics whether objects of this class should be saved when a checkpoint is created.

In C/C++, registration of classes is usually done from within the mandatory init_local function. A simple init_local initialization function could look like the example in Listing 6.17.

The function SIM_register_class returns a pointer to a conf_class_t structure, which is used internally by Simics to keep track of the class information. This pointer can be used when referring to the class in calls to other functions, such as when creating new objects of the class.

For each instance of a Simics class defined using the C++ API, there will be a C++ object created to correspond to that Simics configuration object. This C++ object is an instance of a model-defined class that must inherit from the SimicsObject class. The C++ class must have a constructor taking a single parameter of type SimicsObjectRef, which is passed on to the SimicsObject constructor. Listing 6.18 shows the corresponding init_local function in C++. Using C++, a class is added to Simics by creating an instance of the template class ClassDef in the init_local function. When the instance goes out of scope the class is registered with Simics automatically (using the class' destructor).

```
1    void init_local(void) {
2        class_data_t cdata;
3        conf_class_t *my_class;
4        memset(&cdata, 0, sizeof(cdata));
5        cdata.init_object = my_init_object;
6        cdata.description = "This is my class";
7        cdata.kind = Sim_Class_Kind_Session;
8        my_class = SIM_register_class("my-class", &cdata);
9        // Other initializations...
10   }
```

LISTING 6.17

Example init_local Function in C.

In Python, the class registration is done when the global statements of the module are executed (at load time), but use of some convenience classes provided by the `pyobj` module is recommended. The `pyobj.ConfObject` class defines a new Simics class using the `SIM_register_class` function. It is possible to call `SIM_register_class` and all the related functions for attribute and interface registration directly, but `ConfObject` will make the code much more concise, as shown in Listing 6.19.

The name of the Simics class is identical to the Python class. The class description is the same as the Python class description. The class implements the methods `_initialize`, `_finalize`, and `_pre_delete`. All of these methods can be overridden if required.

The `_initialize` method is called when an object of the class is instantiated. The `_finalize` method is called when the object is finalized. The `_pre_delete` method is called right before an object of the class is deleted.

```
1    extern "C" void
2    init_local()
3    {
4        simics::ClassDef<sample_instance>(
5        // Simics class name
6        C++ Device API 10
7        5.1. Defining the Simics Class
8        "sample_device_auto",
9        // short description
10       "Sample C++ Device",
11       // class documentation
12       "This is a sample Simics device written in C++.");
13   }
```

LISTING 6.18

Example `init_local` function in C++.

```
1    class foo(pyobj.ConfObject):
2        """This is the long-winded documentation for this Simics
3    class. It can be as long as you want."""
4        _class_desc = 'One-line doc for the class'
5
6        def _initialize(self):
7            pyobj.ConfObject._initialize(self)
```

LISTING 6.19

Registering a class in python.

OBJECTS

In C and C++, it is necessary to maintain an object structure that is used to hold data about individual objects for each Simics class. In C++, this is automatically managed by any object inheriting from the SimicsObject class. The corresponding conf_object_t is available through the object method in the SimicsObject class. This allows easy access to the underlying conf_object_t if it is needed— for example, to call a Simics API function.

In C, it is convenient to add a conf_object_t pointer in the structure so that Simics' own private object can be easily found from the object structure. A Simics object (the conf_object_t) contains all the information related to its class and its attributes. When an object is created, the init_object function declared in the class definition is called. The init_object function is responsible for allocating an object structure for the new object and initializing all the fields, including the conf_object_t pointer, which is passed as an argument to the init_object function. The pointer to the allocated and initialized structure should be returned. Using C, a typical function would look like Listing 6.20.

Just as in C++, Python automatically manages the configuration object reference for subclasses of ConfObject. The ConfObject provides an obj member that is the reference to the conf_object_t object associated with a ConfObject instance.

ATTRIBUTES

For checkpointing and reverse execution to work properly it is important to expose the entire model's state in attributes. In C, the function SIM_register_typed_attribute can be used to register attributes on a class. The function takes a number of parameters, such as the name and type of the attribute, as well as a callback function for setting and getting the attribute's value. It is important to note that Simics attributes operate on an explicit get and set model. When an attribute is read from the Simics CLI or while taking a Simics checkpoint, the getter function defined for the attribute is called. It is the job of the getter function to convert the runtime representation stored in the object data structure to a Simics attribute format that can be displayed to the user and saved in a

```
1    static lang_void *
2    my_init_object(conf_object_t *obj, lang_void *data)
3    {
4        my_object_t *mo = MM_ZALLOC(1, my_object_t);
5        mo->obj = obj;
6        // Initializations...
7    }
```

LISTING 6.20

Creating an object in C.

checkpoint. When an attribute is set, the `setter` function is used to convert from the external attribute format into the internal representation. This separation means that the internal representation of an object can change, even as the external representation is kept the same. This simplifies checkpoint portability and allows for the use of arbitrary data structures in the internal representation of an object. If the Simics core had directly accessed the internal representation, that representation would have been much more limited.

The C++ API provides a number of ways to define the attributes, depending on which method of accessing the internal state is convenient. Generally, the attribute definition needs a way to extract the state from the C++ object, and then a way to convert this state to a Simics attribute value. These two parts are handled separately, and the ways to extract the state are described first.

The attribute is defined by creating an object of type `Attribute` and adding it to the `ClassDef` instance using the `<<` operator. The `Attribute` type is never instantiated directly. Instead, one of its subclasses is used, depending on how the state is accessed. They all share a few common features, and are created like this: `simics::SomeAttribute<sample_instance, mapper>("value", "A value.", ...)`. The mapper is covered later. The first string is the attribute name, which must be unique for the class and stable between revisions of the model. The second string is the documentation. The rest of the arguments depend on which kind of attribute is defined.

A mapper translates between C++ values and the data representation used by Simics attributes. Simics attribute values are stored in values of the type `attr_value_t`, and it can contain numbers (both integer and floating point), Booleans, strings, object references, or binary data. It can also be a list of attribute values, or a dictionary that maps attribute values to other attribute values.

The different types of attributes supported by the C++ API are `Simple Attribute`, `GetSetAttribute`, `LocateAttribute`, and `ProxyAttribute`. The `Simple Attribute` class is used when the state is represented directly as a public member variable in the C++ class. The `GetSetAttribute` class is used when the top-level object has methods to get and set the state variables that correspond to the attribute. The `LocateAttribute` class is used when there is a state variable that contains the state to export through the attribute, but it isn't as readily available as when `SimpleAttribute` is used. Instead of a member pointer to the variable, a function is given that returns a reference to the state variable. This is, for instance, useful when the state variable is in another object that is referenced from the main object. The `ProxyAttribute` class is the most versatile, and uses `getter` and `setter` functions. These functions are not member functions, but instead get the main object as a function parameter. Other than that, it works in a very similar way to `GetSetAttribute`.

In Python, the `ConfObject` class can contain inner classes that define attributes, interfaces, and the like. The `Attribute` class defines an attribute that will be registered for the containing `ConfObject` class. The class methods named `getter` and `setter` will be used when registering the attribute. The attribute

```
1    class foo(pyobj.ConfObject):
2        """This is the long-winded documentation for this
3        Simics class. It can be as long as you want."""
4        _class_desc = 'One-line doc for the class'
5
6        def _initialize(self):
7            pyobj.ConfObject._initialize(self)
8            self.my_val = 4711
9
10       def _info(self):
11           return [("Python device info",
12                    [("my_val", self.my_val)])]
13
14       def _status(self):
15           return [("Python device status",
16                    [("woot", self.woot.val),
17                     ("signal", self.signal.val)])]
18
19       class woot(pyobj.SimpleAttribute(0, 'i|n')):
20           """A four-letter attribute"""
21
22       class lost(pyobj.Attribute):
23           """A pseudo attribute"""
24           attrattr = simics.Sim_Attr_Pseudo
25           def getter(self):
26               return self._up.my_val
27
28       class signal(pyobj.Interface):
29           def signal_raise(self): self.val = True
30           def signal_lower(self): self.val = False
31           def _initialize(self): self.val = False
```

LISTING 6.21

Python attributes.

description is the same as the Python class description. Listing 6.21 shows an example of a simple Simics class with attributes defined in Python. As in C++, there are different types of attributes. The SimpleAttribute class has predefined getter and setter functions that simply store and retrieve the value without further side effects, and the Attribute class allows arbitrary getter and setter functions to be implemented.

INTERFACES

An object that wants to interact with another object through an interface uses the SIM_get_interface function to retrieve the interface structure. It can then call the other object using the functions defined in the structure, as shown in Listing 6.22.

In Python, the interface methods are available directly in the iface member of the ConfigObject: val = mem.iface.memory_space.read(conf.cpu0, 0x1234, 4, 0).

```
1    conf_object_t *obj = SIM_get_object("phys_mem");
2    memory_space_interface_t *ifc;
3    ifc = (memory_space_interface_t *) SIM_get_interface(obj,
4                                         "memory_space");
5    attr_value_t val;
6    val = ifc->read(obj, SIM_get_object("cpu0"), 0x1234, 4, 0);
```

LISTING 6.22

Calling an interface from C or C++.

```
1    static cycles_t
2    my_operate(conf_object_t *mem_hier, conf_object_t *space,
3            map_list_t *map, generic_transaction_t *mem_op)
4    {
5        // do something
6    }
7
8    static conf_class_t *my_class;
9    static timing_model_interface_t ifc;
10
11   void init_local(void)
12   {
13       // . . .
14       ifc.operate = my_operate;
15       SIM_register_interface(my_class, "timing_model",
                                (void *)&ifc);
16       // . . .
17   }
```

LISTING 6.23

Implementing an interface in C.

In Python, the first argument to the interface method should be omitted because it is automatically added by Simics based on the object on which the method is invoked.

When using interfaces inside an object, it is often necessary to define which object to call via an attribute. The classic way of doing that is to define an attribute with type "o|n" and check if the object implements the necessary interface.

The implementation of an existing interface requires the population of all the function pointers that are listed in the interface definition with the functions that should be called. The interface should then be registered using the SIM_register_interface function, as shown in Listing 6.23.

In C++ the << operator of the ClassDef class is used to register an interface. To do this, the class derived from SimicsObject needs to define C++ methods that implement the different methods in the interface, as well as an interface declaration. The interface method declarations are straightforward. They should have the same signature as the interface, except that the first argument of type conf_object_t * is left out, as it corresponds to the C++ class instance. The interface declaration consists of a typedef of a template. The name of the class is the name of the interface, suffixed with _interface. The template arguments are the instance class followed by the interface methods in the order they appear in the interface definition. The typedef name can be anything and will be used later to refer to this declaration. An example of implementing an interface in C++ is shown in Listing 6.24. The interface definition on line 17 is a C++ preprocessor macro call that ties the interface declaration in Listing 6.24 to an object that is used to register the interface with the model's ClassDef. This creates a dev_io_memory object tied to the interface defined by the io_memory_iface typedef in the instance class. The macro corresponding to the name interface is called DEFINE_NAME_INTERFACE.

```
1    class sample_interface : public simics::SimicsObject {
2      public:
3        sample_interface(simics::SimicsObjectRef o)
4            : simics::SimicsObject(o) { }
5
6        // interface method declarations
7        int map(addr_space_t memory_or_io, map_info_t map_info);
8        exception_type_t operation(generic_transaction_t *mem_op,
9                                   map_info_t map_info);
10       // interface declaration
11       typedef simics::io_memory_interface<
12           sample_interface,
13           &sample_interface::map,
14           &sample_interface::operation> io_memory_iface;
15   };
16
17   DEFINE_IO_MEMORY_INTERFACE(dev_io_memory,
18                              sample_interface::io_memory_iface);
19
20   exception_type_t sample_interface::operation(
21       generic_transaction_t *mop,
22       map_info_t info)
23   {
24       // implement behavior here
25       return Sim_PE_No_Exception;
26   }
27
28   extern "C" void
29   init_local()
30   {
31       simics::ClassDef<sample_interface>("sample_interface",
32                                          "Sample interface", "N/A")
33           << dev_io_memory;
34   }
```

LISTING 6.24

Implementing an Interface in C++.

In Python, the `Interface` class defines an interface that will be registered for the containing `ConfObject` class. The interface is registered using the `SIM_register_interface` function. The interface name is taken from the class name. An example is shown for the `signal` interface in Listing 6.23.

LOGGING

Logging in C or Python is handled by `SIM_log_register_group` and the `SIM_log_info`, `SIM_log_spec_violation`, `SIM_log_unimplemented`, and `SIM_log_error` functions. A single call to `SIM_log_register_groups` registers all groups for the class. For example, in C:

```
static char *groupnames[] = { "config", "request", "response", NULL };
SIM_log_register_groups(my_class, &groupnames)
```

or in Python:

```
SIM_log_register_groups("sample-device", ("config", "request",
"response"))
```

To issue a log message, call the corresponding log function, such as:

```
SIM_log_info(4, obj, 0, "get_counter_array")
```

Logging from a Simics module written in C/C++ should be done with the following macros: `SIM_LOG_INFO`, `SIM_LOG_ERROR`, `SIM_LOG_UNDEFINED`, `SIM_LOG_SPEC_VIOLATION`, and `SIM_LOG_UNIMPLEMENTED`. These macros use the corresponding `SIM_log_<type>` function internally, and should always be used instead for performance reasons. Note that the macros take a variable number of arguments to allow `printf`-like strings.

EVENTS

For events, the API is identical for Python, C, and C++. Event classes are created with the `SIM_register_event` function, which should be called at module load time from the `init_local` function. The event class holds a pointer to the callback function. Listing 6.25 shows an example from a UART (universal asynchronous receiver/transmitter) model. To post an event in the future, based on time, the `SIM_event_post_time` or `SIM_event_post_cycle` function is used as follows:

```
SIM_event_post_time(obj, transmit_event, obj, 0.00001, NULL);
```

In Python, the `Event` class can also be used in conjunction with the `ConfObject` class. The `Event` class defines an event that will be registered for the containing `ConfObject` class. Internally, registration is done with `SIM_register_event`.

```
1    static event_class_t *transmit_event;
2    static void
3    uart_transmit(conf_object_t *obj, void *param)
4    {
5        uart_device_t *uart = (uart_device_t *)obj;
6        SIM_LOG_INFO(4, &uart->log, 0, "event called");
7    }
8
9    void init_local(void)
10   {
11       conf_class_t *uart_class;
12       // ...
13       uart_class = SIM_register_class(. . . );
14       // ...
15       transmit_event = SIM_register_event("transmit character",
16        uart_class, 0, uart_transmit,
17        0, 0, 0, 0);
18       // ...
19   }
```

LISTING 6.25

Registering an event.

```
1    class foo(pyobj.ConfObject):
2        class ev1(pyobj.Event):
3            def callback(self, data):
4                do_something(data)
5        class ev2(pyobj.Event):
6            def callback(self, data):
7                self.do_something_else(data)
8            def get_value(self, data):
9                return str(data)
10           def set_value(self, val):
11               return int(val)
12           def describe(self, data):
13               return 'ev2 with %s' % data
14       class ev3(pyobj.Event):
15           flags = simics.Sim_EC_Notsaved
16           def callback(self, data):
17               self._up.do_this_third_thing(data)
```

LISTING 6.26

Registering an event in python using the event subclass.

Events are posted with the post(clock, data, <duration>) method. The clock object determines which clock the event is posted on, and data is the event data. The duration is the number of seconds, cycles, or steps until the event triggers, specified with the appropriate keyword argument—for example, ev.post (a_clock, some_data, seconds = 4.711). Listing 6.26 shows an example of a Python class implementing events based on the Event subclass.

DMA: A concrete modeling example

Example is the school of mankind, and they will learn at no other.
—Edmund Burke, Letters on a Regicide Peace

Following the introduction to modeling in the previous chapter, this chapter provides a tutorial-style example on how to develop a model of a direct memory access (DMA) controller, properly connect it to a virtual platform, and enable a device driver to interact with it.

A DMA model is used because it is a relatively simple model to understand and implement, yet it contains many important aspects of modeling, such as delays (timing), interrupts, MMIO, DMA, and parsing of target data structures in target memory.

A programmer's reference manual or similar document typically provides the information a modeler needs to create a device model. Having access to driver source code can often help as well, because the programmer's reference manuals sometimes lack in detail or clarity. However, access to driver source code may not be an option when developing models of hardware in the pre-silicon phase. The next section describes the DMA device that will be used as an example throughout this chapter. You may wish to skim the next section and then refer back to it as the implementation of the DMA model is expanded throughout the following sections.

DMA DEVICE DESCRIPTION

The DMA device can act as a bus master and can read and write physical memory. The DMA device can be used to offload the software and processors from copying large chunks of data from one place in memory to another. This DMA device supports two modes of operation: contiguous transfer and scatter-gather lists. In contiguous transfer mode the DMA device copies a number of bytes sequentially, starting at one physical address and transferring the same number of bytes to another physical address. In scatter-gather mode the bytes are instead copied from a data structure known as a scatter-gather list into a contiguous area of memory starting at the destination address. The scatter-gather list is described later in this section.

Table 7.1 Register Overview

Offset	Register	Documentation
00	DMA control	Control register
04	DMA source	Source address
08	DMA destination	Destination address

The DMA device is controlled through a set of 32-bit memory-mapped registers described in Table 7.1. The device uses big-endian (network) byte order and little-endian bit order.

The DMA control register consists of the following fields, where the numbers in brackets indicate the bit or bit range in little-endian bit order:

- *EN[31]—Enable DMA.* Enable the DMA device by writing a 1 to this field. If the device is not enabled, registers are still updated but no side effects occur.
- *SWT[30]—Software Transfer Trigger.* Starts a DMA transaction if the EN bit is set. The result of writing a 1 to SWT when there is a transaction in progress is undefined.
- *ECI[29]—Enable Completion Interrupt.* If set to 1, an interrupt is generated when a transfer completes. If set to 0, no interrupt is generated.
- *TC[28]—Transfer Complete.* This bit is used to indicate whether a transfer has completed. This bit is set to 1 by the DMA device when a transfer is completed, and if the ECI bit is also set to 1, an interrupt is raised at this time. Software is only allowed to write a 0 to this bit to clear the status. Clearing the TC bit also lowers any interrupt that is currently active.
- *SG[27]—Scatter-Gather List Input.* If set to 1, the DMA source register points to the first entry in a scatter-gather list and not a contiguous block of data.
- *ERR[26]—DMA Transfer Error.* This bit is set by the DMA device if an error has occurred during the transfer—for example, if an incorrect scatter-gather data structure has been supplied to the device.
- *TS[15:0]—Transfer Size.* The number of 32-bit words to transfer from the address (or scatter-gather list) pointed to by the DMA source register to the address pointed to by the DMA destination register.

FUNCTIONAL DESCRIPTION

To initiate a DMA copy operation, software first writes a physical address to the DMA source and DMA destination registers. The address in the DMA destination register is the start address where the data will be copied and is always a contiguous block. The DMA source register can hold the address to either a contiguous block or to a scatter-gather list. The SG bit in the DMA

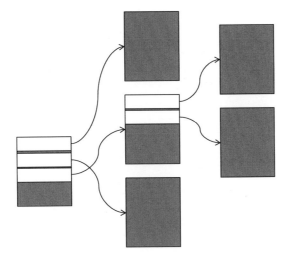

FIGURE 7.1

Scatter-gather list data structure.

control register determines how the DMA device interprets the data at the source address.

To start the copy operation, the software writes the DMA control register with a nonzero value for the EN bit, the SWT bit, and the TS field. Upon completion the DMA controller sets the TC bit and, if the ECI bit is set, raises an interrupt.

If the device is configured in scatter-gather mode (SG bit set), the copy procedure works as follows. In a scatter-gather list, data is spread out over several blocks. These blocks can be of two types: data blocks and extension blocks. A data block is simply a chunk of application-specific data, while an extension block contains references to other blocks. Extension blocks can only be referenced from the last row in another extension block. An example of a scatter-gather data structure is shown in Figure 7.1.

The layout of an extension block is shown in Figure 7.2. The individual fields are as follows:

- *Address:* Pointer to a block.
- *Length:* The length of valid data at the address + offset.
- *Offset:* Data begins at the address + offset.
- *Flags:* If bit 0 is set, address points to an extension block. If bit 0 is not set, address points to a data block.

When using the scatter-gather mode, the DMA source register contains the address of a scatter-gather head block. The head block is illustrated in Figure 7.3. The head block points to the first scatter-gather block, which is always an extension block. The length field is the length of valid data in the first extension block.

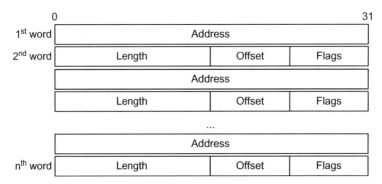

FIGURE 7.2

Scatter-gather list block descriptor.

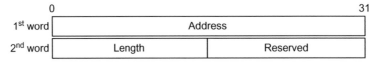

FIGURE 7.3

Scatter-gather list head descriptor.

IMPLEMENTING THE BASIC DMA DEVICE MODEL

Just as in the previous chapter, the first step is to map out all the registers based on the specification and to mark them as unimplemented. Listing 7.1 shows the "translation" of the description of the DMA device into a DML model. This is already a complete model that can be instantiated, and unit tests can be written for the features added.

Because the DMA device needs to access target memory and raise interrupts, it is necessary to create connections to the relevant objects that implement the memory space and signal interfaces. The memory space interface is used for reading and writing target memory and the signal interface is used for interrupts, as described in Chapter 6. The code shown in Listing 7.2 adds these connections and implements the basic functionality of the DMA model. Scatter-gather lists are left as unimplemented and are marked as such in the code, so that if software should try to use the functionality the user will be notified that the model does not support it. Of course, the model should be developed in parallel with tests, but they are left out of this example for the sake of brevity.

UNIT TESTING

To test the device a simple test can be added that tells the device to copy a few words of data from one place in a memory to another. This is shown in

```
1    dml 1.2;
2
3    device c7_dma_device;
4
5    parameter desc = "DMA Device (Example)";
6
7    parameter documentation =
8      "Example of a DMA device supporting contiguous"
9      + " memory or scatter-gather lists. The device"
10     + " has a controllable throughput (words per"
11     + " second) and supports either polling mode or"
12     + " interrupt-based signalling upon DMA"
13     + " completion.";
14
15   import "utility.dml";
16
17   parameter byte_order = "big-endian";
18
19   bank regs {
20     parameter register_size = 4;
21     register DMA_control @ 0x00 is (unimplemented)
22       "Control register";
23     register DMA_source  @ 0x04 is (unimplemented)
24       "Source address";
25     register DMA_dest    @ 0x08 is (unimplemented)
26       "Destination address";
27   }
```

LISTING 7.1

DMA model register map.

Listing 7.3, which is not intended to be a complete test but serves as illustration only. It is interesting to note the use of the Memory class provided by the dev_utils module. It acts as a convenient target memory, implementing the memory space interface, that will have all memory uninitialized when it is instantiated. This means that if a read happens to an address that has not previously been written, an exception is thrown. This is very useful when writing tests.

Running this test shows an interesting result: the DMA device has copied the contents of memory in zero virtual time. The simulation cannot even be started because there is no clock or processor object in the simulation. This behavior is somewhat unrealistic; software may expect that performing a DMA transfer will take some amount of time. If the software can work with an infinitely fast DMA controller without running into timing issues or races, the code can be left as is. If not, a delay needs to be introduced between the time when the SWT bit is written and the result is available.

SIMULATING TIME

To simulate time in a device model, *events* are used. A naïve approach would be to post an event every N cycles and then copy a word at a time. However, this would result in very poor simulation performance, because the ISS would need to constantly switch to running device code, and frequent switches may prevent JIT compilation and will have negative effects on code locality.

```
1    dml 1.2;
2
3    device c7_dma_device;
4
5    parameter desc = "DMA Device (Example)";
6
7    parameter documentation =
8        "Example of a DMA device supporting contiguous"
9        + " memory or scatter-gather lists. The device"
10       + " has a controllable throughput (words per"
11       + " second) and supports either polling mode or"
12       + " interrupt-based signalling upon DMA"
13       + " completion.";
14
15   import "utility.dml";
16   import "simics/devs/memory-space.dml";
17   import "simics/devs/signal.dml";
18
19   parameter byte_order = "big-endian";
20
21   // Memory-space connection for DMA work
22   connect target_mem_space {
23       parameter documentation =
24           "The memory space on which the DMA engine"
25           + " operates. Data will be read from and copied"
26           + " to the memory associated with this memory"
27           + " space.";
28       parameter configuration = "required";
29       interface memory_space;
30   }
31
32   // CPU connection for interrupting
33   connect intr_target {
34       parameter documentation =
35           "Interrupt target to signal on DMA interrupts.";
36       parameter configuration = "required";
37       interface signal;
38   }
39
40   bank regs {
41       parameter register_size = 4;
42       register DMA_control @ 0x00 "Control register";
43       register DMA_source  @ 0x04 "Source address";
44       register DMA_dest    @ 0x08 "Destination address";
45
46       // Internal register not mapped to any memory
47       // location
48       register DMA_interrupt_posted @ undefined
49           "Internal register to track if interrupts are"
50           + " posted.";
51   }
52
53   method lower_interrupt() {
54       if ($regs.DMA_interrupt_posted != 0) {
55           log "info", 3: "clearing interrupt";
56           $intr_target.signal.signal_lower();
57           $regs.DMA_interrupt_posted = 0;
58       }
59   }
60
61   method raise_interrupt() {
62       if ($regs.DMA_interrupt_posted == 0) {
63           log "info", 3: "raising interrupt";
64           $intr_target.signal.signal_raise();
65           $regs.DMA_interrupt_posted = 1;
```

LISTING 7.2

Basic DMA model.

```
66          }
67        }
68
69        // Read len bytes of target memory from the address src
70        // in the memory $target_mem_space. The result is put in
71        // memory pointed to by dst, which must be large enough
72        // to hold at least len bytes. If a memory access error
73        // occurs, this method will print an error message and
74        // throw an exception.
75        method read_mem(void *dst,
76                        physical_address_t src,
77                        physical_address_t len) {
78          local exception_type_t exc;
79          exc = $target_mem_space.memory_space
80            .access_simple($dev.obj, src, dst, len,
81                           Sim_RW_Read, Sim_Endian_Target);
82
83          if (exc != Sim_PE_No_Exception) {
84            log "error": "an error occurred when reading"
85              + " target memory";
86            throw;
87          }
88        }
89
90        // Write len bytes to target memory from the memory
91        // pointed to by src. The data is written to the memory
92        // space $target_mem_space at address dst. If a memory
93        // access error occurs this method will print an error
94        // message and throw an exception.
95        method write_mem(physical_address_t dst,
96                         const void *src,
97                         physical_address_t len) {
98          local exception_type_t exc;
99          exc = $target_mem_space.memory_space
100           .access_simple($dev.obj, dst,
101                          cast(src, uint8*), len,
102                          Sim_RW_Write, Sim_Endian_Target);
103
104         if (exc != Sim_PE_No_Exception) {
105           log "error": "an error occurred when writing to"
106             + " target memory";
107           throw;
108         }
109       }
110
111     bank regs {
112       register DMA_control {
113         field EN  [31] "Enable DMA";
114         field SWT [30] "Software Transfer Trigger";
115         field ECI [29] "Enable Completion Interrupt";
116         field TC  [28] "Transfer complete" {
117           // Set to 1 by device when transfer has completed
118           // Clear by writing a zero.  If interrupts are
119           // enabled and interrupt status is one also clear
120           // the interrupt in the processor.
121           method write(value) {
122             if (value != 0) {
123               log "spec_violation":
124                 "write one to TC - ignored";
125               return;
126             }
127
128             if (!$this)    // Already cleared
129               return;
130
```

LISTING 7.2

(Continued.)

```
131          log "info", 3:
132            "write zero to TC - clearing TC";
133          $this = 0;
134
135          call $lower_interrupt();
136        }
137      }
138      field SG  [27] is (unimplemented)
139        "Scatter-gather list input";
140      field ERR [26]    "DMA transfer error";
141      field TS  [15:0] "Transfer size (32-bit words)";
142
143      method after_write(memop) {
144        call $do_dma_transfer();
145      }
146    }
147
148    method do_dma_transfer() {
149      if (!$DMA_control.SWT)
150        return; // No need to do anything if we are not
151                // asked by software
152
153      // Software asked us to initiate a DMA transfer
154      if(!$DMA_control.EN) {
155        // enable bit not set, so we cannot transfer
156        log "info", 2:
157          "EN bit not set, SWT = 1 has no effect";
158        return;
159      }
160
161      log "info", 3:
162        "EN bit set, SWT written, initiating DMA";
163      log "info", 3:
164        "Transferring %d 32-bit words from 0x%x to"
165        + " 0x%x", $DMA_control.TS, $DMA_source,
166        $DMA_dest;
167
168      local uint18 count = $DMA_control.TS * 4;
169      try {
170        if ($DMA_control.SG) {
171          log "unimplemented", 1:
172            "Scatter-gather is not implemented";
173          return;
174        }
175
176        log "info", 4: "Contiguous Transfer";
177        call $copy_contiguous($DMA_dest,
178                              $DMA_source,
179                              count);
180      } catch {
181        log "error": "DMA memory access failed";
182        return;
183      }
184
185      call $complete_dma();
186    }
187
188    method copy_contiguous(physical_address_t dst,
189                           physical_address_t src,
190                           uint18 count) {
191      local uint8 buf[count];
192      call $read_mem(buf, src, count);
193      call $write_mem(dst, buf, count);
194    }
195
```

LISTING 7.2

(Continued.)

```
196     method complete_dma() {
197         // Log that completion is done
198         log "info", 2: "DMA transfer completed";
199
200         // clear SWT bit, update TS
201         $DMA_control.SWT = 0;
202         $DMA_control.TS = 0;
203         $DMA_control.TC = 1;
204
205         // raise interrupt towards CPU
206         if(!$DMA_control.ECI) {
207             log "info", 3: "ECI is zero, no interrupt raised";
208             return;
209         }
210
211         call $raise_interrupt();
212     }
213 }
```

LISTING 7.2

(Continued)

Lines 75, 95: The `read_mem` and `write_mem` functions are responsible for copying the data in the target memory by calling functions on the memory space interface on the connected object—typically the physical memory of the processor. The functions work in a similar way to the normal C `memcpy` function, but for target addresses instead.

Line 181: The documentation is not clear under what conditions the `ERR` bit should be set. For this reason the implementation will log an error message and stop the simulation if a memory access error occurs. It can be debated what the right approach should be, but in the authors' experience the conservative approach where the end user is made aware of the problem is usually better than guessing and potentially providing a silent but incorrect behavior.

In most cases software does not care about intermediate results; only the end state matters. That means it is enough to calculate the delay of the *complete* transfer, post a single event, and then copy all the data at once. There are rare cases where this leads to the wrong behavior. For example, if the software is polling the destination address, the write pattern will again look strange (but will still function according to the specification).

A more severe case is if the source and target memory areas overlap. In this case the result will be wrong because the source memory would have changed during the copying process if it was done on a word-by-word basis. However, this is a very rare and unlikely case, and it is most likely not worth trading simulation performance for this. If desired, the model can detect this condition and warn the user (because it is quite likely a programming error), or fall back to the slow approach. This is a good example of the tradeoffs the modeler has to do when picking an abstraction level, and in this example the problem with overlapping memory areas is simply ignored.

```
1    import dev_util as du
2    import stest
3    from stest import expect_equal
4
5    # Create fake Memory and Interrupt objects; these are
6    # required
7    mem = du.Memory()
8    intr_dev = du.Dev([du.Signal])
9
10   # Create DMA device and connect with memory and
11   # interrupt
12   dma = simics.pre_conf_object('mydma',
13                                'c7_dma_device')
14   dma.target_mem_space = mem.obj
15   dma.intr_target = intr_dev.obj
16
17   # Create the configuration
18   simics.SIM_add_configuration([dma], None)
19   mydma = conf.mydma
20
21   # Define the register objects
22   dma_src_reg = du.Register_BE((mydma, 'regs', 4), 4)
23   dma_dst_reg = du.Register_BE((mydma, 'regs', 8), 4)
24   ctrl_fields = du.Bitfield({'en': 31,
25                              'swt': 30,
26                              'eci': 29,
27                              'tc': 28,
28                              'sg': 27,
29                              'err': 26,
30                              'ts': (15,0)})
31   dma_ctrl_reg = du.Register_BE((mydma, 'regs', 0), 4,
32                                 ctrl_fields)
33
34   # Init 12 words of 0xb0b0b0b0 to address 0xadd9
35   src_addr = 0xadd9
36   dst_addr = 0xde57
37   data = [0xb0]*4*12
38   mem.write(src_addr, data)
39
40   # Configure DMA to copy from src_addr to dest_addr
41   dma_src_reg.write(src_addr)
42   dma_dst_reg.write(dst_addr)
43   dma_ctrl_reg.write(en = 1, swt = 1, ts = 12)
44   expect_equal(dma_ctrl_reg.tc, 1,
45                'The transfer did not complete'
46                + ' (TC bit not set)')
47   result = mem.read(dst_addr, 4*12)
48   expect_equal(result, data,
49                'Memory contents mismatch after DMA')
50   print tuple(hex(x) for x in result)
```

LISTING 7.3

Simple test for the DMA model.

Line 43: Writing to the DMA control register initiates the copy.

Lines 44–46: Verify that the transfer was completed and the DMA device set the TC bit to 1.

Lines 47–49: Verify that the memory content at the destination was updated with the content from the source.

```
1     ...
2
3     // Timing parameter
4     attribute transfers_per_second {
5       parameter documentation =
6         "Number of 32-bit words that can be transfered in a"
7         + " second; default is one million.";
8       parameter allocate_type = "int64";
9       parameter configuration = "optional";
10
11      method set(value) {
12        if (SIM_attr_integer(value) < 1) {
13          log "error": "%s must be positive.", $qname;
14          throw;
15        }
16
17        call default(value);
18      }
19    }
20
21    ...
22
23    method init() {
24      // a really slow DMA device
25      $transfers_per_second = 1e6;
26    }
```

LISTING 7.4

Adding a timing attribute.

To implement the timing delay in the DMA model, a timing attribute is added to configure the performance of the model, and the completion of the operation is delayed with an amount of time corresponding to the number of words copied and the timing attribute.

The code required to add the timing attribute is shown in Listing 7.4, and it is chosen to be the number of transfers, in 32-bit words, the device can do per second. Because this value must be positive and nonzero, the set method in the transfers_ per_second attribute has been overridden to check that a valid value is supplied before calling the default implementation of set to update the attribute's value. Because the default value is zero, the init method has been added to provide a reasonable default value. The init method is called before the model is completely instantiated and provides a hook for performing this type of initialization. The init method is called before any attributes are set by the configuration system or by the checkpoint-loading mechanism, allowing the value to be overridden.

To delay the completion of the transfer, the call to the complete_dma method is prefixed with an after statement:

```
after (count / $transfers_per_second / 4.0) call $complete_dma;
```

The after statement can be used to produce delays in seconds where no data needs to be associated with the event. For more advanced types of events that need to carry data or to be posted on cycles or steps, an explicit event object must be used.

Running the test from Listing 7.3 again results in an error:

```
[mydma error] Attribute 'queue' is not set, ignoring delayed call to
method 'regs.complete_dma'.
```

This is because there is no clock or processor object in the simulation, and thus no concept of time. Refer to Chapter 2 for details on time in Simics.

To resolve the error it is necessary to add a clock object to the test from Listing 7.3. The updated code is shown in Listing 7.5.

Running the test again produces a test error in the expect statement on line 44 in Listing 7.3, Because the completion flag will not be set until some time has passed. Figure 7.4 shows the failed test in the TestRunner View in Eclipse. The log provides the details for the error, in this case an unfulfilled expectation.

To fix the test failure it is necessary to run the simulation for some time after the DMA control register has been written but before the TC bit is read out. Listing 7.6 shows the updated code where a call to the new helper function run_seconds has been inserted between the write and the read of the DMA control register. The function run_seconds calculates the number of cycles to advance the clock to run for a specified amount of seconds and calls SIM_continue to run the simulation.

SCATTER-GATHER LIST SUPPORT

Adding support for scatter-gather lists highlights two important aspects of device modeling: how to parse target data structures, and how to avoid deadlocking a discrete event simulation.

To efficiently manage data structures in target memory, DML provides two constructs known as *bit fields* and *layouts*. Layouts were briefly described in the previous chapter and provide a mechanism for managing data copied from target memory. A bit field provides an easy way to manipulate bits or fields (bit ranges)

```
1    ...
2    # Create clock object for timing
3    clock = simics.pre_conf_object('clock', 'clock')
4    clock.freq_mhz = 1000
5
6    # Create DMA device and connect with clock, memory, and
7    # interrupt
8    dma = simics.pre_conf_object('mydma',
9                                 'c7_dma_device')
10   dma.target_mem_space = mem.obj
11   dma.intr_target = intr_dev.obj
12   dma.queue = clock
13
14   # Create the configuration
15   simics.SIM_add_configuration([clock, dma], None)
16   mydma = conf.mydma
17   ...
```

LISTING 7.5

Adding a clock to the test.

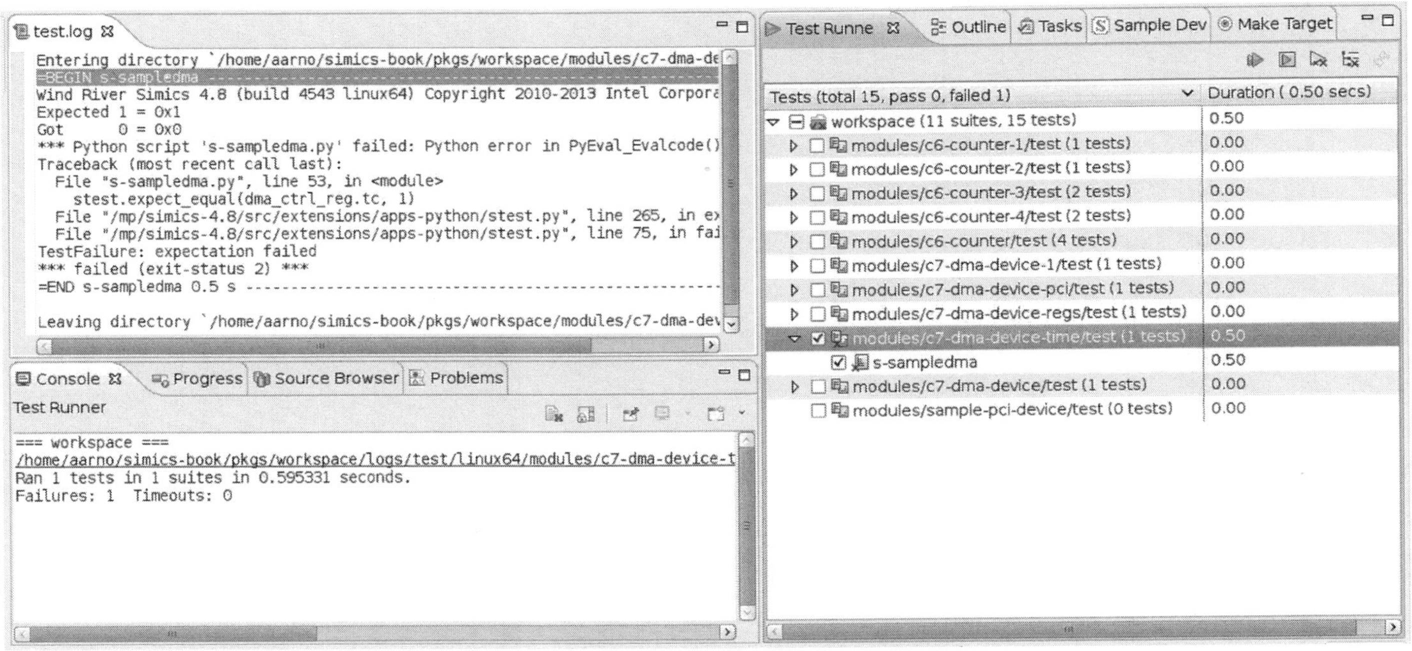

FIGURE 7.4

Failing test.

```
1     ...
2     def run_seconds(s):
3         steps = s * clock.freq_mhz * 1e6
4         SIM_continue(steps)
5
6     # Configure DMA to copy from src_addr to dest_addr
7     dma_src_reg.write(src_addr)
8     dma_dst_reg.write(dst_addr)
9     dma_ctrl_reg.write(en = 1, swt = 1, ts = 12)
10    run_seconds(1)
11    expect_equal(dma_ctrl_reg.tc, 1,
12                    'The transfer did not complete'
13                    + ' (TC bit not set)')
14    result = mem.read(dst_addr, 4*12)
15    expect_equal(result, data,
16                    'Memory contents mismatch after DMA')
17    print tuple(hex(x) for x in result)
18    ...
```

LISTING 7.6

Advancing the time.

```
1     ...
2     typedef layout "big-endian" {
3        uint32 addr;
4        uint16 len;
5        uint16 reserved;
6     } sg_list_head_t;
7
8     typedef layout "big-endian" {
9        uint32 addr;
10       uint16 len;
11       uint8 offset;
12       bitfields 8 {
13          uint1 ext @ [0:0];
14       } flags;
15    } sg_list_block_row_t;
16    ...
```

LISTING 7.7

Layouts and bit fields.

on a sub-byte granularity. To support scatter-gather lists, two layouts are used by the DMA model, one of which includes a bit field. These layouts are shown in Listing 7.7.

These layouts correspond directly to the data structures defined in Figures 7.2 and 7.3. Layouts are similar to structs in C but explicitly map directly to the data layout in memory with no padding. Layouts also have explicit big- or little-endian byte order, making it easy to work with data from targets that have a different endian from the host.

To support copying from scatter-gather lists we replace the unimplemented log message from Listing 7.2 with a call to a new method, copy_scatter_gather, which handles the copying from the scatter-gather list. The code that performs the copying is shown in Listing 7.8, which is an interesting example for how the model can detect programming errors in the form of cyclic scatter-gather lists.

```
1      ...
2          // next_row - Returns the address to next row to be
3          // processed.  end_addr is the address after the end
4          // of the block, if this address is reached the
5          // transaction should have finished
6          method next_row(physical_address_t addr,
7                          physical_address_t end_addr)
8            -> (physical_address_t next_addr,
9                physical_address_t next_end_addr,
10               bool finished) {
11          local sg_list_block_row_t block_row;
12          call $read_mem(&block_row, addr,
13                          sizeof block_row);
14          if (block_row.flags.ext) {
15            next_addr = (block_row.addr
16                          + block_row.offset);
17            next_end_addr = next_addr + block_row.len;
18          } else {
19            next_addr = addr + sizeof block_row;
20            next_end_addr = end_addr;
21          }
22          finished = next_addr == end_addr;
23        }
24
25        // Copy Scatter Gathered data.
26        method copy_scatter_gather(physical_address_t dst,
27                                   physical_address_t src)
28          -> (uint18 copied_bytes) {
29          // Get the header data
30          local sg_list_head_t head;
31          call $read_mem(&head, src, sizeof head);
32          copied_bytes = 0;
33
34          local physical_address_t addr = head.addr;
35          local physical_address_t end_addr =
36            head.addr + head.len;
37          local physical_address_t hare_addr = addr;
38          local physical_address_t hare_end_addr =
39            end_addr;
40
41          // Continue running through the lists until the end
42          // is reached or an error has been detected
43          local sg_list_block_row_t row;
44          local bool finished = false;
45          local bool hare_finished = false;
46          while (!finished && !$DMA_control.ERR) {
47            call $read_mem(&row, addr, sizeof row);
48
49            if (!row.flags.ext) { // Data block
50              log "info", 4: "Data block of length %d"
51                + " at 0x%x with offset %d",
52                row.len, row.addr, row.offset;
53              // Copy a block of data
54              call $copy_contiguous(dst,
55                                     row.addr + row.offset,
56                                     row.len);
57              dst += row.len;
58              copied_bytes += row.len;
59            } else {
60              log "info", 4:
61                "Extension block of length %d at 0x"
62                + "%x with offset %d", row.len,
63                row.addr, row.offset;
64            }
65
```

LISTING 7.8

Adding support for scatter-gather lists.

```
65
66              call $next_row(addr, end_addr)
67                -> (addr, end_addr, finished);
68
69           // Check for loops.
70           if (!hare_finished) {
71             local int8 i;
72             // Hare moves through lists at double the speed
73             // of addr.  If the hare ends up at the same
74             // address as addr, a loop has been detected, if
75             // the hare reaches the end there is no loop.
76             for (i = 0; i < 2; i++) {
77               call $next_row(hare_addr,
78                              hare_end_addr)
79                 -> (hare_addr,
80                     hare_end_addr,
81                     hare_finished);
82               if (hare_finished) {
83                 log "info", 4:
84                   "Loop checker finished, no loops";
85                 break;
86               }
87             }
88             if (hare_addr == addr) {
89               log "spec_violation": "Stuck in a loop.";
90               $DMA_control.ERR = 1;
91             }
92           }
93         }
94       }
```

LISTING 7.8

(*Continued*).

AVOIDING DEADLOCK

One potential problem with scatter-gather lists is that it is possible to program *cycles* in the list, where one extension block points back to a previous extension block. Such a configuration is most likely a programming error, and on real hardware this could cause the DMA controller to enter an infinite loop, copying data to the destination address until finally overwriting some critical data in memory and crashing the machine. This type of error can lead to hard-to-find bugs. On the simulator all the memory is copied at once, and Because there is an infinite amount to copy, due to the cyclic nature of the list, the simulation will appear to hang. This is a common concern when writing models for discrete event simulators. Because the various models are not actually running in parallel as on real hardware, entering an infinite loop in one of them blocks the entire simulation and prevents virtual time from progressing.

A simple solution to this problem would be to only copy a few bytes of data, post an event to copy a few more, and then yield. However, as discussed before this will lead to poor simulation performance. In some cases this can be the right approach, but most often it is not. Consider the case of the scatter-gather list; most likely any cycles are a programming error, so instead of behaving like the real hardware, the model should alert the developer to the fact that a cycle has been detected. A simple way that is often used in practice is to introduce a loop counter that the user can configure through an attribute. If the loop counter expires, the model aborts the operation and logs an error.

In the case of the scatter-gather list it is not difficult to detect actual cycles using a basic algorithm known as *the tortoise and the hare*, or Floyd's cycle-finding algorithm (Floyd, 1967). In the example in Listing 7.8 the model logs a spec violation and sets the error flag of the control register to indicate an invalid scatter-gather list. Again, the specification does not properly describe exactly what constitutes an error, and the modeler has to make an interpretation. Therefore, it is important to log the spec violation to show the user that the model believes that a violation has occurred.

CREATING A PCI EXPRESS (PCIe) MODEL

The model is now complete and can be mapped into the address space of a target machine. However, often devices are not directly accessible in the address space; rather, they are accessed through some sort of bus, such as PCIe (Wilen et al., 2003). In this section the device model is transformed into a PCIe device, capable of being plugged into a PCIe bus on a real target model.

Simics provides most of the code required to create a model of a PCIe device, so the transformation is straightforward. All that is necessary is to import the file `pci/common.dml`, configure a few things, and implement some standard registers in the `pci_config` bank. The `pci_config` bank corresponds to the configuration space of the PCIe device and is read and written by early firmware to enumerate and map the device's register into the address space of the processor. The additional code required to turn the DMA model into a PCIe device is shown in Listing 7.9. The complete code listing is available in Appendix A. Most noteworthy is that interrupts and DMA are done slightly differently, Because the transactions need to propagate the PCIe bus hierarchy. Because DMA and interrupts are managed by the PCIe infrastructure, the `intr_target` and the `target_mem_space` connect object can be removed.

CREATING A COMPONENT FOR THE DMA MODEL

Adding a PCIe device to the system is a bit more complex than simply mapping a device into the physical address space as was done in the previous chapter. The user needs to understand the PCIe bus hierarchy and how it is implemented in Simics. To encapsulate this logic the DMA model is wrapped in a *component*, as described in Chapter 4.

```
1     ...
2     import "pci/common.dml";
3     is pcie_device;
4
5     parameter pci_hotplug = false;
6
7     ...
8
9     bank pci_config {
10      // This attribute should contain a list of all BAR
11      // registers
12      parameter base_address_registers =
13        ["base_address_0"];
14
15      register vendor_id {
16        parameter hard_reset_value = 0x8086;
17      }
18      register device_id {
19        parameter hard_reset_value = 0xABBA;
20      }
21
22      register base_address_0 @ 0x10
23        is (memory_base_address_32)
24      {
25        parameter size_bits = 8;
26        parameter map_func = 1;
27      }
28      register base_address_1 @ 0x14
29        is (no_base_address_32);
30      register base_address_2 @ 0x18
31        is (no_base_address_32);
32      register base_address_3 @ 0x1C
33        is (no_base_address_32);
34      register base_address_4 @ 0x20
35        is (no_base_address_32);
36      register base_address_5 @ 0x24
37        is (no_base_address_32);
38
39      register interrupt_pin {
40        parameter hard_reset_value = 1;
41      }
42    }
43
44    ...
45
46    method lower_interrupt() {
47      if ($regs.DMA_interrupt_posted != 0) {
48        log "info", 3: "Clearing interrupt";
49        call $pci_config.pci_lower_interrupt();
50        $regs.DMA_interrupt_posted = 0;
51      }
52    }
53
54    method raise_interrupt() {
55      if ($regs.DMA_interrupt_posted == 0) {
56        log "info", 3: "raising interrupt";
57        call $pci_config.pci_raise_interrupt();
58        $regs.DMA_interrupt_posted = 1;
59      }
60    }
```

LISTING 7.9

Creating a PCIe device.

```
61
62    . . .
63
64    method read_mem(void *dst,
65                    physical_address_t src,
66                    physical_address_t len) {
67      local exception_type_t exc;
68      call $pci_data_from_memory(Sim_Addr_Space_Memory,
69                                  dst, src, len) -> (exc);
70      if (exc != Sim_PE_No_Exception)
71        throw;
72    }
73
74    method write_mem(physical_address_t dst,
75                     const void *src,
76                     physical_address_t len) {
77      local exception_type_t exc;
78      call $pci_data_to_memory(Sim_Addr_Space_Memory,
79                                src, dst, len) -> (exc);
80      if (exc != Sim_PE_No_Exception)
81        throw;
82    }
83
84    . . .
85
86    bank regs {
87      // For PCI devices each bank need to have a unique
88      // function number,which should match with the
89      // map_func parameter in one BAR
90      parameter function = 1;
91
92    . . .
```

LISTING 7.9

(Continued)

Line 3: This statement turns the device model into a PCIe device. Another option is to use pci_device to make the device a PCI (not PCIe).

Line 9: The definition of the PCIe configuration register bank, which includes a set of standard registers.

Line 22: The device has a single base address register (BAR) that will contain the address of where the regs bank is mapped, and thus where the DMA control register is accessible. The value of the parameter map_fun must match that of the parameter function in the regs bank. When firmware writes the BAR, the regs bank is automatically mapped at the corresponding location.

Line 39: The interrupt_pin register defines the PCI interrupt that the device will use. Interrupts work a bit different in PCI, so the methods to raise and lower interrupts need to be updated as shown on lines 46–56. It also means that the intr_target connect object can be removed.

Lines 64, 74: The read_mem and write_mem methods have been updated to access the system memory though the PCIe bus.

```
1    # MODULE: c7_dma_comp
2    # COMPONENT: c7_dma_comp
3
4    from comp import *
5
6    class c7_dma_comp(StandardConnectorComponent):
7        """DMA PCI Express Component"""
8        _class_desc = "DMA PCI Express Component"
9        _help_categories = ()
10
11       def setup(self):
12           StandardConnectorComponent.setup(self)
13           if not self.instantiated.val:
14               self.add_objects()
15           self.add_connector('pci',
16               PciBusUpConnector(0, 'dma'))
17
18       def add_objects(self):
19           self.dma = self.add_pre_obj('dma',
20                                       'c7_dma_device')
```

LISTING 7.10

DMA Component.

Lines 1–2: Comments used by Simics to determine the name of the Simics module and the components it defines.

Lines 6–9: Define the component class together with documentation and help text that shows up in the online help.

Line 11: The `setup` method is called when an object of the component class is instantiated. It adds the relevant objects and connectors.

Lines 15–16: Create a PCI connector, named `pci`, that can connect to a PCI bus. This is a standard connector type provided by Simics.

Line 19: Create a preconfiguration object for the `c7_dma_device` class.

As described in Chapter 4, components are Python classes that consist mainly of two aspects. A component instantiates and connects all the internal device models, and the component defines its external interface by defining a set of connectors. In the DMA example, there is only a single object, the DMA model, and a single connector, the PCI connector. This is not uncommon, but components often encapsulate many objects that together form a logical unit, such as an SoC. The complete source code for the DMA component is shown in Listing 7.10.

Components make heavy use of preconfiguration objects. Preconfiguration objects are objects that are not fully instantiated. The use of preconfiguration objects is required when objects have circular dependencies. Using preconfiguration objects, all objects can be created (as preconfiguration objects) and their attributes can be connected before they are instantiated. When the component is instantiated, all the preconfiguration objects are turned into real Simics objects.

```
1    load-module c7_dma_comp
2    create-c7-dma-comp dma_comp
3    connect dma_comp.pci "viper.mb.nb.pci_slot[1]"
4    instantiate-components
```

LISTING 7.11

Connecting a Component.

Lines 1–2: Load the c7_dma_comp module into Simics and create a uninstantiated component. Because the DMA device does not support hot-plugging, it is not possible to create an instantiated component that is not connected to a system.

Line 3: Connect the pci connector of the component to a free slot on the PCIe bus on the Northbridge of the viper target. The PciBusUpConnector takes care of setting all the required attributes in the preconfiguration object of the dma device model.

Line 4: Instantiate all uninstantiated components and replace all preconfiguration objects and their references with the real Simics objects and their references.

```
1    run-command-file ("%simics%/targets/x86-x58-ich10"
2                       + "/viper-busybox.simics")
3
4    load-module c7_dma_comp
5    create-c7-dma-comp dma_comp
6    connect dma_comp.pci "viper.mb.nb.pci_slot[1]"
7    instantiate-components
8    alias dma dma_comp.dma
9
10   $src = 0x7c300000
11   $dst = 0x7c400000
12   $con = $system.serconsole.con
13   script-branch {
14       $con.wait-for-string "~ #"
15       dma.log-level 4
16       dma->regs_DMA_source = $src
17       dma->regs_DMA_dest = $dst
18       viper.mb.phys_mem.write $src  0x900dc0ffe 8 -b
19       viper.mb.phys_mem.write ($src + 8) 0xbadc0ffe 8 -b
20       $con.wait-for-string "PS/2 Generic Mouse"
21   }
```

LISTING 7.12

Testing the DMA Device.

Once the component has been created, the user can easily add the DMA device to the PCIe bus of the system, as shown in Listing 7.11.

The device can now be manually tested by executing the script shown in Listing 7.12. The script loads a standard viper target and adds the DMA model to the PCIe bus. Next, the script waits for the system to boot, using a script branch. A *script branch* is run in parallel with the target and is useful when scripting interactions with the target. Once the system has booted, the script branch configures the DMA source and destination registers to point to some unused memory areas and initialize the source area with some interesting pattern.

Once the system has booted, it is possible to test the DMA device; for example, executing `lspci` in the target serial console shows that the device has been discovered and initialized by the firmware:

```
...
00:05.0 Class 0604: 8086:340c
00:07.0 Class 0604: 8086:340e
00:0c.0 Class 0000: 8086:abba
00:0f.0 Class 0300: 1234:1111
00:10.0 Class 0000: 8086:3425
...
```

With the simulation still running, the target memory can be examined:

```
running> viper.mb.phys_mem.x $src
p:0x7c300000 0000 0009 00dc 0ffe 0000 0000 badc 0ffe
running> viper.mb.phys_mem.x $dst
p:0x7c400000 01c2 0600 0000 0000 01c2 0600 0000 0000
```

The magic pattern (`0000 0009 00dc 0ffe 0000 0000 badc 0ffe`) from Listing 7.12 is visible at the source address and the destination address contains some other data. To transfer the data from the source to the destination, the DMA control register must be written. Note that Because setting the associated attribute will not trigger any side effects, a memory write must be simulated:

```
running> viper.mb.nb.pci_mem.write 0xfd736000 0xc0000010 4 -b
[dma_comp.dma  info]  Write  to  register  regs.DMA_control  (addr
0xfd736000) <- 0xc0000010
[dma_comp.dma info] EN bit set, SWT written, initiating DMA
[dma_comp.dma info] Transferring 16 32-bit words from 0x7c300000 to
0x7c400000
[dma_comp.dma info] Contiguous Transfer
[dma_comp.dma info] reading 64 bytes from PCI memory space
[dma_comp.dma info] Reading 64 bytes from address 0x7c300000
[dma_comp.dma info] writing 64 bytes to PCI memory space
[dma_comp.dma info] Writing 64 bytes to address 0x7c400000
[dma_comp.dma info] DMA transfer completed
[dma_comp.dma info] ECI is zero, no interrupt raised
running> viper.mb.phys_mem.x $dst
p:0x7c400000 0000 0009 00dc 0ffe 0000 0000 badc 0ffe
```

Of course, in the real system the target software would be responsible for configuring and using the DMA device. An example of this is shown in the next section where a Linux device driver is created for the DMA device.

CREATING A DEVICE DRIVER

To bring everything together it is necessary to have some software that can interact with the device model. This section shows how a simple Linux driver can be developed and added to the target system. To understand the details, some familiarity with Linux device drivers and PCI is required. However, even without that knowledge it should be possible to understand the gist of the material presented. For an introduction to Linux device drivers, the book *Linux Device Drivers* provides an excellent resource (Corbet et al. 2005).

The first step is to obtain the source code for the Linux kernel. Throughout this section Linux kernel version 2.6.39 is used. It was obtained from kernel.org using Git and the following command:

```
git   clone   git://git.kernel.org/pub/scm/linux/kernel/git/torvalds/
linux.git
```

Once the kernel sources are available they need to be configured for the target and built. In addition, support for SimicsFS will also be added to simplify copying files in and out of the simulation. Finally, the device driver will be added.

Detailed instructions for adding SimicsFS are included in the Simics Installation Guide. Basically, the code must be extracted into .../fs/simicsfs, where .../ denotes the top-level directory of the Linux kernel source, and the files .../fs/Kconfig and .../fs/Makefile must be updated to include SimicsFS support by adding the lines

```
source "fs/simicsfs/Kconfig"
```

and

```
obj-$(CONFIG_SIMICSFS) + = simicsfs/
```

respectively. Once this is done the kernel can be built as usual, and SimicsFS can be configured and included.

The driver that is used as an example in this chapter is very simplistic and is not a good example of how to write device drivers for Linux. It is included to show the basic steps that need to be taken to provide a fully functional system, all the way down from the device model and through the target system, operating system, and user-space software. The functionality of the driver is described in more detail in the following section.

To add the driver to the Linux kernel a new file is created in .../drivers/char/simics-c7-dma.c, and .../drivers/char/Kconfig and .../drivers/char/Makefile are updated to include the new device, as shown in Listing 7.13. The full source code for the device driver is available in Appendix A, and is not covered in detail here.

- File.../drivers/char/Kconfig:

```
1   ...
2   config SIMICS_DMA
3       bool "Simics book chapter 7 example DMA driver"
4       help
5         DMA Device driver.
```

- File.../drivers/char/Makefile:

```
1   ...
2   obj-$(CONFIG_SIMICS_DMA) += simics-c7-dma.o
```

LISTING 7.13

Adding a new driver to the Linux kernel.

DRIVER OVERVIEW

The device driver is a character device that will expose a simple interface to user space. Three device files will be added to the /dev/ portion of the file system, one for each register of the device. The DMA source address will be available in /dev/dma_src, and the DMA control register will be available in /dev/dma_ctrl. Both these files can be read and written by user-space software. The driver will simply forward reads and writes to the corresponding device register. The DMA destination register will be exposed as read-only through /dev/dma_dst, because copying memory to an arbitrary location could easily lead to system memory corruption.

When software initiates a transfer by writing the appropriate bits into /dev/dma_ctrl, the driver will allocate a chunk of memory large enough to hold the result of the copy operation and place the address in the DMA destination register before issuing the copy command to the DMA control register. With this approach the target software can write an address to /dev/dma_src and then initiate a transfer by writing /dev/dma_ctrl. Once the copy is completed, the software can read /dev/dma_dst to find out where the result was copied to. This is, of course, useless in practice, but serves to illustrate the workflow.

To support both interrupt and polling modes, the driver will make sure that the transfer's complete status is available in /dev/dma_ctrl. If interrupts are enabled, reads will block until the transfer is complete. In polling mode, reads will return directly with the current value of the DMA control register.

BRING IT ALL TOGETHER

To test the driver with the model the script branch in Listing 7.12 can be updated as shown in Listing 7.14. The script branch now waits for the system to boot, mounts the host's file system using SimicsFS, creates the nodes in /dev, writes a magic pattern (0000 0009 00dc 0ffe 0000 0000 badc 0ffe) to the source memory, configures the driver, and prepares the copy operation.

```
1     . . .
2     $system.mb.hfs.root (lookup-file "%script%")
3     script-branch {
4         $con.wait-for-string "PS/2 Generic Mouse"
5         dma.log-level 4
6         $con.input "mount /host\n"
7         $con.input "sh /host/mknod-dma.sh\n"
8
9         $src = 0x7c300000
10        viper.mb.phys_mem.write $src   0x900dc0ffe 8 -b
11        viper.mb.phys_mem.write ($src + 8) 0xbadc0ffe 8 -b
12
13        $con.wait-for-string "~ #"
14        $con.input "echo " + (hex $src) + " > /dev/dma_src"
15        $con.input "\n"
16        $con.wait-for-string "~ #"
17        $con.input "echo '0xc0000010' > /dev/dma_ctrl"
18        enable-real-time-mode
19    }
```

LISTING 7.14

Testing the driver.

Line 2: Configure the SimicsFS virtual device to have its root file system located at the same place as the current Simics script.

Line 6: Mount the host file system under /host on the target using SimicsFS. The configuration is provided in /etc/fstab as simicsfs /host simicsfs defaults, noauto 0 0.

Line 7: Execute the mknod-dma.sh script from the host's file system. The script will parse /proc/devices to find out what major device number to use and set up the device files as appropriate.

Line 14: Write the source address to the DMA source register; only hexadecimal values are allowed by the driver.

Line 17: Prepare the command to write the control word to the driver that initiates a transfer, but do not press Enter. The user can press Enter to start the DMA transfer.

Line 18: Enable real-time mode to prevent the simulation from running too fast. This is useful when working interactively with the target, because Simics can simulate a mostly idle target several orders of magnitude faster than in real time, making it difficult to interact with it.

Listing 7.14 illustrates how easy it is to use Simics scripts for automation of test scenarios. To trigger the copy operation the user only has to press Enter in the target console. The output from the target console and the Simics CLI is shown in Listing 7.15. Note how the kernel log messages are intermixed with the user input and script output, just like they would be on a real system. This is due to the fact that Simics simulates the hardware and runs a real operating system with a real TTY driver, preemptive scheduler, and timing behavior. The complementary view in Simics' CLI shows the log output of the DMA model and is a good help for the driver developer in determining that indeed the driver works as expected.

To verify that the copy operation worked as expected the memory at the source and destination address can be examined. The destination address was

```
                ▪ Target Console Output
1    ~ # [    4.955882] input: PS/2 Generic Mouse as
     /devices/platform/i8042/serio1/input/input1
2    mount /host
3    [    4.970827] [simicsfs] mounted
4    ~ # sh /host/mknod-dma.sh
5    ~ # echo 0x7c300000 > /dev/dma[    4.986001] Simics DMA: Read from
     ffffc9000034a004
6    _src
7    ~ # echo '0xc0000010' > /dev/dma_ctrl [    7.376861] Simics DMA: Read
     from ffffc9000034a008
8
9    [    7.382381] Simics DMA: Read from ffffc9000034a000
10   ~ #

                ▪ Simics CLI Output
11   [dma_comp.dma info] Write to register regs.DMA_source (addr 0xfd736004)
     <- 0x7c300000
12   [dma_comp.dma info] Write to register regs.DMA_dest (addr 0xfd736008) <-
     0x7c33a000
13   [dma_comp.dma info] Write to register regs.DMA_control (addr 0xfd736000)
     <- 0xc0000010
14   [dma_comp.dma info] EN bit set, SWT written, initiating DMA
15   [dma_comp.dma info] Transferring 16 32-bit words from 0x7c300000 to
     0x7c33a000
16   [dma_comp.dma info] Contiguous Transfer
17   [dma_comp.dma info] reading 64 bytes from PCIe memory space
18   [dma_comp.dma info] Reading 64 bytes from address 0x7c300000
19   [dma_comp.dma info] writing 64 bytes to PCIe memory space
20   [dma_comp.dma info] Writing 64 bytes to address 0x7c33a000
21   [dma_comp.dma info] DMA transfer completed
22   [dma_comp.dma info] ECI is zero, no interrupt raised
```

LISTING 7.15

Initiate DMA copy operation.

```
                ▪ Target Console
~ # cat /dev/dma_dst
[   17.176857] Simics DMA: Read from ffffc9000034a008
0x7c33a000~ #

                ▪ Simics CLI Output
simics> dma_comp.dma->regs_DMA_dest
0x7c33_a000
simics> viper.mb.phys_mem.x $src
p:0x7c300000  0000 0009 00dc 0ffe 0000 0000 badc 0ffe .............
simics> viper.mb.phys_mem.x 0x7c33_a000
p:0x7c33a000  0000 0009 00dc 0ffe 0000 0000 badc 0ffe .............
simics>
```

FIGURE 7.5

Verify DMA copy result.

determined by the driver, and it can be obtained, either by reading the corresponding attribute in the model or by querying the driver through the /dev/dma_dst device file. The result shown in Figure 7.5 demonstrates that the DMA device model and driver are working together and the full system has now been completed.

Simulator extensions

8

No one can do everything, but everyone can do something.
—Swedish proverb

INTRODUCTION

From the very beginning, Simics was designed to be an extensible and programmable system. The goal was to enable a user to do anything with the simulator without having to modify the actual source code, and thus cause huge support headaches and potentially divergent branches of code. In hindsight, this goal has indeed been achieved, and Simics has proven extremely flexible for users (Intel, 2013). Over the years, Simics has been used for things and in situations that were not intended or even imagined by its developers.

Any Simics user is able to build not just new device models and system configurations, but also arbitrary Simics extensions. With the *Extension Builder* product, users have access to the complete Simics API and can basically implement any functionality they want to. New functionality often starts out as scripts, but over time it migrates into custom Simics modules to make the setup more robust and to achieve higher performance.

APPLICATIONS OF EXTENSIONS

Technically, almost every part of the Simics tool itself is an extension. The core Simics executable is really small, and it loads everything else from Simics modules. For example, the Simics Python interpreter, command-line system, and text and graphics consoles are all dynamically loaded extensions. It is hard to imagine Simics running without them, but they are not part of the core Simics binary. An extension can quite literally be or do anything.

Some common categories of extensions are:

- *Analysis tools:* Tools that trace instructions, monitor the execution of the system, and dump the results to a file for offline analysis, or perform some analysis inline. Analysis tools might set up and listen to software breakpoints, follow software using OS awareness, pull instruction traces out of processors, or read and write target memory. Simics comes with quite a few such tools, like the trace module.

- *Debugger connections:* Connections between Simics and external debuggers. The Simics Eclipse debugger is driven from one tool connection, and Simics also comes with the gdb-remote module to connect Simics to an external gdb debugger. Other debug connections have been built over the years, such as for Intel® In-Target Probe (Intel® ITP) and Freescale CodeWarrior[†].
- *Bug provocation and bug-finding tools:* Tools that build on top of Simics to steer and observe the target system to find bugs in the software are further examples of Simics extensions. The application of such tools was already discussed in Chapter 3. Technically, they are extensions because they use parts of the Simics API that are not part of the device API.
- *Configuration and inspection tools:* Some Simics users have built their own tools to manage the Simics configuration and inspect the currently running configuration. Because access to object attributes is considered bad form for device models, such tools are by definition extensions.
- *Fault injection:* Injecting faults into the target system can be done from scripts, but most persistent faults and most classes of faults require an implementation as a Simics extension. See the section on fault injection later in the chapter for more details.
- *Simulator integrations:* One large class of Simics extensions is simulator integrations, which connect Simics to other simulators. Simulator integration is a large topic in its own right, and it is discussed in more depth in Chapter 9.
- *Simics remote control:* If another tool wants to control Simics, an extension can be built that talks to the other tool over network sockets and performs actions using the Simics API. Such modules are sometimes used when Simics is part of a larger simulation system or when Simics is run from an automation system.
- *Network links:* New types of network links are defined by extensions, because they need to interact with Simics time, the Simics configuration, and the Link library. Network links are discussed in detail in Chapter 5.
- *Real-world connections:* Connections between Simics networks and physical real-world networks need to be realized as extensions. Examples included with Simics include Ethernet networking, as well as serial ports and various embedded buses as discussed in Chapter 5.
- *Cache and memory simulation:* Simics provides users with the ability to simulate caches and memory timing. Such models are considered extensions, because they do not model the functional part of the system and will need to access interfaces that are not needed by normal devices. They are discussed in more detail later in the chapter.

The applications of extensions are boundless, and over the years many surprising and enterprising uses of the Simics API have been made. For example, one research group embedded an entire Java Virtual Machine inside of Simics (Wright et al., 2006), while others have controlled the Simics reverse execution API to do backtracking searches over program executions (Blum et al., 2013).

SCRIPT OR EXTENSION

While many tasks in Simics can be automated using CLI scripts, scripts are in practice limited in what they can do. The Simics script engine and CLI commands are designed to be easy to use interactively, but not necessarily to expose all the details of what Simics can do. Even if it is possible to inline Python code in Simics scripts, this quickly becomes unmanageable as the size and complexity grows. At that point it is better to create a proper extension module in Python or C.

A Simics CLI script is a sequence of commands that act on Simics and the target system. Using inline Python, it is possible to call the Simics API directly, as well as invoke interface functions provided by objects. However, many APIs are built around the concept of *callbacks*, and callbacks require a function to call and a Simics object in which that callback exists. Also, a Simics configuration object is needed when setting up operations that rely on being called from Simics objects when things happen, such as capturing memory operations or network packets. Whenever a configuration object is needed, using an extension is necessary.

Scripts are not saved as part of checkpoints, because they are considered session state. If the desire is for some instrumentation or operation to be part of the system setup for the duration of the system life, it is necessary to use a configuration object defined by a compiled Simics class, which entails writing a Simics extension.

Any persistent functionality in Simics that is not a device model is per definition an extension, and it should be built as a Simics module with full support for all Simics features.

DEVICE OR EXTENSION

The Simics API is split into two main groups of functions: the device API and the simulator API. The device API has been designed to only allow operations that make sense in the context of building device models, and it is intentionally limited to the API calls that are consistent with well-behaved device models that adhere to Simics modeling guidelines. The device API is also isolated from the outside world, which makes devices very easy to port to new Simics versions and across host platforms.

The restrictions imposed by the device API include reading or writing attributes in other devices. All communication between devices should be over properly defined and declared interfaces, because that makes communications channels visible in device metadata and explicitly supported in DML code. Devices should not use their own threads or directly access anything outside their own object data to ensure thread safety and portability. Devices should not do things like call `SIM_run_command`, as that has global effects and is unlikely to work well as devices are ported around between different target setups.

If the need to use something not in the device API comes up during the development of what is supposed to be a device model, it probably indicates that the device model should be split into one part that is a pure device model, and another part that does whatever requires the full simulation API. This fits with the overall Simics architecture of devices being inside the simulator and only specially crafted modules interacting with the outside world. It could also be the case that the modeling architecture needs to be reconsidered—the device API has proven sufficient to model the absolute majority of all devices ever encountered.

IMPLEMENTING EXTENSIONS

Extensions are built just like Simics device models, in a Simics project. They are compiled into Simics modules, and when loaded they are used to create Simics objects that implement their functionality. Once compiled, an extension can be distributed to other Simics users as a binary module, with no need to include the source code.

C OR PYTHON

Simics extensions are normally written using C or Python. Python offers a quick way to create Simics modules, while C offers maximum performance and the full power to create low-level data structures and access arbitrary C-language APIs. DML is better for writing device models, but typically does not add much convenience to extensions, because extensions would not be expected to expose programming registers to software.

The dynamic typing and powerful library often make it much quicker to write an extension in Python than in C. Most of the Simics API is available in Python, except for a few functions with argument types that cannot be mapped to Python in a reasonable way. Simics simulator data structures like attribute values are easy to manipulate in Python. However, there is a simulator execution time cost involved in calling into Python from the C-based Simics core. This overhead can dominate the execution time of Simics if Python is invoked too often. Thus, Python is best suited for operations that are invoked comparatively rarely, such as operating on network packets, dealing with processor exceptions, or handling software breakpoints.

If extensions are invoked very often, such as when tracing memory operations or instruction execution, it makes sense to write them in C. C also allows access to a few APIs and data structures that are at too low a level to express in Python. C is also necessary if the extension is to invoke external libraries only available in C. There have been quite a few integrations between Simics and external tools where the interface was a C library for creating files or passing data, and in such cases using Python is not feasible. It is also possible to mix C and Python in the implementation of the same module, which offers the ability to use each language where it is most suitable.

ATTRIBUTE VALUES

Simics attribute values are used to represent the values you get from and use to set the attributes in Simics objects, and in quite a few API calls as a convenient way to pass complex variable-size data. Attribute values are built from a set of simple primitive types such as Boolean, signed and unsigned 64-bit integers, floating-point values, Simics object references, strings, and raw binary data. These primitive types can be put into arbitrarily nested lists. There is also a special value for NIL values and an invalid value to use for reporting errors. Values are created, inspected, and decomposed using Simics API calls.

Attribute values are a fundamental feature of the Simics C API, where they are represented as the opaque `attr_value_t` type. Attribute values are also automatically mapped into Python values. In DML, attribute values are often automatically handled by the DML compiler, but it is sometimes necessary to directly manipulate attribute values using the C API. Simics provides built-in conversions between attribute values and text for use in checkpoints, as well as to present and input values from the CLI and GUI.

CALLBACK FUNCTIONS

Callback functions are very common in the Simics API and in Simics extensions. Because Simics is an event-driven simulator, most things happen as a result of events, and events are realized by callbacks.

In a callback function, a key issue is to get hold of the Simics object that the callback code belongs to. A callback function is just a plain function with no way to know about any particular object. Global or static variables are not an appropriate solution in a system where each type of object can be instantiated any number of times. Thus, it is necessary to pass the object pointer to the callback function. Any Simics callback function or interface function that logically belongs to an object will have an object pointer as its first argument. This pointer is used by the called function to establish its local object so that it can read and modify its state.

Another issue with callback functions is how to pass some form of context from the point where a callback is requested to the point where the callback happens. If an object only has a single callback of a certain type active at any one point, this can be handled by data in the object. However, if multiple callbacks need to be active, some form of context needs to passed along. To support this, Simics callback functions tend to have a user data argument as their last argument. This user data is just a C void pointer, and this pointer will carry a pointer value from the registration point to the callback function. Typically, a struct of data is allocated on the heap and a pointer to the data used as the user data. In Python, any data structure can be passed as the user data argument.

A typical example of a Simics API function taking a callback function is `SIM_run_unrestricted`, which is declared like this:

```
void SIM_run_unrestricted(conf_object_t * NOTNULL obj, void (* NOTNULL
func)(conf_object_t *obj, lang_void *param), lang_void *user_data);
```

When called, `SIM_run_unrestricted` takes three arguments: the object that the callback belongs to, the callback function itself, and the user data parameter. The callback function is of the type shown in bold in the middle of the declaration: a function that does not return anything and takes an object pointer (`obj`) and a user data parameter (`param`).

Simics API functionality that relies on callbacks are things like reacting to simulator haps, OS awareness detecting changes in the target system, handlers for breakpoints, recorders, memory simulation, notifications on sockets, and many others. Callbacks can normally be written in C, Python, or C++. In DML, the best solution is to use inline C code to declare callback handlers.

GETTING TO A SAFE CONTEXT

Callback functions in extensions are often called in the middle of Simics instructions, known as *instruction context* in Simics. In instruction context, the set of APIs available is severely restricted to avoid corrupting the state of the simulator. If such actions need to be performed as a result of a callback, the API call `SIM_run_unrestricted` has to be used. This schedules another callback function to run after the current instruction has finished and before the next instruction starts. This is known as *execution context* in Simics.

In execution context, it is possible to access all objects in the current cell, but it is not legal to access objects in other cells, because they are not synchronized and the results would be nondeterministic and possibly fatal to the simulator. Most extension work can be carried out in execution context. Some API calls can only be used when the simulator is completely synchronized, in what is known as *outside execution context* (OEC). To get to OEC, the `SIM_run_alone` API call is used.

The Simics reference manuals list the execution context for all Simics API calls, as well as the execution context of the callbacks resulting from the API calls. Typically, the more local an operation is, the less restricted it is. For example, registering a callback that catches magic instructions on all processors in a simulation has to be done outside execution context, but registering a callback for magic instructions in a particular processor can be done from instruction context.

It is possible to create separate execution threads within a Simics simulation, using threads in Python or using the host's API for threads. Such threads are not managed by Simics, and thus care must be taken so that the threads do not interfere with the deterministic behavior of Simics or damage Simics' state. For this purpose, there is a single callback function, `SIM_thread_safe_callback`.

This function can be called by any thread at any time and will result in the callback function being called when Simics is in a consistent and safe state. The callback function can then use the Simics API to access the state of the Simics simulation, such as reading attributes.

SPECIAL CONCERNS WHEN CREATING EXTENSIONS

When creating extensions, special care has to be taken to maintain some of Simics' core features. For example, if an extension is reading and writing data to files on the disk, these files must be part of the checkpoint. Similarly, if an extension is not deterministic, the repeatability of the simulation is lost. Special concern typically has to be given to the following items:

- *Repeatability and reverse:* Extensions should support determinism, repeatable simulation, and reverse execution if it is at all possible. Repeatable execution is the key to the efficient debugging of issues discovered in the target system when using the extension.
- *Recording:* If an extension receives inputs from the outside world, it has to *record* those inputs using a Simics *recorder*, as discussed in Chapter 2. The way the recorder is used in an extension is to always pass all inputs through the recorder and have the recorder call a callback function in the extension each time an input arrives. In this way, a replay session looks identical to a live session from the perspective of the downstream logic.
- *Randomness:* Extensions that provide "random" input to the Simics simulation need some special care to ensure that repeatability is maintained. Examples of random inputs are extensions that randomly drop network packets or that vary memory timing or interrupt arrival times to create and explore variations in the system behavior. It is highly desirable to be able to repeat any run to facilitate the debugging of issues found thanks to the random input.

   There are two ways to handle such repeatability. Either all input values are recorded using a Simics recorder, or the randomness is generated by a pseudo-random system with a checkpointable state. The checkpointable state method is very simple and effective and results in a minimal saving of state. It assumes that each run is started with an assignment of a random value as the seed of the pseudo-random number generator (PRNG), and then the state of the PRNG is saved any time a checkpoint is taken. When the checkpoint is opened, the state is restored into the extension, and the PRNG will continue generating the exact same sequence of numbers as it did in the original run.
- *Output suppression:* If an extension has side effects that are visible outside of Simics, such as adding data to a log file or sending network packets to an external program, it needs to suppress these outputs during reverse execution and replay of recorded sessions. If not, duplicate or corrupt data or communications errors are likely to occur.

Extensions need to check both for reverse execution and recording replay. Replay of recorded data can happen without reverse execution, and Simics will tell an extension whether it is replaying data from a file (in a new Simics session). Reverse execution is used within a Simics session, and thus the recorder will not consider itself to be replaying from a file.

Note that if an extension has complete control over the state of some external component, it is advisable to update this in reaction to reverse execution or replay scenarios. For example, if an extension is drawing an image based on the simulation state into an external window, it should keep this window updated to reflect the current state. Nothing would break due to such an update.

ON-THE-FLY PYTHON OBJECTS

For quick hacks that do not require checkpointing, there is an intermediate level of implementation between full modules and CLI scripts: the on-the-fly Python object. These objects are not defined as Simics configuration classes, but rather as standard Python classes. The classes are defined in Python files called from CLI scripts at runtime and are not compiled before being used. Python methods can be used as callbacks for most Simics APIs, in particular those from OS awareness and the debugger system.

Listing 8.1 shows an example of an on-the-fly object that listens to OS awareness events. It uses a plain Python class and employs functions defined in the class as the callback functions from the Simics OS awareness API. Note how data can be stored in the object created from the class, avoiding the need for either global variables or passing data around between callbacks.

CACHE AND MEMORY SIMULATION

A hardware cache is normally a hardware performance optimization that is not relevant for the functionality of the software. Therefore, Simics does not model any cache system by default. It uses its own memory system to achieve high-speed simulation, and modeling a hardware cache model would only slow it down.

However, Simics optionally exposes the flow of memory transactions coming from the processor and thus allows users to attach cache models, write tracing tools, and collect statistics on the memory behavior of their simulations. Simics also allows users to write *timing models* to control how much virtual time each memory transaction takes. Stalling transactions, as it is called in Simics, helps improve the timing accuracy of the simulation, when compared to a real system running the same software.

These properties make Simics very suitable for various types of cache simulation:

```
1     class data_collector:
2         "Simics on-the-fly OS awareness-using extension"
3         # When the object is created, we install our callbacks
4         def __init__(self,name,software_tracker,program_name):
5             self.name = name
6             # Save tracker and pipe
7             self.tracker       = software_tracker
8             self.program_name  = program_name
9             # Install callback for program start
10            self.sw = self.tracker.iface.software
11            self.npc_id = self.sw.notify_property_change(self.sw.root_node_id(),
12                                                   "name", True,
13                                                   self.pstart_cb, None)
14
15            ...
16
17        #-----------------------------------------
18        # Program starting (expressed as node name change) callback
19        #-----------------------------------------
20        def pstart_cb(self, _dummy, tracker, curcpu, node_id, key, old_val,
21                      new_val, status):
22            # Check if the program starting is the program we are
23            # waiting for
24            if self.program_name.startswith(new_val):
25                print "Program %s started (node %d) " %
26                      (self.program_name, node_id)
27                # Catch program switch in and out
28                # This assumes a single-threaded program where the main thread is
29                # the only thread
30                self.activate_id = self.sw.notify_cpu_move_to(node_id,
31                                                       self.activate_cb,
32                                                       None)
33                self.deactivate_id = self.sw.notify_cpu_move_from(node_id,
34                                                       self.deactivate_cb,
35                                                       None)
36        #-----------------------------------------
37        # Callback for program thread activate
38        #-----------------------------------------
39        def activate_cb(self, _dummy, tracker, curcpu, _node_path):
40            now = SIM_cycle_count(curcpu)
41            print "Activate callback! ", _node_path, curcpu, now
42            self.process_activated(curcpu,now)  # do something
43        #-----------------------------------------
44        # Callback for program thread deactivate
45        #-----------------------------------------
46        def deactivate_cb(self, _dummy, tracker, curcpu, _node_path):
47            now = SIM_cycle_count(curcpu)
48            print "Deactivate callback! ", _node_path, curcpu, now
49            # Do something now that the process is switching out
50
51    ...
52
53    # Creation of the object, at the top-level of the Python file
54    # Assume tracker is the name of the software tracker to talk to,
55    # and cmdname the program to follow.
56    data_collect_object = data_collector("packet stats",
57                                  tracker,
58                                  cmdname)
```

LISTING 8.1

Reacting to OS awareness callbacks.

- *Cache profiling:* The goal is to gather information about the cache behavior of a system or an application. Unless the application runs on multiprocessors, takes a lot of interrupts, or runs a lot of system-level code, the timing of the memory operations is often irrelevant, thus no stalling is necessary.

The memory interfaces are used to be informed of all transactions sent by the processor. Note that this type of simulation does not change the execution of the target program. It could be performed by using Simics as a simple memory transaction trace generator and then computing the cache state evolution afterwards. However, doing the cache simulation at the same time as the execution enables a number of optimizations that Simics models make good use of.

- *Cache timing:* The goal is to study the timing behavior of the transactions, in which case a transaction to memory should take much more time than, for example, a transaction to an L1 cache. This is useful when studying interactions between several CPUs, or to estimate the number of cycles per instruction (CPI) of an application. Simics models can be used for such simulation. This type of simulation affects the software execution, because interrupts and multiprocessor interaction will be influenced by the timing provided by the cache model. However, unless the target program is not written properly, the execution will always be correct, although different from the execution obtained without any cache model.

- *Cache content simulation:* It is possible to change the Simics coherency model by allowing a cache model to contain data that is different from the contents of the memory. Such a model needs to properly handle the memory transactions because it must be able to change the values of loads and stores.

When simulating with caches, it is imperative to start Simics with the `-stall` flag to get correct cache statistics. It is possible to start Simics without it, but no transactions will then be stalled, and not all transactions may be visible to the cache.

For simplicity and performance, Simics does not model incoherence. In Simics, the memory is always up to date with the latest CPU and device transactions. This property holds even when doing cache simulation with Simics' standard model, because the model does not contain any data, only cache line status information.

Cache control instructions and the use of caches as temporary memory during early boot can be simulated without implementing a full cache model—one must only ensure that the cache control operations have the appropriate effect on which values are mapped at which addresses in memory. This functional modeling is separate from the timing modeling addressed in this section.

SIMICS' GENERIC CACHE MODEL

Simics comes with a cache model called g-cache, which allows cache profiling and timing simulation. The g-cache handles one transaction at a time; all needed operations (copy-back, fetch, and so on) are performed in order and at once. The cache returns the sum of the stall times reported for each operation. The g-cache provides the following features:

- Configurable number of lines, line size, and associativity. Note that the line size must be a power of 2, and that the number of lines divided by the associativity must be a power of 2.
- Physical/virtual index and tag.
- Configurable write allocate/write back policy.
- Random, true Least Recently Used (LRU) or cyclic replacement policies. It is easy to add new replacement policies.
- Sample Modified-Exclusive-Shared-Invalid (MESI) protocol.
- Support for several processors connected to one cache.
- Configurable penalties for read–write accesses to the cache, and read–write accesses initiated by the cache to the next level cache.
- Cache-miss profiling.

Adding a g-cache to a processor is easily done using a small Python script, as illustrated in Listing 8.2. The script starts by creating a preliminary cache object with a number of parameters: 256 lines of 32 bytes each, with no associativity, physical index and tags, and random replacement policy. No stalling is enabled, because all penalties are 0. All the cache parameters are described in more detail in the *Wind River Simics Accelerator User's Guide* (Wind River, 2014d). Next, the script adds the preliminary cache object to the current configuration, and then connects it as a listener object on the memory space representing the physical memory of the processor in the system. From now on, accesses to main memory will go through the cache and cache hits and misses will be simulated.

It is worth noting that connecting the caches to the memory space can be done separately from defining the caches. Thus, it is possible to connect and disconnect the caches at any time during the simulation. For example, the OS boot and work-load setup can be done with Simics in normal mode to create a checkpoint. The checkpoint is then reloaded in -stall mode with cache simulation enabled.

```
1    cpu = conf.viper.mb.cpu0.core[0][0]
2    cache = pre_conf_object('cache', 'g-cache',
3                            config_line_number = 256,
4                            config_line_size = 32,
5                            config_assoc = 1,
6                            config_virtual_index = 0,
7                            config_virtual_tag = 0,
8                            config_replacement_policy = 'random',
9                            penalty_read = 0,
10                           penalty_write = 0,
11                           penalty_read_next = 0,
12                           penalty_write_next = 0,
13                           cpus = cpu)
14
15   SIM_add_configuration([cache], None)
16
17   cpu.physical_memory.timing_model = conf.cache
```

LISTING 8.2

Adding a g-cache to a processor.

After running the simulation for a while, information about the cache is available using the cache.status and cache.statistics commands. To get decent cache statistics, it is important to run at least a few million instructions to warm up the caches before actually starting to do measurements. Note that this is only rough advice; the precise warm-up time needed will depend on the cache model and the workload. The following statistics are available in a g-cache:

- *Total number of transactions:* Count of all transactions received by the cache, including all transactions listed in the following.
- *Device data read—write:* Number of transactions, such as DMA transfers, performed by devices against the memory space to which the cache is connected. Device accesses are otherwise ignored by the cache and passed as-is to the next level cache.
- *Uncacheable data read—write, instruction fetch:* Number of uncacheable transactions performed by the processor. Uncacheable transactions are otherwise ignored by the cache and passed as-is to the next level cache.
- *Data read transactions:* Cacheable read transactions counted by the cache.
- *Data read misses:* Cacheable read transactions that were missed in the cache.
- *Data read hit ratio:* 1 (cacheable read misses/cacheable read transactions).
- *Instruction fetch transactions:* Cacheable instruction fetch transactions counted by the cache.
- *Instruction fetch misses:* Cacheable instruction fetch transactions that were missed in the cache.
- *Instruction fetch hit ratio:* 1 (cacheable instruction fetch misses/cacheable instruction fetch transactions).
- *Data write transactions:* Cacheable write transactions counted by the cache.
- *Data write misses:* Cacheable write transactions that were missed in the cache. This is not directly related to the number of transactions sent to the next level cache, which also depends on the write allocation and write-back policies selected for the cache.
- *Data write hit ratio:* 1 (cacheable write misses/cacheable write transactions).
- *Copy-back transactions:* Copy-back transactions performed by the cache to flush modified cache lines.
- *Lost stall cycles:* Number of cycles the processor model should have stalled but did not, because the memory transaction was not allowed to. This number represents how the model limitations—in this case, nonstallable transactions—are preventing timing from being fully taken into account.

Using g-cache it is possible to model more complex cache systems, such as the one shown in Figure 8.1 where there are separate instruction and data caches at level 1 backed by a level 2 cache. The dotted components in the diagram represent elements that are introduced in Simics to complete the simulation. The id-splitter is used by Simics to separate instruction and data accesses and send them to separate L1 caches. Although unlikely, accesses that cross a cache-line boundary can be received. To avoid that, a splitter is placed before

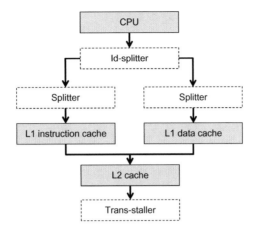

FIGURE 8.1

A more complex cache system.

each cache. The splitter will let uncacheable and correctly aligned accesses go through untouched, whereas others will be split in two accesses. The `trans-staller` simulates memory latency and will stall all accesses by a fixed amount of cycles.

FAULT INJECTION

The nature of the faults that Simics can inject into a system has already been discussed in Chapter 3. This chapter will address how fault injectors can be implemented in Simics. There is a wide variety of ways to implement fault injection, and most of them require using Simics extensions. Using extensions is recommended, because it puts no limitations on the mechanisms that can be used.

Using extensions also makes the faults part of the system setup, and thus part of checkpoints and reverse execution. A fault-injection module should use a recorder to enable precise replay of faults ordered from outside the module. If a random number generator is used to drive errors, it has to be deterministic and checkpointable so that the same fault sequence is repeated each time the same scenario is run. Chapter 9 has a deeper discussion on record–replay debugging and recorders, which also applies to fault-injection modules.

A fault-injection module should register some custom commands to allow a user to write scripts to control its execution. It is also common to use external files with lists of errors to inject (Bastien, 2004; Yu et al., 2013).

MODIFYING MEMORY AND REGISTERS

The most basic type of fault injection is to modify the value of processor registers, device registers, or memory contents to present bad data to the software rather than good data. Such modifications can be performed from scripts, but they can also be done using extensions. The interfaces used to achieve such changes can either be object attributes, the Simics memory write APIs, or in some cases special interfaces on processors and devices that provide access to register names and contents.

It should be noted that errors in memory error-correcting codes (ECCs) are most commonly modeled as error reporting, and not memory contents modifications. Typically, the ECC systems manage to correct most errors that appear in memory, and only very rarely will the errors be so severe that the values read by software will be affected.

ERROR REPORTING REGISTERS IN DEVICES

Most hardware errors in a real system end up being reported to software via error-reporting registers in the hardware, along with an interrupt to tell a processor core that an error has occurred. For Simics, this requires modeling the error-reporting registers in the hardware device that reports errors, which is really just a set of regular devices. Because all registers should be backed by attributes, changing the attributes is the easiest way to change the values visible to software in the error registers. The hardest part is usually generating a coherent set of values for the registers that will be correctly interpreted by the error-handling code. The processor core must also implement the error-reporting register, such as the System Management Interrupt (SMI) on Intel® Architecture systems, or the Machine Check exception on Power Architecture systems.

Once the device- and processor-side infrastructure are in place, an extension can be written that both generates the appropriate values for the registers and sends the interrupt to the processor core. Figure 8.2 shows a general setup for this type of work. By implementing the fault-injection system as an extension, it is much easier to encapsulate all its intelligence and to activate errors.

Error-reporting registers are common in systems such as PCIe, and it is often sufficient to only implement the parts closest to the processor. The key is to cover all the places that the software reads to determine what has happened, but there is usually no need to implement the fault mechanisms themselves in Simics. The key is to model the behavior visible to software, not the actual errors taking place in the hardware.

INTERCEPTING TRAFFIC

Another common type of fault injection is the interception of traffic in the system, such as network packets, bus transfers, or memory reads. In these cases, the goal

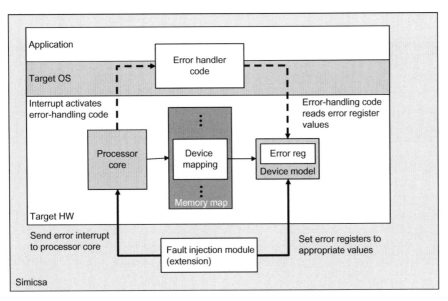

FIGURE 8.2

General device error register fault injection.

is to modify the data being transmitted, to remove transactions altogether, or to add new "spurious" transactions.

Chapter 5 discusses how network fault injection could be performed using Ethernet probes and instrumentation modules. Such modules are implemented as Simics extensions, because they need to be objects inside the simulation. They receive callbacks from the network simulation system when packets arrive, and they need to call into the network simulation system to pass packets on, inject modified packets, and inject new packets of their own that did not originate with any actual network devices.

For simpler Simics buses and network models where no special interface is provided for traffic intercept, fault injection can usually be implemented in the manner shown in Figure 8.3. The fault-injection module in this case looks like a network or bus model to the communications device in the target system, and like a device to the network.

The fault-injection module accepts calls from the device model and sends the traffic on to the network, and it accepts calls from the network and sends the traffic on to the device, unless it modifies the traffic before passing it on or drops it entirely. A setup like this is also able to inject spurious traffic into the system. Most Simics interfaces can be subjected to this type of intercept, including network models, bus models, or even custom interfaces used for communicating between tightly coupled devices.

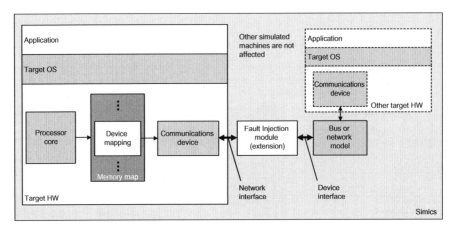

FIGURE 8.3

Man-in-the-middle intercept.

INTERCEPTING MEMORY ACCESSES

Memory accesses can be intercepted and changed in Simics. They are different from network transactions, in that a memory transaction originates with a processor as a function call into the memory system, and a reply is always needed. To "drop" a memory transaction, it has to be modified to hit something different from where it was originally targeted. Figure 8.4 shows how to set up a memory intercept using a fault-injection module. To simplify the implementation, a separate memory map has been inserted between the main memory map and the target device or memory. Any memory access that hits this memory map will generate a call into the fault-injection module, and this module will be able to use Simics API calls to modify the contents of the memory operation.

This method can be used to model a *persistent* fault in memory. The basic idea is to apply an error to any value written, such as using logical AND to clear certain bits or using logical OR to set certain bits in a byte. This would model bits stuck at 0 or 1 in a bad memory. In Simics, this is done using the timing_ model interface. It is the same interface that is used by a cache simulation to see all memory accesses and manipulate the value in the memory operation, and it gets called after the processor executes the store, but before the value arrives in memory. Memory reads just return what was last stored, and need not be intercepted.

Memory operation intercept also makes it possible to simulate *transient data bus faults*, where a value being written or read is modified before it reaches its target. This means modifying write values in the same way as for persistent faults, but only occasionally. To modify values being read, the Simics snoop_device interface provides the fault-injection module with a callback when a value has

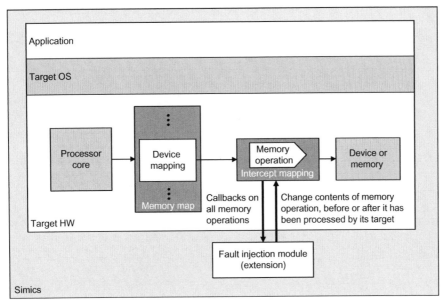

FIGURE 8.4

Intercepting memory operations.

been read and is on its way back to the processor, allowing modification of the read value seen by the processor.

When modeling a *permanent device malfunction*, the assumption has to be that the values returned by reads from the device are generated dynamically and are not set by any previous write. Thus, it is necessary to intercept the value read from the device on its way back to the processor in the same way as a transient data bus error.

REAL-WORLD STORY: L33T SERIAL PORT

A couple of years ago, we built a funny little demo showing what could be done using a memory map–based intercept of device accesses. The purpose was to simulate a serial device with flaky interface circuitry, or a device connected to a bus that would sometimes fail to correctly pass the data from the device to the processor. The device operation itself was not affected, only the traffic between it and the processor. Note that if an error is injected on a transaction that targets the configuration or control registers of the device, it might well misconfigure device, causing it to misbehave.

On the surface, this might seem trivial to implement: just pass all transactions from the main memory map through an intercept module and have that module corrupt the transactions as it sees fit. However, this would burden all transactions with a cost and remove the ability of the simulator to cache values and optimize accesses to memory and other devices that are not affected by the fault injection. Instead, we introduced a separate memory map to only hit accesses to the targeted device.

The setup looked like this illustration, essentially the same as Figure 8.4.

This target system modification was done in a few lines of Simics scripting and could be done in the middle of a simulation to simulate a bus that goes bad after some time has passed in the system. Changing the memory map to point to something new and introducing of a new memory map and fault-injection module can both be done and undone at runtime.

If we program the fault injector to replace some output characters with other characters, we get something like the illustration shown further below. On line 11 of the serial output, we activated the error module.

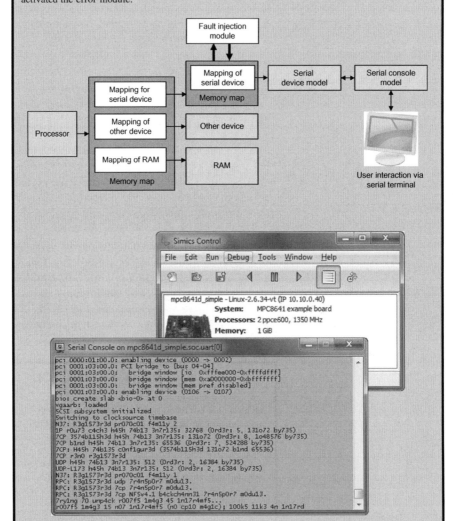

Note how the output is suddenly corrupted with a bit of L337-style text. This is achieved by changing the values written to the serial port transmission register on their way from the processor to the device. From the device, the modified characters are then passed on to the serial console and displayed to the user. It was also possible to set the module to change values read from the serial port, making typing commands exceedingly hard.

To enable the various types of faults, the module provided three attributes (assuming `$finj` in a Simics CLI variable holding the name of the fault-injection object):

- `$finj->zzz_write_fault` = TRUE, which would replace all characters written with z.
- `$finj->l33t_write_fault` = TRUE, which resulted in the effect shown in the illustration.
- `$finj->l33t_read_fault` = TRUE, which would make characters typed by the user be converted to L33T style.

CHAPTER

Simulator integration

Nature laughs at the difficulties of integration.
—Pierre-Simon Laplace

INTRODUCTION

Simics provides an excellent simulation tool for digital computer systems running software, with a focus on simulating complete platforms very quickly and running large software stacks for a long time. However, this is not the end of all that you might want to simulate. Often, Simics users need to model the physical world or look deep into the implementation of computer components. Rather than using Simics itself to create such models, it makes more sense to integrate Simics with other simulators, leaving each simulator to do what it does best. This chapter addresses the reasons for and the main issues involved in creating such simulator integrations. In Simics terms, most simulator integrations are built as *extensions*, as discussed in Chapter 8, because they need to do more than a typical device model.

PHYSICS AND THE ENVIRONMENT

Simics does not natively simulate analog electronics, mechanical or physical systems, or other aspects of the world in which embedded computer systems operate. Instead, Simics users employ various external simulator engines to build true full-system setups. System engineering companies have usually worked with simulations of their physical systems for decades, using a variety of tools from hand-coded simulators in C, to mathematical modeling tools like MATLAB, to model-based design tools like Simulink and LabVIEW. These existing mechanical and physical simulators provide the environment for the control computers simulated by Simics.

The value that Simics brings is the ability to run the actual deployed control software in the context of the full system. In particular, the ability to run the full and integrated software stack on a model of the real target system provides a new ability where the target control computer system can be integrated with the system simulation. With Simics, it is possible to perform the whole system integration in simulation.

As shown in Figure 9.1, Simics can simulate a system with control algorithms running as OS tasks on top of a real-time operating system. The operating system contains device drivers that drive simulated input and output devices. These inputs and outputs are then connected to the simulation of the system being built, in

257

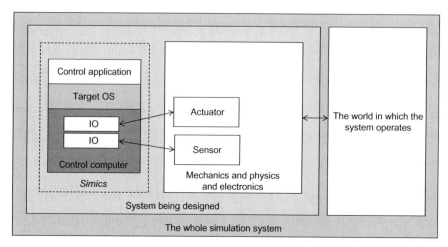

FIGURE 9.1

Generic system simulation with physics.

particular to the sensors and actuators found in the system. This lets the control computer interact with the system just like it would in the real world. Finally, the model of the system is often connected to a simulation of the world around the system.

For example, for a satellite, the "system being designed" in Figure 9.1 would be the satellite itself with power supplies, cameras, attitude thrusters, heaters, cooling systems, and communications systems. Simics would simulate the onboard computer system and the control code. The world simulation would encompass the orbital dynamics of the satellite in orbit around Earth, as well as the most important objects in the sky like the sun and the moon. This simulation could be used to check that the satellite correctly positions its solar panels toward the sun and maintains a stable alignment in orbit by watching the stars in the sky.

COMPUTER ARCHITECTURE

As discussed in Chapter 2, computer simulation has been used for computer architecture studies since the late 1950s (Brooks, 2010). The objects under study in such circumstances typically need to be simulated at the cycle level, because the goal is to understand how the details of the microarchitecture affect the computation latency, overall throughput, multicore scaling, power consumption, or other nonfunctional aspects of the system. Sometimes this evaluation is performed by simulating the complete system at the cycle level, because that provides the most accurate picture of the performance. As computer systems have grown larger and more complex, such complete-system cycle-level simulations have become impractical. Rather, the focus has turned to simulating subsystems or individual components in full detail, with the rest of the system simulated in a more abstract way. What has also become clear is that the runtime system and operating system have a huge impact on the overall performance of a system (Alameldeen et al., 2003a; Skadron et al., 2003; Peterson et al., 2006; Chen et al., 2007).

Today, the most common computer architecture research setup used in industry and academia is a transaction-level fast platform like Simics, alongside detailed models of particular subsystems. The fast platform provides the ability to run the complete software stack and real benchmark programs, providing the context and realistic input streams for the detailed simulators. Typically, checkpoints are used to boot the system and position the workload at the start of an interval of interest. Then, gear shifting is applied to change from a fast model to a detailed model at interesting points in the workload (Rosenblum and Varadarajan, 1994; Magnusson et al., 2002; Neifert and Kaye, 2012). Another necessary optimization used for computer architecture studies is the use of sampling techniques to only run a small but representative subset of a large workload through the detailed simulator (Yi et al., 2005).

For processor core architecture work, there are three different types of setups used with Simics:

- Use the Simics processor core to *generate a trace* of instructions, which is sent to a trace-driven processor model. Such an approach has the downside that the timing from the detailed simulation cannot feed back to the execution of the system, potentially missing some variability (Alameldeen and Wood, 2003b). Trace-based simulators are quite common in industrial computer architecture design teams. The advantage is that the integration can be quick and simple, while gaining most of the benefit of a full cycle-accurate model of the processor (Werner and Magnusson, 1997). It is possible to extend trace-based integrations to do more than just consume traces of instructions, such as evaluating speculative paths by retrieving memory contents from Simics dynamically (Chen et al., 2007), or importing cache state from the fast-functional simulator (Werner and Magnusson, 1997).

- *Direct execution*, where the Simics processor core models are *replaced with a detailed processor core model*, using the Simics processor API. This assumes the detailed model is complete enough to run an operating system and react to interrupts. Such processor models are mostly found in industry, where they have been the mainstay of processor design teams for many decades. They are the design tools discussed in the section "Cycle-Accurate Simulation" in Chapter 2. Simics has been integrated with a variety of such tools over the years, but the only public case is the Freescale P4080, where Virtutech and Freescale provided users access to detailed processor and device models via a combination of Freescale detailed models and a Simics model of the processor (Freescale, 2007; Halfhill, 2008; Liong, 2008).

- Using a *timing-first model*, where the Simics functional model is run alongside a detailed model. The timing simulator is capable of functionally executing the instructions most important to performance, but as it executes, it is followed by the standard Simics processor core simulator to ensure correctness. This approach allows the timing simulator to skip instructions that are unimportant to timing fidelity without introducing functional errors in the system's simulation (Mauer et al., 2002; Martin et al., 2005).

At the purely functional level, Simics has been used to *study the effect of new instructions* on the runtime of benchmarks. Sometimes magic instructions are used as a stand-in for new instructions (Moore et al., 2006), while in other cases the user decoder feature of the Simics processor models is used to add new instructions. In the case that the architects have their own complete functional simulator integrated with Simics, it is very easy to add new instructions.

The study of *memory hierarchies and cache systems* is closely related to processor core simulation, but it can be performed separately. Indeed, it has been shown that once memory instructions are filtered by a level 1 cache, the resulting stream of accesses is very similar for a detailed cycle-level processor model and a simple in-order functional model. Most of the speculation and out-of-order behavior is absorbed by the first levels of cache, and by exploiting this, cache system and memory system exploration can be performed about 100 times faster than a full processor core cycle-level simulation (Wallin et al., 2005; Malani and Tamhankar, 2013).

Computer architecture setups have also been used as the basis for *power simulation* with Simics. Because power is intimately related to time, some level of processor and cache modeling has been shown to be needed to get decent power estimates. Power estimation usually involves combining multiple simulators, with Simics providing the functional platform and sometimes the memory system simulation. A separate simulator is used to provide the detailed processor core model (Chen et al., 2007, Bartolini et al., 2010), and yet another simulator is used to estimate the power consumed (Chen et al., 2007, Bartolini et al., 2010, Malani and Tamhankar, 2013).

Apart from the processors, modern computer systems contain a large number of complex devices that need to be designed and optimized. In particular, accelerators for complex and processing-intense tasks like cryptography, pattern matching, network protocol processing, and network packet management have become common in recent years. The software interface and microarchitecture of such devices have to be designed, and because the designs often approach the complexity of processor cores, powerful design tools are needed.

- *Standard Simics models* can be used to study the interaction between devices and the software drivers, validating that programming interfaces make sense and investigating how much work the processor has to do based on instruction counts.
- Detailed performance evaluation requires the *integration of other simulators* that can model the microarchitecture and timing of the accelerators. Typically, the starting point is a complete Simics model of the system that can be used to quickly boot and position the workloads. Then, a device or set of devices is replaced by a detailed model run by a second simulator. The software stack keeps running on the Simics processors and mostly using Simics devices,

while feeding realistic operation sequences to the accelerators (Liong, 2008; Khan and Wolfe, 2013). Integrating a detailed device simulator is usually simpler than integrating a full processor core model, because a processor core tends to have much more complex behavior.

HARDWARE VALIDATION

Another use case for simulator integration is hardware validation. Just like with computer architecture, some parts of a Simics setup are replaced by detailed simulations. The purpose, however, is different. For hardware validation, the design is known, and the goal is to validate and verify that the actual implementation of the design works as intended. The integrated simulation is usually at a much lower level than computer architecture models, because the purpose of computer architecture is to explore the performance design space, which requires flexible and quite general models that cannot reflect the particulars of register-transfer level implementation.

The role of Simics in hardware validation is generally to run validation and testing software on the processor simulated by Simics, driving tests into the more detailed models of various peripheral devices and I/O units. The testing software is typically developed using transaction-level modeling of the hardware, long before the RTL or silicon is available. The same testing software is used to validate the RTL and to test the silicon implementation once it arrives (Veseyi and Ayers, 2013). It should be noted that Simics is used in addition to other hardware validation tools, such as classic test generators and low-level test benches. Simics adds the ability to develop testing software and test hardware using software, which extends the breadth and depth of testing.

For hardware validation, the integrated simulators normally operate with the actual design RTL. This level is cycle-accurate and bit-accurate, and expects bus interfaces to play out the complete bus protocol. To use such simulators, the transactions from a TLM simulator like Simics have to be converted into cycle-level operations by a *transactor*. A transactor is a small active machine that takes a single TLM operation, such as a memory write, and turns it into a sequence of bus cycles, including arbitration, address and data phases, and pipelined operations. Transactors are almost by definition highly purpose-specific, but can be reused for all devices attached to the same type of bus.

Several Simics users have built their own hardware validation setups over the years, integrating Simics with RTL simulators from various vendors, as well as cycle-accurate implementation-accurate SystemC, hardware emulators, FPGA prototyping boards, and RTL compiled into C.

REUSING EXISTING MODELS

When modeling a new customer-specific platform in Simics, it makes sense to reuse any existing machine-readable information, code, or virtual platform models. Reuse of information and algorithms was covered previously in Chapter 6. However, when complete models are available, the task becomes one of simulator integration.

Running TLM device models designed for other simulators in Simics is often quite easy, as long as they operate at an abstraction level similar to that of Simics. It then becomes a matter of translating transactions between the two simulators, including inbound memory-mapped register writes from Simics, and outbound interrupts and DMA operations. Other data-exchange operations are sometimes needed, such as sending and receiving Ethernet packets. Compared to "inside chip" operations like memory, DMA, and interrupts, such interfaces are less standardized and often implemented in more complicated ways, such as bouncing all traffic through a TCP/IP socket. It is unfortunately the case that most other virtual platform frameworks lack Simics' set of interfaces for things like networks.

If a model is written in a more detailed way, such as cycle-accurate (CCA) or SystemC TLM approximately timed (AT), the benefit of integrating it into Simics is often doubtful. Because the speed of a virtual platform is dictated by the slowest component in the system, using a CCA or AT-level model in Simics will tend to slow down the entire simulation. In such cases, writing a native Simics model from scratch is typically the best choice. However, the more detailed model can often be useful as a reference to facilitate testing and implementation of the more abstract Simics model.

Device models are not the only type of models that can be reused. Processor core models have also been integrated with Simics. When no Simics ISS is available, using an existing ISS can shorten the time required to create a complete platform. There are also cases such as configurable processor cores, where it is difficult to build a Simics model at all, because the users generate new instruction sets on-the-fly as part of their development flow. To support such integrations, Simics features a *processor API*, described later.

REAL-WORLD EXAMPLE: TENSILICA CORES IN SIMICS

In 2009, a Simics customer needed to add a Tensilica processor to their system model. It was yet another type of core needed to build a true system model capable of running all the code from the real system. Usually, such processors are modeled as Simics native models, but the Tensilica core added the twist that it was configurable and user-extensible. Because the Simics users in this case were using such features and reconfiguring their Tensilica processor core as part of their hardware tuning process, the best method was to use the existing Tensilica TurboXim simulator inside of Simics. The Tensilica simulator would be regenerated by the Tensilica design tools each time the processor was reconfigured, and thus automatically track the design being used. By incorporating this ISS in Simics, the users immediately got the ISS that they needed, with no need to wait for the Simics team to change or configure an ISS for them. The downside was a certain loss of features, in particular checkpointing and reverse execution.

A general issue with reusing existing models in Simics is that the key features of Simics, such as multithreaded execution, checkpointing, deterministic execution and repeatability, reverse execution, and debugging, all pose requirements on the models. The Simics framework cannot transparently make a model become checkpointable—it only provides the interfaces to enable checkpoints to be created (Montón et al., 2009). The integration layer between Simics and the models can often arrange to meet some of these requirements, but in general it is rare to find models not written with Simics in mind that fully support checkpointing, multithreading, and reverse execution. In such cases, some Simics features will be limited in their applicability. One way to get around this, and to allow Simics software debugging, is to do record—replay debugging, as discussed later.

PROBLEMS AND SOLUTIONS

When integrating multiple simulators, there are a number of issues that have to be solved.

- *Run control:* Which simulator is in charge?
- *Launching and embedding:* How are the simulators launched and connected?
- *Time synchronization management:* How should time be handled between the simulators?
- *Communications:* How is data moved between the simulators?
- *Frontends:* Which frontend is being used?

The following sections address various aspects of these issues. Most of them can have asymmetric master—slave solutions, or symmetric peer-to-peer solutions.

RUN CONTROL

The most common way to integrate two simulators is to designate one simulator as the *master* and the other as the *slave*. The master simulator determines when the simulation is to be run and when it is stopped, controls the progress of virtual time, and is the main point of user interaction. Deciding which simulator is the master in a particular setup depends on many factors, including what is technically convenient and what is semantically reasonable. Often, the simulator that simulates the largest part of the integrated system is considered the master, or the simulator that the user is the most used to working with. If one simulator interacts with the outside world and the other does not, it makes sense to assign the interacting simulator as the master, because it will tend to have tougher requirements on interactivity and availability.

It is also possible to construct a peer-based integration, where the simulators collaborate around control. Typically, the model is that each simulator keeps its own simulated time within a fixed bound of the other simulator, by some kind of sync protocol. This means that progress is bounded by the slowest simulator and that either simulator can pause the simulation. Getting the simulation started requires starting it on both sides, which in turn requires some kind of coordination during the startup phase. The *Simics Time Synchronization library* already mentioned in Chapter 5 enables peer-to-peer time synchronization and data exchange between multiple simulators. When using the library, the simulators essentially apply the same efficient synchronization logic as a distributed Simics simulation.

When Simics is integrated with a physics simulator, it is quite common to have the physics simulator be the master with Simics hidden as a component inside a larger simulation setup. When Simics is being used for computer architecture and hardware validation, it is normal to use Simics as the master simulator. Simics simulates the overall platform and runs the software that the user interacts with, and Simics interaction is needed to set up and boot the target system. When building large network simulations, peer-to-peer synchronization has been successfully used, because the network connection offers a natural peer-level connection between the simulators.

LAUNCHING AND EMBEDDING

There are several options for how and where to run the simulators being integrated. As shown in Figure 9.2, the simulators can be integrated into a single process, run as separate processes on the same host, or even run on separate hosts in the same network.

The embedded solution has primarily been used for computer architecture simulations. In such simulations, it is crucial to have short latencies between the simulators and the detailed simulator's model hardware that is logically part of the overall system. Embedding also requires that it is possible to embed *simulator*

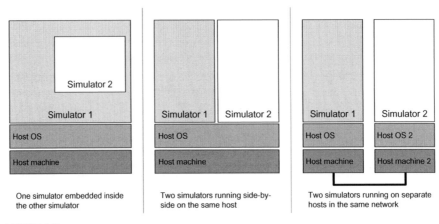

One simulator embedded inside the other simulator

Two simulators running side-by-side on the same host

Two simulators running on separate hosts in the same network

FIGURE 9.2

Simulator physical integration alternatives.

2—not all simulators have that ability. It is very common to find simulators that are built to run as standalone programs with no provision for being embedded.

Running the simulators as separate programs is probably the most common model for physics simulators. Often, the physics simulation system where Simics is being integrated already runs on multiple machines and contains multiple simulators, and adding Simics as yet another program to the overall setup is natural and facilitated by the overall simulation framework. Indeed, seeing setups that contain tens of separate simulators running on multiple hosts is not uncommon for mature simulation-based development setups.

When using separate programs, one simulator might launch the other simulator, or the two simulators might be started independently and then linked up. Both approaches are possible, and both approaches have been used. It comes down to how programs are launched, and how multiple program launches can be coordinated.

EMBEDDING SIMICS

It should be noted that Simics has the ability to be embedded as a slave inside another master simulator. There is a special library that can be loaded into another program, allowing it to start a Simics simulation. In this mode, the master simulation uses function calls to ask Simics to execute Simics commands, which in turn can make Simics run. Simics does not return to the caller until it has stopped, so usually the master simulator asks Simics to run for a bounded period of time. Note that it is possible to create more sophisticated setups where Simics keeps running, communicating with the master simulator using some other mechanism.

Simics embedding has been employed both to use Simics as a component in a larger computer-focused simulation, as well as a way to use Simics as an execution engine controlled from some a physics simulator.

TIME MANAGEMENT

Dealing correctly with time is very important to make a simulator integration work well. In most systems, semantics is closely tied to time. For example, when using a simulation of a physical process alongside a Simics simulation of a computer system, it is important to make sure that when Simics computes for one virtual second, the same amount of time passes in the physics simulation. If this is not the case, results will quickly deviate from what could be expected.

Time is often the most difficult thing to get right, because different simulators can handle time in rather different ways. In Simics, time is a set of temporally decoupled clocks, each with a local time expressed in cycles but convertible to seconds. In other computer simulators, time can be the count of instructions executed or the number of cycles spent. For a physics simulation, time is typically a continuous variable expressed in seconds. There are also simulations where logical event counts provide the time base, with no relationship to any concept of real time. In some simulators such as QEMU or virtual machines like VMware and VirtualBox, the host clock is used to provide time to the simulated system, with no attempt made to use a virtual time internal to the simulator. Thus, when integrating a simulator, the type of time kept and how it is kept have to be taken into consideration.

Time must always be kept as a property of the simulation. For Simics this is achieved by using virtual time as described in Chapter 2. If time is measured as the real time of the combined system as it runs on the host, it will be impossible to produce repeatable results and to control the data rates. For example, generating sensor readings or network packets at a certain rate is trivial as long as all times are kept virtual—it would not matter how much time it takes to compute each value or packet. If host time is used, the execution speed of the simulators would limit the achievable data rates and also make them essentially unpredictable and uncontrollable. A simulator needs a concept of simulated or virtual time to make sense.

SYNCHRONIZATION INTERVALS

For performance, it is necessary to let the integrated simulators run decoupled for some time before synchronizing their time. If time is synchronized at each atomic time unit, almost all time will be spent synchronizing and no time will be spent actually running the simulation forward. Thus, it is necessary to apply some amount of temporal decoupling to the simulators involved, just like Simics itself applies temporal decoupling to multiple processors within a single Simics process. The larger the time quanta, the faster the simulation can be expected to run, as discussed for Simics internally in Chapter 2.

Time synchronization is closely tied to run control—in a master–slave setup, the master simulator usually orders the slave simulator to run for a certain amount of time before stopping. If a simulator is embedded inside another simulator, this is done using a simple function call. If the simulators run side by side, it is part of the communications protocol between the simulators. In a peer-to-peer setup, the two simulators will continuously update each other on how far they have run and thus how far ahead they are allowed to run.

This use of temporal decoupling between simulators has implications for when the simulators are allowed to and able to exchange information. The simplest solution that often works well is to have the simulators exchange information at the end of each time quantum. This means that all events crossing between the simulators will happen at a discrete and quantified time in the other simulator, but as long as the time quanta are kept reasonable with regard to the domain being studied, this should not skew the overall simulation results. For example, with control systems, there is often a given sample rate for each algorithm. Keeping the time quanta shorter to or equal to the sample time produces a working integration where the temporal decoupling is not really visible to the software and the controlled system. There are designs for parallel event simulations that try to roll back time if an interaction happens within a time quantum, but in practice such rollback is difficult to achieve and of limited value compared to the cost of implementation.

SIMICS TEMPORAL DECOUPLING

When using Simics with a detailed computer architecture simulator to study detailed performance characteristics of a target system, in particular for caches, shared memory, and other shared resources, temporal decoupling should not be used, or used with very short time quanta. Using a long time quantum of several thousand cycles, as is commonly done in Simics, will give a false picture of the contention for shared resources, as each processor, or other active component, will see itself as alone in the system for its entire time slice. This has been shown to produce dramatically skewed results. A good rule of thumb is that the time quantum needs to be less than the shortest time in which contention can occur. Most computer architecture researchers tend to set the time quantum to a single cycle or a few cycles, as that provides the most realistic simulation results.

Another effect of temporal decoupling is that if an external simulator looks at the virtual Simics time when observable events occur, it might see time jump back and forth. For example, if all data sent from Simics is time stamped with the time of the processor generating it, the sequence of data could have later data items time stamped with a time earlier than the data preceding it. This tends to break simulators that assume that time increases monotonically. The solution is to make sure that the communications module that connects Simics to the outside world does the time stamping, and ensures that time increases monotonically.

SIMICS AND SYSTEMC TIME

The integration of Simics simulations with SystemC simulations provides a good case study of how to deal with simulator time. The SystemC kernel has a single global time that is used in all parts of a SystemC simulation, while Simics has a set of local times, one for each processor or clock in the system. As shown in Figure 9.3, when SystemC is used inside of Simics, a complete SystemC kernel with its scheduler is present as a subsystem. The time of the SystemC device (or set of devices) is synchronized with the time of the Simics processor core to which it is associated, just like any Simics device gets its time from a particular processor in the system. This means that the SystemC subsystem has a single internal time, but at the same time, other times exist in the Simics system.

When it comes to synchronization, the standard approach is to precisely synchronize the simulation time of the SystemC kernel and the Simics processor core time. SystemC time is always in the past or at the current Simics time, and it is never allowed to run ahead of Simics. When an access from Simics to SystemC happens, the SystemC system is run forward to the current Simics time. At such a

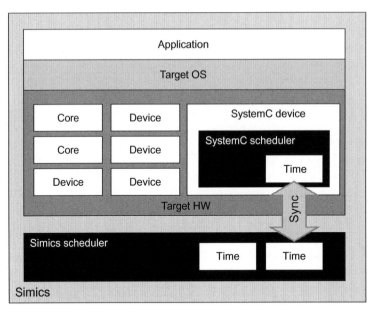

FIGURE 9.3

SystemC in Simics.

point, SystemC time and Simics time are equivalent, and reading the current virtual time on either side results in the same value. If the SystemC device needs to create events that happen in the future, Simics will schedule Simics events matching the time of these future events. When the events happen in Simics, Simics calls the SystemC subsystem to bring time up to date, just like for other accesses from Simics to SystemC. This model is implemented in the Simics SystemC Bridge and its research precursors (Montón et al., 2009).

Such tight time synchronization might not always be the correct answer. When the main goal is to simulate the functional effect of software running on Simics on the hardware simulated in SystemC, it is often sufficient to get the right *sequence* of events. The precise time of memory accesses and interrupts does not matter to get the desired result. This makes it possible to optimize the performance of detailed SystemC models running within Simics by making time run slower in SystemC than in Simics. If the SystemC simulator needs to run an event at time t, the simulator integration schedules it at some multiple of t. This increases locality and increases performance quite significantly. The drawback is that certain polling loops will run slower, because the SystemC subsystem will evolve slower in virtual time (Khan and Wolfe, 2013).

SystemC models that post very frequent events will cause severe performance degradation using the aforementioned scheme. The reason is that the Simics processor that is acting as the event queue on behalf of SystemC will constantly context-switch into and out of SystemC. This causes bad code locality and can prevent JIT compilation from taking place. In such a case it can make sense to run the SystemC kernel as its own Simics clock, assigning it a quantum of its own. This situation is typically most common for *active* device models that must continuously be activated to perform some activity. Most Simics device models are passive, meaning that they are only activated when a rare event is triggered or when they are accessed through an interface.

COMMUNICATIONS

Communicating information between the integrated simulators is necessary to get any value out of the integration. Almost every existing mechanism for interprocess communication has been used at some point to integrate simulators. For embedded simulators, function calls, global variables, and other variants of shared memory are the most common.

For separate simulators, standard networking sockets are probably the most common transport, with shared files being second. Shared memory between processes is also used where large amounts of data need to be shared and the simulators are running on the same host OS instance. APIs that are specific to the host's operating system, such as Windows RPC, have also been used. When Simics replaces specific embedded hardware boards, real-network mechanisms like host-serial have been used where Simics presents a virtual serial port on the host, to which host-based programs connect just like they would connect to a real board.

DEDICATED COMMUNICATIONS MODULES

As mentioned in Chapters 2 and 5, a Simics device module should never interact directly with the outside world. Instead, as shown in Figure 9.4, all external communications should be handled by a separate communications module. Such a

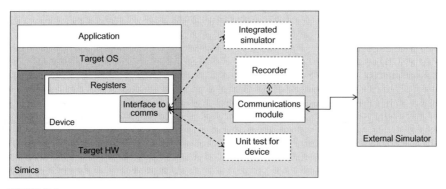

FIGURE 9.4

Isolate the device from the environment.

split simplifies the implementation of the Simics device model, and it makes it possible to reuse the same communications module with many different devices that talk to the same simulator. It allows the device to be tested within Simics without having the external simulator available; unit tests can feed data directly to the device via the interface. The communications interface will most likely be a custom Simics interface appropriate for the semantics of the simulator in use, just like discussed for custom networks in Chapter 5.

As shown in Figure 9.4, this architecture makes it easy to apply a recorder to the interaction with the outside world, because the communications module will look identical to the device whether it is replaying an old session or feeding it a live session. This enables record–replay debugging, as discussed later. It is also possible to move the implementation of the external simulator into Simics and keep the device unchanged. Typically, the communications module that talks to the outside uses TCP/IP via network sockets and the `SIM_notify` family of calls to react to asynchronous inputs. These functions allow a callback function to be called with an argument whenever a specific I/O event occurs on the host machine.

DEVICES FOR I/O

The ultimate goal of integrating physics simulators with Simics is usually to test and assess the behavior of the target software when interacting with the environment. In particular, control loops where the target software reads some values from the environment, computes control law outputs, and sends the outputs to the world via some actuator.

The most straightforward way to handle the input and output is via simulated I/O devices in the target system. Simics would model the full target system, including its I/O hardware devices, and the software runs on it just like it would on the physical hardware. Figure 9.5 shows a typical setup, where sensor readings

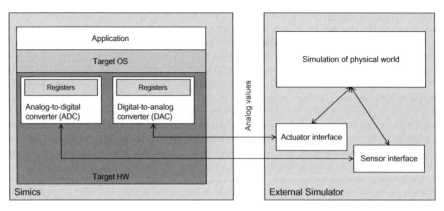

FIGURE 9.5

Typical I/O integration.

are brought into the software stack via an analog-to-digital converter (ADC), and actuator outputs are sent out via a digital-to-analog converter (DAC). The ADC and DAC accesses are either done directly from the application software, or more commonly via some device driver layer. The same code for input and output is being used as would be used in the real system. Note that for simplicity, Figure 9.5 does not show the simulator integration module that handles the communication between Simics and the external simulator.

In Figure 9.5, the values are transported to and from the external simulator as virtual analog values, usually floating-point values within some specified range. In the external simulator, some kind of model of the sensor and actuator is needed to convert between the values exchanged with Simics and the internal variables and state representation of the physics model. The inputs and outputs could also be digital values, in case the interface to the external simulator is in communication via GPIO, I^2C, CAN, MIL-STD-1553, or similar control buses. It depends on the design of the physical target system and the nature of the external simulator.

BYPASSING DEVICES

Another way to achieve input and output is to use the *Simics debugger functionality* to read and write memory locations directly, as shown in Figure 9.6. The target software defines its output and input in terms of global variables located somewhere in the target memory. The simulator integration module would read the output variables to tell the external variables what the software is trying to do, and write values to the input variables to provide input to the software. The values read would then be passed on to the external physics simulator, and values from the physics simulator would be written to the input variables.

Reading and writing global variables to drive software is actually quite common on hardware test setups, where hardware debuggers are used to drive tests of

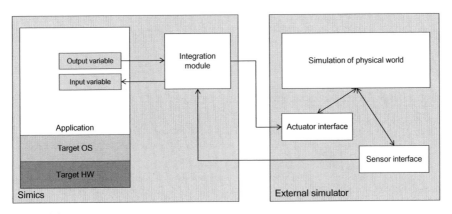

FIGURE 9.6

Reading and writing variables.

control software without the need for simulating real I/O streams over real I/O ports. When such setups exist, it makes sense to use the same methods with Simics to achieve commonality between the Simics setup and the hardware setup.

PUSH OR PULL

The data flow between the information generator and consumer can be orchestrated in a number of ways. At a high level, communications can be orchestrated using push or pull. Which mode of interaction to use depends on the latency of communications and the nature of the simulator being integrated with Simics.

In a *pull* setup, the Simics-side consumer of data requests information whenever it needs new data. Pull works best if the communications have low latency, because it essentially pauses the requesting device or module until a value has been returned. Thus, it is most commonly used for embedded simulators or simulators communicating using shared memory. Figure 9.7 shows an example of an ADC in a virtual platform connected to a sensor in a physics simulator. Using a pull method, each read from the ADC would result in a request to the physics simulator, which would need to reply before the read could be completed. If this communication was realized over a network socket, and something happened to the reply, the main Simics thread could get stuck hanging on a network socket indefinitely.

In general, any memory access call from a processor to a device in Simics needs to return as quickly as possible. Performing a complete network send—receive cycle inside the device is bad practice. If the semantics of the processor integration requires a pull model, it is best to do the pulling from a separate communications module as depicted in Figure 9.4. The communications module would regularly pull values from the attached simulator, and then store the latest value for the device model to read. From the perspective of the device, this is equivalent to the push model.

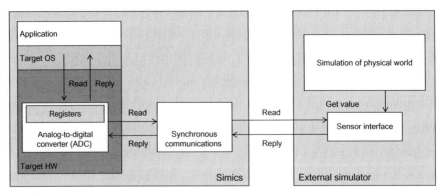

FIGURE 9.7

Pull communications.

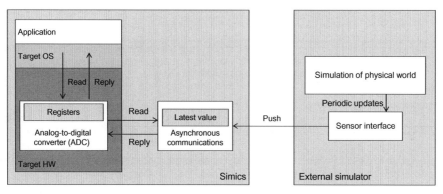

FIGURE 9.8

Push communications.

In a *push* setup, the generator of data pushes updates to Simics whenever a new piece of data is produced. This requires that Simics is able to accept data asynchronously, having some thread running waiting for input at all times. In Simics, the best way to realize this is a dedicated communications module as discussed before. The incoming data is buffered until such time that it is needed. In the ADC example shown in Figure 9.8, the physics simulator would send a steady stream of current values for the sensor to the computer simulator, typically one value for each time step of the simulator. Every time an ADC read was done by the software, the device would reply with the latest value seen. The main issue with a push communications model is to avoid sending lots of information that will never be used—something like a clock signal that changes value rapidly is not suitable for a push communications model.

The preceding discussion focuses on the issue of reading data from the external simulator in the Simics system. Writing is normally simpler, because it is a one-way process and Simics does not need to get a reply back before the simulation can continue. Obviously, this means that Simics expects the other simulator to be able to accept pushed data asynchronously. This has been found to be the common case, but if it is not, the Simics communications module will have to buffer outgoing writes until such a time that the other simulator requests them. That is, when it does a pull to get new data.

ABSTRACTION LEVEL CHANGE AND TRANSACTORS

When integrating different simulators, and in particular different computer simulators, the abstraction level of the simulators needs to be bridged and data translated.

For physics simulations, this is often just a matter of format conversion: there has to be agreement on how to communicate values from the physical world to and from Simics, but value exchange happens as a single transaction in a

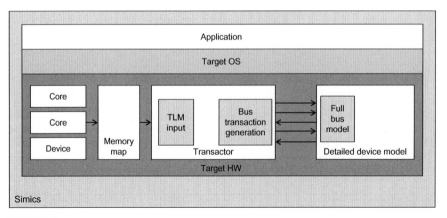

FIGURE 9.9

Functionality of a transactor.

TLM-friendly manner. For network systems, network packets provide a natural exchange level. However, even here it might be necessary to convert from one representation of a network packet to another, including dealing with issues like adding or removing checksums and translating hardware addresses.

For computer architecture simulations where Simics transaction-level modeling is integrated with a more detailed computer architecture model, the translation is complicated by the additional need to *change the abstraction level*. While Simics just delivers a single transaction for a memory access, a detailed model requires a series of bus transactions to be performed. The translation is handled by a module called a *transactor*, as shown in Figure 9.9. The transactor generates the details left out of the transaction-level model. This provides a sufficient level of detail for the device under test without burdening the entire simulation system with the detail level.

A transactor by nature deviates from the standard Simics model that memory operations take no virtual time from start to finish. The way that this is typically resolved is to let the transactor play through the whole transaction with the detailed model, and once it is done, push time in Simics forward to match the time the operation took. This can be done by either using a processor in stall mode or by using the SIM_stall API call to make the calling processor jump forward in time without executing any more instructions. If there is no desire to keep the time in the detailed device model and in Simics itself in sync, the whole operation can be allowed to take zero time on the Simics side and multiple cycles on the detailed side.

STATE TRANSFER IN CHECKPOINTS

When using gear-shifting with checkpoints, it is necessary to map or transfer the state from the Simics model to the detailed model. The implementation-independent design of Simics checkpoints greatly facilitates this, because all information is encoded in a text format that can be parsed by other simulators and that clearly defines and describes the functional architectural state of the target system.

Because Simics only models the functional architectural state of the target system, there will be details missing when changing to a detailed simulator. Figure 9.10 shows a conceptual picture of the state kept by Simics and a general detailed processor core simulator. The functional architectural state of the processor is much smaller than the detailed state and is typically straightforward to map into the detailed model. There is also some state peculiar to the Simics implementation of the processor core, and this will either need to be stripped out or converted to the simulator-internal state of the detailed simulator.

The basic translation from a fast function model like Simics to a detailed model leaves a large part of the detailed simulator state in a blank state. Aspects like the cache, branch predictor, pipeline, and prefetching mechanisms need to get to a realistic state before timing and power measurements can be made. Thus, it is standard practice to run the detailed simulator for some time before starting to take measurements in order to warm up its state.

Trying to go in the other direction, from a detailed to functional state, is much harder. The problem is that the many speculative mechanisms in a modern processor core leave the instantaneous architectural state somewhat difficult to find. For example, there is really no "current instruction" when there are dozens of instructions simultaneously in various stages of execution, and where an instruction yet to start execution might trigger an exception that requires squashing many instructions that have been speculatively finished. The only practical way to get to a clearly defined architectural state is to drain all pipelines and buffers by executing a large number of NOPs or similar operations. This obviously

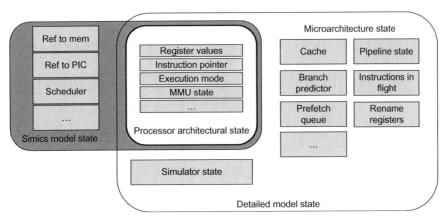

FIGURE 9.10

State of Simics core model and detailed core model.

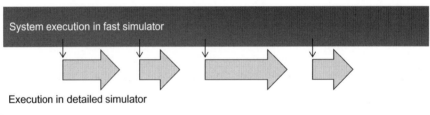

System execution in fast simulator

Execution in detailed simulator

FIGURE 9.11

Dropping into detailed mode.

changes the program flow, making it fairly pointless to move back into the functional simulator in this manner.

Therefore, it tends to be simpler and faster to let the fast simulator simulate the entire run of a system, and use checkpoints taken at various points as the starting point for detailed simulations, as shown in Figure 9.11. Instead of switching back from detailed to functional mode, the simulation is simply reset to the point in time before the simulation was switched from functional to detailed mode. The simulation is then continued from this point. Because the functional model is typically orders of magnitude faster than the detailed model, the time required to run the portion of the simulation that was run in detailed mode twice, once in detailed mode and once in functional mode, is negligible.

FRONTENDS

When a simulator is embedded inside another simulator or at least controlled from it, its user interface tends to be hidden. Ideally, the slave simulator can display its status to the user for inspection, even if the slave simulator cannot control the status. Any control to the slave simulator would have to be passed through the master, or things would quickly get out of control.

When Simics is used as a slave simulator, it is quite common to see the master simulator issue Simics commands to control Simics and often provide the end user with access to Simics features through its own interface. Simics modules are able to execute Simics CLI commands using the SIM_run_command function, and they can also use the Simics API to control Simics and inspect and change the simulation state. The Simics debugger is typically not available, nor is interactive Simics simulation control. The simplest way to get the full set of Simics features for software debugging available is to use a record–replay debugging as discussed later.

When Simics is used as the master, it is standard procedure to add Simics CLI commands to control and configure the slave simulator. This makes it possible to script scenarios in Simics that affect both the target system simulated in Simics and the system simulated in the other simulator.

RUNNING SIMICS FROM OTHER PROGRAMS

When running Simics as part of a larger simulation consisting of multiple separate simulators, from a test management system, and similar, Simics needs to be started from some other program. This is basically achieved by using Simics as a command-line program, using scripts and command-line parameters to set up the simulation.

The most common method is to start Simics using the host command line and then use some mechanism, as discussed before, to communicate with Simics. Simics typically starts by running a Simics script file that creates an appropriate target system and instantiates the communications channel to the external simulator. Arguments are provided using the Simics command-line -e option to pass Simics variable values, like this:

```
./simics  -e  "$variable=value"  start-integrated-system.simics  -e
"continue".
```

This command first sets up a Simics variable called $variable to have a certain *value*. It then runs the Simics script start-integrated-system.simics, and once that script is done it tells Simics to start the simulation with the continue command.

To simplify the management of the target system and software issues found during a run on Simics, it is recommended that the start script creates a checkpoint of the target setup and uses a Simics recording to provide a session checkpoint. This makes it possible to later reproduce the run without the involvement of the external simulator, as discussed later in the section "Record–Replay Debugging of Target Software."

VIRTUAL LAB MANAGEMENT

Starting Simics from the command line can be accomplished from any kind of launcher, and this has been done many times to run Simics from various execution and scheduling engines. Simics has been run on a wide variety of clusters, compute grids, and cloud computing infrastructures, because it is essentially just a regular user-level program that can be run from a CLI. A key part of such a setup is having a daemon that can start Simics.

An overview of a typical daemon system is provided in Figure 9.12. There is a client that connects to the daemon and asks the daemon to start a Simics session for it. Once the Simics session is started, the daemon hands back the information needed to connect and control Simics to the client. The client can then connect to Simics and perform whatever tasks it wants.

The daemon provides the persistent process that is always available, while the Simics sessions come and go. Simics is used in the same way as any other tool: it is invoked to do some work, it does the work, and it is then terminated. It does

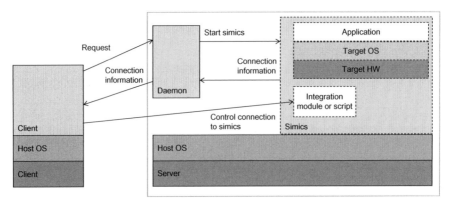

FIGURE 9.12

Simics started by a daemon.

not make sense to have Simics running as a virtual board that is active all the time and managed exactly like a virtual board, because that does not enable most of the benefits from using a virtual platform. The Simics launch daemons typically have to be created by Simics users to fit in whatever lab management and user authentication systems they are using.

Another issue that needs to be handled via the daemon or some other system is to provision the Simics system with the files it needs and to collect any resulting files. Any Simics run needs to start from some particular setup, be it a checkpoint of a running system or a fresh boot from a new system image. These files need to be made available on the server running Simics. This can be achieved in many different ways: shared file systems on file servers, checking out virtual file systems from systems like ClearCase, pulling files from version control like Git or Subversion, grabbing files from software build servers, or uploading files using a protocol like HTTP or FTP—it comes down to what is most convenient in a particular working environment.

RECORD–REPLAY DEBUGGING OF TARGET SOFTWARE

When running Simics together with another simulator or from a lab management system, it is often difficult to use Simics as an interactive environment and in particular as an interactive debugger. The other simulator typically requires Simics to be running to make the integration work, and it might be expecting to control Simics' terminal inputs and outputs. There can be scripts running that do not appreciate the user entering text into target consoles. Simics might be terminated once a run is complete or a particular output is achieved. Simics often has no visible user interface at all, being that it is used as a background process by another program or it is possibly running on a remote machine.

Thus, trying to get into the target system to debug its software and functionality as the simulation session is running is generally difficult. However, it is still possible to debug the target code and inspect the simulated system by taking advantage of Simics' session checkpoints to do record–replay debugging of the Simics part of the simulation, as discussed in Chapter 3.

As shown in Figure 9.13, during the run with the external simulator attached, the simulator integration module records all relevant inputs from the external simulator. This is typically all input data coming from the outside, as well as other events such as synchronization messages and the opening and closing of the connection. During the replay run, the integration module gets its input from the recording instead of from the external simulator. The key is to record everything that is relevant for the integration, so that exactly the same simulator state appears in the replay session. During the replay session, the integration must not open any external ports or try to interact with the outside world—all it should do is accept input from the recording and make sure that any outputs from Simics are squashed. There is no other simulator there to accept them, anyhow. All Simics debugging features are available in the replay run.

Record–replay can also be used when integrating device models into Simics. When a foreign device model does not support checkpointing or reverse execution, the integration code can still record all operations passing between Simics and the device model. The simulation session can then be replayed using the recording instead of the foreign device model, enabling full software debugging and reverse execution for the recorded slice of time.

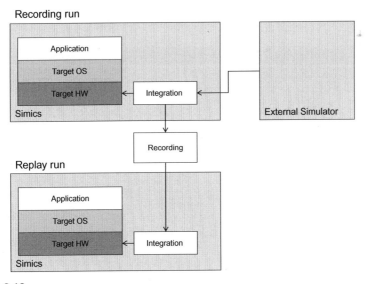

FIGURE 9.13

Record–replay debugging with external simulator.

RUNNING ON A SIMICS TARGET

One approach to using an existing simulation tool with a Simics target is to run the existing simulation tool *on* a Simics target. This makes sense when, in the real world, there already is an existing simulator that runs on some utility machine, and where the application can talk to this simulator over a network. If the network and utility machine needed are available as Simics models, it makes perfect sense to mimic the real-world setup inside of Simics and bring the simulator into Simics as a simulated machine. The resulting setup is shown in Figure 9.14.

The utility machine can be a generic PC running Windows or Linux, corresponding to a case where a generic PC is used in the lab to run simulators, traffic generators, and other such software. However, it is also fairly common for the utility machine to be the same kind of embedded hardware as the target hardware. It is very popular in the networking space to use instances of network equipment as the traffic generator or rest-of-network simulator for the network equipment itself. In a real lab, you would have two instances of the target system connected over a network, and the Simics setup is also two instances of the target system.

Time synchronization is trivial for this setup. Because it is essentially cloning a real-world setup into Simics, as long as the execution on the main target and the utility machine have the same relative speed as in the real world, it will just work. Time can also be used to play tricks on the target system—by varying the virtual speed of the utility machine relative to the target machine, it is possible to create much heavier network loads than are possible in the real world, in particular when the target machine is built to handle large loads.

The main cost of running the simulator on a Simics target is that it requires more work to simulate the utility machine inside of Simics rather than running

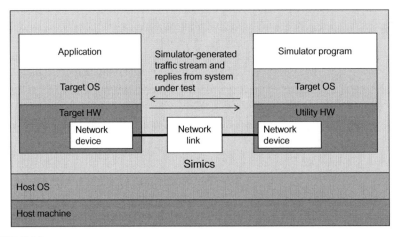

FIGURE 9.14

Running a simulator on a simulated machine.

the simulator program directly on the Simics host. On the other hand, it has the benefit of bringing the external simulator into Simics, producing instant check-pointability and reversibility. Simics is clearly the master in this case, because the other simulator literally runs under its control. For the common case where the additional machines are standard Intel®-based PCs, the fast VMP execution mode together with Simics' multithreading typically makes the overhead negligible, and the benefits far outweigh the drawbacks.

MULTIPLE SIMULATOR APIS

When models are to be used in multiple simulator contexts, one possible approach is to create an interposer API or a shim layer. This API is used to create models, and an implementation for the API is provided both for Simics and for other sim-ulator APIs such as SystemC. This approach makes it possible to reuse the same model code in multiple types of simulators without having to maintain multiple versions of the same model. The language of such multiple-simulation-system models is usually plain C or C++, but it can also be full SystemC (Khan and Wolfe, 2013).

The facilities exposed by the API that is used to target multiple simulators can either be common subset, or the features of most expressive simulators. For Simics, the best results are achieved when the API exposes important Simics fea-tures such as checkpointing, reverse execution, logging, and breakpoints. Features not available in other simulators can simply be compiled to dummy code that does nothing.

This single-API approach is very similar to what is commonly used for devel-oping real-time and embedded systems code, where a company creates their own generic API, and all their programs are written targeting this API. The API is then implemented for various real-time operating systems, providing code porta-bility across operating systems and architecture (Möller et al., 2005).

SIMICS PROCESSOR API

Simics has a dedicated API available for integrating external processor simulators into Simics target systems. This API allows for a simulator provided by a user to take the place of a Simics processor in the Simics system, including driving time queues and step queues. It is the method of choice for integrating an existing pro-cessor simulator into Simics, both for computer architecture studies and to use an existing processor simulator instead of writing a Simics processor model.

The API consists of a number of separate APIs, not all of which need to be implemented. The more of the APIs that are implemented, the more Simics func-tionality will be enabled for the processor. It is thus possible to use the API with different levels of ambition, from basically just enabling the processor to run code, all the way up to processors that support debugger breakpoints, checkpointing, and reverse execution.

The result of using the Simics processor API fully is a Simics module that is indistinguishable from a native Simics processor core model. From the perspective of Simics, it is a processor model like any other—even if it internally contains a full separate simulation framework. A user can also program directly to the Simics processor API, creating a Simics processor model without any other simulator being involved. There have been cases where existing simulator frameworks have been stripped out of processor models and replaced with the Simics processor API, creating what is essentially a native Simics processor core even if the starting point was a separate simulator.

Intel® architecture bring-up

10

Contributed by Alexey Veselyi and Denis Vladimirov

*People will realize that software is not a product;
you use it to build a product.*
—Linus Torvalds

At Intel, one of the major use cases of Simics is to help software and hardware bring-up, starting from the early pre-silicon stages. With the help of Simics, a functional model of future Intel hardware can be made available to BIOS and driver developers a year or even more ahead of engineering hardware samples. This approach allows development of hardware-dependent low-level software in parallel with the development of the hardware. Additionally, close collaboration with hardware developers allows the team of Simics engineers to perform a certain amount of validation of early hardware specifications, speeding up the hardware development process as well. These practices lead to cost savings by reducing product time-to-market—that is, the "shift left."

This chapter describes the collaboration processes that are established to speed up Intel® Architecture bring-up, as well as examples of what Simics has to offer in the world of modern Intel Architecture software and hardware. Starting with work performed pre-silicon, the chapter also covers use cases and scenarios implemented in the post-silicon stage—Simics continues to be very useful even after actual hardware becomes available.

PRE-SILICON PROCESS

Developing a model of pre-silicon hardware requires a different approach from modeling existing hardware. The process is more iterative because the hardware specification and the model evolve in parallel. The pre-silicon modeling process outlined in Figure 10.1 is commonly used at Intel and is in line with the general recommendations in Chapter 6.

Development of a new platform generally consists of a new Platform Controller Hub (PCH, previously commonly known as a southbridge), new uncore devices and feature set, new core functionality, and requirements for new BIOS/ OS support. Depending on the platform, some devices can be taken from a

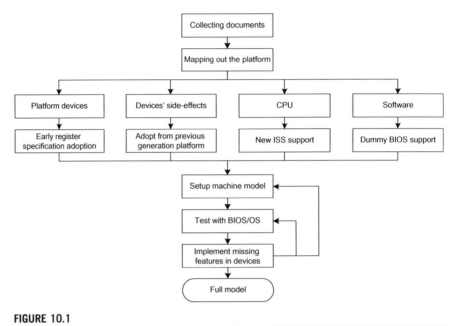

FIGURE 10.1

Pre-silicon modeling process.

previously developed platform. The hardware block reuse across different Intel Architecture platforms makes model reuse quite likely. Simics itself can be used as a big part of the pre-silicon process, allowing adoption of early drops of new device register layouts provided by the hardware architects, new instruction set support, and early BIOS/OS bring-up.

EARLY COLLABORATION WITH HARDWARE ARCHITECTS

Simics model developers can start implementation of the hardware model using the earliest available device register specifications. The model that appears during the early specifications period is only an outline of the future model, although parts that resemble those of a legacy platform can be fully functional already at this stage. In many cases, Intel® Architecture hardware is developed incrementally, and functionality is inherited from legacy platforms where possible.

The Simics model developers become one of the first consumers of the register specification and they are able to find several types of specification errors significantly earlier than it is possible using other validation options. In some cases, model developers provide a perspective unavailable to other options (Veseyi and Ayers, 2013). This increases the hardware architects' confidence in the maturity of the specifications and ensures that software will be able to make use of the hardware features.

The approach detects not only register construction errors, but also validate key architectural specifications against legacy-derived behavioral assumptions.

Additionally, Simics creates the possibility to define high-level functional tests for the new platform based on the same legacy assumptions. These tests can cover most of the platform's functionality with the exception of features that are new or being heavily redefined. Being part of an integration test system, such an approach gives the opportunity to provide feedback to hardware architects for every register definition release.

Based on the experience from such collaborations between Simics model developers and hardware architects within Intel® during development of Intel® Xeon® chips, Simics can find bugs in both the register address attributes and the PCI/PCIe device configuration settings. The ability to have early validation testing provides timely feedback on the project specification documents and helps shift earlier the delivery of key external specifications. More information on such collaboration between hardware architects and Simics teams is described by Veseyi and Ayers (2013).

NEW INSTRUCTION SET SUPPORT AND USAGE

With almost every new announced Intel® processor core, new instruction sets are being added to the Intel® Architecture. Internally, even more instruction set extensions are being explored and evaluated. Every new instruction set extension usually brings a number of new operations with complex semantics and ever-increasing variants of machine encoding.

It is crucial to have simulator support for new instruction sets at an early stage of exploration, because this opens the path for development of essential software tools, such as compilers, firmware, and binary translators.

However, supporting all new instructions in a software simulator is a challenging task. Defining new instruction semantics and expanding existing decoders and disassemblers is nontrivial and very costly. The requirements for instruction set simulator (ISS) quality are usually much higher than those for a platform model, making it crucial to properly test each one of the instructions. In addition, some instructions can break legacy design assumptions in the ISS. Because of this, implementing new instructions can lead to massive rewrites of stable code and performance degradation.

To avoid this, the Simics team has created a tool chain to generate decoder, disassembler, and simulation service routines of individual instructions from a single definition. The method allows keeping all instruction definitions together in one place in a consistent form, automatically checking for conflicts and generating code.

The implementations of certain ISA subsets are shared with another Intel-developed ISS called *zsim*. Such instructions do not use the normal Simics tool chain, so another way is needed for the simulator to recognize these instructions during simulation. For this, a high-quality decoder called XED is used. XED is also used in such Intel® products as Pin and Intel® Software Development Emulator (Intel® SDE). The ability to use several decoders and interpreters in the same system is achieved by invoking them in a defined order. External decoders are called only when an internal one fails to recognize an instruction, as shown in

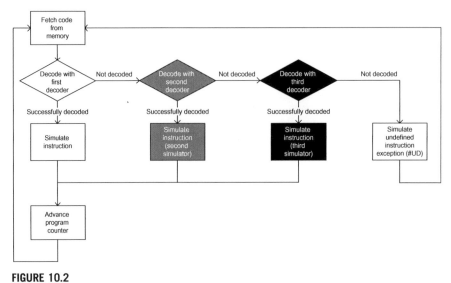

FIGURE 10.2

Intel® architecture instruction decode flow.

Figure 10.2. This approach allows the Simics team to quickly extend CPU models without the need to modify the core model code.

With Simics, it is easy to use a new CPU model with a previous-generation platform model. Some new instructions, such as vector computation extensions, are independent of the overall platform architecture. In this case, developers of compilers, binary translators, and other code can make use of the model very early in the product lifecycle.

COLLECTING REQUIREMENTS FROM CUSTOMERS

As the specifications mature, the modeling team approaches the BIOS development stage, and later the driver development stage, with a functional model that already works. The early pre-silicon work on model development naturally leads on to pre-silicon software and hardware codevelopment and, subsequently, post-silicon validation. The model is built incrementally, addressing each use case in turn, keeping it agile in the early stages and moving toward a stable and well-tested model for the later stages.

By the time the specification for a new hardware platform is set, at least on the high level, software developers, validators, and other future users of the Simics model create a requirements list for the platform model. The document with such requirements scope and schedule is called a *model development request* (MDR). The primary purpose of the MDR is to capture all requirements necessary to understand the scope of the simulator, schedule and prioritize the work, and fully productize the virtual platform.

The first draft of the MDR contains the requirements as they are seen at the time of the platform's creation. As the platform design progresses, requirements can be added, removed, or changed. During development, it is required that customers provide timely updates of the MDR, and that the simulation solution and its development schedule remain up-to-date with the latest requirements.

The MDR should contain links to the hardware documentation and instructions on how to obtain access to it. The general approach here is as follows: it is better to have maximum specifications available before development starts; full document coverage makes it possible to deduce the required scope of work, even if some of the documentation is not used for actual model development.

The model development process is usually split into stages, or *phases*, that target to approximately match those of BIOS and other software development. This helps prioritize and schedule work on a higher level. Table 10.1 shows an example of model development milestones in some typical phases.

Note how the development timeframes are specified relative to the specifications availability. However, if specifications are already available or a strict date exists for their release, it is possible to have specific dates in these fields: in the example, phase 4 can be tied to a hardware-specific milestone (tape-in).

Also note that the timeframe is specified in a "desired date/too late after" fashion: meeting the "desired date" point allows the model to contribute to software development shift left and save time and resources required for software development. Failure to provide the required solution until the "too late after" date will lead to software developers failing to meet their schedule as well.

Table 10.1 Example Phase Breakdown for a Simics MDR

Phase 1

Summary: Basic register support—no side effects, basic register access
Desired date: Register availability + 2 weeks
Too late after: Register availability + 5 weeks

Phase 2

Summary: Basic single socket, dual-core platform support, BIOS boot
Desired date: Phase 1 + 4 weeks
Too late after: Phase 1 + 8 weeks

Phase 3

Summary: Basic dual-socket, full core-count support + Linux boot support
Desired date: Phase 2 + 6 weeks
Too late after: Phase 2 + 10 weeks

Phase 4

Summary: Multisocket, max-core platform support + Windows boot support
Desired date: April 25
Too late after: June 10

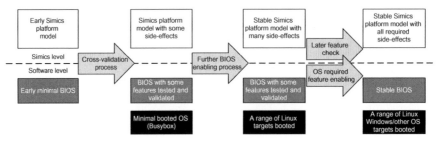

FIGURE 10.3

General BIOS process development using Simics.

BIOS DEVELOPMENT AND ENABLING CAPABILITIES USING SIMICS

BIOS development using Simics is one of the most common use cases of Intel® Architecture–based Simics platforms, for both internal and external teams. Although each team can have its own development process, the general steps for BIOS development using Simics can be found in Figure 10.3. As described earlier, the exact timeframes and Simics platform required features are defined in the specific customer MDR.

The following sections present an overview of several processes related to BIOS development and enabling using Simics: software and simulator cross-validation, UEFI BIOS debugging, specific feature checking, and OS enabling.

SOFTWARE AND SIMULATOR CROSS-VALIDATION

The development phases are set up in such a way that the development of the BIOS and the Simics model are performed simultaneously. This leads to the following issue: it is impossible to validate the correctness of either the Simics model or the BIOS, because there is nothing stable to validate against.

Attempting to overcome this limitation (which is inherent to the use-case scenario itself) leads to the establishment of *cross-validation* between the software and the model. BIOS and Simics engineers are working independently from the same hardware specifications, so the same functionality is implemented twice: once in the BIOS and once in the model.

If the model reacts the way the BIOS expects it to, and, equivalently from the other perspective, the BIOS behaves in a way expected by the model, a certain amount of confidence in both the BIOS and the model is established. Whenever a run does not go as expected, both teams perform debugging—separately or together within a joint debugging session—to figure out the root cause.

Because of this, it is not recommended to provide Simics engineers with BIOS source code. Having access to the sources can tempt the Simics engineers to start *enabling the code* instead of creating a model *from the actual specifications* that can run and validate any software. In addition, the BIOS code is complex and often requires BIOS engineering expertise to properly understand the behavior. Thus, the best approach is to work closely with BIOS and driver engineers as more and more features are enabled in software and in the model.

Simics does not offer complete validation of the BIOS code. There are two reasons for this: Simics does not attempt to implement 100% of the hardware functionality, and the model and the BIOS can share the same bug, either by accident or because of some ambiguity in the documentation. Some errors are found using emulation (a very resource-consuming process involving register-transaction-level full-chip, or at least full-block, emulation), or even on real hardware engineering samples. After they are corrected in the BIOS, Simics should change its behavior as well if the error is within the scope of the model.

Both software and Simics engineers can find errors in hardware specifications during this collaboration scenario. Errors that are missed will be found during emulation runs or in actual hardware. The later a bug is found, the more expensive it is to find and fix it. Using Simics has proved to dramatically decrease the number of bugs found after power-on, because of both the input from the Simics team and increased maturity of the BIOS code at the power-on stage.

Simics can engage in a similar process with a driver development team. The difference for the Simics team is mostly the width and breadth of the required focus: while the BIOS development requires whole platform and board setup, and system-wide development and testing, collaboration with driver developers requires focus on one or several devices, but usually in much more detail.

UEFI BIOS DEBUG

As discussed already in Chapter 3, UEFI BIOS debugging is an application of the general Simics debugger. The same debugger is used for BIOS code, OS code, and application code.

Going deeper to the required steps for UEFI BIOS support, several steps can be defined:

1. Special Simics packages must be installed on the customer side to enable UEFI BIOS debugging capabilities.
2. UEFI BIOS should be compiled with optimizations turned off.
3. BIOS image and its `.map` file have to be provided to Simics:

```
if not defined bios { $bios = "UEFI_BIOS.fd" }
if not defined map_file { map_file = "SimicsUefiBios.map" }
```

4. After the instantiation phase (see Chapter 3), the `.map` file has to be provided to the `enable-uefi` command: `enable-uefi mapfile = $map_file`.

As UEFI debugging is a part of a common Eclipse integration, it allows using all Simics functionality for debugging: setting source-level breakpoints, saving checkpoints, enabling reverse execution, and so on.

JEDEC MEMORY MODULE SUPPORT

Modern DDR4 modules run with a frequency of up to 2 GHz (4 GHz effectively) and have a parallel I/O bus. Thus, having different delays for each of the wires connecting a memory module to the processor can cause disruption of transactions. The JEDEC DDR specification describes that complex delay measurements are required to interface with memory modules. The delays are specific to the board layout and depend heavily on physical wire length. Delay measurements are conducted by hardware driven by the corresponding low-level firmware. The goal of this firmware code is to fine-tune JEDEC DDR signal delays so that all parallel signals arrive at the DDR modules synchronously.

The firmware code that performs delay measurement is very complex, because it must handle many different boards, DIMM module configurations, and memory slot population schemes. Testing all possible configurations is a challenging task, especially because real hardware is lacking at the early development stages.

The Simics simulation environment provides unique system configuration flexibility, which allows users to create memory configurations of any required complexity. Simics platform models allow altering parameters such as:

- DIMM sockets population
- Memory types: LRDIMM, UDIMM, RDIMM, SODIMM, and so on
- Number of ranks
- Ranks density
- Number of chips
- Direct adjusting memory modules Serial Presence Detect (SPD) data

To test the dependency of firmware behavior on board-line delays, Simics exposes a set of configuration attributes that alter wire feedback, as reported by the model to the software. By providing these capabilities, the Simics simulation environment provides the ability to test all required memory configurations. This also allows increasing firmware code coverage by running firmware on an unsupported configuration and validating firmware error-recovery scenarios.

FAULT INJECTION AND RAS

Simics Intel® Architecture platforms have fault-injection capabilities that allow testing of error handling in the software stack. This functionality is required for the bring-up of reliability, accessibility, and serviceability (RAS) features in Intel® Architecture platforms. The software that benefits from this includes BIOS and OS drivers at both pre-silicon and post-silicon stages. Fault injection is implemented as part of specific device models, like PCIe/IIO (integrated I/O), as well as general mechanisms, like machine check error (MCE) injection. The latter allows covering most error sources in modern Intel® Architecture platforms.

On physical hardware, testing error handling usually requires a lot of additional effort, because it involves implementation of special fault injection or poisoning blocks; this takes silicon space and engineer time. In contrast, a developer using Simics can just intervene in an already available fault propagation path and inject a fault into it. It is as simple as issuing a CLI command once the fault-injection functions have been implemented and packaged. This method has all of Simics' features like predictability and reproducibility, and allows the integration of error testing into an automated test suite (and the ability to run it, for example, as part of continuous integration).

MACHINE CHECK ERRORS

Using the Simics scripting environment, developers can tie a fault injection to specific events in memory or inside a device. Listing 10.1 shows an example of how to inject an MCE when a specific memory range is accessed.

The flow of activity in the simulation when the fault injection from Listing 10.1 happens is illustrated in Figure 10.4. When the target software accesses physical address 0x7ca73000, a CMCI (correctable machine check interrupt) error is generated. As can be seen, the hsx-mca-cmci command takes the Machine Check Architecture (MCA) bank index and the value of the MCA Model-Specific Register (MSR) registers, which include error codes and other information, and generates a CMCI fault in the hardware. This command is device-agnostic; it does not have any knowledge about the error, except what was provided by the user. This allows more flexibility, because if the MCE error-code format is changed in the future, it does not require updating the Simics model; simply providing new values to the command is sufficient. For users close to the hardware design, such a flexible solution makes sense. However, for users downstream, it might be

```
1     # choose an address for breaking
2     $mce_on_address = 0x7ca73000
3
4     # set a 64-byte-long read/write/execute breakpoint on the address
5     $break_id = (break p:$mce_on_address 64 -r -w -x)
6     script-branch {
7        wait-for-breakpoint breakpoint-id = $break_id
8
9        # Using "help" on any command will show
10       # you its arguments and a usage example
11       HaswellServer.mb.nb0.hsx-mca-cmci -reach-threshold \
12                                   index = 1 \
13                                   MCACOD = 0x1234 \
14                                   MSCOD = 0x5678 \
15                                   Other_Info = 0x123 \
16                                   ADDR = $mce_on_address \
17                                   MISC = 0 \
18                                   CET = 3
19    }
```

LISTING 10.1

Injecting an error on memory access.

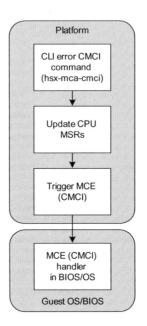

FIGURE 10.4

MCE injection from CLI.

better to build the knowledge of the error into the fault-injection command for better ease-of-use.

DEVICE-SPECIFIC FAULTS

Injection of *device-specific* faults is also supported. Sometimes the injection flow is a bit more complex than to generate an interrupt or an MCE and update a couple of status registers. It may involve analyzing the content of multiple control/mask registers. In that case, a software developer may want to verify that all of these control/mask registers are programmed correctly by the software, in addition to just verifying the correctness of error handling after injection. In an Intel® Architecture platform, PCIe/IIO fault injection is such a case.

AER (advanced error reporting in PCIe) faults injected in PCIe ports propagates to IIO, which, in turn, checks severity/control/mask registers to classify errors and choose the right way to signal it to software. It may be an System Management Interrupt (SMI), an Non-Maskable Interrupt (NMI), or a simple interrupt to the Advanced Programmable Interrupt Controller (APIC) device. Figure 10.5 illustrates the flow. Here is an example command that injects a correctable PCIe error into a Direct Memory Interface (DMI) port: `HaswellServer.mb.nb0.ras_mem. write address = 0x80 value = 0x1 size = 1`.

In this case, an error corresponds to a byte in a special memory space. The user should consult the platform model documentation on the exact mapping of

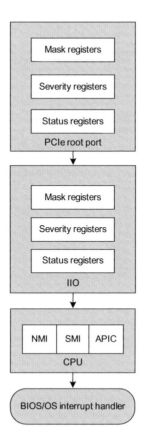

FIGURE 10.5

IIO error injection.

the possible errors to bytes. This mapping would include the complete range of PCIe and IIO errors.

EARLY OS ENABLING

As the BIOS code becomes more or less stable, the OS bring-up process can begin. At the start, drivers are not available for new hardware devices. Early OS enabling is not focused on OS driver development, but is rather focused on checking and removing BIOS errors, which might cause the OS boot sequence to fail on real hardware. There are several methods to make new hardware work with an OS that does not yet support it. The OS enablement process starts pre-silicon and should enable an OS to boot on hardware as soon as the hardware becomes available.

COMPATIBILITY HARDWARE LEVEL FOR LEGACY DRIVERS

Many hardware devices are designed for register-level compatibility with previous generations. They simply add additional capabilities, which are not mandatory to use by default. Even if the register map has changed, devices can provide register aliases or shadow registers to be backward-compatible with legacy (previous-generation) drivers. Even if new functions are not yet supported, the first step for post-BIOS setup is to check that BIOS does not have regression errors and that those devices are still working with the operating system. Ensuring that backward compatibility works is very important for the Intel® Architecture ecosystem.

New devices can be easily modified to be supported by already working legacy drivers of the current operating system. The idea is to replace the PCI configuration *device ID* register of the new device with a value from the previous-generation platform, for example: `dev->pci_config_device_id=0x1234`. This makes an old driver identify the new hardware as old hardware, so it will use the new hardware device in the same way it would use the old hardware device.

The same approach of changing some registers can be used as a common technique of checking that the device is still working although the driver is not updated right now. For example, some device capabilities registers can be changed to their values from previous-generation platforms.

The general limitation of this approach is that device ID (or any other register) might change after the reset routine (platform-based or device-based). Simics provides a capability to break on such events, giving the ability to change the registers every time a reset happens.

Common examples of devices with such "compatibility" capabilities are network interface controllers (NICs), SATA controller devices, and different PCH legacy devices. The hardware-driven creation of a legacy shadow register layer to support previous driver versions, as well as Simics capabilities of manual register overloading, is often helpful for early OS bring-up. It is very useful to be able to "patch" such registers in runtime without having to update or rebuild the model.

BIOS SATA MODE SWITCHING

Before enabling any operating system, it is very convenient for enabling engineers to have the following two BIOS images:

- Image of BIOS in Advanced Host Controller Interface (AHCI) mode (ahci.bin).
- Image of BIOS in Legacy IDE mode (ide.bin).

The reason to create them is the operating system might not have the required AHCI capabilities, or those capabilities are turned off by default, but the BIOS usually runs in AHCI mode by default. This step is also dependent on whether the SATA controller (or the controller model) supports AHCI mode: a legacy platform might not have AHCI support. The images can be created using the following procedure:

1. Run the target script in AHCI mode: `./simics -e '$bios = "ahci.bin"' target-script.simics`.
2. Once BIOS is booted, enter BIOS Setup.
3. In SATA settings, change the mode from AHCI to IDE.
4. Save the changes and reset the platform from the BIOS menu.
5. After the reset, save the BIOS image: `$system.mb.spi_image.save filename = "ide.bin"`.

This shows how Simics can be used to save and reuse persistent software configurations. Creating separate images for every set of often-used BIOS parameters can save a lot of developer time, because a preconfigured BIOS image can simply be pulled into the simulator and used immediately. It also makes it possible to ensure that all settings are set up—a developer manually doing the same configuration over and over is likely to forget something, leading to really hard-to-debug errors.

COMMON OS INSTALLATION STEPS

Because Simics is a full-platform simulator capable of running an unmodified software stack, OS installation can be performed in the same way as on real hardware. This section describes how to install any operating system from a CD-Rom image. We assume that the Simics model provides a variable, `$cd_image`, which points to a CD-Rom or DVD containing an OS installation image file.

1. Set the `$cd_image` parameter and run the script: `./simics -e '$cd_image = "ubuntu12.iso"' target-script.simics`.
2. In the BIOS Boot manager, choose the relevant "Boot from CD/DVD" option.
3. Follow the usual OS install procedure. Some hints:
   - Some operating systems reboot several times during installation, and after the first time they are required to boot from HDD (not CD). CD boot is required only the first time.
   - The installation process can take time (up to 30 minutes depending on host hardware). Using the Simics VMP execution mode, as discussed in Chapter 2, can make this process significantly faster.
4. After installation is complete, save the disk image for future use: `$system.disk.hd_image.save filename = "os.raw"`.

POST-SILICON PROCESS

Even in the post-silicon phase of hardware rollout, when developer boards or real hardware devices are available to the final customer, Simics can be very useful.

Following are several examples for how Simics is used as a post-silicon virtual platform.

- *Architecture exploration.* A customer wants to switch their servers from non-Intel-based server boards to boards based on Intel® Architecture. To try Intel® Architecture possibilities and see the benefits of switching, the customer takes a Simics virtual board, enables the required software stacks, and runs their custom tests to define the advantages of using the Intel-based solutions.
- *Software stack validation.* A customer wants to use a next-generation Intel-based server board, and is already using a board based on an older generation. The whole software stack was already enabled on the old board, but the customer might not have detailed knowledge about the changes in drivers that would be required. To solve this problem, the customer can use Simics: they will validate the whole software stack on a Simics virtual platform for the next-generation server, note required changes in the software stack, and shift left software stack readiness before the actual next-generation Intel-based server board arrives. The Simics ability to warn on bad register accesses and check the details of the hardware—software interaction makes this process run much smoother than just trying it on hardware.
- *Customer BIOS development.* Most Intel Software stack validation Architecture systems actually have customized BIOS. For example, server vendors and embedded systems vendors tend to add reliability, error reporting, and manageability features, while desktop and laptop vendors use BIOS to add differentiating features to their systems. Such a custom BIOS is built starting with a validated BIOS from a BIOS vendor, and adding features particular to the system being built. The customized BIOS has to be validated and debugged. Simics makes it possible to work on a custom board model, developing the BIOS in parallel to the actual board development, as well as providing many more test systems for the developers to use. This saves time and results in less bring-up time being needed on the actual hardware board.
- *Hardware shortage.* New hardware is out in the market, but it is expensive to supply all developers with new machines, especially in a variety of configurations. With Simics, adding additional sockets or inserting a dozen new DDR4 memory modules is as easy as changing a variable in the setup script.
- *Early system integration.* New boards built on new Intel® Architecture platforms can be modeled in Simics and integrated into an existing customer system before hardware is available. This shortens the time to actual production and deployment of new hardware. If a customer has a model of their existing system, adding a new model of a new Intel® Architecture platform on a new board provides a very fast path to integration.

POST-SILICON MODELING

As Simics is a very flexible framework, the list of possible use cases for it is almost limitless—from running it as part of a virtual platform farm to playing games on new Windows. However, enabling each possible use case is likely to cost additional developer resources.

The general approach for Simics development post-silicon is to clarify the customer-required features and devices that are actually needed for the customer use cases. Given the use cases, it is necessary to understand priorities, tests, and target dates for them and, finally, to divide them into a list of delivery phases. This is essentially the same MDR procedure as used for pre-silicon, but with requirements driven by an external user building their systems, rather than internal users focusing on the early bring-up. These two groups have many overlapping concerns, but also have unique requirements. I/O tends to be more important for external users, for example.

Although the structure of pre-silicon and post-silicon MDR looks similar, there are differences between them in the whole modeling process flow. For example, parts of the model are already complete at the time of writing of a post-silicon MDR, and the MDR has to take this into account. To fully understand the difference, look at the states of the modeling process overview in Figure 10.6:

1. *Collect documents.* At the post-silicon stage a fully functional virtual platform with many use cases working is already in place. However, additional use cases and device models might be required for the customer compared to the base platform. In this stage, additional required documents are needed according to the customer's needs.

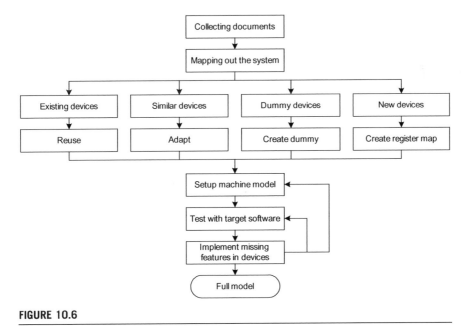

FIGURE 10.6

Modeling process overview.

The first part of the documents covers additional *hardware model requirements*. Every new device has to have an available specification; the whole platform itself might have a specification that contains hardware differences from a base board, such as strap values and GPIO pin setup.

Another part of collecting documents is to collect *software requirements*. The software stack required to run on a virtual platform is very dependent on the specific customer needs and, in the general case, software enabling might take an amount of time comparable to that of model development. Thus, collecting the requirements for the software stack is very important. Software stack support might change between the delivery phases, and those changes have to be defined as well.

The final part is to collect a list of *specific required use cases* to run on a virtual platform and software stack. Even once hardware and software documents are in place, some hardware development and software enabling parts might take a lot of time on a virtual platform, which might not fit into a customer's required schedule. That is why the customer might want to limit required functionality to specific use cases to test and support. The step of clearly defining use cases and tests is critical for developing, enabling, and providing support for the model.

The consideration here is the following: *an untested feature equals a nonworking feature*. If any required use case is not clearly outlined inside of the MDR, it will not be tested. If the use case is not tested, the developer and enabler might not be aware of possible pitfalls inside of the model. Finally, it might lead to customer dissatisfaction from using the platform.

Example: Network interface controller (NIC) specifications, customer board X extended architecture deviation, driver version X.X, OS Linux version X.

2. *Map the system.* The customer has to provide their vision on what is finally needed from the board model, at a high level. Although the mapping itself is generally done on the customer's side, the supplier of a virtual platform must outline and divide the system into the following blocks:

   a. *Existing devices.* There might be previously developed devices that were used in other virtual platforms. Although they are developed and tested, it is worth noting that some functionality of the devices might be missing or limited, and the final use-case requirements have to be negotiated with the customer. For example, a customer needs IPSec support in a network adapter, which was not initially implemented inside of the NIC model for Intel-internal use. Furthermore, devices might not have been tested with the customer's required software stack. For example, there might be fixes required in a model to work with a driver from a Linux 3.1-series kernel when it was previously only tested using a 2.6-series kernel.

   b. *Similar devices.* There might be devices that can be easily adopted to match the customer's requirements. The adoption schedule negotiation results must be described in the MDR, as well as the list of requirements for the final device (after adoption it will be an *existing device* with the same considerations required). For example, a customer wants the new generation of XYZ controller, and a very similar older generation was previously implemented. In this case, it will be faster to adopt a new model from a previous one compared to doing it from scratch.

  c. *Dummy devices.* All base platform devices usually exist at least as dummies in the post-silicon phase. The customer has to be aware of the list of dummy devices and understand that only a register map and very limited side-effect support will be provided for them—this is usually listed in the platform's limitations document. It is very important to identify cases where devices need to be made functional rather than dummies so that this can be planned.

  d. *New devices.* All new devices have to be defined in the MDR as well. The MDR has to be filled in with the delivery schedule of such devices as well as required support for the customer's use cases. Generally, a new device is delivered in stages, starting with a register map dummy, then making it work with the BIOS during boot, and finally adding OS driver and application use cases.

     At this stage the MDR is filled and agreed upon by both the customer and the Simics platform supplier, all required documents are collected, the system is mapped out, and development/enabling can start. The following three steps are considered to be iterative:

3. *Set up machine model.* This step can be considered similar to the MDR phases: set up first delivery virtual platform with some of the devices not in place yet, update it after some device is ready, and so on.

4. *Test with target software.* Once the current machine model is set up, it can be tested with a required OS/software/use case. Test case−driven development helps save time: instead of developing all possible functionality, the modeling team can outline and focus only on the required features, and, finally, shift left delivery time of the final platform. Test cases must be added to an automated test system to make sure that new implemented functionality does not break anything that has already been tested.

5. *Implement missing features in devices.* This step is taken if some of the test cases are not working and specific feature development is required. The developer focuses on implementing specific features to unblock the software enablers with their use cases, providing functional tests for the feature and making sure previous functionality is not broken.

After all delivery phases are complete and the model has been successfully deployed to the customer, the customer should verify that it is working so that the platform can go to the final stage:

6. *Final model.* The virtual platform project goes into the support phase, which means that bugs will be fixed, but that, in general, development of the platform is complete.

It should be noted that the post-silicon development and enabling process can take just the same amount of time as pre-silicon. It is quite possible for the development scope and MDR to change during the post-silicon program to keep track of hardware design changes and changing use-case requirements, which can have a drastic effect on the delivery timeline. Work on the product might not be complete after the delivery of the final model: the customer can have another MDR with new features or use cases. As the same model is used in more and more systems, the incremental work needed to support each new customer, system, or use case goes down as more and more gets covered. This is the iterative nature of Simics development, as discussed in Chapter 6.

POST-SILICON CASE STUDY: PXE

PXE stands for *Preboot eXecution environment*, and it is used to boot computers using a network interface, independently of any local data storage devices or installed operating system. The PXE use case shows the following capabilities of Simics:

- Simics flexibility on the division of a big use case into several small parts, the isolation of these smaller parts, the enabling of each part separately, and then the integration of small parts with each other.
- Different types of software working together through the network: BIOS network stack, Gigabit Ethernet (GbE) Option ROM network stack, and the target operating system.
- Unique Simics capabilities of network stack support and network traffic inspection.

The Simics PXE illustrated in Figure 10.7 shows two different platforms (client and server) interconnected through a Simics Ethernet network link, and a *service node* device with TFTP and DHCP settings (for more information, please refer to Chapter 5).

PXE OVERVIEW

An overview of PXE is needed to understand what the specific requirements are for Simics to enable it on a target platform. The PXE boot sequence is shown in Figure 10.8.

Figure 10.8 illustrates the simplest route of PXE. First, the client tries to find a PXE-capable DHCP server on the network. To do this, it sends a DHCP discovery message with the class identifier field as `PXEClient:Arch:xxxxx:UNDI:yyyzzz`. The `Arch` identifier specifies what bootstrap file the client is waiting for: Extensible Firmware Interface (EFI) or legacy. The client understands that that server is capable of a PXE boot when it receives a DHCP-offer message with

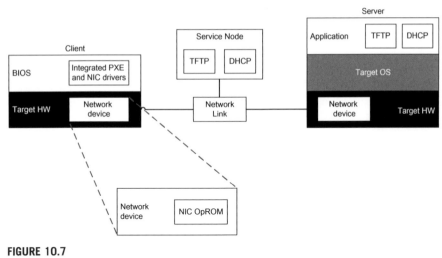

FIGURE 10.7

General PXE setup in Simics.

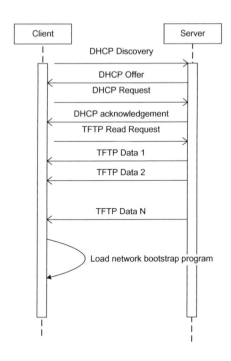

FIGURE 10.8

PXE boot sequence.

PXE options and the bootstrap file name. After that the client, depending on their own policy, chooses one of the detected PXE-capable DHCP servers and sends a DHCP request message. After receiving a DHCP acknowledgment, the client initiates a TFTP read, getting a number of TFTP data answers from the server. After the file is downloaded, the client loads it into a special RAM location and executes it. For detailed information please refer to Intel® (1999).

Several steps can be defined from the software stack requirements:

- Correctly configured server.
- Correctly configured client.
- Configuration with client and server.

The following sections will define how to configure it all in Simics.

SERVER-SIDE SOFTWARE SUPPORT

There are several different configurations to choose from for creating a working server, such as a TFTP/DHCP server using a service node or a TFTP/DHCP server using a separate virtual machine. Another consideration here is how to use a server. There are two possibilities: legacy PXE capabilities or UEFI PXE capabilities.

SERVICE NODE AS SERVER

Listing 10.2 shows the common service node creation commands that can be used to create a valid configuration for PXE. This is a minimal required configuration of the service node for a PXE boot. The service node currently implemented in Simics has a limitation: it only supports a legacy (non-UEFI) PXE setup. If the user needs UEFI PXE boot supports, the PXE server should be a virtual platform.

```
1    $sn = new-std-service-node
2    $sn.add-connector ip = $service_node_ip_address
3    connect $sn.connector_link0 $eth_link.deviceX
4    $sn.dhcp-add-pool ip = $dhcp_ip \
5                                pool-size = $dhcp_size
6    $sn.sn->default_boot_filename = "pxelinux.0"
7    $sn.set-tftp-directory dir = tftpboot
8    $sn.set-ftp-directory dir = tftpboot
```

LISTING 10.2

Configure service node for PXE.

Line 1: Instantiate a new service node.

Lines 2–3: Specify an IP address for the service node and connect the node to the Ethernet link of the target.

Line 4: Set up DHCP through the service node.

Lines 6–8: Provide the TFTP host directory and a boot file name.

```
1    if option arch == 00:06 {
2    filename "pxelinux/bootia32.efi";
3    } else if option arch == 00:07 {
4        filename "pxelinux/bootx64.efi";
5    } else {
6        filename "pxelinux/pxelinux.0";
7    }
```

LISTING 10.3

Server PXE Configuration.

VIRTUAL PLATFORM AS SERVER

Although the service node can be used for many network-related use cases, it is sometimes necessary to use a real server platform with a custom software stack running on it. The service node is intended to cover simple general cases; it provides a quick way for easy problems. However, a case like UEFI PXE boot is such that it makes more sense to run the full server on a target system, which essentially provides validation for the entire client–server system within the simulator. General requirements for this server are the following:

- *DHCP server application/service*. This is required for providing the IP address and the name of the network bootstrap program for download through TFTP.
- *TFTP server application/service*. This is required for providing the PXE client with a network bootstrap program.

Any custom image with these two features enabled can be used as a server. Depending on the DHCP discover message received from the client, the server side might be required to have several options to respond with: EFI and legacy boot files. Example pseudo-code of such a switch for Red Hat Enterprise Linux 6 (Red Hat, 2013) is shown in Listing 10.3. Any additional PXE settings are dependent on the specific DHCP/TFTP stack on the customer side.

CLIENT-SIDE SOFTWARE SUPPORT

There are a couple of options to set up a PXE client:

- Using a BIOS with integrated NIC drivers and PXE support. In this case, everything is relying on the BIOS, with no external software needed.
- Using a NIC Option ROM (OpROM). In this case, the BIOS will just execute the NIC OpROM. The drivers for the NIC and other PXE-required software are part of the NIC OpROM.

INTEGRATED BIOS APPROACH

The BIOS vendor has to provide the customer with a list of available NIC drivers and PXE environment support so that they are sure that their NIC is supported by

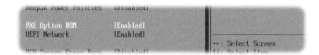

FIGURE 10.9

BIOS option for PXE and PXE + UEFI.

FIGURE 10.10

NIC in BIOS boot devices.

the BIOS. Although some steps might be BIOS-specific, this section outlines the steps commonly required:

1. As a preliminary step, the user must have a configuration script with the NIC connected to the virtual platform, and the BIOS with a NIC driver and PXE support.
2. Once the configuration script is done, run it and boot to the BIOS setup menu.
3. Enter BIOS setup and enable "PXE Option ROM" (see Figure 10.9). In contrast with the separate NIC-based OpROM approach, BIOS will try to use its integrated generic PXE OpROM.
4. If it is required to validate PXE + UEFI support, another option has to be enabled as well: "UEFI Network" (see Figure 10.9).
5. Save the changes and reset the platform to make changes appear on the next boot.
6. As an optional step, it can be convenient to save a new BIOS image with the saved settings for further use: `$motherboard.spi_image.save BIOS_PXE_enabled.rom`.
7. After the second BIOS boot, go to the BIOS setup menu again and check that NIC is visible in the boot device list (see Figure 10.10). The NIC can now be used for booting through PXE.

NIC OpROM APPROACH

The NIC OpROM approach is more complex and is divided into several major steps:

1. Prepare a BIOS image with NIC OpROM boot enabled.
2. Prepare a NIC OpROM itself.
3. Put everything together and verify that it is working.

To prepare the BIOS:

1. As a preliminary step, the user must have a configuration script with BIOS that has NIC OpROM boot support.
2. Once the configuration script is done, run it and boot to the BIOS setup menu.
3. Enter BIOS setup and enable option "Boot from GbE ROM" (see Figure 10.11). The name of the option can differ depending on the BIOS vendor.
4. Save changes and reset, saving the BIOS image for further use:

   `$motherboard.spi_image.save BIOSPXE_NIC_OpROM_enabled.rom.`

After preparing the BIOS, it is necessary to obtain an option ROM image for the chosen NIC. For an Intel® NIC, the software can be obtained via downloading the Intel® Ethernet Connections Boot Utility, Preboot Images, and EFI Drivers package. Once the package has been downloaded, it is necessary to build a configured OpROM using the Intel-provided BootUtil program. The configuration needs to specify the type of the boot (legacy or UEFI) and the PCI ID of the network card itself. An example execution of BootUtil on Windows is shown in Figure 10.12.

FIGURE 10.11

BIOS option for "Boot from GbE ROM".

```
C:\Intel18.6\APPS\BootUtil\Winx64>BOOTUTILW64E.EXE -di=pxe -devid=10F7 -lom

C:\Intel18.6\APPS\BootUtil\Winx64>dir
Volume in drive C is OSDisk
Volume Serial Number is 245D-9DEC

Directory of C:\Intel18.6\APPS\BootUtil\Winx64

10.06.2014  10:29    <DIR>          .
10.06.2014  10:29    <DIR>          ..
10.06.2014  10:29            63 488 10F703.LOM
20.08.2013  19:27         1 158 807 BootIMG.FLB
26.06.2013  20:27         2 915 840 BOOTUTILW64E.EXE
01.10.2013  13:49             1 078 BOOTUTILW64E.EXE - Shortcut.lnk
26.06.2013  20:27             2 915 install.bat
26.06.2013  20:27            33 616 iqvw64e.sys
24.01.2012  09:24               370 Readmefirst.txt
01.10.2013  13:47                36 run.bat
               8 File(s)      4 176 150 bytes
               2 Dir(s)  21 741 178 880 bytes free

C:\Intel18.6\APPS\BootUtil\Winx64>
```

FIGURE 10.12

Example of BootUtil output.

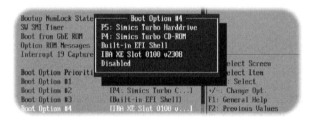

FIGURE 10.13

OpROM boot option.

Given the file that results from the configuration step, the Simics hardware setup has to specify that the NIC should load this newly created ROM file. Assuming the name is DEVID.NIC, you would use a command similar to this:

```
$eth_dev = (create-nic-comp name = $motherboard.nic  \

                   lan_cnt = $port_count  \
                   mac_list = [$mac_address] \
                   dev_id = $dev_id      \
                   expansion_rom_file = "DEVID.NIC")
```

Finally, verify that BIOS and the OpROM can work with each other:

1. Set up the client configuration with the new BIOS image (BIOSPXE_NIC_OpROM_enabled.rom) and a NIC using the new OpROM file.
2. Run this configuration to the BIOS setup and check the available boot options to see the OpROM boot option enabled, as shown in Figure 10.13.

PXE FINAL RESULTS

Once the client and the server have been prepared, they have to be put into a single configuration. Here are several hints for creating it correctly:

- As the process of booting the server to the operating system can require a lot of time, it can be loaded once, configured, and saved as a Simics checkpoint. That can save a lot of user time. Each user test-run would then start from a setup containing a booted server plus a target system under testing that is about to start booting.
- The Wireshark and Tcpdump tools can be used to examine network traffic inside of the simulated environment. Those tools can help, for example, to check that the correct PXE options are transferred over the network. Information about using these tools in Simics can be found in Chapter 5.
- Simics OS/UEFI debugging capabilities can be used to debug erroneous behavior of the software stack. High log-level output from devices can be used to discover erroneous behavior of hardware or software.

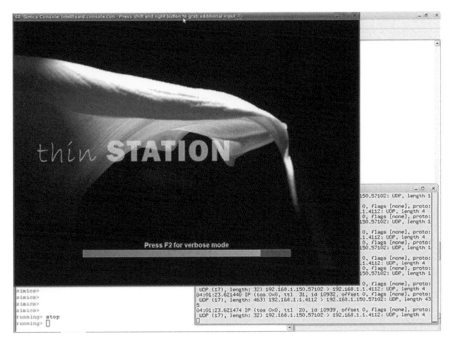

FIGURE 10.14

Loading Thinstation on a Simics client through PXE.

- Simics cell synchronization latency settings can be tuned to set up the simulated network speed, as discussed in Chapter 5. TFTP is a protocol that likes fairly short latencies, because each packet is acknowledged before the next packet is sent.
- VMP usage is strongly recommended for better performance.

After putting everything together, the user will be able to test PXE capabilities in Simics. An example of this is shown in Figure 10.14. Figure 10.14 shows a *Thinstation* distribution loading on Simics through the network.

Appendix A: Source code

Chapter 6: Counter Device

```
1    dml 1.2;
2
3    device c6_counter;
4
5    parameter desc = "Counter Example Device";
6
7    parameter documentation =
8        "This device implements a register that can be read and
     written and two counters that keep track of the number of
     times the device is read and written. When one of the counters
     overflow the device can optionally raise an interrupt.";
9
10   import "simics/devs/signal.dml";
11   import "utility.dml";
12
13   connect irq {
14       parameter documentation =
15           "Connection to an interrupt controller that"
16           + " implements level triggered interrupts"
17           + " through the signal interface.";
18       parameter required = true;
19       interface signal;
20   }
21
22   attribute is_interrupt_raised {
23       parameter documentation =
24           "Keeps track of the interrupt signal's state.";
25       parameter allocate_type = "bool";
26   }
27
28   bank regs {
29       parameter register_size = 1;
30       parameter byte_order = "big-endian";
31
32       register data size 4 @ 0x00 "Data";
33       register icr @ 0x4 "Interrupt control";
34       register isr @ 0x5 "Interrupt status";
35       register rd_count @ 0x08 "Read counter for 'data'";
36       register wr_count @ 0x09 "Write counter for 'data'";
37   }
38
39   template irq_updater {
40       method after_write(mop) {
41           call $update_interrupt();
42       }
43   }
44
45   template overflow_ctr {
46       parameter interrupt_status default undefined;
47       parameter mask_bit default undefined;
48
```

LISTING A.1

Counter Example Device Model Code.

```
49              method inc() {
50                  if (++$this == 0)
51                      call $overflow();
52              }
53
54            method overflow() {
55                if (!$icr.mask[$mask_bit])
56                    $interrupt_status = 1;
57
58                call $update_interrupt();
59            }
60          }
61
62      bank regs {
63          method update_interrupt() {
64              if (($isr.wr || $isr.rd) && $icr.enable) {
65                  if (!$is_interrupt_raised) {
66                      $is_interrupt_raised = true;
67                      $irq.signal.signal_raise();
68                  }
69              } else {
70                  if ($is_interrupt_raised) {
71                      $is_interrupt_raised = false;
72                      $irq.signal.signal_lower();
73                  }
74              }
75          }
76
77          register data {
78              method after_write(mop) {
79                  call $wr_count.inc();
80              }
81              method after_read(mop) {
82                  call $rd_count.inc();
83              }
84          }
85
86          register icr is (irq_updater) {
87              parameter hard_reset_value = 0x06;
88              parameter soft_reset_value = $hard_reset_value;
89
90              field reserved[7:3] is (reserved);
91              field mask[2:1];
92              field enable[0];
93          }
94
95          register isr is (irq_updater) {
96              field reserved[7:2] is (reserved);
97              field wr[1];
98              field rd[0];
99          }
100
101         register rd_count is (overflow_ctr) {
102             parameter interrupt_status = $isr.rd;
103             parameter mask_bit = 0;
104         }
105
106         register wr_count is (overflow_ctr) {
107             parameter interrupt_status = $isr.wr;
108             parameter mask_bit = 1;
109         }
110     }
```

LISTING A.1

(*Continued*).

- **File** s-counter.py:

```
1    # Test that the counter registers increment when the
2    # data register is read/written.
3
4    from c6_counter_common import *
5    dut = create_c6_counter()
6    regs = Registers(dut)
7
8    # Reading data should increase rd_count...
9    for n in xrange(10):
10       expect_equal(regs.rd_count.read(), n)
11       expect_equal(regs.data.read(), 0)
12       # ... but not wr_count
13       expect_equal(regs.wr_count.read(), 0)
14
15   # Writing data should increase wr_count...
16   for n in xrange(10):
17       expect_equal(regs.wr_count.read(), n)
18       regs.data.write(n)
19       expect_equal(dut.regs_data, n)
20       # ... but not rd_count
21       expect_equal(regs.rd_count.read(), 10)
```

- **File** s-reset.py:

```
1    # Test that registers have correct reset values.
2
3    from c6_counter_common import *
4    regs = Registers(create_c6_counter())
5
6    # Check reset values, data last to avoid affecting
7    # rd_count
8    expect_equal(regs.icr.read(), 0x6)
9    expect_equal(regs.isr.read(), 0)
10   expect_equal(regs.rd_count.read(), 0)
11   expect_equal(regs.wr_count.read(), 0)
12   expect_equal(regs.data.read(), 0)
```

- **File** s-data-read-write.py:

```
1    # Test that values can be written and read back from the data
2    # register.
3
4    from c6_counter_common import *
5    dut = create_c6_counter()
6    regs = Registers(dut)
7
8    for n in (4711, 0xdeadbeef, 0, 0xabba, 0xffffffff):
9        regs.data.write(n)
10       expect_equal(regs.data.read(), n)
11       expect_equal(dut.regs_data, n)
```

- **File** s-interrupt.py:

```
1    # Test that interrupts are raised when counters overflow
2    # depending on ICR.
3
4    from c6_counter_common import *
```

LISTING A.2

Counter Example Device Tests.

```
5        dut = create_c6_counter()
6        regs = Registers(dut)
7        irq = dut.irq
8
9        def interrupt_check(wr, rd, count):
10           expect_equal(regs.isr.wr, wr)
11           expect_equal(regs.isr.rd, rd)
12           expect_equal(irq.count, count)
13
14       # After reset interrupts are masked and
15       # disabled. Nothing should happen on overflow.
16       for n in xrange(0xff):
17           regs.data.write(n)
18           expect_equal(regs.data.read(), n)
19           interrupt_check(0, 0, 0)
20       expect_equal(regs.wr_count.read(), 0xff)
21       expect_equal(regs.rd_count.read(), 0xff)
22
23       # Write to wrap wr_count
24       regs.data.write(0xabba)
25       expect_equal(regs.wr_count.read(), 0)
26       expect_equal(regs.rd_count.read(), 0xff)
27       interrupt_check(0, 0, 0)
28       # Read to wrap rd_count
29       expect_equal(regs.data.read(), 0xabba)
30       expect_equal(regs.wr_count.read(), 0)
31       expect_equal(regs.rd_count.read(), 0)
32       interrupt_check(0, 0, 0)
33
34       # Disable interrupt masking for writes (still no
35       # interrupts should trigger)
36       regs.icr.write(mask = 1)
37       dut.regs_rd_count = 0xff    # Force wrap
38       dut.regs_wr_count = 0xff    # Force wrap
39       regs.data.read()
40       expect_equal(regs.rd_count.read(), 0)
41       interrupt_check(0, 0, 0)
42       regs.data.write(0xdabbad00)
43       expect_equal(regs.wr_count.read(), 0)
44       interrupt_check(1, 0, 0)
45
46       # Enable interrupts, an interrupt should be triggered
47       regs.icr.write(enable = 1)
48       interrupt_check(1, 0, 1)
49       # Clear ISR should lower interrupts
50       regs.isr.write(0)
51       interrupt_check(0, 0, 0)
52       # Clear read mask and wrap read counter
53       regs.icr.write(mask = 0)
54       dut.regs_rd_count = 0xff    # Force wrap
55       dut.regs_wr_count = 0xff    # Force wrap
56       regs.data.read()
57       interrupt_check(0, 1, 1)
58       regs.data.write(0xfaceb00c)
59       interrupt_check(1, 1, 1)
```

LISTING A.2

(*Continued*).

Chapter 7: DMA Device

```
1      dml 1.2;
2
3      device c7_dma_device;
4
5      parameter desc = "DMA Device (Example)";
6
7      parameter documentation =
8        "Example of a DMA device supporting contiguous"
9        + " memory or scatter-gather lists. The device"
10       + " has a controllable throughput (words per"
11       + " second) and supports either polling mode or"
12       + " interrupt-based signalling upon DMA"
13       + " completion.";
14
15     import "utility.dml";
16     import "pci/common.dml";
17     is pcie_device;
18
19     parameter pci_hotplug = false;
20
21     typedef layout "big-endian" {
22       uint32 addr;
23       uint16 len;
24       uint16 reserved;
25     } sg_list_head_t;
26
27     typedef layout "big-endian" {
28       uint32 addr;
29       uint16 len;
30       uint8 offset;
31       bitfields 8 {
32         uint1 ext @ [0:0];
33       } flags;
34     } sg_list_block_row_t;
35
36     parameter byte_order = "big-endian";
37
38     // Timing parameter
39     attribute transfers_per_second {
40       parameter documentation =
41         "Number of 32-bit words that can be transfered in a"
42         + " second, default is one million.";
43       parameter allocate_type = "int64";
44       parameter configuration = "optional";
45
46       method set(value) {
47         if (SIM_attr_integer(value) < 1) {
48           log "error": "%s must be positive.", $qname;
49           throw;
50         }
51
52         call default(value);
53       }
54     }
55
56     bank pci_config {
57       // This attribute should contain a list of all BAR
```

LISTING A.3

DMA Device Model.

```
58        // registers
59        parameter base_address_registers =
60          ["base_address_0"];
61
62        register vendor_id {
63          parameter hard_reset_value = 0x8086;
64        }
65        register device_id {
66          parameter hard_reset_value = 0xABBA;
67        }
68
69        register base_address_0 @ 0x10
70          is (memory_base_address_32)
71        {
72          parameter size_bits = 8;
73          parameter map_func = 1;
74        }
75
76        register base_address_1 @ 0x14
77          is (no_base_address_32);
78        register base_address_2 @ 0x18
79          is (no_base_address_32);
80        register base_address_3 @ 0x1C
81          is (no_base_address_32);
82        register base_address_4 @ 0x20
83          is (no_base_address_32);
84        register base_address_5 @ 0x24
85          is (no_base_address_32);
86
87        register interrupt_pin {
88          parameter hard_reset_value = 1;
89        }
90
91        register command {
92          field m {
93            parameter hard_reset_value = 1;
94          }
95        }
96      }
97
98    bank regs {
99        // For PCI devices each bank need to have a unique
100       // function number,which should match with the
101       // map_func parameter in one BAR
102       parameter function = 1;
103
104       parameter register_size = 4;
105       register DMA_control @ 0x00 "Control register";
106       register DMA_source  @ 0x04 "Source address";
107       register DMA_dest    @ 0x08 "Destination address";
108
109       // Internal register not mapped to any memory
110       // location
111       register DMA_interrupt_posted @ undefined
112         "Internal register to track if interrupts are"
113         + " posted.";
114     }
115
116   method lower_interrupt() {
```

LISTING A.3

(Continued).

```
117        if ($regs.DMA_interrupt_posted != 0) {
118          log "info", 3: "Clearing interrupt";
119          call $pci_config.pci_lower_interrupt();
120          $regs.DMA_interrupt_posted = 0;
121        }
122      }
123
124      method raise_interrupt() {
125        if ($regs.DMA_interrupt_posted == 0) {
126          log "info", 3: "raising interrupt";
127          call $pci_config.pci_raise_interrupt();
128          $regs.DMA_interrupt_posted = 1;
129        }
130      }
131
132      // Read len bytes of target memory from the address src
133      // in the PCI memory space. The result is put in
134      // memory pointed to by dst, which must be large enough
135      // to hold at least len bytes. If a memory access error
136      // occurs, this method will print an error message and
137      // throw an exception.
138      method read_mem(void *dst,
139                      physical_address_t src,
140                      physical_address_t len) {
141        local exception_type_t exc;
142        call $pci_data_from_memory(Sim_Addr_Space_Memory,
143                                   dst, src, len) -> (exc);
144        if (exc != Sim_PE_No_Exception)
145          throw;
146      }
147
148      // Write len bytes to target memory from the memory
149      // pointed to by src. The data is written to the PCI
150      // memory space at address dst. If a memory access error
151      // occurs this method will print an error message and
152      // throw an exception.
153      method write_mem(physical_address_t dst,
154                       const void *src,
155                       physical_address_t len) {
156        local exception_type_t exc;
157        call $pci_data_to_memory(Sim_Addr_Space_Memory,
158                                 src, dst, len) -> (exc);
159        if (exc != Sim_PE_No_Exception)
160          throw;
161      }
162
163      bank regs {
164        register DMA_control {
165          field EN  [31] "Enable DMA";
166          field SWT [30] "Software Transfer Trigger";
167          field ECI [29] "Enable Completion Interrupt";
168          field TC  [28] "Transfer complete" {
169            // Set to 1 by device when transfer has completed
170            // Clear by writing a zero.  If interrupts are
171            // enabled and interrupt status is one also clear
172            // the interrupt in the processor.
173            method write(value) {
174              if (value != 0) {
175                log "spec_violation":
```

LISTING A.3

(*Continued*).

```
176                      "write one to TC - ignored";
177                   return;
178                }

179
180            if (!$this)     // Already cleared
181               return;

182
183            log "info", 3:
184               "write zero to TC - clearing TC";
185            $this = 0;

186
187            call $lower_interrupt();
188          }
189        }
190      field SG  [27]   "Scatter-gather list input";
191      field ERR [26]   "DMA transfer error";
192      field TS  [15:0] "Transfer size (32-bit words)";

193
194      method after_write(memop) {
195         call $do_dma_transfer();
196      }
197    }

198
199    method do_dma_transfer() {
200       if (!$DMA_control.SWT)
201          return; // No need to do anything if we are not
202                  // asked by software

203
204       // Software asked us to initiate a DMA transfer
205       if(!$DMA_control.EN) {
206          // enable bit not set, so we cannot transfer
207          log "info", 2:
208            "EN bit not set, SWT = 1 has no effect";
209          return;
210       }

211
212       log "info", 3:
213          "EN bit set, SWT written, initiating DMA";
214       log "info", 3:
215          "Transferring %d 32-bit words from 0x%x to"
216          + " 0x%x", $DMA_control.TS, $DMA_source,
217          $DMA_dest;

218
219       local uint18 count = $DMA_control.TS * 4;
220       try {
221          if ($DMA_control.SG) {
222             log "info", 4:
223                "Scatter Gather Transfer";
224             call $copy_scatter_gather($DMA_dest,
225                                       $DMA_source)
226                -> (count);
227          } else {
228             log "info", 4: "Contiguous Transfer";
229             call $copy_contiguous($DMA_dest,
230                                   $DMA_source,
231                                   count);
232          }
233       } catch {
234          log "error": "DMA memory access failed";
```

LISTING A.3

(Continued).

```
235          return;
236        }
237
238      after (count / $transfers_per_second / 4.0)
239        call $complete_dma();
240    }
241
242    method copy_contiguous(physical_address_t dst,
243                           physical_address_t src,
244                           uint18 count) {
245      local uint8 buf[count];
246      call $read_mem(buf, src, count);
247      call $write_mem(dst, buf, count);
248    }
249
250    // next_row - Returns the address to next row to be
251    // processed.  end_addr is the address after the end
252    // of the block, if this address is reached the
253    // transaction should have finished
254    method next_row(physical_address_t addr,
255                    physical_address_t end_addr)
256      -> (physical_address_t next_addr,
257          physical_address_t next_end_addr,
258          bool finished) {
259      local sg_list_block_row_t block_row;
260      call $read_mem(&block_row, addr,
261                     sizeof block_row);
262      if (block_row.flags.ext) {
263        next_addr = (block_row.addr
264                     + block_row.offset);
265        next_end_addr = next_addr + block_row.len;
266      } else {
267        next_addr = addr + sizeof block_row;
268        next_end_addr = end_addr;
269      }
270      finished = next_addr == end_addr;
271    }
272
273    // Copy Scatter Gathered data.
274    method copy_scatter_gather(physical_address_t dst,
275                               physical_address_t src)
276      -> (uint18 copied_bytes) {
277      // Get the header data
278      local sg_list_head_t head;
279      call $read_mem(&head, src, sizeof head);
280      copied_bytes = 0;
281
282      local physical_address_t addr = head.addr;
283      local physical_address_t end_addr =
284        head.addr + head.len;
285      local physical_address_t hare_addr = addr;
286      local physical_address_t hare_end_addr =
287        end_addr;
288
289      // Continue running through the lists until the end
290      // is reached or an error has been detected
291      local sg_list_block_row_t row;
292      local bool finished = false;
293      local bool hare_finished = false;
```

LISTING A.3

(*Continued*).

```
294              while (!finished && !$DMA_control.ERR) {
295                call $read_mem(&row, addr, sizeof row);
296
297                if (!row.flags.ext) { // Data block
298                  log "info", 4: "Data block of length %d"
299                    + " at 0x%x with offset %d",
300                    row.len, row.addr, row.offset;
301                  // Copy a block of data
302                  call $copy_contiguous(dst,
303                                        row.addr + row.offset,
304                                        row.len);
305                  dst += row.len;
306                  copied_bytes += row.len;
307                } else {
308                  log "info", 4:
309                    "Extension block of length %d at 0x"
310                    + "%x with offset %d", row.len,
311                    row.addr, row.offset;
312                }
313
314                call $next_row(addr, end_addr)
315                  -> (addr, end_addr, finished);
316
317                // Check for loops.
318                if (!hare_finished) {
319                  local int8 i;
320                  // Hare moves through lists at double the speed
321                  // of addr.  If the hare ends up at the same
322                  // address as addr, a loop has been detected, if
323                  // the hare reaches the end there is no loop.
324                  for (i = 0; i < 2; i++) {
325                    call $next_row(hare_addr,
326                                   hare_end_addr)
327                      -> (hare_addr,
328                          hare_end_addr,
329                          hare_finished);
330                    if (hare_finished) {
331                      log "info", 4:
332                        "Loop checker finished, no loops";
333                      break;
334                    }
335                  }
336                  if (hare_addr == addr) {
337                    log "spec_violation": "Stuck in a loop.";
338                    $DMA_control.ERR = 1;
339                  }
340                }
341              }
342            }
343
344      method complete_dma() {
345        // Log that completion is done
346        log "info", 2: "DMA transfer completed";
347
348        // clear SWT bit, update TS
349        $DMA_control.SWT = 0;
350        $DMA_control.TS = 0;
351        $DMA_control.TC = 1;
```

LISTING A.3

(*Continued*).

```
352
353              // raise interrupt towards CPU
354              if(!$DMA_control.ECI) {
355                log "info", 3: "ECI is zero, no interrupt raised";
356                return;
357              }
358
359              call $raise_interrupt();
360            }
361          }
362
363          method init() {
364            // a really slow DMA device
365            $transfers_per_second = 1e6;
366          }
```

LISTING A.3
_____

(*Continued*).

```
1        from cli import *
2
3        def info(obj):
4            return [(None,
5                       [("Memory Space", obj.target_mem_space)]
6                       )]
7
8        def status(obj):
9            sg = "Yes" if obj.regs_DMA_control & (1 << 27) else "No"
10           c_int = "Enabled" if obj.regs_DMA_control & (1 << 29) else "Disabled"
11           enabled = "Yes" if obj.regs_DMA_control & (1 << 31) else "No"
12           return [ (None,
13                       [("Speed (transfers/s)",
14                         obj.transfers_per_second),
15                        ("DMA enabled", enabled),
16                        ("Completion Interrupt", c_int),
17                        ("Scatter-gather transfer", sg),
18                        ("DMA source addr", "0x%x" % obj.regs_DMA_source),
19                        ("DMA destination addr", "0x%x" % obj.regs_DMA_dest)])]
20
21       new_info_command("c7_dma_device", info)
22       new_status_command("c7_dma_device", status)
```

LISTING A.4
_____

DMA Device Commands.

```
1       import random as r
2       import dev_util as du
3       import stest
4
5       def run_seconds(s):
6           steps = s * clock.freq_mhz * 1e6
7           SIM_continue(steps)
8
9       class PidSignal(du.Signal):
10          def __init__(self):
11              self.raised = False
12          def signal_raise(self, sim_obj):
13              self.raised = True
14          def signal_lower(self, sim_obj):
15              self.raised = False
16
17      # Create fake Memory and Interrupt objects, these are required
18      mem = du.Memory()
19      intr_dev = du.Dev([PidSignal])
20
21      # Create clock object for timing
22      clock = simics.pre_conf_object('clock', 'clock')
23      clock.freq_mhz = 1000
24
25      # Create DMA device and connect with clock, memory and interrupt
26      dma = simics.pre_conf_object('mydma', 'sample_dma_device')
27      dma.target_mem_space = mem.obj
28      dma.intr_target = intr_dev.obj
29      dma.queue = clock
30
31      # Create the configuration
32      simics.SIM_add_configuration([clock, dma], None)
33      mydma = conf.mydma
34
35      dma_src_reg = du.Register_BE((mydma, 'regs', 4), 4)
36      dma_dst_reg = du.Register_BE((mydma, 'regs', 8), 4)
37      dma_ctrl_reg = du.Register_BE((mydma, 'regs', 0), 4, du.Bitfield(['en': 31,
38                                                                        'swt': 30,
39                                                                        'eci': 29,
40                                                                        'tc': 28,
41                                                                        'sg': 27,
42                                                                        'err': 26,
43                                                                        'ts': (15,0)]))
44
45      def dma_transfer_test(in_data, interrupt = False):
46          pad = (4 - len(in_data) % 4) % 4
47          # mem.write wants data as a tuple. (always a multiple of 4)
48          test_data = tuple(list(ord(c) for c in in_data) + [0]*pad)
49          test_words = len(test_data) / 4
50          mem.write(0x20000, test_data)
51
52          # Set control register to enable dma and enable/disable interrupts
53          dma_ctrl_reg.write(0, en = 1, eci = interrupt)
54
55          # Load source and target addresses and transfer size
56          dma_src_reg.write(0x20000)
57          dma_dst_reg.write(0x30000)
58          dma_ctrl_reg.ts = test_words
59
60          # Initiate transfer and check result
61          dma_ctrl_reg.swt = 1
62          # TC should not be set because no time passed
63          stest.expect_equal(dma_ctrl_reg.tc, 0)
64
65          # Nothing should happen because not enough time has passed
66          if test_words > 1:
67              run_seconds((test_words - 1) * mydma.throttle)
68          stest.expect_equal(dma_ctrl_reg.tc, 0)
69          stest.expect_equal(intr_dev.signal.raised, False)
```

LISTING A.5

DMA Device Tests.

```
70              # Run forward until transfer should complete
71              run_seconds(1.01 * mydma.throttle)
72              if interrupt:
73                  stest.expect_equal(intr_dev.signal.raised, True)
74              else:
75                  stest.expect_equal(intr_dev.signal.raised, False)
76
77              # TC should be set if transfer is complete
78              stest.expect_equal(dma_ctrl_reg.tc, 1)
79
80              # Transferred data should match written data
81              out_data = tuple(mem.read(0x30000, test_words * 4))
82              stest.expect_equal(out_data, test_data, "Outdata does not match indata")
83
84              if interrupt:
85                  # Clear TC to notify that data is read, should lower interrupt
86                  dma_ctrl_reg.tc = 0
87                  stest.expect_false(intr_dev.signal.raised)
88
89          for length in (0, 1, 4, 10, 30, 50, 121):
90              in_data = ""
91              for i in range(length):
92                  in_data += chr(ord('a') + (i % (ord('z') - ord('a') + 1) ))
93              # Test without interrupts
94              dma_transfer_test(in_data, False)
95              # Test with interrupts
96              dma_transfer_test(in_data, True)
97
98      def write_scatter_block(start_addr, indata, extension):
99          addr = start_addr
100         junk = [0xba]
101         for data in indata:
102             write_addr = data[0]
103             write_data = junk * data[1] + data[2]
104             mem.write(write_addr, write_data)
105             flags = du.Bitfield_BE({"ext" : 7}, bits = 8)
106             blockrow = du.Layout_BE(mem, addr, {"addr"  : (0, 4),
107                                                 "len"   : (4, 2),
108                                                 "offset" : (6, 1),
109                                                 "flags" : (7, 1, flags)})
110             blockrow.clear()
111             blockrow.addr = data[0]
112             blockrow.len = len(data[2])
113             blockrow.offset = data[1]
114             addr += 8
115         if extension:
116             extrow = du.Layout_BE(mem, addr, {"addr"  : (0, 4),
117                                               "len"   : (4, 2),
118                                               "offset" : (6, 1),
119                                               "flags" : (7, 1, flags)})
120             extrow.clear()
121             extrow.addr = extension[0]
122             extrow.len = extension[2]
123             extrow.offset = extension[1]
124             extrow.flags.ext = 1
125
126     def setup_scatter_block(start_addr, startnr, datalen, offslen):
127         ret = []
128         for i in range(len(datalen)):
129             (addr, offs, data) = (start_addr + i * 0x100,
130                                   offslen[i],
131                                   [(startnr + i * 10) & 0xff] * datalen[i])
132             ret.append([addr, offs, data])
133         return ret
134
135     def write_head_block(src_addr, block_addr, block_len, total):
136         header = du.Layout_BE(mem, src_addr, { "addr"    : (0, 4),
137                                                "len"     : (4, 2),
138                                                "tot_len" : (6, 2)})
139         header.addr = block_addr
```

LISTING A.5

(Continued).

```
140            header.len = block_len
141            header.tot_len = total
142
143        # Test with no extensionblocks
144        def setup_scatter_list_noext(src_addr):
145            datalen = (100, 10,  5,  8, 20, 15)
146            offslen = (10,    5,  1, 20,  0, 11)
147            totlen = sum(datalen, 0)
148            data = setup_scatter_block(0x30000, 0, datalen, offslen)
149            write_scatter_block(0x20000, data, 0)
150            write_head_block(src_addr, 0x20000, len(datalen) * 8, totlen)
151            expdata = []
152            for a in range(len(datalen)):
153                expdata += data[a][2]
154            return expdata
155
156        # Test where dma should get stuck in loop
157        def setup_scatter_loop(src_addr):
158            print " == DMA SG - Loop test"
159            blockaddr = 0x20000
160            dataaddr = 0x40000
161
162            datalen = (10, 20, 30, 20, 10, 15)
163            offslen = (10,    5,  1, 20,  0, 11)
164            totlen = sum(datalen, 0) * 2
165
166            ext1 = (blockaddr + 0x100, 0, 7 * 8)
167            ext2 = (blockaddr, 0, 7 * 8)
168
169            data = setup_scatter_block(dataaddr, 0, datalen, offslen)
170            write_scatter_block(blockaddr, data, ext1)
171            write_scatter_block(blockaddr, data, ext2)
172
173            write_head_block(src_addr, blockaddr, (len(datalen) + 1) * 8, totlen)
174            expdata = []
175            for a in range(len(datalen)):
176                expdata += data[a][2]
177            expdata = expdata * 2
178            return expdata
179
180
181        # Test with random values
182        def setup_scatter_list_rand(src_addr, seed):
183            blockaddr = 0x20000
184            dataaddr = 0x40000
185
186            r.seed(seed)
187            expdata = []
188            blocklengths = []
189            datalengths = []
190            offsetlengths = []
191            blockoffsets = [0]
192            # Randomize sizes for blocks and data
193            nr_blocks = r.randrange(1, 20)
194            for i in range(nr_blocks):
195                blocklengths.append(r.randrange(1, 20))
196                if i > 0:
197                    blockoffsets.append(r.randrange(1, 20))
198                dlen = []
199                offslen = []
200                for j in range(blocklengths[i]):
201                    dlen.append(r.randrange(1, 100))
202                    offslen.append(r.randrange(0, 20))
203                datalengths.append(dlen)
204                offsetlengths.append(offslen)
205            count = 0
206
207            print " == Random SG: seed %d  %d blocks" % (seed, nr_blocks)
208            print " == Blockslengths: ", blocklengths
209            print " == Blockoffsets : ", blockoffsets
```

LISTING A.5

(Continued).

```
210            # Write blocks and data
211            for i in range(nr_blocks):
212                data = setup_scatter_block(dataaddr, count,
213                                           datalengths[i],
214                                           offsetlengths[i])
215                for a in range(len(datalengths[i])):
216                    expdata += data[a][2]
217                if i < nr_blocks - 1:
218                    next_len = blocklengths[i + 1] * 8
219                    if i != nr_blocks - 2:
220                        next_len += 8
221                    ext = (blockaddr + 0x100, blockoffsets[i + 1], next_len)
222                else:
223                    ext = 0
224                write_scatter_block(blockaddr + blockoffsets[i], data, ext)
225                if blockoffsets[i]: # Write junkdata
226                    mem.write(blockaddr, [0xba] * blockoffsets[i])
227                dataaddr += 0x100 * blocklengths[i]
228                blockaddr += 0x100
229                count += blocklengths[i] * 10
230            first_len = blocklengths[0] * 8
231            if(nr_blocks > 1):
232                first_len += 8
233            write_head_block(src_addr, 0x20000, first_len , len(expdata))
234            return expdata
235
236
237    def test_scatter_gather(src_addr, dst_addr, expect_data, interrupt = True,
238                            looptest = False):
239        data_len = len(expect_data)
240        test_words = (data_len + 3) / 4
241        # Configure DMA for Scatter Gather
242        dma_ctrl_reg.write(0, en = 1, eci = interrupt, sg = 1)
243
244        # Set source and destination addresses
245        dma_src_reg.write(src_addr)
246        dma_dst_reg.write(dst_addr)
247
248        # set length (in words) to transfer and start transmitting
249        dma_ctrl_reg.ts = test_words
250        dma_ctrl_reg.swt = 1
251
252        # TC should not be set because no time passed
253        if test_words > 1:
254            run_seconds((test_words - 1) * mydma.throttle)
255        if looptest:
256            stest.expect_equal(dma_ctrl_reg.err, 1)
257            return
258        stest.expect_equal(dma_ctrl_reg.tc, 0)
259        stest.expect_equal(intr_dev.signal.raised, False)
260        # Run forward until transfer should complete
261        run_seconds(1.01 * mydma.throttle)
262        if interrupt:
263            stest.expect_equal(intr_dev.signal.raised, True)
264        else:
265            stest.expect_equal(intr_dev.signal.raised, False)
266
267        # TC should be set if transfer is complete
268        stest.expect_equal(dma_ctrl_reg.tc, 1)
269
270        stest.expect_equal(dma_ctrl_reg.err, 0)
271        # Transferred data should match written data
272        out_data = mem.read(dst_addr, data_len)
273        # sum(in_data, [])
274        stest.expect_equal(out_data, expect_data,
275                           "Outdata does not match indata")
276        if interrupt:
277            # Clear TC to notify that data is read, should lower interrupt
278            dma_ctrl_reg.tc = 0
279            stest.expect_false(intr_dev.signal.raised)
```

LISTING A.5

(*Continued*).

```
280
281     srcaddr = 0x10000
282     dstaddr = 0x60000
283     mem.clear()
284     expdata = setup_scatter_list_noext(srcaddr)
285     # Test Scatter Gather without interrupts
286     test_scatter_gather(srcaddr, dstaddr, expdata, False)
287     # Test Scatter Gather with interrupts
288     test_scatter_gather(srcaddr, dstaddr, expdata, True)
289
290     mem.clear()
291     expdata = setup_scatter_list_rand(srcaddr, 1)
292     test_scatter_gather(srcaddr, dstaddr, expdata, False)
293
294     mem.clear()
295     expdata = setup_scatter_list_rand(srcaddr, 10)
296     test_scatter_gather(srcaddr, dstaddr, expdata, False)
297
298     mem.clear()
299     expdata = setup_scatter_list_rand(srcaddr, 0xabba)
300     test_scatter_gather(srcaddr, dstaddr, expdata, False)
301
302     mem.clear()
303     expdata = setup_scatter_loop(srcaddr)
304     stest.expect_log(test_scatter_gather, (srcaddr, dstaddr, expdata, False, True),
305                      log_type = "spec-viol")
```

LISTING A.5

(*Continued*).

```
1       # MODULE: c7_dma_comp
2       # COMPONENT: c7_dma_comp
3
4       from comp import *
5
6       class c7_dma_comp(StandardConnectorComponent):
7           """DMA PCI Component"""
8           _class_desc = "DMA PCI Component"
9           _help_categories = ()
10
11          def setup(self):
12              StandardConnectorComponent.setup(self)
13              if not self.instantiated.val:
14                  self.add_objects()
15              self.add_connector('pci',
16                  PciBusUpConnector(0, 'dma'))
17
18          def add_objects(self):
19              self.dma = self.add_pre_obj('dma',
20                                          'c7_dma_device')
```

LISTING A.6

DMA Device Component.

```
1     #include <linux/pci.h>
2     #include <linux/init.h>
3     #include <linux/cdev.h>
4     #include <linux/fs.h>
5     #include <linux/interrupt.h>
6     #include <linux/wait.h>
7     #include <linux/sched.h>
8     #include <linux/module.h>
9
10    enum {
11      DMA_CTRL_ERR_BIT = 26,
12      DMA_CTRL_SG_BIT,
13      DMA_CTRL_TC_BIT,
14      DMA_CTRL_ECI_BIT,
15      DMA_CTRL_SWT_BIT,
16      DMA_CTRL_EN_BIT,
17    };
18
19    enum {
20      DMA_CTRL_ERR_MASK = (1 << DMA_CTRL_ERR_BIT),
21      DMA_CTRL_SG_MASK = (1 << DMA_CTRL_SG_BIT),
22      DMA_CTRL_TC_MASK = (1 << DMA_CTRL_TC_BIT),
23      DMA_CTRL_ECI_MASK = (1 << DMA_CTRL_ECI_BIT),
24      DMA_CTRL_SWT_MASK = (1 << DMA_CTRL_SWT_BIT),
25      DMA_CTRL_EN_MASK = (1 << DMA_CTRL_EN_BIT),
26      DMA_CTRL_TS_MASK = 0xffff,
27    };
28
29    enum {
30      DEV_DMA_CTRL,
31      DEV_DMA_SRC,
32      DEV_DMA_DST,
33      DEV_LAST,
34    };
35
36    enum {
37      OSET_REG_CTRL = 0,
38      OSET_REG_SRC = 4,
39      OSET_REG_DST = 8,
40    };
41
42    typedef struct {
43      void *vptr;
44      dma_addr_t dma_handle;
45      size_t size;
46    } dma_region_t;
47
48    typedef u32 (*reg_get_fun_t)(void);
49    typedef void (*reg_set_fun_t)(u32);
50
51    // ----------------------------------------
52
53    static const int EOF = 0;
54    static const char *DEV_NAME = "Simics-DMA";
55
56    static struct {
57      struct cdev *cdev;
```

LISTING A.7

DMA Device Driver.

```
58        struct pci_dev *pdev;
59        void __iomem *base_addr;
60        int major;
61        dma_region_t dma_dst_region;
62        u8 irq;
63    } dma_dev;
64
65    static const struct pci_device_id id_table[] = {
66        { PCI_DEVICE(PCI_VENDOR_ID_INTEL, 0xabba) },
67        { 0, },
68    };
69
70    static DECLARE_WAIT_QUEUE_HEAD(ctrl_read_wq);
71
72    // ---- Register accessors ----
73    static u32
74    reg_read(int oset) {
75        return be32_to_cpu(ioread32(dma_dev.base_addr + oset));
76    }
77
78    static void
79    reg_write(int oset, u32 value) {
80        iowrite32(cpu_to_be32(value),
81                  dma_dev.base_addr + oset);
82    }
83
84    static u32
85    reg_src_get(void) {
86        return reg_read(OSET_REG_SRC);
87    }
88
89    static void
90    reg_src_set(u32 val) {
91        reg_write(OSET_REG_SRC, val);
92    }
93
94    static u32
95    reg_dst_get(void) {
96        return reg_read(OSET_REG_DST);
97    }
98
99    static void
100   reg_dst_set(u32 val) {
101       reg_write(OSET_REG_DST, val);
102   }
103
104   static u32
105   reg_ctrl_get(void) {
106       return reg_read(OSET_REG_CTRL);
107   }
108
109   static void
110   reg_ctrl_set(u32 val) {
111       reg_write(OSET_REG_CTRL, val);
112   }
113
114   // ----
115
116   static bool
```

LISTING A.7

(Continued).

```
117     read_should_block(void) {
118       u32 ctrl = reg_ctrl_get();
119       return ((ctrl & DMA_CTRL_ECI_MASK)
120               && (ctrl & DMA_CTRL_SWT_MASK));
121     }
122
123     static irqreturn_t
124     irq_handler(int irq, void *dev_id) {
125       u32 dma_ctrl;
126
127       dma_ctrl = reg_ctrl_get();
128       if (!(dma_ctrl & DMA_CTRL_TC_MASK)) {
129         printk(KERN_DEBUG
130                "Transfer not complete 0x%x!\n", dma_ctrl);
131         return IRQ_NONE;
132       }
133
134       printk(KERN_DEBUG
135              "%s: transfer complete 0x%x!\n",
136              DEV_NAME, dma_ctrl);
137       wake_up_interruptible(&ctrl_read_wq);
138       reg_ctrl_set(dma_ctrl & ~DMA_CTRL_TC_MASK);
139
140       return IRQ_HANDLED;
141     }
142
143     static void
144     free_dma_dst_region(void) {
145       dma_region_t *dst = &dma_dev.dma_dst_region;
146       if (dst->vptr != NULL) {
147         dma_free_coherent(&dma_dev.pdev->dev,
148                           dst->size,
149                           dst->vptr,
150                           dst->dma_handle);
151         dst->vptr = NULL;
152         dst->size = 0;
153       }
154     }
155
156     static void
157     alloc_dma_dst_region(size_t bytes) {
158       if (dma_dev.dma_dst_region.size < bytes) {
159         dma_addr_t dma_handle;
160         void *vptr;
161
162         free_dma_dst_region();
163         vptr = dma_alloc_coherent(&dma_dev.pdev->dev,
164                                   bytes, &dma_handle,
165                                   GFP_KERNEL);
166         dma_dev.dma_dst_region.vptr = vptr;
167         dma_dev.dma_dst_region.dma_handle = dma_handle;
168         dma_dev.dma_dst_region.size =
169           vptr == NULL ? 0 : bytes;
170       }
171     }
172
173     /* Allocate a scratch pad large enough to hold the
174      * transfer size as specified by the DMA_CTRL_TS_MASK
175      * bits of val, if it is not already allocated. Then
```

LISTING A.7

(*Continued*).

```
176      * set the DMA_control register to val, posibly
177      * initiating a DMA transfer. */
178     static void
179     reg_ctrl_alloc_and_set(u32 val) {
180       u16 ts = val & DMA_CTRL_TS_MASK;
181       alloc_dma_dst_region(ts * 4);
182       if (dma_dev.dma_dst_region.vptr == NULL) {
183         printk(KERN_ERR
184               "%s: Failed to allocate DMA buffer\n",
185               DEV_NAME);
186         return;
187       }
188
189       reg_dst_set(dma_dev.dma_dst_region.dma_handle);
190       reg_ctrl_set(val);
191     }
192
193     // ---- Char device access functions ----
194     static ssize_t
195     read_reg(loff_t start, loff_t end, char __user *buf,
196             loff_t *off, reg_get_fun_t getter) {
197       char addr[11];    // Can hold "0x11223344"
198       size_t size;
199
200       if (start >= sizeof(addr))
201         return EOF;
202       if (end >= sizeof(addr))
203         end = sizeof(addr);
204       size = end - start;
205
206       snprintf(addr, sizeof(addr), "0x%08x", getter());
207       if (copy_to_user(buf, addr + start, size))
208         return -EFAULT;
209
210       *off += size;
211
212       return size;
213     }
214
215     static ssize_t
216     write_reg(loff_t start, loff_t end,
217               const char __user *buf,
218               loff_t *off, reg_set_fun_t setter) {
219       static char addr[11];    // Can hold "0x11223344"
220       size_t size;
221
222       if (start >= sizeof(addr)) {
223         return EOF;
224       }
225
226       if (end >= sizeof(addr))
227         end = sizeof(addr);
228       size = end - start;
229
230       if (copy_from_user(addr + start, buf, size))
231         return -EFAULT;
232
233       if (end == sizeof(addr)) {
234         // Trigger write to device
```

LISTING A.7

(Continued).

```
235        long val = 0;
236        int err;
237        addr[10] = '\0';   // Make sure 0-terminated
238        err = kstrtol(addr, 16, &val);
239        if (err) {
240          printk(KERN_ERR
241                 "%s Invalid register value: %s\n",
242                 DEV_NAME, addr);
243          return err;
244        }
245
246        setter(val);
247      }
248
249      return size;
250
251    }
252
253    static ssize_t
254    read_src(struct file *f, char __user *buf,
255             size_t size, loff_t *off)
256    {
257      return read_reg(f->f_pos, f->f_pos + size, buf,
258                      off, reg_src_get);
259    }
260
261    static ssize_t
262    write_src(struct file *f, const char __user *buf,
263             size_t size, loff_t *off)
264    {
265      return write_reg(f->f_pos, f->f_pos + size,
266                       buf, off, reg_src_set);
267    }
268
269    static ssize_t
270    read_dst(struct file *f, char __user *buf,
271             size_t size, loff_t *off)
272    {
273      return read_reg(f->f_pos, f->f_pos + size,
274                      buf, off, reg_dst_get);
275    }
276    // write_dst not supported
277
278    static ssize_t
279    read_ctrl(struct file *f, char __user *buf,
280             size_t size, loff_t *off)
281    {
282      int rc = wait_event_interruptible(ctrl_read_wq,
283                                        !read_should_block());
284      if (rc != 0)
285        return rc;
286
287      return read_reg(f->f_pos, f->f_pos + size,
288                      buf, off, reg_ctrl_get);
289    }
290
291    static ssize_t
292    write_ctrl(struct file *f, const char __user *buf,
293             size_t size, loff_t *off) {
```

LISTING A.7

(Continued).

```
294      return write_reg(f->f_pos, f->f_pos + size, buf,
295                    off, reg_ctrl_alloc_and_set);
296    }
297
298    static int
299    open(struct inode *inode, struct file *filp)
300    {
301      static struct file_operations dma_src_fops = {
302        .owner = THIS_MODULE,
303        .read = read_src,
304        .write = write_src,
305      };
306
307      static struct file_operations dma_dst_fops = {
308        .owner = THIS_MODULE,
309        .read = read_dst,
310      };
311
312      static struct file_operations dma_ctrl_fops = {
313        .owner = THIS_MODULE,
314        .read = read_ctrl,
315        .write = write_ctrl,
316      };
317
318      int minor = iminor(inode);
319      switch (minor) {
320      case DEV_DMA_CTRL:
321        filp->f_op = &dma_ctrl_fops;
322        break;
323      case DEV_DMA_SRC:
324        filp->f_op = &dma_src_fops;
325        break;
326      case DEV_DMA_DST:
327        filp->f_op = &dma_dst_fops;
328        break;
329      default:
330        return -EINVAL;
331      }
332
333      return 0;
334    }
335
336    // ---- PCI initialization code ----
337
338    static void __devexit
339    dma_remove(struct pci_dev *pdev)
340    {
341      printk(KERN_DEBUG "Remove %s device", DEV_NAME);
342      if (dma_dev.base_addr) {
343        free_irq(dma_dev.irq, &dma_dev);
344        pci_iounmap(pdev, dma_dev.base_addr);
345        pci_release_regions(pdev);
346      }
347    }
348
349    static int __devinit
350    dma_probe(struct pci_dev *pdev,
351            const struct pci_device_id *id)
352    {
```

LISTING A.7

(Continued).

```
353      int err;
354      printk(KERN_DEBUG "%s: probe device\n", DEV_NAME);
355
356      err = pci_request_regions(pdev, DEV_NAME);
357      if (err) {
358        printk(KERN_ERR
359               "%s: Failed request regions: %d\n",
360               DEV_NAME, err);
361        return err;
362      }
363
364      dma_dev.base_addr = pci_iomap(pdev, 0, 1);
365      if (dma_dev.base_addr == NULL) {
366        err = -ENOMEM;
367        goto out;
368      }
369
370      printk(KERN_DEBUG
371             "%s: BAR0 = %p\n",
372             DEV_NAME, dma_dev.base_addr);
373
374      err = pci_read_config_byte(pdev, PCI_INTERRUPT_LINE,
375                                 &dma_dev.irq);
376      if (err) goto out;
377
378      err = request_irq(dma_dev.irq, irq_handler,
379                        IRQF_NO_THREAD, DEV_NAME, &dma_dev);
380      if (err) goto out;
381
382      err = pci_enable_device(pdev);
383
384      out:
385      if (err) {
386        if (dma_dev.irq)
387          free_irq(dma_dev.irq, &dma_dev);
388
389        if (dma_dev.base_addr)
390          pci_iounmap(pdev, dma_dev.base_addr);
391
392        pci_release_regions(pdev);
393        dma_dev.base_addr = NULL;    // Failed probing
394        printk(KERN_ERR
395               "%s: Failed to initialize PCI device: %d\n",
396               DEV_NAME, err);
397      } else {
398        dma_dev.pdev = pdev;
399      }
400
401      return err;
402    }
403
404    // ---- Module initialization ----
405
406    static struct pci_driver dma_driver = {
407      .name = "simics-c7-dma",
408      .id_table = id_table,
409      .probe = dma_probe,
410      .remove = __devexit_p(dma_remove),
411    };
```

LISTING A.7

(Continued).

```
412
413    static void
414    free_cdev(void) {
415      if (dma_dev.cdev) {
416        cdev_del(dma_dev.cdev);
417        dma_dev.cdev = NULL;
418      }
419    }
420
421    static int __init
422    dma_init(void)
423    {
424      static struct file_operations major_fops = {
425        .owner = THIS_MODULE,
426        .open = open,
427      };
428
429      dev_t dev;
430      int err = alloc_chrdev_region(&dev, 0,
431                                    DEV_LAST, DEV_NAME);
432      if (err) {
433        printk(KERN_ERR
434              "alloc_chrdev_region failed for %s\n",
435              DEV_NAME);
436        return err;
437      }
438      dma_dev.major = MAJOR(dev);
439
440      err = pci_register_driver(&dma_driver);
441      if (err) {
442        printk(KERN_ERR
443              "pci_register_driver failed for %s\n",
444              DEV_NAME);
445        goto err_1;
446      }
447
448      dma_dev.cdev = cdev_alloc();
449      if (!dma_dev.cdev)
450        return -1;
451
452      dma_dev.cdev->ops = &major_fops;
453      dma_dev.cdev->owner = THIS_MODULE;
454      err = cdev_add(dma_dev.cdev,
455                     MKDEV(dma_dev.major, 0), 3);
456      if (err) {
457        printk(KERN_ERR "Failed to add device\n");
458        goto err_2;
459      }
460
461      return 0;
462
463    err_2:
464      free_cdev();
465
466    err_1:
467      unregister_chrdev_region(dev, DEV_LAST);
468
469      return err;
470    }
```

LISTING A.7

(Continued).

```
471
472    static void __exit dma_exit(void)
473    {
474      pci_unregister_driver(&dma_driver);
475      unregister_chrdev_region(MKDEV(dma_dev.major, 0),
476                               DEV_LAST);
477      free_cdev();
478      free_dma_dst_region();
479    }
480
481    module_init(dma_init);
482    module_exit(dma_exit);
483
484    MODULE_DESCRIPTION("Simics chapter 7 sample"
485                      " DMA controller driver");
486    MODULE_AUTHOR("Daniel Aarno <daniel.aarno@intel.com>");
487    MODULE_LICENSE("GPL v2");
488    MODULE_DEVICE_TABLE(pci, id_table);
```

LISTING A.7

(*Continued*).

References

Alameldeen, A., Wood, D., 2003b. Variability in architectural simulations of multi-threaded workloads. Proceedings of the Ninth Annual International Symposium on High-Performance Computer Architecture (HPCA-9), February 2003, Anaheim, CA, USA

Alameldeen, A.R., Martin, M.M.K., Mauer, C.J., Moore, K., Min, X., Hill, M.D., et al., 2003a. Simulating a $2M commercial server on a $2K PC. IEEE Comput. 36 (2), 50−57.

Albertsson, L., 2006. Entropy injection. SICS Technical Report T2007:02, August 2006.

Aynsley, J., 2009. OSCI TLM-2.0 Language Reference Manual. Open SystemC Initiative (OSCI).

Bartolini, A., Cacciari, M., Tilli, A., Gries, M., 2010. "A virtual platform environment for exploring power, thermal and reliability management control strategies in high-performance multicores," in Proceedings of the 20th Great Lakes Symposium on VLSI, GLSVLSI '10. New York, NY, USA: ACM, pp. 311−316. http://doi.acm.org/10.1145/1785481.1785553.

Bastien, B., 2004. A technique for performing fault injection in system level simulations for dependability assessment. M.Sc. Thesis. Blacksburg: University of Virginia.

Black, D.C., Donovan, J., Bunton, B., Keist, A., 2010. SystemC: From the Ground Up, second ed. Springer, New York.

Blum, B., Eckhardt, D., Gibson, G., 2013. Landslide: a Simics extension for dynamic testing of kernel concurrency errors. Intel Technol. J. 17 (2), 84−89.

Brooks, F., 2010. Stretch-ing is great exercise—It gets you in shape to win. IEEE Ann. Hist. Comput. (January−March), 4−9.

Canon, M.D., Fritz, D.H., Howard, J.H., Howell, T.D., Mitoma, M.F., Rodriguez-Rosell, J., 1980. A virtual machine emulator for performance evaluation. Commun. ACM 23 (2), 71−80. http://dx.doi.org/10.1145/358818.358821.

Carbonari, S., 2013. Using virtual platforms for BIOS development and validation. Intel Technol. J. 17 (2), 32−52.

Chen, J., Dubois, M., and Stenström, P. "Integrating Complete-System and User-level Performance/Power Simulators: The SimWattch Approach", IEEE Micro, Vol. 27, No. 4, pp 34-48, July/August 2007.

Chessin, S., 2010. Injecting errors for fun and profit. Commun. ACM 53 (9), 48−54.

Condon, J., Kernighan, B., Thompson, K., 1980. Experience with the Mergenthaler Linotron 202 Phototypesetter, or How We Spent Our Summer Vacation, Bell Laboratories Technical Memorandum 80-1270-1, Bell Laboratories, Murray Hill, NJ.

Corbet, J., Rubini, A., Kroah-Hartman, G., 2005. Linux Device Drivers, third ed. O'Reilly Media, Sebastopol, CA.

Cornet, J., Maraninchi, F., Maillet-Contoz, L., 2008. A method for the efficient development of timed and untimed transaction-level models of systems-on-chip. DATE '08: Proceedings of the Conference on Design, Automation and Test in Europe, March 2008, Munich, Germany, pp. 9−14.

Doran, M., Zimmer, V., Rothman, M., 2011. Beyond BIOS: Exploring the many dimensions of the unified extensible firmware interface. Intel Technol. J. 15 (1), 8−21.

Duvall, P., Matyas, S., Glover, A., 2007. Continuous Integration: Improving Software Quality and Reducing Risk. Addison-Wesley, Boston.

Eclipse TCF, 2013. Eclipse TCF homepage. Retrieved from <http://www.eclipse.org/tcf/>.

Engblom, J., 2002. Processor pipelines and static worst-case execution time analysis. Ph.D. Thesis, Acta Universitatis Upsaliensis, Uppsala Dissertations from the Faculty of Science and Technology, Uppsala, Sweden.

Engblom, J., 2008. The 1970 rule strikes again: Virtual platform principles in 1967. Observations from Uppsala blog, May 30, 2008, from <http://jakob.engbloms.se/archives/130>.

Engblom, J., 2010b. Transporting bugs with checkpoints. Proceedings of the System, Software, SoC and Silicon Debug Conference (S4D 2010), Southampton, UK, September 15−16, 2010.

Engblom, J., 2012a. A review of reverse debugging. Proceedings of the System, Software, SoC and Silicon Debug Conference (S4D 2012), Wien, Austria, September 19−20, 2012.

Engblom, J., 2012b. "Eagle" cycle-accurate simulator Anno 1979. Observations from Uppsala blog, July 12, 2012, from <http://jakob.engbloms.se/archives/1712>.

Engblom, J., Kågedal, D., Moestedt, A., Runeson, J., 2005. Developing embedded networked products using the Simics full-system simulator. Proceedings of the 16th IEEE International Symposium on Personal Indoor and Mobile Radio Communications (PIMRC 2005), Berlin, Germany, September 2005.

Engblom, J., Aarno, D., Werner, B., 2010a. Full-system simulation from embedded to high-performance systems. In: Leupers, R., Temam, O. (Eds.), Processor and System-on-Chip Simulation. Springer, New York.

Floyd, R.W., 1967. Nondeterministic algorithms. J. ACM 14 (4), 636−644.

Freescale 2007. A Smarter Approach to Multi-Core: Freescale's Next-Generation Communications Platform, Freescale White Paper MULTICOREFTFWP, rev 1, 2007.

Fuchi, K., Tanaka, H., Manago, Y., Yuba, T., 1969. A program simulator by partial interpretation. SOSP '69: Proceedings of the Second Symposium on Operating Systems Principles, pp. 97−104, October 1969. http://dx.doi.org/10.1145/961053.9610.

Ghenassia, F. (Ed.), 2005. Transaction-Level Modeling with SystemC. Springer, New York.

Gill, S., 1951. The diagnosis of mistakes in programmes on the EDSAC. Proc. R. Soc. Lond. A Math. Phys. Sci. 206 (1087), (May 1951).

Gottbrath, C., 2009. Reverse debugging with the TotalView debugger. Cray User Group Conference, Helsinki, Finland, May 2009.

Guenzel, R., 2013. Using Simics in education. Intel Technol. J. 17 (2), 158−177.

Halfhill, T. "Freescale's Multicore Makeover - New QorIQ Processors Will Eventually Supersede PowerQUICC Chips", Microprocessor Report, July 7, 2008.

Hardavellas, N., Somogyi, S., Wenisch, T.F., Wunderlich, R.E., Chen, S., Kim, J., et al., 2004. SimFlex: a fast, accurate, flexible full-system simulation framework for performance evaluation of server architecture. SIGMETRICS Perform. Eval. Rev. 31 (4), 31−34.

1666-2011 IEEE Standard for Standard SystemC Language Reference Manual, IEEE, New York, USA, 3 January 2012.

Intel, 1999. Preboot Execution Environment (PXE) specification, Version 2.1.

Intel, 2013. Simics unleashed: applications of virtual platforms. Intel Technol. J. 17, (Intel Press).

Kågström, S., 2008. Tools, techniques, and trade-offs when porting large software systems to new environments. Doctoral Dissertation Series No. 2008:07, Bleking Institute of Technology, Karlskrona, Sweden.

Kågström, S., Grahn, H., Lundberg, L., 2006. The application kernel approach—A novel approach for adding SMP support to uniprocessor operating systems. Softw. Pract. Exp. 36 (14), 1563–1583.

Khan, A., Wolfe, C., 2013. Simics-SystemC integration. Intel Technol. J. 17 (2), 54–65.

Kidder, T., 1981. The Soul of a New Machine, Little, Brown and Company, NY.

Knuth, D.E., 1969. The Art of Computer Programming, Volume 2: Semi-numerical Algorithms. Addison-Wesley, Boston.

Koerner, S., Kohler, A., Babinsky, J., Pape, H., Eickhoff, F., Kriese, S., et al., 2009. IBM System Z10 firmware simulation. IBM J. Res. Dev. 52 (3), 12:1-12:12. (paper 12), DOI: http://dx.doi.org/10.1147/JRD.2009.5388577.

Kraemer, S., Leupers, R., Petras, D., Philipp, T., 2009. A checkpoint/restore framework for systemc-based virtual platforms. International Symposium on System-on-Chip (SoC), October 2009, Tampere, Finland, pp. 161–167.

Liong, M. "Performance Analysis with Hybrid Simulation", Presentation at the Freescale Technology Forum (FTF), 2008.

Magnusson, P., Dahlgren, F., Grahn, F., Karlsson, M., Larsson, F., Lundholm, F., et al., 1998. SimICS/sun4m: A virtual workstation. Proceedings of the 1998 USENIX Annual Technical Conference, June 1998, New Orleans, LA.

Magnusson, P., Christensson, M., Eskilson, J., Forsgren, D., Hallberg, G., Hogberg, J., et al., 2002. Simics: A full system simulation platform. IEEE Comput. 35 (2), 50–58.

Magnusson, P. "The Virtual Test Lab", IEEE Computer, Volume 38, Issue 5, pp 95-97, May 2005.

Magnusson, P., 2013. Foreword: Simics—The early years. Intel Technol. J. 17 (2), 7.

Malani, P., and Tamhankar, M., "Software Power and Performance Correlation on Simics", Intel Technology Journal, Volume 17, Issue 2, pp. 112–123, 2013.

Martin, M., Sorin, D., Beckmann, B., Marty, M., Xu, M., Alameldeen, et al., "Multifacet's general execution-driven multiprocessor simulator (GEMS) toolset", ACM SIGARCH Computer Architecture News – Special issue: dasCMP'05, Volume 33 Issue 4, pp 92–99, November 2005. http://dx.doi.org/10.1145/1105734.1105747.

Mauer, C., Hill, M., Wood, D. "Full-System Timing-First Simulation", Proceedings of the 2002 ACM Sigmetrics Conference on Measurement and Modeling of Computer Systems, pp. 108-116, 2002.

Menzies, T., 2002. The Raw and the Uncooked: The Windows XP Raw Sockets Saga, Final Words (Hopefully). SANS Institute, Bethesda, MD.

Möller, A., Åberg, P., Löwenhielm, F., Brundin, J., Engblom, J., Nolin, M., 2005. Developing and testing distributed CAN-based real-time control-systems using a single PC. 10th International CAN Conference, CAN in Automation, Roma, Italy, March 2005.

Montón, M., Engblom, J., Burton, M., 2009. Checkpoint and restore for SystemC models. Proceedings of International Forum on Specification and Design Languages (FDL), pp. 1–6, Sophia Antipolis, France, September 2009.

Moore, K., Bobba, J., Moravan, M., Hill, M., Wood, D. "LogTM: Log-Based Transactional Memory", Proceedings of the 12th Annual Symposium on High-Performance Computer Architecture (HPCA-12), 2006.

Neifert, B., Kaye, R., 2012. High Performance or Cycle Accuracy? You Can Have Both. ARM White paper ATC 100.

Peterson, J., Bohrer, P., Chen, L., Elnohazy, E., Gheith, A., Jewell, R., et al., "Application of full-system simulation in exploratory system design and development", IBM Journal of Research and Development, Vol 50, no 2/3, pp 321−332, March/May 2006.

Phillips, S., 2010. Simplicity betrayed—Emulating the TRS-80 graphics system. Commun. ACM 53 (6), 52−58.

Rechistov, G., 2013. Simics on the shared computing clusters: The practical experience of integration and scalability. Intel Technol. J. 17 (2), 124−135.

Red Hat, 2013. Red Hat Enterprise Linux 6 Installation Guide: Installing Red Hat Enterprise Linux 6.5 for All Architectures, Edition 5, Red Hat, Inc.

Rosenblum, M., Varadarajan, M., 1994. SimOS: A Fast Operating System Simulation Environment, CSL-TR-94-631. Stanford University, Stanford, CA.

Skadron, K., Martonosi, M., August, D., Hill, M., Lilja, D., and Pai, V. "Challenges in Computer Architecture Simulation", IEEE Computer, Volume 36, Issue 8, pp. 30-36, August 2003.

Thomas, J., Engblom, J., 2012. Getting code coverage with LDRA tools on Simics. Wind River blog post, April 20, 2012, from <http://blogs.windriver.com/tools/2012/04/getting-code-coverage-with-ldra-tools-on-simics.html>.

Tian, T., 2013. Post-silicon impact: Simics helps the next generation of network transformation and migration to a software-defined network (SDN). Intel Technol. J. 17 (2), 66−82.

UndoDB, 2013. UndoDB man page. Retrieved from <http://undo-software.com/product/undodb-man-page>.

Veseyi, A., Ayers, J., 2013. Early hardware register validation with Simics. Intel Technol. J. 17 (2), 100−111.

Wallin, D., Zeffer, H., Karlsson, M., Hagersten, E. "Vasa: A Simulator Infrastructure with Adjustable Fidelity", Proceedings of the 17th IASTED International Conference on Parallel and Distributed Computing and Systems (PDCS 2005), Phoenix, Arizona, USA, November 2005.

Weinstock, J., Schumacher, C., Leupers, R., Ascheid, G., Tosoratti, L., 2014. Time-decoupled parallel SystemC simulation. Proceedings of Conference on Design, Automation & Test in Europe (DATE 2014), Dresden, Germany, March 2014.

Werner, B., Magnusson, P. "A Hybrid Simulation Approach Enabling Performance Characterization of Large Software Systems", Proceedings of the Fifth International Symposium on Modeling, Analysis and Simulation of Computer and Telecommunication Systems, Haifa, Israel, pp. 73-80, January 12-15, 1997.

Wilen, A., Schade, J., Thornburg, R., 2003. Introduction to PCI Express: A Hardware and Software Developer's Guide. Intel Press, Hillsboro, OR.

Wind River, 2014a. Wind River Simics Hindsight User's Guide, Revision 4559. Wind River, Alameda, CA.

Wind River, 2014b. Wind River Simics Model Builder User's Guide, Revision 4559. Wind River, Alameda, CA.

Wind River, 2014c. Wind River Simics Installation Guide, Revision 4559. Wind River, Alameda, CA.

Wind River, 2014d. Wind River Simics Accelerator User's Guide, Revision 4559. Wind River, Alameda, CA.

Wright, G., McGachey, P., Gunadi, E., Wolczko, Ma. Introspection of a Java Virtual Machine under Simulation, Sun Labs Technical report SMLI TR-2006-159, September 2006.

Yi, J., Kodakara, S., Sendag, R., Lilja, D., Hawkins, D. "Characterizing and Comparing Prevailing Simulation Techniques", Proceedings of the 11th Int'l Symposium on High-Performance Computer Architecture (HPCA-11), San Francisco, California, USA, 2005.

Yu, T., Witawas, S., Gregg, R., 2013. Sim-O/C: An observable and controllable testing framework for elusive faults. Intel Technol. J. 17 (2), 178–197.

Index

Note: Page numbers followed by "*f*", "*b*" and "*t*" refers to figures, boxes and tables respectively.

Printed and bound by CPI Group (UK) Ltd, Croydon, CR0 4YY

09/10/2024

01042813-0001